Enriching Collaboration and Communication in Online Learning Communities

Carolyn N. Stevenson
Purdue University Global, USA

Joanna C. Bauer
Claremont Lincoln University, USA

A volume in the Advances in Mobile and Distance Learning (AMDL) Book Series

IGI Global
DISSEMINATOR OF KNOWLEDGE

Published in the United States of America by
IGI Global
Information Science Reference (an imprint of IGI Global)
701 E. Chocolate Avenue
Hershey PA, USA 17033
Tel: 717-533-8845
Fax: 717-533-8661
E-mail: cust@igi-global.com
Web site: http://www.igi-global.com

Library of Congress Cataloging-in-Publication Data

Names: Stevenson, Carolyn N., 1968- editor. | Bauer, Joanna C., 1968- editor.
Title: Enriching collaboration and communication in online learning communities / Carolyn N. Stevenson and Joanna C. Bauer, Editors.
Description: Hershey, PA : Information Science Reference, [2020] | Summary: "This book examines communication and collaboration in online settings by focusing on the ways all members of an educational institution can create community fostering personal and professional growth for all"-- Provided by publisher.
Identifiers: LCCN 2019010593 | ISBN 9781522598145 (hardcover) | ISBN 9781522598152 (paperback) | ISBN 9781522598169 (ebook)
Subjects: LCSH: Distance education--Computer-assisted instruction. | Communication in education. | Professional learning communities. | Online social networks.
Classification: LCC LC5803.C65 E57 2020 | DDC 371.35/8--dc23
LC record available at https://lccn.loc.gov/2019010593

This book is published in the IGI Global book series Advances in Mobile and Distance Learning (AMDL) (ISSN: 2327-1892; eISSN: 2327-1906)

British Cataloguing in Publication Data
A Cataloguing in Publication record for this book is available from the British Library.

For electronic access to this publication, please contact: eresources@igi-global.com.

Advances in Mobile and Distance Learning (AMDL) Book Series

Patricia Ordóñez de Pablos
Universidad de Oviedo, Spain

ISSN:2327-1892
EISSN:2327-1906

Mission

Private and public institutions have made great strides in the fields of mobile and distance learning in recent years, providing greater learning opportunities outside of a traditional classroom setting. While the online learning revolution has allowed for greater learning opportunities, it has also presented numerous challenges for students and educators alike. As research advances, online educational settings can continue to develop and advance the technologies available for learners of all ages.

The **Advances in Mobile and Distance Learning** (AMDL) Book Series publishes research encompassing a variety of topics related to all facets of mobile and distance learning. This series aims to be an essential resource for the timeliest research to help advance the development of new educational technologies and pedagogy for use in online classrooms.

Coverage

- Course Design
- Economics of Distance and M-Learning
- Snack Learning
- Managing Sustainable Learning
- Tablets and Education
- Educational Apps
- Administration and Organization
- Pedagogy and Design Methodology
- Virtual Universities
- Technology Platforms and System Development

IGI Global is currently accepting manuscripts for publication within this series. To submit a proposal for a volume in this series, please contact our Acquisition Editors at Acquisitions@igi-global.com or visit: http://www.igi-global.com/publish/.

The Advances in Mobile and Distance Learning (AMDL) Book Series (ISSN 2327-1892) is published by IGI Global, 701 E. Chocolate Avenue, Hershey, PA 17033-1240, USA, www.igi-global.com. This series is composed of titles available for purchase individually; each title is edited to be contextually exclusive from any other title within the series. For pricing and ordering information please visit http://www.igi-global.com/book-series/advances-mobile-distance-learning/37162. Postmaster: Send all address changes to above address.

Titles in this Series

For a list of additional titles in this series, please visit: www.igi-global.com/book-series

Advancing Mobile Learning in Contemporary Educational Spaces
Dominic Mentor (Columbia University, USA)
Information Science Reference • ©2019 • 350pp • H/C (ISBN: 9781522593515) • US $195.00

Student Support Toward Self-Directed Learning in Open and Distributed Environments
Micheal M. van Wyk (University of South Africa, South Africa)
Information Science Reference • ©2019 • 300pp • H/C (ISBN: 9781522593164) • US $195.00

Administrative Leadership in Open and Distance Learning Programs
Koksal Buyuk (Anadolu University, Turkey) Serpil Kocdar (Anadolu University, Turkey) and Aras Bozkurt (Anadolu University, Turkey)
Information Science Reference • ©2018 • 378pp • H/C (ISBN: 9781522526452) • US $195.00

Empowering Learners With Mobile Open-Access Learning Initiatives
Michael Mills (University of Central Arkansas, USA) and Donna Wake (University of Central Arkansas, USA)
Information Science Reference • ©2017 • 357pp • H/C (ISBN: 9781522521228) • US $190.00

Handbook of Research on Mobile Devices and Applications in Higher Education Settings
Laura Briz-Ponce (University of Salamanca, Spain) Juan Antonio Juanes-Méndez (University of Salamanca, Spain) and Francisco José García-Peñalvo (University of Salamanca, Spain)
Information Science Reference • ©2016 • 608pp • H/C (ISBN: 9781522502562) • US $300.00

Handbook of Research on Mobile Learning in Contemporary Classrooms
Dominic Mentor (Teachers College, Columbia University, USA)
Information Science Reference • ©2016 • 475pp • H/C (ISBN: 9781522502517) • US $300.00

Mobile and Blended Learning Innovations for Improved Learning Outcomes
David Parsons (The Mind Lab by Unitec, New Zealand)
Information Science Reference • ©2016 • 366pp • H/C (ISBN: 9781522503590) • US $185.00

Integrating Touch-Enabled and Mobile Devices into Contemporary Mathematics Education
Maria Meletiou-Mavrotheris (European University Cyprus, Cyprus) Katerina Mavrou (European University Cyprus, Cyprus) and Efi Paparistodemou (Cyprus Pedagogical Institute, Cyprus)
Information Science Reference • ©2015 • 341pp • H/C (ISBN: 9781466687141) • US $190.00

IGI Global
DISSEMINATOR OF KNOWLEDGE

701 East Chocolate Avenue, Hershey, PA 17033, USA
Tel: 717-533-8845 x100 • Fax: 717-533-8661
E-Mail: cust@igi-global.com • www.igi-global.com

Editorial Advisory Board

Table of Contents

Detailed Table of Contents

Civility in computer-mediated communication, especially in the computer-mediated classroom, has been a topic of numerous inquiries. For this reason, teaching of the means and reasons for civil computer-mediated communication has become increasingly necessary. To accomplish this, the chapter will explore past research which indicates major sources of incivility that have emerged in computer-mediated culture. The chapter will then argue that civil discourse is also the most effective and useful form of discourse and show that needs to be communicated to students. This chapter then offers concrete means of teaching civility in computer-mediated communication by teaching civility as tied to the rhetorical concept of ethos already taught in the Public Speaking class.

In the online classroom, email has emerged as a predominant communication method between students and faculty. Despite many benefits of email, including ease of use, familiarity of the technology, and rapid response times, there are numerous challenges faculty face when sending and receiving email correspondence with students. Mainly, due to the medium and format of email, with its lack of cues such as body language, inflection, and other sensory stimuli, it presents a paramount challenge to faculty. However, appropriate tone and attitude in emails can help mitigate the challenges the medium presents. When written and read effectively and purposefully, email is an effective outreach and communication tool for students and faculty.

As virtual teams continue to become more prevalent, educational administrators, faculty, and other members of online communities must discover and employ guidelines for effectively collaborating in online contexts. Applying the same traditional team strategies to those working in dispersed groups of people may hinder communication and prevent optimal results. In today's world, teams need to execute and learn at the same time. It is time to re-define what constitutes a (virtual) team and consider new avenues for cooperating in an increasingly diverse, global, and continuously "plugged-in" society. A set of practical steps for why and how virtual teams can collaborate in digital environments is presented. Tips for implementing the steps are provided. An analysis of technological tools available for facilitating online team collaboration is also shared.

This chapter explores through phenomenological methodology the experiences of nursing faculty who transitioned from live to online teaching. These experiences are further examined through the theory of transformative learning to determine whether participants were able to transform their teaching identity from traditional classroom teacher (sage on the stage) to facilitators of learning. One-on-one interviews were conducted with 16 full-time nursing faculty at four state universities. Findings revealed that most faculty were originally hesitant to teach online and had multiple misconceptions regarding teaching methods and online student communication. With one exception, professional development for online teaching was limited. Most participants described transforming their teaching methods and philosophies as they gained more experience. Results implicate that faculty development should focus not only on educational principles and technology, but also on ways to connect with students and develop course content that helps maintain faculty identities.

Based on a critical re-reading of a study of a community of practice approach to professional development, this chapter uses Engeström's activity theory model to highlight the tensions that arise in a professional development program oriented to change teaching practice through the introduction of ICT and a student-centered pedagogical approach. Despite the community of practice potential, there are many tensions that inhibit this type of professional learning. These tensions can be summarized in four broad categories: institutional structures (division of work), the institutional culture (rules), levels of engagement (differentiations within the community), and faculty readiness (in the appropriation of tools and new pedagogy). By analyzing, in greater depth, the tensions, our goal is to reflect again in the design principles and to further elaborate on developing a professional development strategy based on a community of practice approach that can be used in broader contexts.

This chapter intends to answer the question, "What are some guidelines for working effectively in virtual teams?" To further advance existing literature, the authors utilized a qualitative phenomenological approach with a randomly-sampled group of seven students who had completed master's-level education courses that were conducted in an online format at a private Midwestern University. Students were halfway through their course completion at the time of data collection. In addition, a random sample of one program administrator and four faculty members were interviewed. Specifically, students who enrolled in online Master's in Education courses are required to work in study teams to complete a certain portion of the course work. Study teams can often be difficult to navigate in person and with the added dimension that a virtual experience brings to developing trusting, successful working relationships, different working guidelines are needed. Findings revealed that managerial and social aspects of online learning and teaching were critical for online students' success.

Foreword

It is a pleasure to write this Foreword for so timely a textbook as we are in the historical center of digital online communities, and even better in the era of online courses and programs. This suggests that building online communities in higher education, and doing so collaboratively, is an idea whose time has come. This book provides a rich discussion of the practical use of technology in promoting a collaborative teaching and learning experience. Educators in every profession could easily make use of the collaborative tools described so elegantly here. This book is about teaching and learning in virtual settings through collaboration. This text offers educators and administrators insightful information on promoting student success and increasing communication in the online classroom. Technology today offers the opportunity to promote such increased communication and collaboration if we understand the use of technological tools that truly enable collaboration. The chapters presented in this book highlight the critical importance of staying connected in an online environment and developing an authentic learning community. Key areas include:

- Guidelines for working collaboratively in virtual teams
- Professional Development to Promote Online Communication, Collaboration and Learning
- Overcoming Implicit Bias In Collaborative Online Learning Communities
- Strategies for Meaningful Collaboration in Online Environments

If you are looking for a resource to assist you in understanding today's online communities, this book is a treasure. The book provides valuable information that will not only enhance teaching and learning, but promote student success in terms of what it means to work collaboratively, preparing them for the world of work.

Valerie J. Janesick
University of South Florida, USA

Preface

Today's online educational settings are composed of diverse students, faculty members, and other stakeholders, each with varying degrees of technological expertise, professional experience, cultural backgrounds, and educational expectations. As such, organizational leaders need to identify differences among members of the educational institution and develop a strategic plan for communicating and collaborating with all members of the institution. To facilitate learning in these important areas, chapters are presented that will assist college administrators, faculty members, and others in higher education to improve communication and create collaborative efforts in an online setting with diverse stakeholders. This book builds a foundation to improve communication across cultures, work collaboratively in virtual teams on cross-discipline projects, overcome implicit bias, address tone, attitude, and civility in communication, develop facilitation skills, and use social networking tools for creating community. In the chapters, questions are addressed such as:

- What are strategies for meaningful collaboration in online environments?
- How important are tone, attitude, and civility in email and the online classroom?
- What are ways to overcome implicit bias in collaborative online learning communities?
- What are tactics for developing facilitation skills online?
- How can social networking tools build community and promote collaboration in the online classroom?
- What are some guidelines for working effectively in virtual teams?
- How can faculty and administrators maintain relationships through social media?

Often, members of the online community work in isolation. Collaboration across varying disciplines and departments can foster unique professional development activities as well as create a stronger connection to the entire online community. Effective communication is essential in every organization. Communication topics to be addressed include managing conflict, working effectively in virtual teams, use of social networking tools, critical thinking, intercultural communication, and online leadership. The chapters in the book will advance the current scope of research in support of communication and collaboration in online settings by focusing on the ways all members of the educational institution can create community fostering personal and professional growth.

Since the major topic is communication, the book is applicable across disciplines. There is a considerable amount of interest in effective communication throughout higher education including building learning communities, therefore, faculty members, course designers, student services officers, and other leaders in higher education would be interested in the topic. Collaboration in a virtual setting will also appeal to a wide range of educational leaders and faculty. This book targets those who work in an online setting, manage others from a distance, teach students in an online format, and work together with others across disciplines on collaborative projects. The topics and issues presented in this book will assist the prospective audience (e.g. faculty members, students, researchers, practitioners, college administrators) and other stakeholders in strengthening communication and collaboration in virtual settings.

Major themes of the book include cultural communication, innovative ways for promoting student success in the online classroom, collaborative course design and assessment, social networks promoting successful communication, and collaboration in the classroom through training and faculty development. The critical topics of promoting student success through practical solutions and online learning communities are also addressed. The chapters also discuss various topics such as: online collaboration, cross-discipline initiatives for collaboration, leading and managing virtual employees, learning communities, online learning in a global society, social networking tools for enhancing communication and collaboration, technology tools that enhance learning (separate from social networking tools), and ethical standards for online communication.

Chapter 1: "Strategies for Meaningful Collaboration in Online Environments," by Valerie Beltran, University of La Verne, Jessica C. Decker, University of La Verne, Mark Matzaganian, University of La Verne, Nancy T. Walker, University of La Verne, and Sammy Elzarka, University of La Verne, examines the complexities of creating a collaborative community in online classes. An online Master's of Education program is studied, with students being surveyed regarding their experiences with collaboration in online courses. Results of the study are discussed, along with recommendations for establishing a sense of community in the online environment. Recommendations include structuring introductory activities for the instructor and students, providing opportunities for authentic collaboration and communication through tools such as blogs and wikis, and guidelines for establishing effective group projects in an online class. Suggestions for future research are also included. Overall, a case is made for the importance of creating meaningful collaborative experiences for students within the context of class content in online courses.

Chapter 2: "Overcoming Implicit Bias in Collaborative Online Learning Communities," by Ludmila T. Battista, Claremont Lincoln University and Lisa Wright, University of Missouri, lays the groundwork for exploring implicit bias and the effects in the online higher education environment. The authors analyze privilege, power, oppression, institutionalized bias, and explore examples in higher education, through both student and faculty perspectives. The chapter focuses on collaborative solutions to a diverse variety of case studies on implicit bias across race, culture, gender, ability, and other dimensions. An emphasis is placed on reflective analysis and creating collaborative experiences for online students and educators.

Chapter 3: "Assessment and Civility: Using Ethos as a Tool," by Benjamin J. Cline, Western New Mexico University, discusses civility in computer-mediated communication and computer-mediated classroom, which has been a topic of numerous inquiries. For this reason, teaching civility in online communication has become increasingly necessary. In order to accomplish this, the chapter explores past research which indicates major sources of incivility that have emerged in computer-mediated culture. The chapter also argues that civil discourse is the most effective and useful form of discourse and shows the need to communicate this need to students. The chapter then offers concrete means of teaching civility in computer-mediated communication by tying it to the rhetorical concept of ethos already taught in Public Speaking class.

Chapter 4: “The Importance of Tone and Attitude in Email and the Online Classroom,” by Melissa A. Miller, Purdue University Global, discusses perception in electronic communication. In the online classroom, email has emerged as a predominant communication method between students and faculty. Despite many benefits of email, including ease of use, familiarity of the technology, and rapid response times, there are numerous challenges faculty face when sending and receiving email correspondence with students. Mainly, due to the medium and format of email, with its lack of cues such as body language, inflection, and other sensory stimuli, it presents a paramount challenge to faculty. However, appropriate tone and attitude in emails can help mitigate the challenges the medium presents. When written and read effectively and purposefully, email is an effective outreach and communication tool for students and faculty.

Chapter 5: “Guidelines for Working Collaboratively in Virtual Teams,” by Shelley Stewart, University of South Florida, addresses strategies for working in virtual teams. As virtual teams continue to become more prevalent, educational administrators, faculty and other members of online communities must discover and employ guidelines for effectively collaborating in online contexts. Applying the same traditional team strategies to those working in dispersed groups of people may hinder communication and prevent optimal results. In today’s world, teams need to execute and learn at the same time. It is time to re-define what constitutes a (virtual) team and consider new avenues for cooperating in an increasingly diverse, global and continuously “plugged-in” society. A set of practical steps for why and how virtual teams can collaborate in digital environments is presented, and tips for implementing the steps are provided. An analysis of technological tools available for facilitating online team collaboration is also shared.

Chapter 6: “A Transformative Learning Experience for New Online Nursing Faculty” by Denise Passmore, University of South Florida, explores through phenomenological methodology the experiences of nursing faculty who transitioned from live to online teaching. These experiences are further examined through the theory of transformative learning to determine whether participants were able to transform their teaching identities from traditional classroom teacher (sage on the stage) to facilitators of learning. One-on-one interviews were conducted with 16 full-time nursing faculty at four state universities. Findings revealed that most faculty were originally hesitant to teach online and had multiple misconceptions regarding teaching methods and online student communication. With one exception, professional development for online teaching was limited. Most participants described transforming their teaching methods and philosophies as they gained more experience. Results implicate that faculty development should focus not only on educational principles and technology but also ways to connect with students and develop course content that helps maintain faculty identities.

Chapter 7: “Professional Development to Promote Online Communication, Collaboration, and Learning, among Faculty: A Community of Practice Approach,” by Mayela Coto, Universidad Nacional and Lone Dirckinck -Holmfeld, Aalborg University, uses Engeström’s activity theory model to highlight the tensions that arise in a professional development program oriented to change teaching practice through the introduction of ICT and a student-centered pedagogical approach. Despite the community of practice potential, there are many tensions that inhibit this type of professional learning. These tensions can be summarized in four broad categories: institutional structures (division of work), the institutional culture (rules), levels of engagement (differentiations within the community), and faculty’ readiness (in the appropriation of tools and new pedagogy). By analyzing in greater depth the tensions, the goal is to reflect on the design principles and to further elaborate on developing a professional development strategy based on a community of practice approach that can be used in broader contexts.

Chapter 8: "Online Teaching and Learning in Higher Education Settings: Focus on Team Effectiveness," by Mette L. Baran, Cardinal Stritch University and Janice E. Jones, Cardinal Stritch University, intends to answer the question: "What are some guidelines for working effectively in virtual teams?" To further advance existing literature, the authors used a qualitative phenomenological approach with a randomly sampled group of seven students who completed master's level online Education courses at a private Midwestern University. Students were half way through their course completion at the time of data collection. In addition, a random sample of one program administrator and four faculty members were interviewed. Students who enrolled in online Master's in Education courses are required to work in study teams to complete a certain portion of the course work. Study teams can often be difficult to navigate in person and with the added dimension that a virtual experience brings to developing trusting, successful working relationships, different working guidelines are needed. Findings revealed that managerial and social aspects of online learning and teaching were critical for online students' success.

Chapter 9: "Maintaining Relationships through Social Media and the Way Forward," by Richard H Afedzie, Pentecost University College, Stanford Nartey, Pentecost University College, and James Aller, Georgia Southwestern State University, examines the influence of social media in our global political, social, and business landscape. It underscores the argument that the value of social media in our 21st century social and business lifestyles cannot be overlooked. It explores some of the ways in which social media has shaped and positively maintained friendship, dating, and family relationships. It also highlights some of the growing challenges and emerging moral risks associated with unregulated social media prevalence in the society and offers ways to minimize threats posed by unfettered social media use in society.

Chapter 10: "Effectively Utilizing a Socially-Mediated Network: Facilitating Meaningful Collaboration among Pre-Service Student-Teachers and University EFL Students," by Dustin De Felice, Michigan State University, Wesley A Curtis, University of South Carolina, and Luz María Ortiz Alcocer, Universidad de Quintana Roo, discusses a group who used computer supported collaborative learning through an online socially mediated network. This collaboration served as a bridge between two universities from different countries. Not only did this collaboration link the students from each university together, but it provided language learners and pre-service student-teachers with the ability to benefit from the unique connection between them (i.e. students needing to learn language and teachers needing to practice teaching a language). The collaboration, the framework, and the format of this cooperative learning project is discussed. Much of this discussion is rooted in the experiences of the students who participated in its evolution with the intent to provide a direction for implementing a similar collaboration in other institutions.

Chapter 11: "Utilizing Social Networking Sites for Communication in Higher Education," by Jodi Whitehurst, Arkansas State University- Beebe and Jim Vander Putten, University of Arkansas at Little Rock, analyzes the need for communication and collaboration tools to connect units of higher education. It then examines a popular social networking site, Facebook, as a possible platform of communication. This chapter also discusses findings from a phenomenological study that explored rhetorical roles employed by participants on Facebook, and then connects findings to current research concerning communication and collaboration in higher education. Data indicated that messages on Facebook were used for cooperation and coordination, but not necessarily collaboration. It also indicated that while participants were audience-minded, they were not necessarily audience aware, and participants used audience shaping as a coping mechanism. Finally, composers' inclinations to exercise authority over their personal, representational space (Facebook wall) led the researchers to conclude that use of Facebook in higher education may best be achieved by creating a Facebook page or group for specific communicative purposes.

Chapter 12: "Technology and Culturally Competent Strategies for the Online Classroom," by Justina Elise Kwapy, Grand Canyon University, explores how technology can support a successful online learning experience and impede the dissatisfaction and higher dropout rates among students in distance learning programs. Higher education's online faculty are faced with the task of creating a virtual community of learners, meeting both the academic and social needs of students. This chapter provides strategies to foster successful online learning communities.

Chapter 13: "Learning Together: Confucius and Freire Collaborate to Redefine a Community of Learning," by Sue K Park, Claremont Lincoln University, develops a fundamental praxis of collaboration. Drawing on the wisdom of Freire and Confucius, the author of this chapter on collaboration delineates it from three different perspectives: liberative, practical, and philosophical. Through these three perspectives, she discusses collaboration as a necessary component of online education and offers key principles to shape effective and successful collaborative efforts. Confucian humanism lays the foundation and context for Freire's liberative pedagogy in education, and the writer brings these two theoretical practitioners into conversation to offer practical principles for collaboration between educators and students in online spaces.

Chapter 14: "If You Build It, They Will Come: Student Clubs in the Digital World," by Elizabeth Donnellan, Purdue University Global, provides specific information about tools used to create, administer, and motivate participation in virtual university clubs. To enhance the club experience, suggestions are offered for creating interactive clubrooms, utilizing specific social media tools, and providing unique club events all as a virtual experience. A case study is included to demonstrate how students of a major online university participate in virtual club events. Results of this case study indicate a correlation between students who can easily access club tools and events with participation in those events. Further, students who participate in clubs report greater satisfaction with their overall university experience and increased confidence in professional skills.

Throughout this book, we have focused on the challenges of communicating and collaborating in online settings and forwarded ways all members of higher educational institutions can create community and foster personal and professional growth. Our intention was to elicit diverse faculty and administrative experience, and with our authors writing about their experiences from all over the globe, this was achieved. The book expands existing models of online communication to include cultural considerations, facilitation techniques, successful collaboration, use of technology including social networking tools, and other forms of computer-mediated communication to create collaborative experiences for students, faculty members, administrators, and other supporters of the educational community.

Carolyn N. Stevenson
Purdue University Global, USA

Joanna C. Bauer
Claremont Lincoln University, USA

Acknowledgment

We express our deepest gratitude to the members of the academy who dedicated their time to share dynamic and insightful chapters for this book. The diversity of thought, discerning content, forward thinking andragogy and theory, and additions to the knowledge base on digital communication is inspiring. With your support, this has been a collaborative and fulfilling experience. To the reviewers of the text who shared their expertise in providing valuable feedback on the chapters, we extend our abundant appreciation as well. The members of the IGI Global team should also be acknowledged for providing us with support and guidance throughout the process. Finally, we thank all faculty members around the globe for your continued dedication to serving our students. Education is a community and this work is an addition to the larger context of the canon of knowledge we build together. Through mindful dialogue and collaboration, we are all contributing to the ongoing quest to enhance teaching and learning.

Carolyn N. Stevenson
Purdue University Global, USA

Joanna C. Bauer
Claremont Lincoln University, USA

Chapter 1
Strategies for Meaningful Collaboration in Online Environments

Valerie Beltran
University of La Verne, USA

Jessica C. Decker
University of La Verne, USA

Mark Matzaganian
University of La Verne, USA

Nancy T. Walker
University of La Verne, USA

Sammy Elzarka
University of La Verne, USA

ABSTRACT

This chapter examines the complexities of creating a collaborative community in online classes. A fully online Master's of Education program is studied, with students being surveyed regarding their experiences with collaboration in the online courses. Results of the study are discussed, along with recommendations for establishing a sense of community in the online environment. Recommendations include structuring introductory activities for the instructor and students, providing opportunities for authentic collaboration and communication through tools such as blogs and wikis, and following guidelines for establishing effective group projects in an online class. Suggestions for future research are also included. Overall, a case is made for the importance of creating meaningful, collaborative experiences for students within the context of class content in online courses.

DOI: 10.4018/978-1-5225-9814-5.ch001

INTRODUCTION

Online education presents unique challenges for both learners and educators, including creating a sense of community conducive to peer collaboration. While creating such learning environments has been well-studied in face-to-face settings, creating such learning opportunities in online settings is a continuing topic for research. This chapter explores prior research on collaboration in the online environment as well as best practices to support these efforts. An empirical mixed methods study is described along with strategies found to be effective.

BACKGROUND

Throughout recent history, the education system in the United States has been playing catch-up in terms of its use of technology. As students are becoming more technologically savvy, the need for instructors to increase their use of technology is becoming more and more apparent. Today's students expect and demand more than an instructor lecturing for hours or copying notes off of a whiteboard for the entire class session. Technology can provide alternatives to these traditional ways of teaching. A current technology trend is online teaching. However, if not developed correctly, online classes can turn into an electronic version of the traditional lecture routine. When designing online classes, it is imperative that instructors consider the communication, interaction, and collaboration among students in an effort to provide a supportive and engaging learning environment. Establishing this type of collaborative community is challenging in a traditional face-to-face classroom and is even more so when students are not in the same physical space.

TRENDS IN ONLINE EDUCATION

Online education is a field that continues to expand in both K12 and higher ed. According to Abamu (2018), fully online degree programs are more prevalent than ever. Enrollment in online courses in higher education has increased for the past 14 years. Between 2016-2017, the number of all students who took courses online grew 5.7 percent (Lederman, 2018). Close to 32% of higher education students have taken at least one online course (Seaman, Allen, & Seaman, 2018). According to Seaman et al. (2018), growth of distance enrollments has gone up regardless of both economic trends and overall higher education enrollment trends.

LEARNING AS A SOCIAL ACTIVITY

Many prominent educational theorists have recognized the importance of the social aspect of learning. Dewey (1916) discussed the importance of using conversation, interaction with others, and opportunities to apply new knowledge as keys to the learning process. Vygotsky's (1978) zone of proximal development also recognized the importance of interaction with others who are more knowledgeable and can facilitate one's learning. Kagan's work (2001) in the arena of cooperative learning has demonstrated the mutual gains students receive when they work together to complete a task. However, before groups can be successful, class building and team building have to take place to develop the bonds and support that need to be present. The research on the benefits of cooperative learning has shown strong empirical support for this type of instruction (Marzano, Pickering, & Pollock, 2001). The challenge in an online environment is how to translate what has been effective in face-to-face teaching into plausible and beneficial online techniques.

ESTABLISHING COLLABORATION IN THE LEARNING ENVIRONMENT

In their research on how online learning environments facilitated collaborative learning, Han and Hill (2007) identified three important categories: context, community, and cognition. Context includes providing structural support and opportunities for active participation. Collaboration occurs more readily when a sense of community is present. Indicators of a strong community include group cohesiveness, member specific jargon, willingness to engage in discussion, and developing a social presence. Han and Hill's (2007) research concluded that small discussion groups, multiple modes of communication, nurturing of the community, and encouraging meaningful discussion amongst participants were critical components in a collaborative environment.

Developing a community of learners was the focus of the research of Green, Edwards, Wolodko, Stewart, Brooks, and Littledyke (2010). They found that resource sharing and personal reflection in an online setting created a collaborative knowledge base which allowed students to consider what is possible within their own socio-cultural contexts. In addition, choosing work groups and creating joint documents nurtured this community of learners. Lee, Ngampornchai, Trail-Constant, Abril, and Srinivasan (2016) investigated the impact group work had on student satisfaction among students in online courses. They found that students' perceptions of group work were associated with peer interaction in online courses. In addition, Sadeghi and Kardan (2015) determined that students were more satisfied with their course experience and scored higher on assessments when they self-selected their groups.

Another study by Falls, Bahhouth, Chuang, and Bahhouth (2014) examined factors influencing students' perceptions of online teamwork. The researchers found that online instructors, through their approach to online teaching, can have a significant impact on students' perceptions of their experiences. Effective strategies were used throughout the course experience and included getting to know each other activities, explicit instructions for team projects, opportunities for frequent check-ins with classmates, and ongoing reflection.

There is a plethora of tools that exist to provide interaction in online environments. As with any other resource, the trick is to use them appropriately. There is a misconceived notion that students want online classes to be totally asynchronous. Scheuermann (2010) has collected data from his online students since the 2000 - 2001 academic year and has found that between 70 - 100% of each of his classes thought the synchronous elements of the class were valuable and should be continued. He stresses the importance of scheduling the synchronous meetings ahead of time and with students' schedules in mind.

SOCIAL PRESENCE IN ONLINE COURSES

Building on the constructivist learning theory, the Community of Inquiry model seeks to develop meaningful learning opportunities online through establishing social, cognitive, and teaching presence, all of which have a social base (Garrison, Anderson, & Archer, 2000). Rourke, Anderson, Garrison, and Archer (2001) defined social presence as "the ability of learners to project themselves socially and affectively into a community of inquiry" (p. 1). Researchers have demonstrated a relationship between social presence and perceived learning and student satisfaction in online courses (Richardson & Lowenthal, 2017).

In addition to the social presence of students' peers, the social presence of the instructor is a key component. Arbaugh and Hwang (2006) included several behaviors within the concept of teacher presence such as consistency of interaction with course participants, clearly stated accessibility to students, the provision of quality feedback, and the ability to moderate and guide online discussions between students. Baker (2010) further explored the concept of teacher presence in online courses. Specifically, he found that teacher presence had a predictive influence on students' affective learning. He also emphasized the difficulty of establishing teacher presence in online classes saying, "It may be harder (without the enhancement of nonverbal cues such as smiling, nodding, leaning in, etc.) for an instructor to convey and for students to interpret verbally immediate behaviors as well as they could in a face-to-face learning environment" (Baker, 2010, p. 19).

Students also want to know that the instructor is actively participating in the online class. This gives students a feeling of security and support. In addition, adding audio or video lectures provides a connection between the instructor and the students. Sull (2010) discussed how the instructor sets the tone for a positive, interactive online experience. The communication system the instructor sets up (such as having a frequently asked questions link at the beginning of the course, providing clear instructions, and giving detailed, specific feedback) sets the stage for promoting interaction. He reiterated the importance of the instructor participating in all activities such as blogs and wikis. In addition, he discussed how crucial it is to respond to students' questions within 24 hours so that the students feel supported and know that the instructor is interested in them as students.

With regards to the social presence in the online environment, Rogers and Lea (2005) emphasized the importance of developing a shared group identity among participants. This shared group identity should be established early on. In addition, groups in online settings benefit from the ability to manage their interactions themselves, thereby further developing the group's shared identity and increasing the participants' sense of ownership in group activities.

A study conducted by Kumar and Ritzhaupt (2014) of an online professional doctorate program found that social presence plays an important role in establishing students' sense of belonging which in turn leads to more impactful and intentional communication with peers. The researchers found that these interactions occurred not only within the context of the course, but also on various social media platforms outside the course. Koole (2014) discussed how students' shared sense of belonging and purpose in an online class leads to increased academic success.

Harrington and Floyd (2009) summarized that students classify online classes as positive experiences when lectures are combined with student activities that promote active participation. One way to promote this kind of engagement is through the use of social-networking activities. The authors suggested creating a virtual homeroom on Facebook where instructors and students can get to know each other. They also recommended using Twitter to send and receive short messages regarding immediate issues such as a question about a lecture or upcoming assignment. In addition, Skype provides the opportunity to make voice calls, video conference, and share a desktop via the Internet to provide real-time connections.

CREATING A COLLABORATIVE COMMUNITY

Methods

To determine if the online courses developed as part of a Master's of Education program were providing collaborative experiences, a research study was conducted to collect data from the people who matter the most: the students themselves. The current study is a continuation of a prior study of collaboration in online communities (Decker, Beltran, Matzaganian, Walker, & Elzarka, 2014). An online survey was sent out to 264 Master's of Education students at a small, private university with a traditional central campus and several regional campuses located within a 200-mile radius. The central campus is located in a suburban city in the southwestern US. The students surveyed had completed at least one online course in the program between the Spring 2012 and Fall 2018 terms. One hundred thirty students completed the survey for a completion rate of 49%. The population consisted of 22 males and 108 females. Twenty-six percent were between the ages of 18-25; 41% were between the ages of 26-35, 17% were between the ages of 36-45, and 16% were 46 or older. Forty-eight percent were regional campus students while 52% attended the main campus. The majority of the participants (79%) indicated that they had taken at least three fully-online classes.

The courses in the Master's of Education program are offered in a fully online format. The numbers of students at each of the regional campuses are small. The online format allows for the students at the regional campuses to be combined into a larger group, which allows for more effective course facilitation. The average class size for each course ranges from 8-20 students.

The courses are delivered using the university's adopted LMS, which is Blackboard. Within Blackboard, instructors use a variety of tools to deliver content and engage learners. SoftChalk, a web-based lesson design software, is used in a similar format to lecture in a face-to-face classroom. Students read content, link to Internet resources, watch videos (instructor-made and/or embedded from other sources), and participate in quizzes and activities to check their understanding of the content. In addition to SoftChalk lessons, instructors utilize collaborative tools such as discussion boards, blogs, and wikis to help students process course content. The majority of the online courses are delivered in an asynchronous fashion. Occasionally, students may be asked to attend one to two synchronous sessions throughout the course for the purpose of student presentations or other course activities. Instructors typically use WebEx web conferencing software or Skype for these sessions.

The core curriculum in the Master's of Education program consists of four main content areas: educational assessment, methods of research, current issues in teaching, and a culminating master's project. The focus of these classes is to give educators additional skills that will help them keep current in their respective fields in order to be more effective in the classroom and also to help them develop leadership skills and knowledge to improve the field of education.

The survey given as part of the study consisted of 20 questions: seven demographic, nine Likert scale, and four open-ended. The nine Likert scale questions had a five-point range with '1' being associated with 'strongly disagree' to '5' being associated with 'strongly agree.' In addition, four open-ended questions were asked in order to provide additional insight for the Likert-scale responses. The Likert scale questions were excerpted with permission from the Community of Inquiry Questionnaire. Specifically, the questions selected were from the Social Presence section of the survey. The questions selected were those that most closely matched the intent of the research study. Arbaugh, Cleveland-Innes, Diaz, Garrison, Ice, Richardson, and Swan (2008) tested the instrument through a multi-institutional sample and found

Table 1. Summary of descriptive data

Item	Percent Scoring 4 or 5	Mean	Std. Dev.
How would you rate your ability to use technology?	82%	4.08	0.77
Getting to know other course participants gave me a sense of belonging in the course.	51%	3.35	1.21
I was able to form distinct impressions of some course participants.	45%	3.46	1.10
Online or web-based communication is an excellent medium for social interaction.	44%	3.29	1.09
I felt comfortable conversing through the online medium.	72%	3.93	1.18
I felt comfortable participating in the course discussions.	78%	4.18	1.02
I felt comfortable interacting with other course participants.	77%	4.07	1.02
I felt comfortable disagreeing with other course participants while still maintaining a sense of trust.	59%	3.62	1.21
I felt that other course participants acknowledged my point of view.	68%	3.91	0.95
Online discussions help me to develop a sense of collaboration.	58%	3.56	1.16

it to be a valid, reliable, and efficient measure of the dimensions specified, including social presence. Participants' responses were evaluated using descriptive statistics, correlations, and tests of difference.

Results and Analysis

The results of this study address students' perceptions in several key areas related to social presence, including technological ability, participation, belonging, and collaboration.

Means derived from the 5-point Likert scale questions indicate that students were generally confident in their ability to use technology. Means from responses related to this area was 4.08 with 82% of students indicating either a score of 4 or 5 for this question. Student responses were varied in their perceptions of the ability of the online class to create belonging, form distinct impressions of other students, establish meaningful social interactions, or develop a sense of collaboration. Means from responses related to these areas ranged from 3.29 to 3.56. Standard deviations for these responses were all over 1.0 indicating that scores were widely distributed across the 5-point scale. The percentage of students responding positively to these questions varied widely, ranging from only 44% believing online communication is an excellent medium for social interaction to 58% believing online discussions helped to develop a sense of collaboration.

Tests of difference were conducted based upon several demographic measures, including gender, age, and campus location. These data indicate two significant differences. Men responded more favorably to the question about ability to use technology. The average score for men was 4.41 whereas for women it was 4.01. The difference between men and women was found to be statistically significant ($t=-2.24$, $p=0.027$). Men responded much less positively to the question, "Getting to know others gave me a sense of belonging in the course," ($t = 2.90$, $p = 0.004$) than did women. In effect, men in this group were much less likely to gain a sense of belonging by getting to know others in online classes.

It is also interesting to note that there is a moderate positive correlation ($r = 0.62$, $p<0.001$) between "Getting to know others creates a sense of belonging in the course," and "Online discussions help to develop

Table 2. Gender differences on technology skills and a sense of belonging

	Ability to Use Technology		Getting to Know Others Gave Me a Sense of Belonging	
	Mean	**Std. Dev.**	**Mean**	**Std. Dev.**
Men	4.41	0.96	2.68	1.49
Women	4.01	0.72	3.48	1.11
t	-2.24		2.90	
p	0.027		0.004	

a sense of collaboration." Therefore, students who gain a sense of belonging by getting to know others in online classes also tend to develop a sense of collaboration through online discussions. In addition, there was also a moderate positive correlation ($r = 0.63$, $p<0.001$) between "I felt comfortable interacting with other course participants," and "Online discussions help to develop a sense of collaboration." Therefore, students who feel comfortable interacting with other participants also tend to develop a sense of collaboration through online discussions. Additionally, there were three other moderate correlations: "I felt comfortable disagreeing with others while still maintaining a sense of trust" and "I felt comfortable interacting with other course participants" ($r = 0.67$, $p<0.001$), "I felt comfortable interacting with other course participants" and "I felt other course participants acknowledged my point of view" ($r = 0.66$, $p<0.001$), and "I felt comfortable disagreeing with others while still maintaining a sense of trust" and "I felt other course participants acknowledged my point of view" ($r = 0.62$, $p<0.001$). Therefore, students who are more comfortable with online interactions also feel that their views are acknowledged by others and retain a sense of trust even when disagreeing in an online setting.

Survey Themes

In the Master's of Education classes, a variety of course activities are implemented in an effort to build community and encourage collaboration between students and instructors in the online environment. The four open-ended questions included at the conclusion of the questionnaire were designed to generate additional insight into the topics addressed in the Likert scale questions. These questions were particularly

Table 3. Relationship between collaboration and community

	I Felt Comfortable Disagreeing With Others While Still Maintaining a Sense of Trust	I Felt That Other Course Participants Acknowledged My Point of View	Online Discussions Help Me to Develop a Sense of Collaboration
Getting to Know Others Gave Me a Sense of Belonging			0.62
I Felt Comfortable Interacting With Other Course Participants	0.67	0.66	0.63
I Felt Comfortable Disagreeing With Others While Still Maintaining a Sense of Trust		0.62	

N=130, **p<0.001 for all correlations in Table 3*

helpful in finding out how specific components implemented in the online classes have contributed to a sense of community and collaboration. Students repeatedly indicated that course introductions using presentation software or screencasting, discussion boards and blogs, synchronous communication media, and group work were helpful in developing a social presence.

In several of the courses in the program, students are asked to introduce themselves as part of the first module. Students are instructed to use a variety of tools for their introductions, including presentation software (PowerPoint, Prezi) and screencasting (SnagIt, Screencast-o-matic). The effectiveness of this introductory activity was related to a question on the survey which asked whether getting to know other participants in the course gave students a sense of belonging. Participants' responses to this question indicated mixed feelings; however, it is clear from the open-ended responses that many students found these introductions to be helpful in creating a sense of community. According to Marzano (2007), "Everyone likes to be known by others" (p. 154). This activity can build camaraderie and provide opportunities for the teacher to incorporate this information into class discussions. One student shared, "The introductions required at the beginning of each course made me feel like I knew my classmates. By seeing pictures of their lives and learning about their interests, I was able to identify things we had in common and put a face to their name throughout the semester." Students also commented on the benefit of building this sense of community early on in the course. One student wrote, "With the video introductions, I felt as if I already knew my classmates beforehand, so collaborating with one another came easily." Another student commented, "Initially listening to and reading each classmate's introduction of themselves gave me a sense of who they were and allowed me to make associations between their experiences and my own." Students also found that the introductions facilitated their online discussions throughout the course. "With the getting to know you videos, I was able to see other students' faces and hear about their lives outside of comments that they made on a blog. This also gave a better sense of what experiences in their lives shaped their opinions and comments."

Class activities also required students to interact with each other within the context of the content being studied. These activities included wikis, blogs, and discussion boards on a variety of topics. Students were required to post original content and comment on their classmates' posts to generate dialogue. The effectiveness of these activities was evaluated through several questions on the survey.

When asked specifically about course discussions, responses indicated that students saw the value in these activities. "Being able to comment and discuss with others made me feel comfortable because we were able to comment on our own time. It was also a great way to get a chance to see everyone's point of view which sometimes can get lost in a classroom setting because the quieter students may not have a chance to speak or feel comfortable doing so." Another student commented, "Discussion boards allowed me to state what I thought about the learning in a way that I received feedback from other classmates who had completely opposite views yet acknowledged my opinion as well as providing their reasons for their own thoughts." Still another student reported, "When you have a classmate who is able to speak intelligently, but does so in a way that is relaxed, it creates a great vibe for all of the other participants to engage more freely in online dialogue."

Although the majority of the coursework in the online program is delivered asynchronously, students are occasionally asked to participate in synchronous sessions and collaboration activities through tools such as Skype, WebEx, and Google Hangout. When asked whether they felt comfortable interacting with other course participants, the mean response was 4.07. One student commented, "When we engage in synchronous online meetings/debates, we have the opportunity to share and build our ideas in real time." This reinforces the work of Han and Hill (2007). Another student reported, "During our online video chats, I was able to talk with people about something we all had experienced together. We were able to discuss the different aspects of the book we had read and bounce ideas off of each other."

The core courses of the online program all require some form of partner or group work to complete assignments. These assignments include creating blogs and wikis, giving presentations, participating in debates, and constructing assessments. These assignments provide students with opportunities to collaborate and collectively enhance their understanding of course content via the use of interactive tools. Similar to the findings of Lee, Ngampornchai, Trail-Constant, Abril, and Srivinivasan (2016), we found several positive aspects of group work. Course activities are structured with the intent that students get to know each other and build a sense of community prior to engaging in partner and group work.

The group work then further enhances the connections between students. These efforts combined led to students feeling their viewpoints were acknowledged by other course participants (mean response of 3.91). Students also reported feeling comfortable disagreeing with other course participants (mean response of 3.62) while still maintaining a sense of trust. One student said, "Feedback on my own blogs/discussions from classmates allowed me to feel part of the class community." Another student stated, "The positive about working in groups was seeing other points of view which led to great discussions." An additional student concurred, "Class discussions, via the web, helped me feel as though I was part of a class, not just a singular student going it alone. It was nice to see feedback from classmates both positive and negative on certain topics. I enjoyed seeing what other students thought, shared, or experienced while working the same assignments as I was." These data reveal the necessity for students to be engaged in the discussion and with each other.

Limitations

As with any original data research, this study has limitations. These limitations warrant caution when interpreting the data. They are explained below.

- **Experimental Mortality**: The total number of students in the original sample pool was 264. Of these, 130 completed the survey. While this is a respectable return rate of 49%, there is the possibility of the completers not appropriately representing the student pool.
- **Selection Bias**: The 264 students in the original pool were all students who completed at least one online course in their degree program. Since the few students who began an online course but subsequently dropped have been omitted from the study, the results can only be generalized to those who complete online courses. In addition, many participants had no other choice but to take the online version of the course(s), regardless of their feelings toward online learning. This may have skewed the results, given the possibility that some participants were negatively disposed toward online classes and were only taking them out of necessity.
- **Halo Effect**: Given that some of the student participants were still enrolled in the degree program when they completed the survey, it is possible that responses were given based on what the participants thought the researchers wanted to see.

SOLUTIONS AND RECOMMENDATIONS

Strategies for Effective Collaboration in an Online Environment

Based on online teaching experiences and the feedback received from students, it is clear that effective collaboration in an online environment is not easy to achieve and must be approached in a very systematic way. It is also apparent that not all collaborative tools are equally effective nor is there a one size fits all approach to encourage collaboration in online environments. This section will focus on the strategies that have been found to be the most beneficial in promoting collaboration for students and faculty.

Online environments can be isolating. Including group interaction and projects can enhance students' experiences in online courses. Group activities provide opportunities for students to collaborate with others, build relationships that lessen the isolation of an online course, and work with others to clarify their understanding of course content. As in the face-to-face classroom, group work has many benefits when it is implemented properly. Online educators must consider many factors in designing and implementing group work. They need to have a clear purpose for each group assignment and provide sufficient support to help the group succeed on both the social and academic levels.

Establishing an Online Community

To establish an online course that promotes collaboration, there are three crucial aspects for the instructor to consider. The first is that students need some kind of orientation to the online environment itself. In order for students to fully engage in collaborative activities, they need to feel comfortable navigating the course setup. They need to know where to find course content, how to find and use the collaboration tools that are available to them, and where to go for help when needed. An orientation video illustrating how to access the course and navigate within it is particularly helpful. This, in combination with a copy of the syllabus and early access to the online environment prior to the start of the class, helps set the students up for success.

In addition, the instructor needs to help the students get to know each other. The instructor needs to be intentional about providing opportunities that mimic the natural relationship building that happens in a face-to-face class. One option is to have a synchronous session during the first week of the class. Using web conferencing software, students can log in to a virtual space and introduce themselves to each other. The instructor can also take advantage of this opportunity to engage students in icebreaker-style activities and clarify course expectations. Another activity that helps build a sense of community in the online environment includes having students post an introduction to themselves with pictures. Students can then view the posts and leave comments for each other, beginning an interpersonal dialogue. The instructor can also create a "Getting to Know You" activity or game based on the introductions students have posted.

Finally, the instructor needs to specify clear expectations regarding online etiquette. These expectations govern students' interactions in the class in much the same way as class norms in a face-to-face class would. Due to the perceived informal nature of communication in the online environment, students may need a reminder to be professional and respectful in their interactions with each other. Online etiquette expectations may be specific to the type of activity students are engaged in. There may be occasions where informal language is acceptable, such as group discussions or processing activities. Other activities, such as blog posts and journal entries, may require more formal, grammatically correct writing.

This differentiation should be specified ahead of time. Lastly, a summative statement may help remind students to be considerate of others in their interactions (i.e., "In any and all communication, be sure that whatever you say online you would also be comfortable saying directly to that person.")

Establishing Instructor Presence

Students also need an orientation to the instructor. Prior to the start of the class, the instructor needs to consider their online presence. Simple steps, such as including photos, sharing personal and professional biographical information, and highlighting their teaching philosophy, help the students to get to know the instructor and their style. This also helps students begin to feel more comfortable as they begin to tackle the academic content. These steps help students identify with their instructor as an authentic persona.

It is also critical for the instructor to maintain their presence throughout the course. This can be accomplished through responding to students in ways that incorporate both the instructor's personality and their knowledge of the students in the class. Online instructors should purposefully design course activities that provide opportunities for meaningful interactions with students. For example, instructors can provide feedback that asks open-ended questions to promote ongoing dialogue with their students.

Another way to establish instructor presence is through regular and ongoing communication with students. Sharing how to contact the instructor as well as having virtual office hours provides students a range of methods for communicating. By sending timely communication such as emails, comments on discussions, and course announcements, the instructor's presence is visible to students and creates an atmosphere of support.

Collaborative Project Planning

Group projects are an authentic way to build community in the online classroom. When carefully planned, group projects can help students learn to collaborate with others and deepen their understanding of course content. Prior to assigning online group projects, educators need to think through the following questions:

- What is the instructional purpose or objective for this activity?
- How will doing this assignment as a group benefit students versus students working individually?
- What is the ideal group size for this project?
- How much time will be required from each group member to complete their part of the task?
- What communication tools are available to support group members collaborating?
- What tools are available to help students demonstrate their learning?
- How will I, as the instructor, ensure equal participation from all group members?
- What kind of modeling/support will I need to provide?
- How will I assess both the group and the individual students in relation to the content?
- How will I assess both the group and the individual students in relation to their collaborative efforts?
- How much of the work can be completed in an asynchronous format versus synchronous?

Once the above questions have been considered, the instructor can then move on to the subsequent stages of project planning discussed below.

Directions

After the instructor has carefully thought through the setup of the group activity, the next step is to establish clear directions. Directions need to be thorough and separated into comprehensible steps. The purpose for the assignment should be clearly stated and tied to the learning outcomes of the course. This helps to establish the relevance of the assignment for the students. In addition, it is helpful to provide clear steps students will take through the assignment. Breaking the assignment down in this fashion helps students know where to begin and how to progress. Clear expectations for the final product should also be described and may be supplemented with an assignment rubric. Due dates need to be clearly articulated as well and published in a variety of locations (course syllabus, course calendar, Learning Management System calendar, etc.).

Directions are most effective when they are presented in a variety of ways. One suggestion is to create a screencast giving the overview of the purpose and the directions for the assignment. A benefit to doing this is that students can view the directions as many times as needed as they progress throughout the assignment. In addition, a screencast provides both visual and auditory support. Also, written directions can be posted on the LMS for students to reference.

Roles

One of the keys to implementing effective group projects is establishing clear roles for the students within the group. Failure to establish roles can lead to inequity of workload and responsibility. Roles may vary according to the style and content of the project.

Oftentimes, in the online environment, the roles need to be more specific than they would be in a face-to-face class. For example, if the group will be collaborating through online tools such as Skype or Google Apps, one particular group member should be assigned to initiate the contact. Other potential role responsibilities may include documenting the group's progress, keeping the group functioning within the parameters of the assignment, presenting for the group, or being the contact person for the group. Roles will vary according to the content and format of the project.

Use of Tools

It is important to remember that some tools work better for certain assignments than others. Also, some students will prefer certain tools over others due to their own learning style and preferences. Providing multiple options allows students and groups to select the specific tools that will best their needs.

To promote collaboration, chat systems may be used. Three such systems that are user-friendly and effective are Skype, Google Chat, and WebEx. Skype can be used to hold individual meetings between the instructor and student to clarify assignments and to give specific feedback. In addition, students can use Skype to conference about their group projects. Additionally, students may also use Skype to set up virtual meetings with classmates to dialogue about upcoming assignments and to discuss course content. In fact, students may continue to Skype with each other on a social basis even after the course is completed.

Another tool used to deal with the logistics of online teaching is Doodle. This free online scheduling tool allows us to set up whole group meetings and individual group check-ins. Students can also use it to coordinate meetings for their specific groups.

A third use of tools is for productivity. Google apps such as Google docs and presentations allow students to collaborate and share the same document. These apps also allow the instructor to monitor a group's progress and each group member's participation through the revision history. An important point to remember when setting up an online class is that the instructor needs to model the use of these tools to maximize their effectiveness. Providing short videos with accompanying directions and opportunities for students to try out the tools before using them in the group setting makes students feel more comfortable before the academic content is added.

Accountability and Progress Monitoring

Accountability is an important consideration in group assignments. Students need to have a clear understanding of the instructor's expectations for their participation and how those expectations will be evaluated.

Accountability should be ongoing throughout the project to ensure the group is working together effectively and staying on track for successful completion of the assignment. To this end, it may be helpful to have checkpoints throughout the duration of the assignment for groups to check in and report their progress. This assists the students in monitoring their process and allows for early intervention on the part of the instructor if the group is not working together effectively. These checkpoints may be opportunities for the instructor to evaluate the students or they may be self-evaluations that the students complete independently.

Wikis can be a powerful tool for establishing ongoing accountability throughout a project. For example, while a group is collaborating, they can use a wiki to track and document their process. Multiple pages can be created within the wiki for this purpose. The front page of the wiki can serve as a checklist of steps or tasks for the group as a whole, while additional pages document the efforts of the individual members of the group. By the end of the assignment, the wiki can serve to give the instructor insight into the group's process and collaborative efforts.

Presentations

After students have invested their time and energy into group projects, it is important to give them an opportunity to present their work and to receive feedback from their classmates. In the online environment, these presentations can be presented in both asynchronous and synchronous formats. The synchronous format allows for immediate feedback, which is often more beneficial to students than delayed feedback. One presentation tool is WebEx. This platform allows students to be in the same virtual meeting room. Having students use webcams allows students to see each other while presenting, which students appreciate, and it helps establish the visual connection. This platform also allows presenters to share documents and their screens. Whole class discussions can also take place via students using headset microphones or using the chat boxes provided. Questions that other classmates pose can be quickly answered by the presenters. In addition, the virtual meetings can be recorded which allows any student who missed the presentation to be able to still hear the content. Listening to the presentation also provides the presenters the opportunity to reflect on their delivery style.

Synchronous Opportunities

While some students take online classes wanting to avoid having to interact with others, many students prefer having some synchronous class sessions. These sessions should be noted in advance to help students plan and should be at times that are conducive to the students. These synchronous sessions can be check in events where the instructor does some reteaching, answers students' questions, and talks about upcoming assignments. These sessions can also serve as a way for students to interact with the content. For example, we have used synchronous sessions to have students participate in online debates on current issues in education. Students are in teams and do their research on their topic using their learning management system tools. Then in the synchronous session, they debate their topic while their classmates are watching and listening and are able to ask questions.

Fostering Ongoing Communication

In an online environment, it is crucial to use a variety of tools to maintain communication among the students and between the professor and students. One way to do this is to have a Frequently Asked Questions section in the Learning Management System. Students post their questions, and the instructor adds a response. This prevents the instructor having to respond to multiple students separately on the same issue or concern. The key to this communication being effective is the instructor responding quickly. We have also seen students taking the initiative to answer each other's postings which helps to build collaboration.

It is also important for the class setup to incorporate communication opportunities. For example, students might partner together to create their response to a discussion question or their blog or wiki entry. When assigning these activities, the professor also needs to communicate with the students regarding their responses. When the professor adds an entry into the conversation thread, it validates that the students' work is being read and their participation is important.

In addition to instructor directed communication, students can also initiate communication. Showing students how to use online chat tools to communicate and collaborate allows them to do so without the aid of the instructor. Over the duration of the course, students' comfort with such tools will increase along with the opportunities for naturally occurring interaction.

Evaluation

Evaluation of group projects in an online environment is multifaceted and should include assessment of content as well as the group's collaborative effort. Assessing collaboration can be challenging but provides insight for the instructor and valuable feedback for the students. Having students do both self and peer evaluations for their group can shed light on how well they collaborated. It also encourages students to reflect upon their understanding of the content and learning objectives as well as engage in higher order educational objectives.

Rubrics are a helpful tool for assessment. They allow the instructor to list several components of an assignment that will be assessed, as well as levels of achievement specific to each component. Rubrics can be shared with students at the start of the project. This allows students to understand the specific expectations of the assignment and monitor their progress in relation to those expectations throughout the project.

FUTURE RESEARCH DIRECTIONS

Based on the research presented in this chapter, there are several compelling directions for future research. The field of online education has continued to grow, and there are many factors to consider in evaluating its effectiveness.

One possible area for future research is to look at changes in students' perceptions over time. The tools and approaches used in online education have continued to evolve as technology has evolved. Further study to compare the impact on perceptions of these new tools and approaches could have significant impact on instructional decisions.

Another area to explore is the longitudinal effect of continued participation in online classes on students' perceptions. As students continue to enroll in online courses and have greater experience with different tools and approaches, it would be compelling to note how their perceptions change.

An additional area of research may center on the reasons students select online educational experiences. Future research could examine why students elect online experiences, and how their perceptions of those experiences match the reality.

Many of the above research efforts should also be explored by those wishing to replicate the approach described in this chapter. Populations of students, the impact of geographical locations, and content within programs all vary widely. It is imperative for programs to collect data to study the effectiveness of their specific efforts.

Instructional technology and online education are fields of rapid growth and evolution. New tools and approaches are being implemented regularly. It is the inherent responsibility of those involved in online environments to ensure they are using the most effective approaches in their instruction.

CONCLUSION

While online teaching has existed for two decades and has become embedded into the fabric of modern education, questions persist about its efficacy in producing collaborative learning opportunities. Students and instructors alike sometimes find it a challenge to build a culture of shared learning in an online medium. This study confirms that collaboration can occur in the online environment when interactive strategies are implemented with intentionality. The strategies outlined in this chapter can produce impactful results in connecting students and creating an environment of cooperative learning. Additionally, the creation of a collaborative online environment can provide opportunities for more reserved students to engage with their peers. Therefore, the instructor's challenge is to provide meaningful collaborative experiences that build a learning community and enhance the students' overall online experience.

REFERENCES

Abamu, J. (2018). *The number of students taking online courses is quickly rising, but perceptions are changing slowly.* Retrieved from https://www.edsurge.com/amp/news/2018-06-12-the-number-of-students-taking-in-online-courses-is-quickly-rising-but-perceptions-are-changing-slowly

Arbaugh, J., & Hwang, A. (2006). Does "teaching presence" exist in online MBA courses? *The Internet and Higher Education*, *9*(1), 9–21. doi:10.1016/j.iheduc.2005.12.001

Arbaugh, J. B., Cleveland-Innes, M., Diaz, S. R., Garrison, D. R., Ice, P., Richardson, J., & Swan, K. P. (2008). Developing a community of inquiry instrument: Testing a measure of the community of inquiry framework using a multi-institutional sample. *The Internet and Higher Education*, *11*(3-4), 133–136. doi:10.1016/j.iheduc.2008.06.003

Baker, C. (2010). The impact of instructor immediacy and presence for online student affective learning, cognition, and motivation. *The Journal of Educators Online*, *7*(1), 1–19. doi:10.9743/JEO.2010.1.2

Decker, J. C., Beltran, V., Matzaganian, M., Walker, N. T., & Elzarka, S. (2014). Creating a collaborative community in online environments. In C. N. Stevenson, & J. C. Bauer (Eds.), *Building online communities in higher education institutions* (pp. 369–387). Hershey, PA: IGI Global. doi:10.4018/978-1-4666-5178-4.ch019

Dewey, J. (1916). *Democracy and education*. London, UK: MacMillan.

Falls, I., Bahhouth, V., Chuang, C. M., & Bahhouth, J. (2014). Factors influencing students' perceptions of online teamwork. *SAGE Open*, 1–9. doi:10.1177/2158244014525415

Garrison, D. R., Anderson, T., & Archer, W. (2000). Critical inquiry in a text-based environment: Computer conferencing in higher education. *The Internet and Higher Education*, *2*(2-3), 87–105. doi:10.1016/S1096-7516(00)00016-6

Green, N. C., Edwards, H., Wolodko, B., Stewart, C., Brooks, M., & Littledyke, R. (2010). Reconceptualising higher education pedagogy in online learning. *Distance Education*, *31*(3), 257–273. doi:10.1080/01587919.2010.513951

Han, S. Y., & Hill, J. R. (2007). Collaborate to learn, learn to collaborate: Examining the roles of context, community, and cognition in asynchronous discussion. *Journal of Educational Computing Research*, *36*(1), 89–123. doi:10.2190/A138-6K63-7432-HL10

Harrington, S., & Floyd, K. (2009). *Enhancing engagement and the value of the course to the student through course organization and active learning*. Online Classroom.

Kagan, S. (2001). *Kagan structures: Research and rationale. Kagan Online Magazine*.

Koole, M. (2014). Identity and the itinerant online learner. *International Review of Research in Open and Distance Learning*, *15*(6), 52–70. doi:10.19173/irrodl.v15i6.1879

Kumar, S., & Ritzhaupt, A. D. (2014). Adapting the Community of Inquiry survey for an online graduate program: Implications for online programs. *E-Learning and Digital Media*, *11*(1), 59–71. doi:10.2304/elea.2014.11.1.59

Lederman, D. (2018). *New data: Online environments grow, and share of overall enrollment grows faster.* Retrieved from https://www.insidehighered.com/print/digital-learning/article/2018/11/07/new-data-online-enrollments-grow-and-share-overall-enrollment

Lee, A. J., Ngampornchai, A., Trail-Constant, T., Abril, A., & Srinivasan, S. (2016). Does a case-based online group project increase students' satisfaction with interaction in online courses? *Active Learning in Higher Education*, *17*(30), 249–260. doi:10.1177/1469787416654800

Marzano, R. J. (2007). *The art and science of teaching*. Virginia: ASCD.

Marzano, R. J., Pickering, D. J., & Pollock, J. E. (2001). *Classroom instruction that works. Research-based strategies for increasing student achievement*. Alexandria, VA: Association for Supervision and Curriculum Development.

Richardson, J. C., & Lowenthal, P. (2017). Instructor social presence: Learners' needs and a neglected component of the Communities of Inquiry. In A. L. Whiteside, A. G. Dikkers, & K. Swan (Eds.), *Social Presence in online learning: Multiple perspectives, theories, and practices*. Sterling, VA: Stylus Publishing.

Richardson, J. C., & Swan, K. (2003). Examining social presence in online courses in relation to students' perceived learning and satisfaction. *Journal of Asynchronous Learning Networks*, *7*(1), 68–88.

Rogers, P., & Lea, M. (2005). Social presence in distributed group environments: The role of social identity. *Behaviour & Information Technology*, *24*(2), 151–158. doi:10.1080/01449290410001723472

Rourke, L., Anderson, T., Garrison, D. R., & Archer, W. (2001). Assessing social presence in asynchronous, text-based computer conferencing. *Journal of Distance Education*, *14*(3), 51–70.

Sadeghi, H., & Kardan, A. A. (2015). A novel justice-based linear model for optimal learner group formation in computer-supported collaborative learning environments. *Computers in Human Behavior*, *48*, 436–447. doi:10.1016/j.chb.2015.01.020

Scheuermann, M. (2010, Feb. 24). *Engaging students with synchronous methods in online courses* [Audio podcast]. Retrieved from http://www.facultyfocus.com/seminars/engaging-students-with-synchronous-methods-in-online-courses/?aa=10502

Seaman, J. E., Allen, I. E., & Seaman, J. (2018). *Grade increase: Tracking distance education in the United States*. Retrieved from: http://www.onlinelearningsurvey.com/highered.html

Sull, E. C. (2010, Oct. 28). Online teaching tips for leveraging students' insights and experiences in online education [Web log post]. Retrieved from http://www.facultyfocus.com/topic/articles/online-education/

Vygotsky, L. S. (1978). *Mind in society: The development of higher psychological processes*. Cambridge, MA: Harvard University Press.

ADDITIONAL READING

Bender, T. (2012). *Discussion-based online teaching to enhance student learning: Theory, practice, and assessment*. Sterling, VA: Stylus Publishing.

Boettcher, J. V., & Conrad, R. M. (2016). *The online teaching survival guide*. San Francisco, CA: Jossey-Bass.

Conrad, R., & Donaldson, J. A. (2012). *Continuing to engage the online learner: More activities and resources for creative instruction*. San Francisco, CA: Jossey-Bass.

Ko, S., & Rossen, S. (2010). *Teaching online: A practical guide*. New York, NY: Routledge. doi:10.4324/9780203855201

Lehman, R. (2010). *Creating a sense of presence in online teaching: How to "be there" for distance learners*. San Francisco, CA: Jossey-Bass.

Major, C. H. (2015). *Teaching online: A guide to theory, research, practice*. Baltimore, MD: Johns Hopkins University Press.

Nilson, L. B., & Goodson, L. A. (2018). *Online teaching at its best: Merging instructional design with teaching and learning*. San Francisco, CA: Jossey-Bass.

Palloff, R. M., & Pratt, K. (2011). *The excellent online instructor: Strategies for professional development*. San Francisco, CA: Jossey-Bass.

Simonson, M., Smaldino, S. E., Albright, M., & Zvacek, S. (2011). *Teaching and learning at a distance: Foundations of distance education*. Boston, MA: Pearson.

Stavredes, T. (2011). *Effective online teaching: Foundations and strategies for student success*. San Francisco, CA: Jossey-Bass.

Thormann, J., & Zimmerman, I. K. (2012). *The complete step-by-step guide to designing and teaching online courses*. New York, NY: Teachers College Press.

Vai, M., & Sosulski, K. (2015). *Essentials of online course design: A standards-based guide*. New York, NY: Routledge. doi:10.4324/9781315770901

KEY TERMS AND DEFINITIONS

Chat Systems: Online tools that allow one or more people to chat via text or video chat such as Skype, Google Hangout, or Google Chat.

Learning Management System (LMS): A platform for delivery of online instruction such as Blackboard or Moodle.

Presentation Software: Software used to organize and deliver content to others such as Microsoft PowerPoint or Prezi.

Screencasting: Software that permits users to capture their computer screen with voiceover such as Jing, SnagIt, or Camtasia.

Social Presence: The affective or interpersonal presence of the instructor and students in an online course.

Web Conferencing Software: Tools that facilitate synchronous online interaction in a virtual classroom environment such as WebEx or Adobe Connect.

Chapter 2
Overcoming Implicit Bias in Collaborative Online Learning Communities

Ludmila T. Battista
Claremont Lincoln University, USA

Lisa Wright
University of Missouri, USA

ABSTRACT

This chapter will lay the groundwork for exploring implicit bias and the effects in the online higher education environment. The authors will analyze privilege, power, oppression, and institutionalized bias and explore examples in higher education, through both student and faculty perspectives. The chapter will focus on collaborative solutions to a diverse variety of case studies on implicit bias across race, culture, gender, ability, and other dimensions. An emphasis will be placed on reflective analysis and creating collaborative experiences for online students and educators.

INTRODUCTION

Uncovering implicit bias can be challenging and the intense self-exploration necessary in assessing personal attitudes can be painful, just as discussing them and finding solutions can be overwhelming. This chapter will focus on exploring different types of bias, examining dimensions of power and privilege, considering effects of stereotype threat, utilizing tools for self-examination and uncovering and discussing implicit bias in a collaborative manner.

Both explicit and implicit bias can be found in many aspects of the higher education experience and can be especially challenging to address in the online environment. Implicit bias experiences can range across a variety of contexts including having immediate effects on faculty attitudes and perceptions impacting policies, expectations, communication and grading (Kirwan Institute for the Study of Race and Ethnicity, 2012; Gullo & Beachum, 2017), as well as indirect effects such as through letters of recommendation (Houser & Lemmons, 2018), mentorship opportunities, international service, recruit-

DOI: 10.4018/978-1-5225-9814-5.ch002

ment and engagement (Diversity Abroad, 2016), to name a few. Explicit bias is bias that is easily seen and identified and is most often the bias discussed in the media and in learning contexts. This chapter will include examples of both explicit and implicit bias in an effort to ensure that both are recognized and addressed. In the online environment, recognizing and addressing implicit bias can be especially challenging.

Examining the multiple facets of implicit bias in higher education is necessary for a comprehensive understanding of this issue. The objectives of this chapter are:

1. Distinguish between explicit and implicit bias in a variety of contexts
2. Discuss dimensions of power, privilege and oppression as they influence attitudes and perspectives of both faculty and students
3. Identify how stereotype threat can have profound and far-reaching effects on students
4. Explore case studies on implicit bias along with solutions and resources
5. Provide empowering strategies for communication and collaboration for diverse populations in higher education

BACKGROUND INFORMATION

Consider how subtle underlying perceptions impact behavior and attitudes in the following examples;

- An African American man making a floral delivery to Professor Magee, dean of a law school in a high-priced San Francisco neighborhood expresses confusion and disbelief when the petite, casually dressed black woman answering the door announces, "I am Professor Magee" (Magee, 2015)
- A teacher who considers herself to be impartial to her students, unknowingly conveys lower expectations for students of color, offering less instances of praise and intervenes more frequently with disciplinary action towards students of color. (Kirwan Institute, 2012)
- A female college student taking a math test in a room full of mostly males, scores worse than she would have if the test were given in a room with a balance of males and females (Hill, 2018)
- A student with dyslexia is given less homework and easier assignments
- A female professor is less receptive to a Middle Eastern student and takes offense to some of his comments in the online environment because she believes he does not respect women. While she doesn't voice these perceptions, they do affect her perception of the student.
- A white male in an online classroom comprised of primarily of female women of color does not participate frequently due to his concern of offending someone by saying the "wrong thing."
- An online college professor engages in less discussion with a female student who mentions "her wife" in discussion posts because he feels uncomfortable realizing the student is a lesbian.
- An online instructor does not provide requested letters of reference to students who do not attend graduation where she can meet the student face to face.
- A student who uses a wheelchair for mobility is assured that the study abroad accommodations will be wheelchair accessible and she will be able to participate in all activities. The accommodations were not wheelchair accessible and the student had to be carried into and out of the room each day which was demoralizing for the student.
- Faculty recruit students as mentors for other students based solely on faculty recommendations.

In some cases, these are actual documented findings based on studies, while others are anecdotal experiences. In each of these contexts, while there may not be explicit discrimination or even the awareness of bias, less obvious perceptions come into play influencing reactions. This is implicit bias. Consider how frequently one may be affected by seemingly unexpressed bias.

Distinguishing Bias: Implicit and Explicit

In many circumstances, the brain's tendency to categorize perceptions can be efficient and helpful in a world often overwhelming with constant stimulation. Being able to identify a furry, four-legged creature as a dog and not a bear or adjusting one's behavior based on a context (such as the proper behavior at a wedding as compared to an accident scene) are harmless or even helpful examples of the many ways humans categorize perceptions on a daily basis. This ability to quickly identify or ascertain a situation can save time and lead to appropriate responses (Sack, 2014). However, when one's tendency to categorize leads to negative or harmful attitudes and judgments about individuals or groups that may or may not be accurate, we begin to roam into the realm of bias. For example, is a white woman's fear response of crossing the street when she encounters an African American male a result of a helpful categorization tendency or harmful bias?

Bias is defined as prejudice or judgment (whether positive or negative) based on a characteristic, such as race, gender, age, socioeconomic status, disability, education level or any other dimension. Even a positive judgment or perception based on bias can be problematic if it awards power or privilege to a group at the expense of another. Affinity bias, for example, is an often-unconscious preference for people who share qualities similar to that of the perceiver (Burton, 2017). A professor who engages with a student who is from the same hometown or who is also a yoga enthusiast, may be acting on affinity bias. At face value, this may seem harmless, but if other students perceive a preference on the part of the professor, they may feel the effects of a shift in power or privilege. While possibly unintentional (or even unconscious), the professor may convey a more open, approachable relationship with some, but not other students.

When a preference or bias is reflected in communication or behavior, the individual may or may not be actively aware of his/her attitudes or beliefs, but this is considered "explicit bias" and often occurs as the response to a perceived threat, such as physical safety or economic security (Perception Institute). Explicit bias is often readily identifiable due to the nature of it being expressed through observable behaviors. Blatant discrimination, vocalizing prejudicial beliefs or promoting stereotypes are obvious examples of explicit bias. While societal attitudes towards overt prejudice and discrimination has seemingly declined (most people actively denounce explicit examples of racial and sexual discrimination, for example), some social scientists believe many simply learn to avoid expressing such openly racist views (Beattie, 2013). Even further, implicit or unconscious bias is more difficult to discern and challenging to eradicate, even (or especially) for individuals who consciously reject prejudice and discriminatory attitudes (Myers, 2011). "I'm not racist, I don't see color," or "I love gay people!" one may claim, making it even more challenging to search for and accept deeply hidden implicit bias. Award-winning psychologist, researcher and professor Geoffrey Beattie, author of *Our Racist Heart?* suggests that implicit bias exists in even the most liberal, and educated, seemingly non-biased individuals. Psychologists in the field of implicit social cognition have long recognized the unconscious and automatic perceptions that influence consumers through marketing and advertising, and perhaps this is easier for many to stomach than the equally implicit attitudes towards often socially stigmatized groups such as African Americans, women and LGBTQ (Brownstein, 2015). Of course, unconscious perceptions can affect any group including those with disabilities, the poor, uneducated or those in a particular age group.

Often this bias is deeply rooted in one's subconscious and it can be especially challenging to identify such attitudes and beliefs, especially for those who see themselves as being generally nonjudgmental and without prejudice. However, the very nature of implicit bias means that it is often so deeply ingrained in core values and heavily influenced by personal experiences that implicit bias is not usually recognizable to the individual and research has demonstrated the devastating social and economic impact in areas such as the criminal justice system, education and health care to name a few (Kirwan Institute, 2014).

Power, Privilege, and Types of Bias

It is helpful to consider the role of power and privilege as they relate to bias. While privilege within a society is defined as the unearned advantage or benefit of the dominant group over other groups, typically, the privileged group does not recognize this advantage and often attributes it to personal effort and hard work. Just as implicit bias is so deeply ingrained at an unconscious level that the individual may not even be aware of bias, likewise, the social, cultural, economic or institutional privileges enjoyed by dominant groups can contribute to this subconscious bias, as well. Typically, in contemporary American society privilege is experienced by individuals who are members of one or more of the following groups; white, able-bodied, heterosexual, cisgender, males, Christians, the middle class, middle-aged, and/or English speaking. (Vanderbilt University, 2019) The individual who is a member of one or more of these privileged groups may believe, "I worked hard to get where I'm at," not realizing that while the effort exerted certainly may have contributed to the progress made, simply by being part of one or more of these dominant groups has already given him/her a "head start." Unconscious bias perpetuates this phenomenon. For example, a college professor may erroneously believe that because she was able to work her way through college, a student who struggles to complete coursework because of conflicts with a work schedule is simply not "trying hard enough." A variety of implicit biases may be at work here. The work opportunities and income available to a student who does not enjoy certain dominant group privileges may be exponentially more challenging than the professor's college work experience. Consider how some of these biases may come to play in the classroom environment;

Affinity Bias

Affinity bias is the individual's tendency to hold positive feelings for those that they view as similar to themselves or someone they know. For example, a professor who practices Christianity may learn through casual discussions about a student's affiliation with a Christian church, and as such, may feel a connection and affinity for this student. At face value, this may not appear to be a bias, but if the common factor influences the professor's interaction, comments and expectations of that student, it puts this student in a privileged position over other students. Affinity can be derived from a number of different dimensions- factors such as age, background, ethnicity and religion are some, but also any other number of possibilities such as where the student is from, his/her occupation, the fact that both individuals like Frank Sinatra or are marathon runners....or perhaps the student just reminds the professor of his younger brother! (Burton, 2017)

Attribution Bias

Attribution bias is the tendency to view positive outcomes pertaining to one's self as due to effort and individual skills or qualities, and attribute negative outcomes to situational factors or those beyond one's own control. An example might be the perception that performing poorly on an oral presentation is because of a lack of sleep but earning a high grade on an exam is due to personal effort and intelligence. Conversely, when making these attributions to others, the tendency is to attribute positive outcomes to luck or situational contexts beyond the individual's control ("She just got lucky," or "She's the teacher's favorite") and attributing negative outcomes to personal effort or qualities. In the classroom environment, this might be demonstrated by the instructor's perception that a non-native English speaker does not have the content knowledge or ability to write a high-quality thesis statement, rather than a situational factor, such as a lack of clarity on the assignment. The tendency to correlate positive attributions to the dominant group also contributes to bias. (Levine & Hogg, 2010)

Confirmation Bias

All humans tend to look for confirmation of what they already believe to be true. This is true in personal beliefs, conducting research, hiring practices, and evaluating students. In this way an individual is more apt to recognize and adapt evidence that confirms a point of view (or in this case a perception or bias) then one that contradicts it. Researchers must be very careful about overlooking or putting less emphasis on data that contradicts their research efforts and likewise, in turning a blind eye to examples and experiences that contradict deeply held beliefs is a form of confirmation bias (Dwyer, 2018). Imagine how an instructor who believes females to be inferior in math and science may practice confirmation bias in the face of one example of a struggling female student in a male-dominated class, while failing to note similarly struggling males who tend to be less obvious in a largely male class.

Other forms of unconscious bias that can unwittingly influence perceptions, attitudes and behaviors include beauty bias, halo/horns effect, contrast effect, and perception bias, among others. (Pratt, 2016; Burton, 2017) Being able to eliminate these often unconscious and naturally occurring biases may be challenging but bringing an awareness that these types of biases *exist* is the first step in moving beyond them. Once the tendency to form biases is brought to awareness and accepted, the work of seeking to address the privilege that often accompanies bias can also be addressed.

While the term "privilege" can be traced back to W.E.B. DuBois' exploration of "psychological wage" in the 1930's in the context of racism, it has since come to include any aspect of personal, societal or institutional advantage afforded to the dominant group. Critical to this understanding is that privilege is not requested, nor granted by intent, just as the oppression that consequently results for the nondominant group may not be intentional or actively perpetrated by those that are privileged. This can be a challenging truth for the privileged to accept-- that it has nothing to do with intent and the member of the dominant group cannot deny or reject it, it simply exists. It's often easier to identify oppression, especially in the forms of obvious prejudice or discrimination than it is recognize and accept privilege (Ferguson, 2014).

Privilege is not only activated in personal relationships, however. Privilege affects the power systems of society as well. Economic and institutional power are perpetuated because those with privilege dominate and are able to influence society's hierarchical systems-- in politics, the economy, media, education, and so on. (Ferguson, 2014). In this context it's clear to see how implicit bias perpetuates the power hierarchy, including in the learning environment.

IMPLICIT BIAS IN COLLABORATIVE LEARNING COMMUNITIES

The rich benefits of collaborative learning communities are facilitated through the foundation of both collaboration or the working together on common goals/shared interests as well as in a community setting- where the appreciation of different backgrounds, experiences and perspectives are welcome and celebrated (Cooper & Boyd, n.d.). The assumption that learning is an active engagement, where individuals participate in discussion, engaging in critical thinking and other higher-order thinking skills is predicated on a welcoming environment that encourages active inquiry, dialogue and debate, and respects diverse perspectives, communication styles and acknowledges that unique individual experiences influence perceptions and attitudes. In the ideal learning community, differences are strengths that add rich dimension to the learning experience. After all, what is learning if not the exposure to new knowledge, information, skills and perspectives that differ from what one already knows and experiences?

However, considering the unconscious biases discussed one must consider how does implicit bias impact the learning environment, and in turn the communication and behavior of those experiencing it? How does implicit bias affect a respect for differences, participation of learners, trust, communication, collaboration and openness? How does it impact, relationships, boundaries, and, in the final analysis, the overall quality and effectiveness of the learning community? How does implicit bias impact both the victim of the bias as well as distort the perception of the offender?

Elements of the Learning Environment

Elements of the learning environment include not only the content and delivery methods of the individual course, but also the diversity of faculty, curriculum, classroom policies and protocols, instructor communication style, demographics of students, grouping strategies, assessment/grading, mentorship and systems of support, to name a few. Ideally, each of these elements support all students' experiences and learning, but a closer examination can reveal dimensions of unintentional bias. Much of the learning environment is under the direct influence of the instructor, and therefore any unconscious bias in the instructor can readily be conveyed through elements such as communication style, grouping strategies, assessment, grading and mentorship. Classroom policies, expectations and professor communication may impact some groups more than others by certain assumptions, for example; that all students will speak up and ask for support if they need it, that students from certain backgrounds or social groups have a particular intellectual ability or ambition, that students who speak (or write) with certain dialects/forms are of lesser intellectual capacity, that individuals relate to literature featuring characters that resemble them demographically and that particular groups have certain participation styles (quiet, argumentative etc.) (Yale Poorvu Center for Teaching and Learning, 2018).

Course materials such as texts, articles, PowerPoints, graphics, multimedia and visual images also can convey unconscious bias. Does course content in all forms reflect the diversity of students across a variety of dimensions validating different backgrounds and experiences? Just as the physical classroom environment (access, decor, materials) can convey underlying messages of who is accepted and what is valued, online course content can, as well. Are authors and research utilized in the course diverse representatives of what's available? Do class policies provide equal access to content and support for all students? Are course assignments inclusive? Are groupings appropriately diverse? Do faculty perceptions influence grading? Are expectations equally achievable for all students? Note that equal access does *not* necessarily mean "the same." Consider the case scenarios below to appreciate how access can be limited by perception.

Media and Cultural Influences

It can be an especially daunting task to address implicit bias in course materials and content when the media and cultural makers so heavily influence perception and facilitate continued stereotypes through visual images and language in both digital and print media through entertainment, journalism, advertisement and even in academic sources. Content included in texts and other academic resources is often representative of the dominant culture and societal trends. Unquestionably, society is influenced by the media and in an industry where 80% of TV newsrooms and 92% of radio newsrooms are white, implicit bias influences media narratives. (Savali, 2015). For example, Black and Latino crime suspects are more often represented with mug shots, are frequently shown to be handled aggressively by law enforcement and are often objectified through the press. Rioting and other lawless behavior by African Americans and other minorities is more often depicted in the press than similar violent behavior by other groups, such as riots after a sports game win or concert. Media consumers of all kinds- print, broadcast, advertising, internet, and social media are influenced by the images and narrative conveyed. Implicit bias even infiltrates society as it influences society's view of standards of beauty, art, and culture.

Case Scenarios of Implicit Bias

As noted, the very nature of implicit bias reflects an unconscious tendency to respond in biased ways, whether through verbal communication, behavior or attitudes and the bias may be unrecognized or completely unintentional. But whether the bias is intentional or not, the effects can still be harmful and repeated experiences over time can have accumulating effects. Consider the following examples and note how a student experiencing not just the one instance described here, but repeated instances over the course of many weeks/terms of classes might be impacted.

Race/Ethnicity Bias

Professor Janet Atkins is teaching a communication course at a large online university. The university offers a live seminar once a week where students can engage in synchronous chat while she lectures on the weekly topic using slides, audio and a web camera. Students can see and hear her, but they respond via chat. Recently, the department has taken an initiative to increase student participation in the seminar and Janet has been reviewing her seminar archives to try to determine patterns of engagement in her students. She noticed that while a handful of students appear to be very vocal, many of her students barely comment and even log out early. Janet has worked hard to prepare engaging, interesting lectures including the use of interactive components such as case studies, video "field trips" and even setting up smaller "break out" sessions during the seminar where students can interact in smaller groups. She is frustrated with the seeming lack of interest in certain students and has asked her department chair for a fresh perspective.

After having reviewed the seminar archive and analyzing some of the chat data, her department chair notices some interesting patterns- while Janet takes pains to open her seminar by welcoming students personally by name, her log shows she has been focusing on names that are familiar or easiest for her to pronounce, such as Sue-Ann, Tracy, William, Makayla and Jade, but not names like Chanahvia, Da-Xia, Ayubu, Gurgian, and D'quell. Likewise, the logs seem to show that Janet tends to respond and provide feedback more frequently to students with these names, as well. Janet is shocked as she insists that these findings are coincidental as she takes pains to respond to as many students as possible and goes out of her way to be supportive and welcoming to all students. She notes that she has many friends and colleagues of diverse backgrounds and values the participation of each of her students. Besides, she reasons, not all minority students have names that are difficult to pronounce...she wonders how many of her students of color or diverse backgrounds have easy-to-pronounce names, as well. However, she also wonders if any of her students have noticed the findings of her chat logs, as well. While she certainly never *meant* to be less welcoming or responsive to students based on their names, could the students be perceiving her as preferring certain students?

Age Bias

Anita is 59 years old and is attending college for the first time. She delayed her education in order to raise four children as a single mother. Her children are very proud of her for beginning college later in life. Anita has enrolled in an online university as she lives in a rural area that is not near any campus.

Anita excitedly completes all her enrollment materials, purchases a laptop and asks one of her children to help her log into her online class platform. She isn't good with technology but is excited to learn.

The first discussion board asks students to introduce themselves via a video. Anita is very nervous as she does not know how to make a video and post this and she is not sure she can complete the introduction. Six days go by and she just gives up and doesn't post to the discussion board the first week. Anita does not hear from the instructor, though she wishes the instructor would reach out to her so she could tell her that she is having a hard time getting started.

Anita is determined to do better her second week. The discussion question asks students to discuss their experiences with social media as this is a course on Media and Culture. Anita doesn't use social media and is starting to feel self-conscious that perhaps she does not belong in college as she does not have the same experiences as the rest of the class. Anita does not post the second week, but she reads all her classmates' posts about their social media usage.

Anita's instructor, Ivan, reviews all the course metrics for his students. He has noticed that Anita has spent more hours online than any other student, though she has not posted. He is busy and figures she will post soon.

In week 3, Anita looks at the discussion questions, but does not post. She never enters the online classroom again and soon she withdraws from the university. She never hears from the instructor.

Is there age bias in this case scenario? Is it implicit, explicit, both and why?

Gender and Sexual Orientation Bias

Harsha is a 34-year old undergraduate student enrolled in international studies. He is a first-time college student based on campus and is excited to attend college for the first time. He realizes that one of his courses is only offered online. He is nervous that he must take an online course as he is not confident in his computer skills.

As Harsha begins his online course, he notices that the instructor's email closing states, "my preferred pronouns are she and her." Harsha is excited to see this as he is a gay man who is transgender, and he thinks this professor is going to be someone he connects with and he is excited to get started in her class.

As Harsha begins the introduction thread in his online course, the instructor has asked each student to make a video introduction. He is nervous as using technology is not a strength. As he reads the instructions for making the video, he is dismayed to find out that in addition to the video introduction, students are required to post a picture from elementary school. The course is Aging throughout the Lifespan and the first assignment is to explore growth in early childhood. Harsha is not openly transgender, and he does not want to post a photo from his early childhood years.

Is there gender or sexual orientation bias in this case scenario? Is it implicit, explicit, both and why?

Disability Bias

Online learning platforms are constantly changing, and this technology continues to become more user friendly with many options for course content delivery. Universities that use online learning platforms strive to deliver content in a dynamic environment in order to meet diverse learning styles of students.

Ezar is a new graduate student and is excited to get started in his first online course in Civic Engagement. He discloses to his instructor in an email that he is deaf, and the instructor indicates that she will be sure to ensure that he experiences everything in the class just as his colleagues that are not deaf. He is especially interested in community grass-roots efforts as he is the first elected official who is deaf in his large metropolitan city. Ezar is excited to get started and as he begins orientation to the online platform at his university, he is dismayed to find several glaring limitations to his experience at this university. First, he notes that there are multiple videos in the online platform that are not closed captioned nor are there transcripts. The instructor also stated in her grading instructions to "listen to my audio grading summary" and there was no transcript. Is there disability bias in this case scenario? Is it implicit, explicit, both and why?

Socio-Economic Bias

Nadia is a single mother of two children and is excited to complete her bachelor's degree. She started college after high school but was unable to finish as she got pregnant with her first child her junior year of college. She is now 29 years old and feels stable enough now to go back to school since both of her children are in Head Start where she works as a teacher's assistant.

Nadia is enrolled part time at an online university where she receives financial aid for her courses. Her first three terms went well, and she is on the Dean's List. She is excited to begin her fourth term at this university where she is majoring in Early Childhood Education. Her teacher this term is a male, which is a first for her as she has always had female instructors. Dr. Nguyen is a director of a for-profit child care center and teaches part time at the university.

Nadia posts to the discussion board on the topic of parent-teacher conferences. She recommends that teachers and directors hold parent-teacher conferences on the weekends and in the evenings with childcare provided to meet the needs of all parents or to offer home visits. Dr. Nguyen responds that parents should be able to find their own childcare and that asking staff to come in on both the weekends and at night is too taxing and that home visits would not be permitted. Nadia thinks this response is somewhat uncaring and not meeting the needs of parents, but she does not say anything else about it on the discussion board.

The following week, the instructor states that "many parents do not provide an enriching environment that is required for proper development for their children. Children should attend art shows, go to the zoo, learn how to order at a restaurant and all the things required of our culture." Nadia thinks to herself that her children have not had the opportunity to do any of these things. Is she a bad mother? Are her friends and relatives bad parents?

Is there socio-economic bias in this case scenario? Is it implicit, explicit, both and why?

Effects of Implicit Bias on Students and Instructors

As discussed above, implicit bias is so deeply embedded in individual attitudes, beliefs and behaviors as well as within society's structure that it is an unavoidable reality. To question the existence of bias is missing the point.... it's a natural human tendency that serves the purpose of categorizing and making sense of the overwhelming amount of information individuals are bombarded with constantly. However, what *is* important, especially in the academic realm, is to accept the fact that bias can be implicit, even by those who profess to abhor it and understand how it can affect students and their learning experience.

Professors may hold implicit biases about their students, students may have implicit bias about their professors and each other and institutional bias contributes to the student experience as well. As illustrated in the case scenarios above, implicit bias can chip away at a student's feeling of belongingness, motivation, and self-perception of ability. Over time, the cumulative effects can lead to an internalization of biases that alter targeted students' attitudes, behaviors, speech and self-confidence and come to accept the oppression of the dominant group. (Vanderbilt University, 2019) This can lead to self-doubt, fear and distrust which continues the negative cycle.

While effects of implicit bias within the classroom setting may be unintentional, it can have drastic effects on student learning, beginning from a young age. Research consistently shows that children who are minorities are disciplined more frequently and intensively than their white counterparts for the same behaviors. They are suspended and expelled at greater rates and are involved in more criminal prosecutions (Long, 2016). Stereotype threat occurs when an individual feels he/she will be judged based on a stereotype and will subconsciously reduce effort or disengage participation (Steel & Aronson, 1995). This can negatively impact self-esteem and performance for both positive and negative stereotypes; females in math and science classes may be weighted by the responsibility of proving their ability in a class full of males, Asians may feel threatened by the perception that they must have stellar academic performance and African Americans may feel the need to prove their belongingness in an academic setting.

Instructor expectations of students can be impacted by implicit bias and students may respond to these lowered or negative expectations. Instructors may be less tolerant of struggling students or less likely to provide outreach and support. Instructors and fellow students may convey subtle messages questioning the academic ability and belongingness of victims of implicit bias. These expectations may, in turn affect the motivation and self-perception of the student's ability. Instructors may judge comments or questions from some students as disrespectful or inflammatory. They may engage more frequently with some students conveying the perception that some students' participation is more desirable than others. They may inadvertently grade more harshly for some students than others or be more empathetic of extenuating circumstances for some students than others. Instructors may be completely unaware of these behaviors and communication as a result of implicit bias.

Research by Katherine Milkman at the University of Pennsylvania illustrated how race and gender affected professors' responses to requests for mentorship opportunities. Email requests for mentorship were sent to over 6000 professors at hundreds of universities in the US, identical in content with the exception of different ethnic names of the students. Requests signed with names of typical Caucasian males (such as Brad Anderson) were responded to the most frequently and more positively than African American, Hispanic, Chinese, and Indian names. Chinese female names suffered the most as compared to the Caucasian male group. Responses from private universities and in typically high-paying disciplines were especially biased in response rates. Surprisingly, East Asian and Indian students suffered the most in responses, revealing that even "model minority" students weren't exempt from bias. In fact, even minority faculty members' responses reflected bias (Milkman, 2014). Obviously, even in presumably progressive field of education, implicit bias will impact students' ability to form meaningful relationships with professors.

Most of the research on implicit bias in higher education has focused on racial and gender inequalities, but disparities can be found across virtually all dimensions of biased groups. Both male and female professors are more likely to call on white males and use their names in discussion and refer and expand on the comments of male students as compared to female students. They tend to ask more higher order, critical thinking questions of males and focus on more fact-based questions of females. They are more likely to expand on points made by males rather than females and this disparate climate is internalized by females. While males have the tendency to speak more frequently and contribute to discussions, females speak less and are often less confident or direct in their comments. (Diversity & Social Justice, 2014)

Implicit bias does not only affect instructor perceptions and behaviors. It influences student-to-student interactions and student perceptions of instructors, as well. Microaggression in communication between students, as well as within instructor-student interactions builds accumulating effects. Microaggression is defined as "brief and commonplace daily verbal, behavioral and environmental indignities, whether intentional or unintentional, that communicate hostile, derogatory or negative racial slights and insults that potentially have harmful or unpleasant psychological impact on the target person or group" (Solozano, Ceja, & Yosso, 2000). Examples of this include both unconscious or conscious remarks that are insulting or demeaning, or that invalidate or exclude the thoughts or feelings of the targeted person. They can be so subtle as to not raise immediate or obvious reactions but convey distinct negative attitudes. For example, correcting or demeaning a student's dialect in a class discussion or denying issues of race/color or implying that race or another quality plays a role in one's success are all considered microaggression. (University of Tennessee Knoxville- Teaching & Learning Innovation, n.d.) The aggression is subtle, but the intent is clear and questions the validity and belonging of the targeted individual. Other examples of microaggression include implying intellectual capabilities are related to race, assuming criminal status or using derogatory descriptions to describe criminal acts ascribed to a particular group or implying that physical characteristics denote certain races as foreigners. Denial of personal or institutional racism may be another example of this.

Interestingly, instructors may also be victims to implicit bias. Studies examining student evaluation of instructors revealed bias against female faculty; they tended to be rated higher in smaller, intimate settings such as seminars where gender-stereotypical qualities such as nurturing and empathy could be demonstrated. However, they scored more poorly in larger lecture hall settings where male instructors fared better. The discrepancy was based on the bias that male instructors did not need to be friendly or nurturing to score high ratings but were evaluated primarily on knowledge and skill (Diversity & Social

Justice, 2014). Of course, any implicit bias can impact attitudes and relationships among individuals whether they are directed from teacher to student, from student to teacher or amongst students themselves.

SOLUTIONS AND RECOMMENDATIONS

Developing Awareness

Key to beginning the process of addressing and overcoming implicit bias is a willingness of each individual to accept its pervasiveness and the ability to take a hard, deep look at one's self. Even if one actively rejects explicit bias, it's possible (even likely!) that implicit bias still exists at a subconscious level, but debiasing practices can work to raise a deliberate awareness and lead to change in perceptions, beliefs and behaviors (Kirwan, 2015). While the media and culture makers have a significant responsibility to stop perpetuating stereotypes in the media, faculty at higher education institutions can begin by becoming more mindful of how implicit bias has been affecting behavior and judgments in unintentional ways and start taking deliberate action to avoid acting in ways that are contrary to conscious attitudes and values.

Both instructors and students can begin by recognizing and accepting the privilege and power inherent in society and institutions such as education, politics, and the media. Recognize that privilege exists and seek to extend to *all* groups. Privilege should not be used as a means to shame or guilt one group over another but should be recognized as an opportunity that should be afforded to all. Privilege does not mean a person doesn't have to work hard, it simply means certain opportunities are more easily afforded to one group than another. In the study cited above, being called on personally by one's *name* in class should be a privilege equally afforded to all students. Likewise, equal opportunities for having professors who are the same race or gender as students should be a privilege afforded to all. Changing the mindset that "privilege" immediately results in defensive responses can begin to build an appreciation for the hurdles some students face. Inventories to help raise privilege awareness such as *How Privileged Are You?* at https://www.buzzfeed.com/regajha/how-privileged-are-you can be a transformative experience.

Building self-awareness is critical in countering implicit bias. As an instructor accepting that implicit biases are pervasive and realizing that even with a devout, professed commitment to fairness and equality for all students, it's likely that one still is influenced by implicit bias is vital. Just because a professor does not hold explicit biases does not mean implicit bias isn't operating on a subconscious level. Being more willing to reframe one's perspective and deeply examine the perspective through the lens of race, gender, sexual orientation, socioeconomic status or ability can offer a transformative realization.

Another beneficial tool is the Implicit Association Tests (IAT) which measure unconscious attitudes and beliefs across a variety of dimensions such as race, gender, sexuality, age, disability, physical appearance such as those offered at Project Implicit at Harvard University's https://implicit.harvard.edu/implicit/takeatest.html. The free online tests operate by timing the speed of associations test-takers have between positive and negative concepts with the target bias. For example, is the subject more prone to connect a male face/name with a math/science concept than a female's? Does the subject associate certain sexual identities with stereotypes with greater ease than counter-stereotypes? Both instructors and students can benefit from the insight and discussions that follow self-examination and reflection based on these assessments. If nothing else, it can lead the test taker to be more mindful in his/her decisions, habits, communication and interactions considering the data.

Mindfulness

In that light, mindfulness training has been linked with enhancing focus, clarity and purpose while increasing control over emotions, reducing anxiety and increasing compassion. The practice of mindfulness, often equated with meditation, involves focusing the mind on the present moment, whether that be through breathing exercises, a body scan, concentration on the senses in the present moment or an intense focus on the current activity one is engaged in (walking, washing dishes, having a conversation or eating a meal). This is all done with an emphasis on acceptance and the lack of judgment in any way. (mindful, 2014)

Research has shown that mindfulness can reduce race and age bias, possibly due to reduced tendencies to activate associations as well as reduce stereotype threat (Magee, 2015). "ColorInsight Practices" involve integrating mindfulness with an examination of race and color across dimensions of bias, privilege, and historical contexts. These practices include contemplative exercises in small groups or pairs such as using mindfulness practices to increase focus and reduce judgment by noticing one's tendency to construct a narrative about daily observations. Other exercises such as the "I See You" circle, "Just Like Me" pairs and "MLK's Equanimity" encourage participants in engaging in nonjudgmental interactions and accessing higher perspectives of controversial or emotionally charged experiences. These exercises are described in more detail at *How Mindfulness Can Defeat Racial Bias*, by Rhonda Magee at https://greatergood.berkeley.edu/article/item/how_mindfulness_can_defeat_racial_bias Both professors and students, alike, can benefit from these exercises.

Developing Anti-Bias Routines

Along with developing self-awareness and a willingness to explore potential implicit bias Dr. Alex Madva, author of *An Introduction to Implicit Bias: Knowledge, Justice, and the Social Mind* and an avid researcher and expert on bias and social psychology, recommends developing specific plans of action to actively combat implicit bias in higher education. Creating these "If...then" 'rules of thumb' can reprogram automatic tendencies to support stereotypes unknowingly or convey messages of bias. Some examples;

- If a female is talking, then I will not interrupt
- If a student of color (or other frequently marginalized group) contributes to the discussion, I will make a point of referring to that comment or expanding on it
- If a student says something odd or seemingly out of context, I will assume the problem is that I don't understand, not that the student is at fault
- If a student underperforms, I will consider situational causes first (checking a tendency to ascribe underperformance to laziness or lack of ability)
- If a student acts in a way to confirm a stereotype, I will consider other possibilities.

By putting uniform, automatic responses into practice instructors can guard against implicit bias influences as an unconscious reaction. It should be noted that individuals have a greater tendency to be influenced by their implicit biases when they are tired, hungry, angry or otherwise responding impulsively or under duress, so having these "rules of thumb" for consistent responses can help to avoid mindless reactions.

Diversity in Course Content

Dr. Madva also noted the influence of course materials listed on the class syllabus. In Philosophy classes typically dominated by white males, the tendency for women to drop from higher level classes was attributed to the lack of content on or written by female authors/historical figures. In fact, research indicated that having just 20% of course content inclusive of female philosophers resulted in an increase of female retention. (Diversity and Social Justice, 2014). The implications for including course content representative of diversity (in gender, race, sexual orientation, ability, age, etc.) is obvious. Course content should be specifically reviewed to ensure diversity in all forms- textual, visual and through class discussions.

Some factors to consider in addressing curricular bias include invisibility, stereotyping, imbalance/selectivity, unreality, fragmentation/isolation, linguistic bias, and cosmetic bias (Sadker, n.d.). Invisibility is probably the most common form of bias in content by the total or partial exclusion of representation in course materials. In years past, African Americans, Asian Americans and Latinos were egregiously missing from the narrative and images of texts. Today, these omissions tend to be by gender, disabilities and sexual orientation/identification. Stereotypes in course materials can be represented by both positive and negative examples in terms of power, success, personal appearance and other characteristics. Content that only provides a one-dimensional view of an issue or group reflects imbalance or selectivity. For example, math and science courses that emphasize European innovations and discoveries over other origins. Unreality occurs when content may ignore prejudice, discrimination, exploitation or inter-group conflict in depicting events in history. Fragmentation and isolation is the tendency to isolate non-dominant groups as peripheral contributors to society, such as a "special box" on "Women Achievers in Science." This conveys the perception that the featured positive examples are an exception to their cultural community. Linguistic bias can be subtle, but powerful in conveying bias such as the predominant use of "man" in language (businessman, mankind, forefathers). Cosmetic bias is a more recent phenomenon where marketing publicizes content as "bias free" through superficial means- including token photos, pictures or features, but still is predominantly biased in favor of a dominant group.

Inclusivity conveys the sense of belongingness and validity of contributions to the field. Specifically filtering course content through these lenses can reduce conveyed stereotypical or biased perceptions. Likewise, the subtle messages conveyed to learners can facilitate the continued implicit bias. Instructors and universities can take steps to ensure debiasing in course content and materials.

Bias Cleansing and Counter-Stereotyping

The good news is that developing awareness about implicit bias and taking deliberate debiasing actions, such as mindfulness practices and the "If...then" rule of thumb practices noted above can reduce implicit bias. A bias cleanse is another opportunity to unlearn biases and replace them with alternatives. The Complicity Cleanse (https://www.complicitycleanse.com/) and MTV/Kirwan Institute for the Study of Race and Ethnicity's Bias Cleanse (http://www.lookdifferent.org/what-can-i-do/bias-cleanse) provide users with daily exercises and tools to raise awareness and challenge biased thinking. These initiatives tap into social media to support and spread the anti-bias message. Participation in these activities can enhance self-awareness of implicit bias.

In addition to purposefully resisting stereotypes, exposure to counter-stereotyping examples has been shown to reduce implicit bias (Lin-Sommer & Lucek, 2015). Repeated exposures to examples of individuals or events that support the opposite of the stereotype help to weaken it. Likewise, instructors can make the deliberate effort to individualize students or imagine them as the opposite of a stereotype. If an instructor finds his/her response seems to support a stereotype, conscientiously adjusting the response helps to minimize biases over time. Other "redirection" techniques include taking the individual's point of view by "putting yourself in their shoes," expanding one's interactions with individuals from other groups by making deliberate efforts to expand networks and professional circles and using exposure to diversity with curiosity and a genuine interest to learn more with an open mind (Institute for Healthcare Improvement, 2017)

Bias-Free Learning Climate

Clearly, creating a classroom environment that not only tolerates and respects all forms of diversity, but embraces and celebrates it is a vital first step in combating bias. Instructors are role models and the due diligence necessary in examining one's own potential implicit biases along with putting debiasing strategies into practice will create a climate conducive to overcoming implicit bias. Communication strategies to combat consequences of implicit bias include the following;

- Avoid conveying an expectation that individual or groups of students represent the entire group- don't expect students to be experts on any experiences beyond their own or encourage them to speak on behalf of their entire community
- Avoid the assumption that groups you are talking about are not represented in the classroom
- Set high expectations for all your students
- Consider the possibility that some students will not have proficient knowledge of US culture, slang words or customs
- Provide clear and firm expectations and guidelines surrounding discussions relating to diversity- be especially mindful during debates and dialogues. Avoid permitting one or more groups of students to monopolize conversations
- Consider how the professor expressing his/her own view (political, moral, philosophical, etc.) can alienate or silence students or how challenging student opinions can be an expression of power over them
- Be balanced when including guest speakers or supplemental materials to ensure alternate perspectives are also represented
- Be sure humor does not target or denigrate any particular students or groups
- Recognize microaggressions and address them if they occur- be prepared to interrupt or challenge them
- Encourage students to contact the professor if they feel offended or belittled (The University of Tennessee Knoxville, n.d.)

In addition to affecting communication and classroom interactions, implicit bias can also impact an instructor's grading. Creating a standard, consistent process for grading can ensure validity that is based on merit and skills rather than being influenced by any kind of bias. Some ways instructors can ensure objectivity in grading include the following;

- Grade "blindly." Assign numbers or other coding to avoid identifying information while grading.

- Prepare answer keys/rubrics ahead of time including all criteria expected to earn full credit. Preparing this ahead of time will avoid making subtle changes to criteria as the instructor proceeds through student work
- Be sure to include explanations validating grades with enough detail to verify why points are deducted- this not only provides validity to the student, but requires the instructor to be able to justify objective deductions
- Go through all students' papers and grade one question all at once and then move on to the next question to grade all together. This will increase the likelihood that the same standard is consistently applied, and the instructor will not be influenced by previous responses on a paper. Shuffling all papers in between each session will also reduce the influence of fatigue or rushing through grading.
- Make sure to take frequent breaks to avoid mistakes due to fatigue
- Be transparent with the grading process- if students see the amount of effort to maintain objectivity, they will appreciate it and respond to it (Aldrich, 2017)

CONCLUSION

Educators have a responsibility to serve as change agents with regard to recognizing and combating implicit bias, even if the course content is not related to diversity or social justice. Simply being in a position of power and privilege within the context of post-secondary education behooves educators to raise awareness about the existence and pervasiveness of implicit bias and that explicit and implicit bias are not mutually inclusive. Educators and students alike need to understand that implicit bias, by its very nature, may be unconscious and may affect individuals in ways that are contrary to one's conscious beliefs. Implicit bias can have far reaching, insidious effects in all fields- criminal justice, education, law, health care, business, media, etc. and can become a self-propagating phenomenon. But, because implicit bias *can* be unlearned through deliberate, conscientious effort, it becomes a moral obligation for those who influence the preparation and training of individuals in all these fields to take a stand and take action.

Educators can facilitate self-reflection and awareness in themselves and their students by having difficult conversations, facilitating internal examination and engaging in meaningful dialogue on the topic of implicit bias as it touches all aspects of society. Compassionate communication and thoughtful learning activities can diffuse defensiveness while transforming perceptions. Icebreaker activities that introduce the topic of implicit bias can build a sensitivity to culture and privilege without activating guilt, resistance or frustration. Some examples of tools and icebreaker activities that can be integrated into any classroom are at *Diversity ToolKit: A Guide to Discussing Identity, Power and Privilege* at https://msw.usc.edu/mswusc-blog/diversity-workshop-guide-to-discussing-identity-power-and-privilege/#icebreaker

Institutions of higher learning have a responsibility to provide continuing professional development and training on countering implicit bias, as well. Institutional bias continues through the unconscious bias in recruitment of both students and faculty, in curriculum and courses as well as course materials. Seeking frequent opportunities to review policies and protocols ensures vigilance in combating implicit bias.

As many as 20% of large US companies are now providing implicit bias training in recognition of the prevalence and heavy toll it takes (Giang, 2015), and addressing implicit bias in higher education should be just as much of a priority. Educators and institutions of higher education are in positions of privilege and power and are called to be active in efforts to eradicate bias. Dr. Martin Luther King, Jr.

said, “It may well be that we will have to repent in this generation. Not merely for the vitriolic words and the violent actions of the bad people, but for the appalling silence and indifference of the good people who sit around and say, ‘Wait on time.’” (King, M. L., Jr., 1986). Now is the time and the good people of higher education will no longer wait to be agents of change.

REFERENCES

Aldrich, H. (2017). *Guidelines for Reducing Implicit Bias in Your Grading.* Retrieved from https://howardaldrich.org/2017/07/guidelines-for-reducing-implicit-bias-in-your-grading/

Beattie, G. (2013). *Our Racist Heart? An exploration of unconscious prejudice in everyday life.* New York, NY: Routledge. doi:10.4324/9780203100912

Brownstein, M. (2015, Feb. 26). *Implicit Bias.* Retrieved from https://plato.stanford.edu/entries/implicit-bias/

Burton, L. (2017). *What is unconscious bias in recruitment?* Available at https://www.highspeedtraining.co.uk/hub/types-of-unconscious-bias/

Cooper, C., & Boyd, J. (n.d.). *Schools as Collaborative Learning Communities.* Retrieved at http://www.vision.net.au/~globallearning/pages/lfs/clc_artcle.html

Diversity & Social Justice Teaching Guide Website. (2014). *Understanding and Overcoming Implicit Bias in Higher Education.* Retrieved from https://www.youtube.com/watch?v=FW0XLnvFvgo

Diversity Abroad. (2016). *Unconscious bias in study abroad?* Retrieved from https://www.diversitynetwork.org/blogpost/1437725/253300/Unconscious-Bias-in-Education-Abroad

Dwyer, C. (2018). *12 Common Biases that affect how we make everyday decisions.* Retrieved from https://www.psychologytoday.com/us/blog/thoughts-thinking/201809/12-common-biases-affect-how-we-make-everyday-decisions

Ferguson, S. (2014). *Privilege 101: A Quick and Dirty Guide.* Retrieved from https://everydayfeminism.com/2014/09/what-is-privilege/

Giang, V. (2015). *The growing business of detecting unconscious bias.* Retrieved from https://www.fastcompany.com/3045899/the-growing-business-of-detecting-unconscious-bias

Goldback, E. (2017). *Diversity Toolkit: A Guide to Discussing Identity, Power, and Privilege.* University of Southern California's Suzanne Dworak-Peck School of Social Work. Available at https://msw.usc.edu/mswusc-blog/diversity-workshop-guide-to-discussing-identity-power-and-privilege/#icebreaker

Gullo, G., & Beachum, F. (2017). *The negative effects of implicit bias in schools.* Retrieved from https://whyy.org/articles/essay-the-negative-effects-of-implicit-bias-in-schools/

Hill, C. (n.d.). *Why So Few? Women in Science, Technology, Engineering, and Mathematics.* Retrieved from https://www.aauw.org/research/why-so-few/

Houser, C., & Lemmons, K. (2018). Implicit bias in letters of recommendation for an undergraduate research internship. *Journal of Further and Higher Education*, *42*(5), 585–595. doi:10.1080/0309877X.2017.1301410

Institute for Healthcare Improvement. (2017). *How to Reduce Implicit Bias*. Retrieved from http://www.ihi.org/communities/blogs/how-to-reduce-implicit-bias

King, M. L. Jr, & Washington, J. M. (1986). *A testament of hope: The essential writings and speeches of Martin Luther King, Jr*. New York, NY: Harper Collins.

Kirwan Institute for the Study of Race and Ethnicity. (2012). *Implicit Racial Bias: Implications for Education and Other Critical Opportunity Domains*. A Presentation to the National Association for the Education of African American Children with Learning Disabilities. Retrieved from http://kirwaninstitute.osu.edu/docs/AACLD_implicit_bias_and_education.pdf

Kirwan Institute for the Study of Race and Ethnicity. (2015). *Understanding Implicit Bias*. Retrieved from http://kirwaninstitute.osu.edu/research/understanding-implicit-bias/

Levine, J., & Hogg, M. (2010). *Encyclopedia of group processes & intergroup relations*. Thousand Oaks, CA: Sage. doi:10.4135/9781412972017

Lin-Sommer, S., & Lucek, S. (2015). The Dangerous Mind: Unconscious Bias in Higher Education. *Brown Political Review*. Retrieved from http://www.brownpoliticalreview.org/2015/04/the-dangerous-mind-unconscious-bias-in-higher-education/

Magee, R. (2015). *How mindfulness can defeat racial bias*. Retrieved from https://greatergood.berkeley.edu/article/item/how_mindfulness_can_defeat_racial_bias

Milkman, K. L., Akinola, M., & Chugh, D. (2015). What Happens Before? A Field Experiment Exploring How Pay and Representation Differentially Shape Bias on the Pathway into Organizations. *The Journal of Applied Psychology*, *100*(6), 1678–1712. doi:10.1037/apl0000022 PMID:25867167

Mindful.org. (2014). *What is Mindfulness?* Retrieved from https://www.mindful.org/what-is-mindfulness/

Myers, D. (2011). *Myers' Psychology for AP*. New York, NY: Worth Publishers.

Perception Institute. (n.d.). Retrieved from https://perception.org/research/explicit-bias/

Perception.org. (n.d.). *Transforming Perception: Black Men and Boys*. American Values Institute. Retrieved from http://perception.org/wp-content/uploads/2014/11/Transforming-Perception.pdf

Pratt, S. (2016). *9 types of unconscious bias and the shocking ways they affect your recruiting efforts*. Retrieved from https://www.socialtalent.com/blog/recruitment/9-types-of-bias

Project Implicit. (n.d.). Retrieved from https://www.projectimplicit.net/index.html

Sack, M. D. (2014, May 12). *Destined to Stereotype? How the Mind's Gift for Grouping Gets Us into Trouble*. Retrieved from https://www.huffingtonpost.com/david-sack-md/stereotype_b_4934495.html

Sadker, D. (n.d.). *Some Practical ideas for Confronting Curricular Bias.* The Myra Sadker Foundation. Retrieved from https://www.sadker.org/curricularbias.html

Savali, K. W. (2015). Throw Away the Script: How Media Bias is Killing Black America. Retrieved from https://www.theroot.com/throw-away-the-script-how-media-bias-is-killing-black-1790860024

Solorzano, D., Ceja, M., & Yosso, T. (2000). Critical Race Theory, Racial microaggressions, and Campus Racial Climate: The Experiences of African American College Students. *The Journal of Negro Education, 69*(1/2), 60.

Steele, C. M., Spencer, S. J., & Aronson, J. (2002). Contending with group image: The psychology of stereotype and social identity threat. *Advances in Experimental Social Psychology, 34,* 379-440. Retrieved from http://disjointedthinking.jeffhughes.ca/wp-content/uploads/2011/07/Steele-Spencer-Aronson-2002.-Contending-with-group-image.pdf

University of Tennessee Knoxville- Teaching & Learning Innovation. (n.d.). *Addressing Implicit Bias & its Impact on Teaching & Learning.* Retrieved from https://teaching.utk.edu/wp-content/uploads/sites/78/2018/03/Addressing-Implicit-Bias-and-its-Impact-on-Teaching-Learning.pdf

Vanderbilt University. (2019). Office of Active Citizenship and Service. *Understanding Privilege and Oppression.* Retrieved from https://www.vanderbilt.edu//oacs/students/meaningful-service-toolkit/

Yale Poorvu Center for Teaching and Learning. (2018). *Awareness of Implicit Biases.* Retrieved from https://poorvucenter.yale.edu/ImplicitBiasAwareness

KEY TERMS AND DEFINITIONS

Collaborative Learning Communities: Groups of individuals that meet regularly to share knowledge and actively explore topics of common interest.

Conscious Bias: Attitudes, perceptions or behaviors that are influenced by prejudices or stereotypes that are purposeful and within the awareness of the individual.

Debias: Removing or combatting bias.

Explicit Bias: Attitudes and perceptions that are influenced by prejudices or stereotypes and are actively demonstrated through language or behaviors.

Implicit Association Test: A test to assess implicit attitudes and biases by comparing reactions to associations.

Implicit Bias: Attitudes, perceptions and behaviors that are influenced by prejudice or stereotypes that are unconscious, below the level of awareness, also known as implicit social cognition.

Institutional Bias: Societal structures (such as in health care, education or criminal justice) that support biased outcomes based on prejudices or stereotypes, also known as systematic bias.

Privilege: Opportunities afforded to an individual or group that provides advantages over other (usually marginalized) individuals or groups who do not have access to the same advantages.

Social Cognition Theory: The principle that learning occurs through observation of others and adapting the observed beliefs or behaviors.

Stereotypes: An overgeneralization about characteristics or behaviors attributed to groups of individuals based solely on membership in the group.

Stereotype Threat: The belief that an individual is at risk of confirming a negative stereotype, resulting in underperformance based on this concern.

Unconscious Bias: attitudes, perceptions and behaviors that are influenced by prejudice or stereotypes that are unconscious, below the level of awareness, also known as implicit bias.

Chapter 3
Assessment and Civility:
Using Ethos as a Tool

Benjamin J. Cline
Western New Mexico University, USA

ABSTRACT

Civility in computer-mediated communication, especially in the computer-mediated classroom, has been a topic of numerous inquiries. For this reason, teaching of the means and reasons for civil computer-mediated communication has become increasingly necessary. To accomplish this, the chapter will explore past research which indicates major sources of incivility that have emerged in computer-mediated culture. The chapter will then argue that civil discourse is also the most effective and useful form of discourse and show that needs to be communicated to students. This chapter then offers concrete means of teaching civility in computer-mediated communication by teaching civility as tied to the rhetorical concept of ethos already taught in the Public Speaking class.

INTRODUCTION

An educator's lament about the lack of civility among students is nothing new. As early as 95 AD Quintilian spoke of "Barabarisms" that might occur in students' speech and recommended that educators attempt to educate these linguistic habits out of students (2006). Hogarth's engraving entitled *Students at a Lecture* from 1736 depicts a scene which allows us to know that uncivil behavior among collegiate learners is hardly a recent phenomenon (Hogarth, 1736). If we are to accept the idea that education serves a purpose in preparing our students for civil society, we should probably expect that they come to our classrooms with less than civil habits. It is at least partially our job to help the students to overcome these habits and prepare them for civilized life.

The purpose of this chapter is to discuss one of the ways in which we might do that. This chapter will show that although the lament of educators regarding civility is nothing new, the need to work with our students to produce civil discourse has taken on a new urgency due to the well-publicized instances of cyber bullying and the growth of social media as a means of interacting. As our communities have become increasingly hybrid digital/physical communities there has come a special need to relearn the lessons

DOI: 10.4018/978-1-5225-9814-5.ch003

of civility from the past. This chapter examines the application of one ancient concept and considers the implications of that concept for today's digital communities and the learners in them. Specifically, this chapter looks at the conceptual correlation that exists between civility and the Aristotelian concept of *ethos* in order to find ways to add civility to our curriculum as a learnable and assessable skill. This chapter will use as its example a means of assessing civility as ethos within a computer mediated classroom which focuses on Public Speaking, but we believe that using the concept of *ethos* as a tool for assessing civility will be more broadly applicable.

BACKGROUND

While the necessity of requiring the teaching of civility has been incumbent on educators for millennia, or possibly longer, the need for teaching civil communication, especially civil computer mediated communication, has never been greater. The popular news outlets abound with stories of what is probably the least civil of all computer mediated communication, online bullying. *Fox News* derides "a West Virginia high school's 'Queen of Charm,' who created a Web page that suggested another student had a sexually transmitted disease, and invited classmates to comment" (2012). *MSNBC* talks about a 16-year-old girl, "a self-described atheist, [who] has been the target of cyberbullying and threats" after a judge required that a religious banner at her high-school be taken down (2012). *Headline News* discusses the plight of a young man for whom online bullying "led to despair, self-mutilation and thoughts of suicide" (2011). *CNN* expounds on a litany of such stories:

Such behavior remains in the spotlight after the recent death of Jamey Rodemeyer, a 14-year-old boy from Williamsville, near Buffalo, who last week took his life after what his parents say was years of bullying over his sexual orientation.

Last year, Phoebe Prince, 15, of Massachusetts, took her own life after being continuously bullied at school and online. The online bullying continued even after her death, as people left vindictive comments on her Facebook memorial page.

An 18-year-old Rutgers University student, Tyler Clementi, killed himself by jumping off of the George Washington Bridge in September 2010 after two classmates posted and broadcast a secretly-taped video of his sexual encounter with another man (Debucquoy-Dodley, 2011).

The *New York Times* captures the public outcry when telling the story of a 14-year-old boy bullied online to the point of suicide and claims that: "His story is a classic case of bullying: he was aggressively and repeatedly victimized. Horrific episodes like this have sparked conversations about cyberbullying and created immense pressure on regulators and educators to do something, anything, to make it stop" (Boyd, 2011). This public outcry for civility in computer mediated communication, especially in the computer mediated communication of young people, demands careful attention from those of us working in the education industry.

That is not to say that the academy has been deaf to the pleas of civil society to return civility to our communication. To the contrary, the concept of teaching civility in the classroom (Baldwin, 2007; Braxton, 2004; Gonzalez & Lopez, 2001; Rookstool, 2007; Connelly, 2009; Schneider, 1998; Lampman,

Bancroft, & Beneke, 2009; Plank, McDill, McPartland, & Jordan, 2001), of studying civil discourse in computer mediated communication (Lim & Chin, 2006; Pearson & Porath, 2005; Sipior & Ward, 1999; Lim, Thompson, & Chin, 2008; Thorston, Vraga, & Eckdale, 2010; Cameron, 2000; Denning, 1993) and in civility in contemporary society in general (Brooks & Greer, 2007; Hendrix, 2007; Rau-Foster & Duthka, 2004) has been the subject of a great deal of research.

Much of this research points to the distance in contemporary communication between the subject and the object. Not only does the above research indicate that a certain false assumption of anonymity creates an environment in which uncivil behavior may lack immediate consequences or any consequences at all, but that otherwise civil discourse may take on less than civil nuances in contemporary communication which would not have been assumed in less mediated cultures of the past. The lack of necessary nonverbal cues for interpreting each other's communication creates a sense of incivility: "Because of its lack of social and contextual cues, negative online interactions are likely to generate a stronger adverse effect on victims compared to traditional face-to-face or telephone encounters as individuals lack the opportunity to seek immediate clarification or obtain dynamic feedback" (Lim, Thompson, & Chin, 2008, p. 155). This difficulty in ascertaining information from body language and vocal tone means that "[e] mail comments in an emotionally charged situation are often misinterpreted" (Denning, 1993, p. 170). The misinterpreted emotional data can cause reactions of incivility which reverberate throughout a particular group and ultimately to the whole of society: "Although the intent to harm may be ambiguous, the spillover effect of an uncivil interpersonal workplace encounter on others as well as the organization should not be underestimated" (Lim, Thompson, & Chin, 2008).

CIVIL DISCOURSE AS *ETHOS*

So the teaching of civility has become more salient than ever because it seems that the slightest provocation can degenerate into uncivil behavior. To eliminate these uncivil discourses, the university has become a central social tool for teaching civil behavior to our students: "Despite the challenges, society in general needs to continue to respond to acts of incivility that seem to damage the broader civic community as well as other smaller communities that intersect the lives of individuals. Higher education can help by dedicating more research to measuring the scope of the incivility problem(s) as well as assessing how well civility initiatives offer useful programs for improvement." (Connelly, 2009, p. 55). Thus, civility in the classroom has become an important part of the curriculum.

Issues, Controversies and Problems

Yet, one can argue that civility is not taught at the university in a reasonable manner. Civility is taught in a punitive manner that overcontextualizes civil discourse to the particular class, rather than inculcating civility in general or teaching the advantages to the student of engaging in civil discourse. Students are simply informed that uncivil behavior will not be tolerated and students are punished for behaving in a manner which is less than civil. This does not teach the student about the personal advantages of civil behavior nor does it provide for a true learning experience with regard to gaining civility as a part of a skill set, much like a student gains skills in citation or learns mathematical algorithms. Teaching civility in this way can be compared to an English teacher saying that "improper use of commas will not be tolerated" or a biology professor saying that "mislabeling of organisms will result in the student immediately being removed from the classroom and count as an absence for that day." Rather than insisting on civility with threats, such as saying that a student who engages in uncivil discourse will be ejected from the course or claiming that certain types of language will not be tolerated, educators must find a means of teaching civility as an assessable skill which students can learn and transfer to multiple extra-classroom contexts.

Solutions and Recommendations

Because the civilizing aspects of higher education have been incumbent on educators from the beginning, we can find early on means of teaching civility in to students. One of the earliest teachings on civility can be found in Aristotle's discussion of *ethos*. Aristotle did not simply require his students to be civil, but explained to them about the particular advantages of civility. By explaining that a more civil tongue might be more functional in accomplishing their tasks: "But since rhetoric exists to affect the giving of decisions -- the hearers decide between one political speaker and another, and a legal verdict is a decision -- the orator must not only try to make the argument of his speech demonstrative and worthy of belief; he must also make his own character look right and put his hearers, who are to decide, into the right frame of mind" (Aristotle, 2011). Aristotle does not merely say that his students need to be civilized or they will be ejected from the class, he explains why civil behavior is essential to the students' own rhetoric.

According to Lanius, "credibility and ethos exist in a subjective space: what makes a text suspicious to one reader will reaffirm its credibility in the eyes of another reader. However, the subjective nature of the audience's evaluation does not make credibility and ethos impenetrable" (2017, p.3). The appropriate penetration of ethos comes from Aristotle who explains that in order to be a good speaker, the speaker must be seen by her or his audience a particular way by his or her audience: "when they feel friendly to the man who comes before them for judgment, they regard him as having done little wrong, if any; when they feel hostile, they take the opposite view" (Aristotle, 2011). Aristotle teaches that "There are three things which inspire confidence in the orator's own character -- the three, namely, that induce us to believe a thing apart from any proof of it: good sense, good moral character, and goodwill" (Aristotle, 2011). Enacting these three aspects of *ethos* are simultaneously teaching the students to be civil and to be an effective public speaker.

Hyde argues that ethos is more than a set of tools. Using concepts from both Aristotle and Heideggar, Hyde says that "One can understand the phrase 'the *ethos* of rhetoric' to refer to the way that discourse is used to transform space and time into 'dwelling places' where people can deliberate about and collectively understand some matter of interest. Such dwelling places define the grounds, abodes, and habitats where a person's ethics and moral character take form and develop. Together the contributors define ethical discourse and describe what its practice looks like in particular communities" (Hyde, 2004, p. 14). He explains that the "ethical practice of rhetoric" necessitates the "construction of a 'dwelling place' (ethos) for collaborative and moral deliberation" (p. 18).

Such a "place" can exist within an online classroom. As Gamie states, "In both virtual or real communities and the rhetorical situations that transpire within and outside those discursive spaces, the construction of ethos emerges as a central component" (2017, p. 163). It is the primacy interconextuality that Gamie describes that is important for such a dwelling place for inculcation of ethos and civility to be achieved in the online public speaking class. By assessing *ethos*, we are simultaneously assessing civility and in so doing, we are providing a means whereby civility can be improved. By taking the above three parts of *ethos* and assessing them in all aspects of our students' communication, both in their graded speeches and in their online discourse, we are able to make civility something more than an overcontextualized requirement for the duration of the course, we are able to make civility into a learned skill.

Step One: Assigning Classroom Community Points

The first step in assessing ethos is the construction of a point system that includes the larger functions of *ethos* besides the simple production of points in a small portion of a student's presentation. This chapter advocates assessing such points through the construction of "classroom community" points. The students are informed in the syllabus that they are required to earn a certain number of points over the term of the course and that these points will be included in the student's overall grade. The student is informed the she or he begins with no points and will gain or lose such points depending on their rhetorical actions in the class. In order to be effective, these points should have a significant impact on the overall course grade. While an individual instructor can decide what she or he thinks is adequately significant, 10% is quite reasonable and could easily replace arbitrary "attendance" grades in many grade structures.

It is not good enough simply to say that these are the points that a student earns or loses. The points should be discussed within the course and within an overall discussion of ethos which provides students with the opportunity to learn which things they do improve their capabilities as rhetors and which things they do to actually make themselves less believable. This allows the students to decontextualize the "points" from simply a part of the class. It allows them to see that similar behaviors outside of the classroom also generate "points" or cost the students "points" in their believability and trustworthiness in their careers.

Step Two: Assessing Phronēsis

Phronēsis (φρόνησις), translated in the above quote from Aristotle as "good sense" and often translated as "practical wisdom" or sometimes just as "wisdom" constitutes a rhetor's ability to provide good advice and to heed good advice when given. *Phronēsis* has been described as "the intellectual virtue that enables one to adapt theoretical principles to practical circumstances" (Cherry 1998). As Rorty has famously noted on the concept of *phronēsis* in rhetoric "It is exceedingly difficult to maintain a reputation for *phronēsis* without actually giving a fair amount of sound advice. [...] Since a rhetoricians reputation is, over the course of time, at least in part measured by the consequences of the policies he [sic] recommends" (1980). That means that the "good advice" that a student gives cannot be limited to the advice in the first major presentation. The student has to be given the opportunity to advise his or her audience previous to that communication in order to establish ethos. In so doing, the student establishes credibility as a speaker and develops an important part of civility which is helping people in need, rather than mocking or further harming them.

In order to accomplish this several assessable tools can be built into the online speech class. The first can be accomplished in the message boards. These should not only be used to generate discussion regarding aspects of the text, but should be places where students can seek out and offer advice from each other. In most online speech classes, students are required to find their own audience, for the public performance. It is difficult, if not impossible to judge the interactions that the students have had with that audience before their presentation, however, it is possible to allow the student to build *phronēsis* within the context of the online class and to assess the building and creation of that *phronēsis*.

The message boards available in most of the major learning management systems provide an excellent place for allowing students to develop their *phronēsis*. Tell students that these forums are set up so that they can seek and find help from their fellow classmates. Begin the boards with specific questions such as "what can you do to get people to be part of your audience" or place sections in the boards in which the students can seek technical help. As students seek and offer advice in these columns, the instructor can rate the quality of the advice on a one-point to five-point scale. The more a particular student offers good advice, the more quickly that student can increase the "classroom community points," allowing the students to increase simultaneously their credibility as rhetors and their grade in the class.

Step Three: Assessing Aretē

The second Aristotelian aspect of *ethos*, *Aretē* (ἀρετή) which is translated above as "good moral character" is also an assessable quality that is an important part of civility and can be assessed in an online public speaking class. Many instructors feel uncomfortable assessing the morals of their students in that morality is increasingly seen as a private issue. When understood from Aristotle's point of view, however, moral behavior is an important part of a public persona. McTavish explains "The various virtues listed by Aristotle include: justice, manly [sic] courage, self-control, magnificence, magnanimity, liberality, gentleness, prudence and wisdom" (McTavish, 2010, p. 69). This is not to assess whether or not a student is a good person in his or her heart, but rather that the student enacts public performances of the virtues in the public parts of their lives.

Sometimes it might be tempting to confuse *Aretē* with character all by itself. However, the reason for this possible confusion is because aretae is the most essential aspect of ethos. Many scholars use the term "virtue" to understand aretae "as it preserves the integrity of Aristotle's choice for the word [aretae] instead of ethics (ethika)" (Ward, 2001). However, virtue, with its Latin roots from a word that basically means "an aspect" does not really work either. For Aristotle, aretae meant "goodness or excellence of any kind" (Ledell & Scott, 1925).

This difficulty can be solved by differentiating between *Aretē* and *Ethikon,* a related but other Greek term. Ethikon is a "subdivision of philosophy at least from the time of Aristotle, literally the study of character (ethos)" (Sedley, 2003, p. 377). However, the reason for this possible confusion is because aretae is the most essential aspect of ethos. It is the virtuousness of the rhetor

It should be explained that such virtuous acts can also be a means of earning classroom community points. When a student stands up for another student, puts him or herself forward in a self-sacrificing way, does something extra to help other students or goes out of his or her way to be careful of others in the class, the instructor should make public note of this. That includes telling the student that he or she has earned a certain number of "classroom community" points by doing so. While we often refer to negative behavior euphemistically as a "teachable moment," these events of positive behavior also come to be considered "teachable moments" too. The students learn that their acts of virtue are noticed. The instructor should also explain that these points make the student a more believable speaker.

Step Four: Assessing Eunoia

According to Fortenbaugh (1992), the concept of *eunoia* (εὔνοια), translated above as "goodwill" in Aristotle's rhetoric is related primarily to creating friendship with the audience. Yet, friendship may not be the best terminology. Burke's concept of identification may indeed come closest to Aristotle's concept of eunoia: "A is not identical with his colleague, B. But insofar as their interests are joined, A is identified with B. Or he may identify himself with B even when their interests are not joined, if he assumes they are, or is persuaded to believe so...In being identified with B, A is 'substantially one' with a person other than himself. Yet at the same time, he remains unique, an individual locus of motives. Thus, he is both joined and separate, at once a distinct substance and consubstantial with another" (Burke, 1969, pp. 20-21).

The instructor may grant the students classroom community points in a number of different instances throughout the semester when the student attempts to show consubstantiality with the other students or with the teacher. This form of identification can happen in the assignments or in discussion when the student shows a recognition that her or his interests are the same as the interests of the colleagues. When the student engages in such behaviors, the instructor can once again use it as a teachable moment point pointing out that such behaviors increase the credibility of the speaker in future presentations.

FUTURE RESEARCH DIRECTIONS

From a philosophical or rhetorical perspective, teaching civility by teaching *ethos* seems to be a perfect match. For any person who considers communication from a humanities-based perspective, these continue with a more civil discourse in the online communities that they go on to inhabit after the online class is over. On the other hand, not all parties are swayed by philosophical and humanities-based perspectives on the study of communication. For purposes of accreditation and in order to help with appropriations from funding entities, many need something that is based in a more scientific paradigm.

For that reason, it is probably appropriate that further research into the application be done. While this chapter provides a logical outline by which civility can be understood and inculcated, it might be useful to provide one that is more externally demonstrable. While terms such as *phronēsis, aretē* and *eunoia* have a stellar philosophical pedigree, it is probably necessary for those with the appropriate knowledge and temperament for social scientific research to turn them into terms that are also operational. From such operational terms, it seems possible that one could engage in statistical and observational research which could adjust various pedagogical methods based on hypothesis testing.

Even for those within the rhetorical paradigm, there is still plenty of work yet to do. Aristotle's notion of *ethos* has been considered for two and a half millennia. During that time there have been innumerable alterations, applications and interpretations of the subject. Those considered here provide adequate justification and means for teaching and assessing *ethos* in the classroom, but while adequate they could hardly be considered complete. There are undoubtedly deeper understandings of ethos that would provide even more thorough and complete means of teaching and assessing *ethos* in order to teach civility.

Finally, the teaching of civility should not probably be limited by the teaching of *ethos*. The history of inculcating civility in students neither began nor ended with Aristotle. Philosophical and pedagogical means of teaching civility have come from many thinkers throughout time. While this chapter showed the way one rhetorical concept, *ethos*, can be taught in order to teach civility and showed specifically how that could be applied to online communities, there can be no doubt that other methods can be equally adapted to the digital universe from ancient sources. Platonic and Ciceronian rhetorics may be equally enlightening when applied to creating online communities.

CONCLUSION

While there is certainly more work to be done in the study of improving civility in online communities, this chapter has shown one way as educators we can move in that direction. By assessing the three aspects of Aristotle's concepts of ethos, we are able to allow students to actually learn civility. While this cannot in any way guarantee that all subsequent actions on the part of the students are civil, it goes a long way toward inculcating a set of civil behaviors. Furthermore, it makes civility a part of learning and allows the student to learn that civil action is not just a part of their action within the confines of a class, but that good rhetoric goes beyond the phrases and turns of a single speech.

REFERENCES

Aristotle. (2011, Sept. 27). *Aristotle's Rhetoric.* (L. Honeycutt, Ed.) Retrieved from http://rhetoric.eserver.org/aristotle/index.html

Baldwin, R. G. (2007). *Academic civility begins in the classroom.* Center For Teaching and Learning. Retrieved from http://teaching.uchicago.edu/;d/pod2/97-98/baldwin.htm

Boyd, D. (2011, Sept. 22). Why Cyberbullying Rhetoric Misses The Mark. *The New York Times.* Retrieved from http://www.nytimes.com/2011/09/23/opinion/why-cyberbullying-rhetoric-misses-the-mark.html?scp=2&sq=cyberbullying&st=cse

Braxton, J. M. (2004). Addressing faculty and student classroom improprieties. *New Directions for Teaching and Learning*, 89–95.

Brooks, D. J., & Greer, J. G. (2007). Beyond negativity: The effects of incivility on the electorate. *American Journal of Political Science*, *51*(1), 1–16. doi:10.1111/j.1540-5907.2007.00233.x

Burke, K. (1969). *A Rhetoric of Motives. Berkley, CA*: University of California Press.

Cameron, D. (2000). Small Incivilities. *Critical Quarterly*, *42*(2), 127–131. doi:10.1111/1467-8705.00293

Cherry, R. D. (1998). Ethos Versus Persona. *Written Communication, 15*(3), 384. Retrieved from http://link.galegroup.com/apps/doc/A53994287/PPCM?u=nm_a_wnmu&sid=PPCM&xid=4b7a0469

Connelly, R. J. (2009). Introducing a Culture of Civility In First Year College Classes. *JGE: The Journal of General Education*, *58*(1), 47–64. doi:10.1353/jge.0.0029

Debucquoy-Dodley, D. (2011, Sept. 27). *New York looks to 'modernize' cyberbullying laws.* Retrieved from http://www.cnn.com/2011/09/27/politics/new-york-cyberbullying/index.html

Denning, P. (1993). A World Lit By Flame. *Communications of the ACM*, *36*(12), 170. doi:10.1145/163298.163353

Doctors explain why teens bully, offer advice. (2011, Dec. 6). Retrieved from http://drdrew.blogs.cnn.com/2011/12/06/doctors-explain-why-teens-bully-offer-advice/

Fortenbaugh, W. W. (1992). Aristotle on Persuasion through Character. *Rhetorica*, *10*(3), 220. doi:10.1525/rh.1992.10.3.207

FoxNews.com. (2012, Jan. 17). *Supreme Court declines to take up cases involving online attacks by students on school officials, other students*. Retrieved from http://www.foxnews.com/politics/2012/01/17/us-supreme-court-passes-on-rulings-for-cases-involving-online-attacks-by/

Gamie, S. (2017). Ethos Construction, Identification, and Authenticity in the Discourse of AWSA: The Arab Women's Solidarity Association International. In M. Folk, & S. Apostel (Eds.), *Establishing and Evaluating Digital Ethos and Online Credibility* (pp. 163–189). Hershey, PA: IGI Global. doi:10.4018/978-1-5225-1072-7.ch009

Gonzalez, V., & Lopez, E. (2001). The age of incivility: Countering disruptive behavior. *AAHE Bulletin*, *55*(8), 3–6.

Harrison, T. (2015). Virtuous reality: moral theory and research into cyber-bullying. *Ethics and Information Technology, 17*(4), 275–283. Retrieved from https://link.springer.com/article/10.1007%2Fs10676-015-9382-9

Hendrix, K. (2007). "She must be trippin": The secret of disrespect from students of Color toward faculty of Color. *New Directions for Teaching and Learning*, *110*(110), 85–96. doi:10.1002/tl.277

Hogarth, H. (n.d.). Students at a lecture. *Hogarth's Graphic Works*. London, UK: Heath Edition.

Hyde, M. J. (2004). *The Ethos of Rhetoric*. Columbia, SC: University of South Carolina Press.

Lampman, C., Bancroft, S., & Beneke, M. (2009). Contrapower Harassment in Academia: A Survey of Faculty Experience with Student Incivility, Bullying and Sexual attention. *Sex Roles*, *60*(5/6), 331–346. doi:10.100711199-008-9560-x

Lanius, C. (2017). Telling the Quants from the Quacks: Evaluating Statistical Arguments in Debates Online. In M. Folk, & S. Apostel (Eds.), *Establishing and Evaluating Digital Ethos and Online Credibility* (pp. 1–21). Hershey, PA: IGI Global. doi:10.4018/978-1-5225-1072-7.ch001

Layard, R., & Dunn, J. (2010). *A good childhood, searching for values in a competitive age*. London, UK: Penguin.

Ledell, G. H., & Scott, R. (1925). Arete. Retrieved from *A Greek-English Lexicon*: http://www.perseus.tufts.edu/hopper/text?doc=LSJ%20a)reth/&lang=original

Li, Q. (2010). Cyberbullying in high schools: A study of students' behaviors and beliefs about this new phenomenon. *Journal of Aggression, Maltreatment & Trauma*, *19*(4), 372–392. doi:10.1080/10926771003788979

Lim, V. K., & Chin, J. Y. (2006). Mind Your E-Manners: Impact of cyber incivility on justice, emotions, and individual responses. *66th Annual Academy of Management Meeting*. Atlanta, GA.

Lim, V. K., Thompson, S. H., & Chin, J. (2008). Bosses and their E-Manners. *Communications of the ACM*, *51*(12), 155–158. doi:10.1145/1409360.1409391

Litwiller, B., & Brausch, A. (2013). Cyber Bullying and Physical Bullying in Adolescent Suicide: The Role of Violent Behavior and Substance Use. *Journal of Youth and Adolescence*, *42*(5), 675–684. doi:10.100710964-013-9925-5 PMID:23381779

Lwin, M., Li, B., & Ang, R. P. (2012). Stop bugging me: An examination of adolescents' protection behavior against online harassment. *Journal of Adolescence*, *35*(1), 31–41. doi:10.1016/j.adolescence.2011.06.007 PMID:21767872

McTavish, J. (2010). The Ethos of the Practice of Rhetoric. *PHILIPPINIANA SACRA*, *45*(133), 66–78.

Morrow, A., & Downey, C. (2013). Perceptions of adolescent bullying: Attributions of blame and responsibility in cases of cyber-bullying. *Scandinavian Journal of Psychology*, *54*(6), 536–540. doi:10.1111jop.12074 PMID:24111682

MSNBC. (2012, Jan. 24). *Clergy voice support for student in prayer banner case.* Retrieved from http://www.msnbc.msn.com/id/46122620/ns/local_news-providence_ri/t/clergy-voice-support-student-prayer-banner-case/

Pearson, C. M., & Porath, C. L. (2005). On the nature, consequences and remedies of workplace incivility: No time for "nice.". *Executive*, *19*, 7–18.

Plaisance, P. (2013). Virtue ethics and digital flourishing: An application of Philippa foot to life online. *Journal of Mass Media Ethics*, *28*(3), 91–102. doi:10.1080/08900523.2013.792691

Plank, S. B., McDill, L., McPartland, J. M., & Jordan, W. J. (2001). Situation and Repertoire: Civility, Incivility, Cursing and Politeness in an Urban High School. *Teachers College Record*, *103*(3), 504–524. doi:10.1111/0161-4681.00125

Quintillian. (2006). *Institutes of oratory*. (L. Honeycut, Ed., & J. Watson, Trans.) Retrieved from http://rhetoric.eserver.org/quintilian/

Rau-Foster, M., & Duthka, P. (2004). Workplace Civility and Staff Retention. *Nephrology Nursing Journal*, *31*(6), 702. PMID:15686340

Rookstool, J. (2007). *Fostering civility on campus.* Washington, DC: Community College Press.

Rorty, A. O. (1980). Structuring Rhetoric. In A. O. Rorty (Ed.), Essays on Aristotle's Rhetoric (p. 9). Berkeley, CA: University Of California Press.

Schneider, A. (1998). Insubordination and intimidation signal the end of decorum in many classrooms. *The Chronicle of Higher Education*, *44*(29), A12–A14.

Sedley, D. (2003). *The Cambridge Companion to Greek and Roman Philosophy*. Cambridge, UK: Cambridge University Press. doi:10.1017/CCOL0521772850

Sipior, J. C., & Ward, B. T. (1999). The dark side of employee email. *Communications of the ACM*, *42*(7), 88–95. doi:10.1145/306549.306591

Thorston, K., Vraga, E., & Eckdale, B. (2010). Credibility in Context: How uncivil online commentary affects news credibility. *Mass Communication & Society*, *13*(3), 289–313. doi:10.1080/15205430903225571

Vallor, S. (2010). Social networking technology and the virtues. *Ethics and Information Technology*, *12*(2), 157–170. doi:10.100710676-009-9202-1

Ward, L. (2001). Nobility and Necessity: the problem of Courage in Aristotle's Nicomachean Ethics. *Political Science Review, 95*(1), 71. Retrieved from http://go.galegroup.com/ps/i.do?p=AONE&sw=w&u=nm_a_wnmu&v=2.1&it=r&id=GALE%7CA73021417&asid=b295edb474117734b0f7643af4e2ac8a

ADDITIONAL READING

Adgani, P., Bowen, H., & Daniels, M. (2007). Aristotle's forms of proof: the keys to teaching recreation marketing. *Schole: A Journal of Leisure Studies and Recreation Education, 22*, 47-50.

Alcorn, M. (1994). Self-Structure as a Rhetorical Device: Modern Ethos and the Divisiveness of the Self. In *Narcissism and the Literary Libido: Rhetoric, Text, and Subjectivity* (pp. 29–62). New York, London: NYU Press; Retrieved from http://www.jstor.org/stable/j.ctt9qfnvz.6

Baumlin, J., & Baumlin, T. (1994). *Ethos: New Essays in Rhetorical and Cultural Theory*. Dallas, TX: Southern Methodist University Press.

Cline, B. (2018). Using the Classical Rhetorical Concept of "Ethos" to Solve Online Collaboration Problems of Trust and Presence: The Case of Slack. In D. Kolbaek (Ed.), *Online Collaboration and Communication in Contemporary Organizations*. Hershey, PA: IGI Global. doi:10.4018/978-1-5225-4094-6.ch005

Corbett, E., & Connors, R. (1998). Classical Rhetoric for the Modern Student (4th Edition ed.). New York: Oxford University Press.

Corts, T. (1968). The Derivation of Ethos. *Speech Monographs*, *35*(2), 201–202. doi:10.1080/03637756809375583

Cummings, K., & Stanescu, J. (2007). Argumentation and democratic disagreement: On cultivating a practice of dissent. *Controversia*, *5*(2), 55–76.

Enos, T., & Borrowman, S. (2001). Authority and Credibility: Classical Rhetoric and the Internet and the Teaching of Techno-Ethos. In L. Gray-Rosendale, & S. (. Grubner, Alternative Rhetorics: Challenges to the Rhetorical Tradition (pp. 93-110). Carbondale, IL: Southern Illinois University Press.

Eyman, D. (2015). Defining and Locating Digital Rhetoric. In Digital Rhetoric: Theory, Method, Practice (pp. 12-60). ANN ARBOR: University of Michigan Press doi:10.2307/j.ctv65swm2.5

Fleckenstein, K. (2005). Cybernetics, Ethos and Ethics: The Plight of the Bread and Butter-Fly. *Journal of Advanced Composition*, *25*(2), 323–345.

Folk, M., & Apostel, S. (2016). *Establishing and Evaluating Digital Ethos and Online Credibility*. Hershey, PA: IGI Global.

Frobish, T. (2003). An Origin of a Theory: A Comparison of Ethos in the Homeric Iliad with that Found in Aristotle's Rhetoric. *Rhetoric Review*, *22*(1), 16–30. doi:10.1207/S15327981RR2201_2

Furley, D., & Nehamas, A. (1994). *Aristotle's Rhetoric: Philosophic Essays*. Princeton, NJ: Princeton University Press.

Golden, J., Berquist, G., Coleman, W., & Sproule, J. (2011). The Scientific Approach of Aristotle. In J. Golden, G. Berquist, W. Coleman, & J. Sproule (Eds.), *The Rhetoric of Western Thought* (pp. 67–82). Dubuque, IA: Kendall-Hunt.

Grimaldi, W. (1972). *Studies in the Philosophy of Aristotle's Rhetoric*. Weisbaden, Germany: Franz Steiner Verlag.

Halloran, S. (1982). Aristotle's Concept of Ethos, or if not His, Someone Else's. *Rhetoric Review*, *1*(1), 53–63. doi:10.1080/07350198209359037

Hicks, D., & Langsdorf, L. (1999). Regulating Disagreement, Constituing Participants: A Critique of Procedural Theories of Democracy. *Argumentation*, *13*(2), 139–160. doi:10.1023/A:1007773607213

Howes, R. F. (1961). *Historical Studies of Rhetoric and Rhetoricians*. Ithica, NY: Cornell University Press.

Johnson, N. (1984). Ethos and the Aims of Rhetoric. In R. Connors, L. Ede, & A. Lunsford (Eds.), *Essays on Classical Rhetoric and Modern Discourse* (pp. 98–114). Carbondale, IL: Southern Illinois University Press.

Johnstone, C. (1980). An Aristotelian Trilogy: Ethics, Rhetoric, Politics and the Search for Moral Truth. *Philosophy & Rhetoric*, *13*, 1–24.

Kallendorf, C., & Kallendorf, C. (1985). The figures of speech, Ethos, and Aristotle: Notes toward a rhetoric of business communication. *Journal of Business Communication*, *22*(1), 35–50. doi:10.1177/002194368502200102

Kumar, N. N. (2018, March). Ethos and Values for Students. *Language In India*, *18*(3), 294.

McCroskey, J. C. (1966). Scales for the measurement of ethos. *Speech Monographs*, *33*(1), 65–72. doi:10.1080/03637756609375482

McCroskey, J. C., & Young, T. (1981). Ethos and Credibility: The Construct and its Measurements after Three Decades. *Communication Studies*, *32*, 24–34.

Miller, A. (1974). Aristotle on Habit and Character: Implications for Rhetoric. *Communication Monographs*, *41*(4), 309–316.

Pross, E. (1952). Practical Implications of the Aristotelian Concept of Ethos. *Southern Journal of Communication*, *17*, 257–264.

Reynolds, N. (1993). Ethos as Location: New Sites for Discursive Authority. *Rhetoric Review*, *11*(2), 325–338. doi:10.1080/07350199309389009

Rosenthal, P. (1966). The Concept of Ethos and the Structure of Persuasion. *Communication Monographs*, *14*, 114–126.

Rosenthal, P. (1971). Specificity, Verifiability, and Message Credibility. *The Quarterly Journal of Speech*, *57*(4), 393–401. doi:10.1080/00335637109383084

Sattler, W. M. (1947). Conceptions of Ethos in Ancience Rhetoric. *Communication Monographs*, *14*, 55–65.

Shanahan, F., & Seele, P. (2015). Shorting Ethos: Exploring the Relationship Between Aristotle's Ethos annd Repuation Management. *Corporate Reputation Review*, *18*(1), 37–49. doi:10.1057/crr.2014.19

Sullivan, D. L. (1993). The Ethos of the Epideictic Encounter. Warnick, B. (1989). Judgement, Probablitily and Aristotle's Rhetoric. *The Quarterly Journal of Speech*, *75*, 299–311.

Willams, J. (2009). Aristotle And the Systemization of Rhetoric. In J. Williams (Ed.), *An Introduction to Classical Rhetoric: Essential Readings* (pp. 222–270). Malden, MA: Wiley-Blackwell.

KEY TERMS AND DEFINITIONS

***Aretē*:** An ancient Greek term that is often translated as "good moral character." It is the ability for a communicator to show that she or he is a good person and therefore worthy of being believed.

Civil Discourse: Communication that engages with others in an ethical and socially appropriate way.

Civility: Actions and behaviors in which one acts towards others in an ethical and socially appropriate way.

***Ethos*:** An ancient Greek term for the way in which a communicator shows that he or she has good sense, good moral character and good will in order to make himself or herself more believable to an audience.

***Eunoia*:** An ancient Greek term that is often translated as "good will." It is the ability for a communicator to show that she or he has friendly motives toward the audience and is therefore worthy of being believed.

Inculcate: To create habits in people by teaching them.

***Phronēsis*:** An ancient Greek term that is often translated as "good sense" or "wisdom." It is the ability for a communicator to show that she or he knows what is being discussed and understands it in a practical way.

Chapter 4
The Importance of Tone and Attitude in Email and the Online Classroom

Melissa A. Miller
Purdue University Global, USA

ABSTRACT

In the online classroom, email has emerged as a predominant communication method between students and faculty. Despite many benefits of email, including ease of use, familiarity of the technology, and rapid response times, there are numerous challenges faculty face when sending and receiving email correspondence with students. Mainly, due to the medium and format of email, with its lack of cues such as body language, inflection, and other sensory stimuli, it presents a paramount challenge to faculty. However, appropriate tone and attitude in emails can help mitigate the challenges the medium presents. When written and read effectively and purposefully, email is an effective outreach and communication tool for students and faculty.

INTRODUCTION

As Marshall McLuhan famously said, "The medium is the message." For online educators, the email communication we send to our students and colleagues are extensions of ourselves. Our email correspondence is the lifeline between us and our students, and in an online classroom, it essentially replaces the face-to-face dialogue. We use various means of communication within the classroom platform, but email (and possibly other social media) are the means of closing the personal gaps sometimes lacking for online learners. Reaching out via email is the smile or wave of a professor you see on campus and a quick reply to a student question via email is the feedback a student receives during face-to-face office hours. Due to the importance of the format and its frequency of use, educators must be committed to effective email communication.

It is socially valid to address tone and attitude in email communication between faculty and students because, "more than any other, email is the adjunct faculty member's most important communication

DOI: 10.4018/978-1-5225-9814-5.ch004

tool" (Cooper & Booth, 2011, p. 16). Also, due to the bulk of communication occurring via email, "it is worth asking what effect the email medium will, in the long run, have on students' language use, or, how students' face-to-face language use in the academic domain might affect their email use with their professors" (Biesenbach-Lucas, 2007, p. 74). Because email serves as a main tool of communication, it is vital faculty use it effectively and judiciously. Additionally, emails are often misunderstood or leave the reader (student) more confused than prior to the communication. Kruger et al. (2005) reminds us, "people routinely overestimate how well they can communicate over email," and this is often the case when the meaning is "ambiguous" (p. 926). Even when faculty believe they are communicating effectively, and writing with appropriate tone and attitude, it is prudent to re-examine and fine-tune their practices. Email communication impact student-to-faculty relationships, and impact instruction in the online classroom. To this end, tone and attitude must be considered when improving email communication. This chapter explores these potential challenges and prescribes ways for faculty to bridge the potential gap created by these obstacles.

BACKGROUND

Although email is a relatively new mode of communication, numerous studies have been conducted in this field, particularly regarding email use and the online learning environment and relationships between faculty and students. For example, in a 2010 qualitative study examined faculty members' and students' expectations and perceptions of email communication in a dual pathway pharmacy program, the researchers found "constructive criticism received by email can be misinterpreted as being rude and condescending" (Foral et al., 2010, para. 27). Students also reported feeling "faculty members should be accessible, approachable, and available for email questions" because they are paying for their services via tuition (Foral et al., 2010, para. 28). Yu and Yu (2002) conducted a study which showed "empirical evidence supporting the usefulness of email as a promising aid to promote student cognitive growth" and that "incorporating email into the learning process might be a promising enhancement to instruction that teachers could readily adopt" (p. 117). However, Wood (2002, as cited in Heiman, 2008) found increased positive perceptions of the online community and student-to-faculty relationships, regardless of the number of emails sent (two or 15) (p. 240).

Heiman conducted a 2008 study at The Open University of Israel that looked at *The Effects of Email Messages in a Distance Learning University*, as higher education e-learning is not a frequently examined field, to date. The study found evidence that "students who received email messages expressed higher perceived social support, had a higher task-oriented strategy, and emotion-oriented strategy, and tended to express higher satisfaction with academic courses" (Heiman, 2008, p. 244). A 1999 study by Minsky and Marin found "favorable attitudes toward innovation and change, computer self-efficacy, and computer experience directly and positively influence email use" (Rockwell et al., p. 195). In a survey conducted by Johnson (2000), cited by Pena-Sanchez of Texas A&M University (2008), email was rated highest (over interpersonal and written communication) by students in the context of social presence when defined as personal touch, socializing, and allowing the receiver to get to know someone (p. 196). Pena-Sanchez (2008) then went on to conduct a survey regarding reliability and validity of various communication channels, including email, and found "students considered email to be superior for timeliness, convenience, efficiency, and turning in work," while faculty rated it to be superior for "convenience, retention, and efficiency" (p. 200). Kruger et al. (2005) conducted five studies measuring the email senders' lack of awareness regarding the correct interpretation of their sarcasm, humor, or another emotion or tone, and found that each study confirmed their prediction the email sender overestimates their ability to clearly communicate over email. This has important implications for online faculty because if faculty are over-confident, students are misunderstanding their tone, attitude, and emotion, no professional learning or growth can take place, and the students may be misconstruing information. However, all of the work regarding interpreting tone, attitude, and emotion does not fall solely on the email sender--Kruger et al. (2005) also found that "participants overestimated their ability to interpret email" (p. 933). Certainly, some of the responsibility for effective email relationships lies with the recipient as well.

A theoretical foundation for email and its impact on student and faculty relationships can be found in the Social Presence Theory (SPT). This theory, a subset of communication theory, argues a critical factor of a communication medium is the social presence, degree of interaction, and salience of relationships (Richardson & Swan, 2003). Authors Richardson and Swan (2003) connect Social Presence Theory to a concept of teacher immediacy, which is the measure of a psychological distance the teacher puts (or removes) between themselves and the student or recipient. This has implications for email use, as teacher immediacy can possibly be achieved through email communication with deliberate effort on the part of faculty. "Much as does social presence, information richness declines along a continuum from face-to-face, through telephone, email, and various other kinds of media" (Rockwell et al., 1999, p. 196). A further context for immediacy can include verbal and non-verbal immediacy behavior, including humor, personal connections, cues, etc. (Dickinson, 2017). This immediacy, whether verbal or non-verbal, needs to be deliberately attempted in an online environment where verbal and non-verbal cues are not clearly seen nor heard.

Additionally, Social Presence Theory "suggests that media that are capable of providing a greater sense of intimacy and immediacy will be perceived as having a higher social presence" (Richardson & Swan, 2003, p. 296). If faculty can increase this intimacy and immediacy through email communication, a greater social presence can be achieved. An annual survey of online students (Drexel University) indicated "the more personalized the online educational environment is for students, the more likely students will be engaged throughout their courses and stay connected as alumni" (Betts, 2009, para. 4). Therefore, the goal of improved tone and attitude in faculty emails is greater student collaboration and engagement in the online classroom and beyond.

MAIN FOCUS OF THE CHAPTER

Benefits

Certainly, email use between faculty and students has numerous benefits. Email is "typed, but they are composed in a manner suggestive of or miming characteristics of spoken language" (Weinstock, 2004, p. 367). Email bridges geographic boundaries and can link students and teachers across time zones and countries. Email "translates into more approachable faculty, which, most professors would likely concur, is a good thing" (Hardeman, 2010, para. 23). Additionally, email can be advantageously used to quickly disseminate information to students in an efficient manner, en masse. Email also serves to answer possible student questions, and a pattern of student questions via email alerts an instructor to a missed concept or the need for clarification (Hardeman, 2010). Another benefit of using email as communication between faculty and students is "college students say that email makes it easier to ask questions and helps them to learn" (Glater, 2006, p. 2).

Instructionally, email aids transmission of large files, increasing "communication velocity, supports collaborative work, and sustains both strong and weak ties among communicators" (Wellman et al., 1996, as cited in Minsky and Marin, 1999, p. 194). Faculty can access and process information (received via email) more quickly, and email "facilitates cross-organizational communication" (Minsky & Marin, 1999, p. 195). Additionally, email and other e-tools serve as a means of preserving data, which can benefit both students and faculty (O'Conner, 2012). Email serves as a means of outreach to all students and is a predominant mode of communication in an online classroom. Finally, because of its widespread use, students and faculty alike generally feel comfortable with this use of technology, which in turn leads to more frequent use. In a study of online perceptions and experiences of faculty, instructors noted that "students' preference for email as an online communication tool was perhaps related to their confidence or comfort level using the tool" (Huang & Hsiao, 2012, p. 20). Similarly, many instructors are also confident and comfortable with email technology.

Challenges

The use of email as a primary or even secondary communication method between faculty and students poses several challenges. According to the Harvard Business Review (2012), "the most valuable form of communication is face-to-face", with the least valuable forms being email and texting (Pentland, p. 65). Email is the "least rich" of the communication channels because it is limited to words (Pena-Sanchez, 2008, p. 195). Email is considered "leaner" in communication "because fewer cues are available and because feedback can be delayed and is less obtainable" (Byron, 2008, p. 311). This presents a potential problem for online faculty, as a bulk of student-to-faculty communication is done via email. Therefore, when we do send emails, they must be done correctly and efficiently. When communicating with students, online learning instructors do not receive valuable information such as body language, body positioning, visual cues or facial expressions. We rely on written tone, and some students may be more informal than others; this can lead to confusion and misinterpretation. Additionally, "if a student does not read and write well, there might be a breakdown in communication (Donathan, Dotson, & Hanks, 2017, p. 88). Kruger et al. (2005) believe one underlying cause of this miscommunication lies in "egocentrism, the inherent difficulty of moving beyond one's subjective experience of a stimulus and imagining how the stimulus might be evaluated by someone who does not share one's privileged perspective" (p. 926). For online faculty, this means moving beyond assuming our message is clear, and taking steps to ensure student comprehension. When faculty members send emails to a student, they have a clear message of what they are trying to say, but due to a lack of "paralinguistic cues" and "because it can be difficult to separate one's own experience of a stimulus from the stimulus available to one's audience, one's email message may be more ambiguous than one realizes" (Kruger et al., 2005, p. 926). For example, humor can easily be lost in translation, and students may not pick up on cues left by the faculty (and vice versa). Related to this, students may be unclear about email standards if different professors have different reactions to student emails" (Biesenbach-Lucas, 2007, p. 60). All of these uncertainties may leave students confused about expectations, and they might not have consistent models of appropriate emails to follow.

Another challenge for faculty is email communication does not provide feedback many students are seeking. Feedback is limited and delayed by "the fact that communication partners are not copresent" and this "further complicates the communication of emotion by email" (Byron, 2008, p. 312). For example, in person, faculty may use tone, inflection, attitude, and gestures to give a critique of an assignment. In an email, however, the inflection and gestures "to soften the blow of negative communication" are missing (Kruger et al., 2005, p. 926). In addition, improved technology has led to email being used more frequently (laptop, mobile phone, etc.), and due to its ease of use, "emails typed in haste may not represent clear thought or audience analysis regarding the tone, organization, immediacy, and presentation of a message" (Hardeman, 2010, para. 4). This feedback works both ways, and faculty may not receive the information they need from their students to best serve their needs. An email may not convey the true despair or confusion, or may exaggerate these emotions, where a face-to-face encounter might be clearer and more effective.

Due to the asynchronous format of email, it "has become a primary medium for some students to 'hide' behind technology" (Hardeman, 2010, para. 27). This means students (or faculty) might use email to ask questions, make statements, or broach topics they would not broach via face-to-face. Donathan, Dotson, & Hanks (2017) remind of the possibility that "students feel invisible in the online classroom, which might lead some to behave in disruptive or inconsiderate ways with classmates and instructors they cannot see and might never meet in person" (p. 88). Email tends to be an isolated, solitary endeavor, and this might also contribute to users willing to disregard typical writing norms and conventions, including appropriate tone and attitude (Weinstock, 2004). Weinstock surmises that often, "individuals are willing to say things in an email that they would not express as bluntly or straightforwardly in a formal letter or communication" (2004, p. 367). Students may lose inhibitions, and "there is a tendency to write things one may not ordinarily say to the face" of the person they are communicating with (Hardeman, 2010, para. 34). Related to this, faculty must consider the fact that when students are reading an email, students are often distracted and inundated with other stimuli. Students may be overwhelmed with the information this digital age presents. Kupritz & Cowell (2011) noted that, "the residual effect of increased data points of information is the potential for misinterpretation and miscommunication" (p. 56). For example, perhaps students are reading the email on their phone while waiting at the doctor with a sick child, or they are on a lunch break at work during a particularly stressful time. While those worries might still be present in an on-ground classroom, the teacher and the student having a discussion would have fewer distractions. Email, however, can be read while the student is in a variety of settings and various states of emotion, and students may be multi-tasking and distracted (Bender, 2012). Students, like faculty, are bombarded with data and stimuli and emotion while reading email. Many of these variables are beyond our control, but are the reality of email correspondence. Therefore, faculty should strive to make certain our tone and attitude in the email is clear and delivered as intended.

Impact on Relationships

The predominant use of email in online learning is changing the landscape and boundaries of faculty-to-student relationships. Common faculty complaints about student emails include, but are not limited to, unreasonable requests, inappropriate or impolite tone and greetings, and grammatical errors (Bisenbach-Lucas, 2007, p. 59). Previously, students and faculty interacted face-to-face, or possibly over the telephone, and "few such complaints have been raised about students abusing their professors' phone lines or voice mail" (Bisenbach-Lucas, 2007, p. 59). Email, as a unique means of communication in terms being less personal (compared to speaking over the phone, for example), presents new challenges for faculty. The relationship is often blurred with faculty and student; because it is "not a face-to-face dyad, email itself can bring forth an almost brazen tone in upward communication" (Hardeman, 2010, para. 18). With the proliferation of email as the means of communication for online learners, faculty face unique challenges. "While some research claims that email, due to absence of non-verbal cues, encourages informal language, other research has claimed the opposite" (Bisenbach-Lucas, 2007, p. 59).

Nearly all of today's online students are comfortable with email, by the nature of their surroundings and learning environment, and many are very comfortable with other forms of technology such as social media, texting, and virtual chatting. These technologies deliver quick, immediate results, and instant feedback. Students, therefore, often expect such responses from their professors, as they are "accustomed to being able to reach anyone they wish to contact by home phone, cell phone, email, instant messaging, or pager" (Walmsley & McManemy, 2008, para. 7). This can create a potential problem in the student-professor relationship, as students are expecting immediate responses, and may become angry, frustrated, or feel disappointed when a response deemed too slow is sent. Interestingly, Weinstock (2004) also points out that an additional challenge to email communication is although users know data is saved, many perceive email communication as ephemeral; thus, the stakes "seem smaller" and people feel less committed (p. 370). Users might be less invested in the email relationship and this might increase the informality of tone many email users assume.

Emails often contain emotions, but even with this, tone and attitude can easily be misinterpreted. Emails "may contain nonverbal cues that have parallels in face-to-face communication, such as emoticons to symbolically convey emotion, asterisks to provide emphasis, or all capital letters to indicate emotional intensity" (Byron, 2008, p. 312). The problem for faculty, however, is many of these methods are viewed as unprofessional and too casual. Hardeman (2010) reminds us "email developed so rapidly and is used so pervasively that its true etiquette is still being worked out" (para. 19). Another problem is accepted email use may be subjective to the student; younger students may feel writing casually is acceptable whereas older students may expect a more formal response. Email is used in so many contexts that when it is used in higher education, it does not have a unique set of guidelines to which all parties agree. For example, while some practices are acceptable or encouraged in a business setting, they might be contradicted as inappropriate in a social or education setting (Hardeman, 2010). This can easily lead to miscommunication and misunderstanding.

Emoticons are popular with students, but when sent by faculty, may be perceived as too casual, or faculty may even be uncomfortable using these cues. In addition, "such attempts at precise communication are often foiled by overuse and the lack of standards regarding what the levels of intensity actually mean" (Glendinning, 2006, p. 84). If all users are not aware of the shorthand or emotive meanings, additional confusion is created. Emoticons can be ambiguous for many people, and some are not universal. Additionally, the purposeful use of these emoticons is often irregular and inconsistent (Byron, 2008). Emoticons may be limited in their scope, and Byron (2008) also insightfully reminds us the email recipient may rely more heavily on other cues, such as response time, message length, presence or lack of greeting, or degree of formality, in perceiving emotion via email. Emojis differ from emoticons in that they are "pictographs of faces, objects, and symbols" (Grannan, 2019). The number of emojis grows exponentially each year, and while they are a more direct symbol or picture, the opportunity for misunderstanding is similar to that of the emoticon. These considerations have tremendous implications for online faculty. If faculty attempt a positive tone with words (or choose to use emoticons or emojis), it may not be enough. A comprehensive act, through the actual words as well as response time, tone, attitude, attention to detail (editing and proofreading) sends a more in-depth message of engagement and interest.

Even when a positive tone is attempted, "the informality of emails as a written form of communication, and the often ephemeral quality of emails may contribute to their symbolic meaning such that emails intended to convey positive emotions are interpreted as more neutral (less positive and intense) than the sender intends" (Byron, 2008, p. 313). Or, receivers may interpret content in a negative manner due to the lack of cues and emotional tone.

Numerous other factors play a role in the tone and attitude of emails, and this may impact the student-faculty relationship. For example, gender is a potential variable, as "because men tend to be less emotionally expressive of positive emotion, their emails may tend to be emotionally neutral" (Byron, 2008, p. 315). Or, a female student may misinterpret an email from a male professor as more neutral or negative than he intended. Males tend to have lower accuracy at "encoding" the emotion in their email in general, and have "minimal use of emoticons indicating positive emotion" (p. 315). This can lead to misinterpretation and misunderstanding for the recipient. Walmsley & McManemy (2008) argue that a student unable to conduct a proper email relationship with faculty exhibits a type of character dysfunction, and this can affect the classroom. They state, "a student who is inflexible and has weak impulse control and poor boundary control contributes to a classroom environment that is not conducive to learning" (Walmsley & McManemy, 2008, para. 4).

Age is another factor that influencing perception of tone and attitude in emails. Age can be related to experience, and an older student may have more experience with other forms of communication in which emotion was more clearly defined. Or, a younger student may have grown up using email and may be completely comfortable sharing emotions in this format. Byron (2008) found in general, "age is negatively related to emotional express, regulation, and perception" (p. 317). However, while age may be a variable in tone and attitude reception, faculty need to avoid making assumptions about the age or perceived age of students and their email use. First, the online environment can be a great equalizer, as the instructor may not know student ages based on the information they receive (unless the student shares this). This may help decrease any bias or stereotypes faculty have (such as that older students will use email less effectively, etc.). In using email to improve relationships, faculty should remember to not "hamstring students with pre-conceived notions of ability" (O'Connor, 2012, p. 9). Faculty should have high expectations of appropriate email use for all students, and if a student needs assistance, "instructors can assemble e-resources to help students gain facility with needed communication tools" (O'Connor, 2012, p. 9).

Finally, the length of the relationship impacts the perception of emotion in email communications. Byron (2008) cited findings suggesting impacts of relative relationship length: partners with a longer email history "may be more likely to express and perceive emotion" via email; may communication emotion more accurately; and "may be less likely to negatively evaluate the email and its sender" (p. 316). This is often the heart of the problem for the online instructor--how do we get our students to know us? How do we develop this relationship in this online setting? Can email be used to bridge this gap, or will it continue to widen the divide? Email can be used to create this trusting relationship, and while time cannot be sped up and create a history, through outreach and interest, faculty can establish rapport and connections to build relationships.

Impact on Instruction

Email interactions can impact education and instructional matters of the online classroom. Instructional immediacy is accomplished when teachers are able to reduce or eliminate feelings of aloofness and social distance, which may be perceived by students as lack of caring or even incompetence, and to increase a sense of "approachability" (Foral et al., 2010). Additionally, immediacy has been linked to rapport-building and student satisfaction with students (Legg & Wilson, 2009). A professional, on-going email relationship can help improve instructional immediacy through reduced social distance and relatively quick feedback. Because the online classroom lacks the immediacy achieved in a face-to-face setting, it is important to attempt instructional immediacy with students, and this can be done via email outreach. For example, a professor may send summary emails at the beginning of the unit, or emails in the middle of the week to check on progress, or simply send out a friendly "hello," as you might do if you saw the student walking on campus or in a meeting during office hours. If the friendly tone of a smile you might give when you physically return a paper to a student, or the facial expression of friendliness when the student asks you a question after class can be conveyed via email, faculty goes a long way towards building rapport and solidifying relationships with students. The goal of this, in turn, is to have more engaged, participatory students, and a more collaborative online learning environment. A study conducted by Legg and Wilson (2009) examined student motivation in a course when they received a welcome email one week prior to the course start date. They found the students who received the welcome email, overall, had higher course completion rates, rated more positive indicators on surveys about the course, the instructor, and their motivation.

Another instructional impact of frequent email use between faculty and students relates to the casual format and text of many emails. The fast-pace and casualness of the medium of emails can translate into student work. Thus, "many of these writing problems have exploded in numbers out of habit as opposed to students actually lacking writing skill" (Hardeman, 2010, para. 29). This underlies the important of faculty modeling correct use of the email, and using correct form, grammar, and punctuation. Instructors need to "draw the grammatical and spelling line, not only with papers...but also with email correspondence" (Hardeman, 2012, para. 32). Interestingly, "as norms have made the task easier, etiquettes related to email are supposed to be known and practiced by people who are corresponding through these upgraded technological mediums" (Gupta, 2012, p. 29). However, faculty may encounter students who are ignorant of these norms for email use and proper email etiquette, and instruction and modeling may be needed.

Faculty can use student email as an informal tool of data collection which in turn be used to guide instruction. For example, if 35% of the students email for clarification about a topic, this alerts the instructor about a need to either re-teach, clarify, or direct students to additional resources in the course. Faculty can also use this data to develop future lessons, discussions, and webinars. The benefit of making this "real-time course adjustment" is that faculty can use email to spot patterns, look for areas of strength and weakness, and turn the data into "a true formative assessment" (O'Conner, 2012, p. 16). This helps faculty conduct "ongoing, not just post-mortem, evaluation of the course" (O'Conner, 2012, p. 16).

Content should be considered when sending information via email, as some topics lend themselves to being appropriate for email, while others less so. Byron (2008) also reminds us that using email for "ambiguous messages is less effective and efficient--it increases the likelihood of inaccurate communication and more time is then spent resolving the miscommunication" (p. 313). For this reason, faculty must be selective about sending using email as an instructional versus a communicative tool.

SOLUTIONS AND RECOMMENDATIONS

There are many strategies faculty can use when communicating via email to mitigate many of the potential problems presented in this chapter. First, while this may sound like an obvious recommendation, always re-read the email prior to sending, checking for accuracy and proofreading for errors. If responding to an email, re-read to ensure all questions have been answered.

In this light, it is important to model desired behaviors and written communication for students. Modeling appropriate tone and attitude in email sets the tone for students, and shows them how it should be done correctly. Continuing this idea, "students should be counseled that, as with other forms of written and oral communication, effective email needs to consider the intended audience and its expectations" (Weinstock, 2004, p. 377). This can be done in class, in a discussion board, through a presentation uploaded in the course, or included in the course syllabus. Faculty might conduct a mini-lesson comparing and contrasting emails with different tone, attitude, grammar, content, etc. There is no guarantee this will result in the same tone and attitude in return, however, it lays an important foundation. In addition, "faculty should be clear about setting boundaries, react consequentially to inappropriate behavior, and themselves model expected behaviors" (Walmsley & McManemy, 2008, para. 8).

Subsequently, it is a good idea to alert students when instructors will not be able to respond to emails immediately or quickly (which is preferred, when possible). For example, if it is known that an instructor will be away from the computer for the day, the instructor should let them know they might not receive as quick of a reply as normally would be expected. Letting students know when there is availability to respond to emails, or when there are set virtual office hours, helps students manage their time and expectations. Hardeman (2010) reminds faculty that if they "do not outwardly discourage weekend or late-night calls and emails, for example, students may develop the perception that we are there to serve them at their leisure and adjust their communication accordingly" (para. 5). Therefore, setting the tone of response times and windows will help define such boundaries.

Students seek online education for a variety of reasons, and one is the convenience of the format and delivery. Familiarity or comfort with the technology and the communication strategies therein is not always clearly understood or considered by students; they may incorrectly anticipate what the relationship with the professors will entail, particularly if they have not previously been in an online classroom. In a case study completed at Oklahoma State University (2017), a study of the language of emails for tone that evaluated student success rates and examined data across two semesters found more positive instructor evaluations and increased responses with emails that had more positive, encouraging, and supportive tones. Dickinson (2017) found implications for the online classroom, including students engaging in online course work need to feel socially connected and supported in their academic efforts. Further, the author of the study concluded, "these findings suggest that while students in an online course may be taking the course to fit the demands of their personal lifestyle, it does not mean they do not want to be connected on some level with their professor. In general, online students appear to want a positive connection with their professor and these students need to feel supported in order to be successful" (p. 8). Helping making these connections through the tone our digital communications is vital due to the lack of other interfaces.

Scott Cutlip and Allen Center developed *The 7Cs of Communication* in 1952, and these concepts stand the test of time and are applicable to email correspondence today (Gupta, 2012). These seven elements of communication are: courtesy, coherence, clarity, completeness, conciseness, concreteness, and correctness. Although developed for written and verbal communication modes, these are appropriate guidelines in digital communication as well. Faculty should not only consider and model these elements when crafting their own emails, but also spend time teaching these to students.

Faculty should focus on the greeting and salutation of the email, as this sets the tone for the message. The greeting, such as *Dear Student*, or *Hello Student*, is an important part of the email because it "establishes your relationship to your reader" (Rudick & O'Flahavan, n.d., para. 8). If sending a message to more than one student, name the students or give the group a term, because "a more specific greeting sets a focused tone to the message" (Rudick & O'Flahavan, n.d., para. 9). Additionally, Rudick and O'Flahavan (n.d.) suggest a strong closing that either summarizes points, re-states an action item, and is gracious. A strong closing can leave students with the overall tone of the last sentiment, and puts a finishing touch on the message. It also appears deliberate, less rushed, and less haphazard than just throwing your name at the end might appear. Email etiquette, or netiquette, guidelines vary, but ending with a closing such as *Best Regards* is often an appropriate closure (Gupta, 2012).

Using personal pronouns and writing in the active voice are both suggested methods for personalizing email and establishing a positive tone. Personal pronouns address the reader and "active voice makes your email tone clearer and more direct," and helps email sound less "bureaucratic" (Rudick & O'Flahavan, n.d., para. 14). This impacts faculty because this word choice may help break down potential barriers between the faculty and student. Additionally, setting a positive tone does not mean that faculty, at times, do not need to deliver a less-than-positive message. For example, faculty may need to address student performance or missing work, and an online professor cannot speak face-to-face with a student regarding these issues. Rudick & O'Flahavan suggest directly addressing even negative topics head-on, because "burying the bad news somewhere in the middle or end of the message is harmful; readers may miss it or misinterpret its importance" (n.d., para. 17). However, faculty should affect a positive tone and attitude, and covey a willingness to work in a partnership with the student to resolve the problem.

There are common errors to avoid in writing an email that may be misleading, or make the tone or attitude of the message unclear. Abbreviations should not be used unless they are general knowledge (Gupta, 2012). Keeping the font, color, and capitalization consistent helps to send a clear, concise, and professional message. Another way to make sure students receive the intended information is to alert students to any attachments or forthcoming emails. After the closing, include a reminder of how many attachments (as might be done in a professional written letter). Gupta (2012) reminds faculty to name files appropriately so students do not ignore them or mistake them for a virus.

Students may also be frustrated by the brevity of an email response (Foral et al., 2010). If you have to research an answer or take time to formulate a response, send the student a reply to let them know you received their question and are working on the response. This validation can serve as a recognition and acknowledgement of receipt. "When you give your students your email address, make sure they know how quickly you plan to respond to them, whether that be within 6 hours or 48 hours. (This is important for students to know. If a student has an urgent problem, he or she will need to know how quickly you plan to respond. Otherwise, you may be inundated by a flood of frantic emails from the student.)" (Cooper & Booth, 2011, p. 17). If faculty need to reply to a negative email, and feel they are only going to respond with negative tone and attitude themselves, Weinstock (2004) suggests composing a response off-line and waiting twenty-four hours before deciding to send the email. Often, time for reflection to craft the appropriate tone and attitude is needed.

Additionally, it is important to use validation and acknowledgement when responding to student emails. "With less feedback available, email senders have less information available to construct effective messages" and faculty can begin by acknowledging what has been received and use "I" messages to state how they are interpreting the message (Byron, 2008, p. 314). For example, *I can see that you are frustrated with this task, and we can work together to solve question number six in the book so that you can better understand the concept.* Another suggestion, when possible, is to specifically state the emotion the writer wishes to convey, as "the most straightforward way of encoding a message to convey the sender's emotion is to verbalize it" (Byron, 2008, p. 319). For this need, the educator could write, *I am happy you reached out to me to clarify this question.*

There are several questions to consider when responding to a student email, particularly if it is not a quick answer, yes-or-no request for information. Things to consider include:

- Would I provide a more detailed answer if I were speaking with the student face-to-face? If yes, what is preventing me from writing out the information needed?
- Does my email reflect the tone I am attempting to convey? Have I attempted to objectively re-read the email from the point-of-view of the student?
- Am I taking the time the student deserves, and what is really needed to fully answer the question?

Word choice, stating specific emotions, and deliberate structuring of an email are ways faculty can decrease the perceived distance between themselves and their students.

Another way to decrease perceived distance using email is that faculty might consider hosting dedicating email office hours, or virtual office hours, in which emails would be answered immediately, or instant messaging such as Skype could be used. Information including response times, office hours, and possibly alternative methods of communication can be included in the faculty signature line (Bradley et al., 2011). In one study, faculty and students responded positively to two-way web conferencing (Skype, face-time chat, etc.) because it "helped to reduce communication barrier" and establish connections (Huang & Hsiao, 2012, p. 23). In a two-way web-conference, tone of voice, facial expressions, and body language can be more accurately paired with the language.

FUTURE RESEARCH DIRECTIONS

As technology changes, the scope and use of email may change and further research may be warranted. Chen, Jones, and Xu (2012) note "email appears to have reached a 'maturity' phase, and might be on the decline as other forms of communication, such as texting, have come into vogue" (p. 66). If students move from using email as a predominant communication tool in the online classroom, instructors may need to focus on communication outreach via social media. However, many of these best practices for email use may still apply to new technologies such as chat rooms, Skype, texting, and instant messaging. Kruger et al. (2005) predict many of these new technologies will have similar challenges to email because "they are largely text-based" and there will likely remain "a rift between the subjective stimuli available to the communicator and the objective stimuli available to the audience that communicators may fail to fully appreciate (p. 934). Additionally, new devices such as mobile phones where students can access email raise new concerns about privacy and password protected accounts that might be more easily penetrated via a mobile device.

Tone and attitude in emails remain an important professional development topic for faculty. The importance of email communication in online classrooms should be discussed in faculty meetings and taught as professional development opportunities. As the technology changes for students, faculty need to be kept abreast of these changes so they can foster and develop communication skills for this new and emerging technology along with their students. Additional research is needed to measure effectiveness in the online classroom as new media emerge. It is suggested future research also be directed into "the issue of what cues receivers rely on to indicate emotion and how they interpret these cues" (Byron, 2008, p. 319).

The impact of email on student and faculty relationships are not only wrought with potential problems; there are rewards and improvements as well. Advantages include that "email technology also allows writers to plan and revise messages before sending them, thus affording the opportunity to edit not only for grammar and mechanics, but also for pragmatic clarity and politeness" (Bisenbach-Lucas, 2007, p. 59). Faculty should focus on these advantages to increase their social presence, when possible. Faculty know "the volume of email [they] answer each day makes it difficult to write each message thoughtfully with the correct tone...but if [they] want [their] messages to achieve [their] goals, [they] must set the tone in email just as [they] do when [they] speak" (Rudick & O'Flahavan, n.d., para. 18).

CONCLUSION

As long as there are asynchronous learners, faculty and students will be using various forms of media to replace the face-to-face interactions of the traditional classroom. The online classroom is not only growing, but "online education enrollment growth in the United States now far exceeds overall higher education growth" (Betts, 2009, para. 2). Faculty are increasingly relying on email as a means of reaching students and maintaining connection. This is particularly true for online faculty, where a major mode of outreach and communication is via email with students. One major problem with the email format is "social and contextual cues that usually regulate and influence group communication dynamics are missing or attenuated" (Kiel & Johnson, 2002, p. 296). However, faculty, through deliberate practice, knowledge of Social Presence Theory, and application of appropriate tone and attitude in their emails, can work to create personalized emails that bridge these potential communication gaps for students. Using appropriate tone and attitude to create personalized emails with high social presence is important to the student-faculty relationship because "personalized communication is critical to recruitment, engagement, and retention of online students" (Betts, 2009, para. 4).

REFERENCES

Bender, T. (2012). *Discussion-based online teaching to enhance student learning: Theory, practice, and assessment*. Sterling, VA: Stylus.

Betts, K. (2009). Lost in translation: Importance of effective communication in online education. *Online Journal of Distance Learning Administration, 12*(2).

Biesenbach-Lucas, S. (2007). Students writing email to faculty: An examination of e- politeness among native and non-native speakers of English. *Language Learning & Technology, 11*(2), 59–81.

Bradley, L. J., Hendricks, B., Lock, R., Whiting, P., & Parr, G. (2011). Email communications: Issues for mental health counselors. *Journal of Mental Health Counseling, 33*(1), 67–79. doi:10.17744/mehc.33.1.05208025375v03r7

Byron, K. (2008). Carrying too heavy a load? The communication and miscommunication of emotion by email. *Academy of Management Review, 33*(2), 309–327. doi:10.5465/amr.2008.31193163

Chen, C. C., Jones, K. T., & Xu, S. (2012). The communication methods of today's students. *The CPA Journal*, *82*(11), 66–71.

Cooper, L. E., & Booth, B. A. (2011). The adjunct faculty handbook. Thousand Oaks, CA: Sage: eBook Collection. Retrieved from EBSCOhost.

Dickinson, A. (2017). Communicating with the online student: The impact of email tone on student performance and teacher evaluations. *The Journal of Online Educators*, *14*(2), 1–10.

Donathan, L. N., Dotson, A. T., & Hanks, M. (2017). Minimizing incivility in the online classroom. *Radiologic Technology*, *89*(1), 88–91. PMID:28904163

Foral, P. A., Turner, P. D., Monaghan, M. S., Walters, R. W., Merkel, J. J., Lipschultz, J. H., & Lenz, T. L. (2010). Faculty and student expectations and perceptions of email communication in a campus and distance doctor of pharmacy program. *American Journal of Pharmaceutical Education*, *74*(10), 10. doi:10.5688/aj7410191 PMID:21436932

Glater, J. (2006, Feb. 21). To: Professor@University.edu Subject: Why it's all about me. *New York Times*. Retrieved from http://www.nytimes.com/2006/02/21/education/21professors.html?_r=1&oref=slo gin.

Glendinning, M. (2006). Email: Boon or bane for school leaders? *Phi Delta Kappan*, *88*(1), 83–86. doi:10.1177/003172170608800115

Grannan, C. (2019). *What's the difference between emoji and emoticons?* Retrieved from www.britannica.com

Gupta, N. (2012). Email etiquettes: Dos and dont's. *The IUP Journal of Soft Skills*, *6*(1), 29–37.

Hardeman, K. T. (2010). *Students and communication competence: A call to professors for establishing appropriate communication boundaries*. Retrieved from http://www.unco.edu/ae-extra/2010/2/hardeman.html

Huang, X., & Hsiao, E. (2012). Synchronous and asynchronous communication in an online environment: Faculty experiences and perceptions. *Quarterly Review of Distance Education*, *13*(1), 15–30.

Keil, M., & Johnson, R. D. (2002). Feedback channels: Using social presence theory to compare voice mail to email. *Journal of Information Systems Education*, *13*(4), 295–302.

Kruger, J., Epley, N., Parker, J., & Ng, Z. (2005). Egocentrism over email: Can we communicate as well as we think? *Journal of Personality and Social Psychology*, *89*(6), 925–936. doi:10.1037/0022-3514.89.6.925 PMID:16393025

Kupritz, V., & Cowell, E. (2011). Productive management communication: Online and face-to-face. *Journal of Business Communication*, *48*(1), 54–82. doi:10.1177/0021943610385656

Legg, A. M., & Wilson, J. H. (2009). Technology and teaching: Email from professor enhances student motivation and attitudes. *Teaching of Psychology*, *36*, 205–211. doi:10.1080/00986280902960034

O'Connor, E. (2012). Next generation online: Advancing learning through dynamic design, virtual and Web 2.0 technologies, and instructor attitude. *Journal of Educational Technology Systems*, *41*(1), 3–24. doi:10.2190/ET.41.1.b

Pentland, A. (2012, April). The new science of building great teams. *Harvard Business Review.* Retrieved from http://hbr.org/2012/04/the-new-science-of-building-great-teams

Richardson, J. C., & Swan, K. (2003). Examining social presence in online courses in relation to students' perceived learning and satisfaction. *Journal of Asynchronous Learning Networks*, *7*(1), 68–88.

Rudick, M., & O'Flahavan, L. (n.d.). *Set the tone in email: How you say it is as important as what you say.* Retrieved from http://www.hodu.com/email-tone.shtml

Walmsley, A., & McManemy, J. (2008). College student character dysfunction: It's time we set some expectations for our students that go beyond the syllabus. *Academe*, *94*, 1.

Weinstock, J. A. (2004). Respond now! Email, acceleration, and a pedagogy of patience. *Pedagogy*, *4*(3), 365–383. doi:10.1215/15314200-4-3-365

Yu, F., & Yu, H. J. J. (2002). Incorporating emails into the learning process: Its impact on student academic achievement and attitudes. *Computers & Education*, *38*(1-3), 117–126. doi:10.1016/S0360-1315(01)00085-9

ADDITIONAL READING

Aylor, B., & Oppliger, P. (2003). Out-of-class communication and student perceptions of instructor humor orientation and socio-communicative style. *Communication Education*, *52*(2), 122–134. doi:10.1080/03634520302469

Baron, N. (2002). Who sets an email style? Prescriptivism, coping strategies, and democratizing communication access. *The Information Society*, *18*(5), 403–413. doi:10.1080/01972240290108203

Baron, N. (2008). *Always on: Language in an online and mobile world.* New York, NY: Oxford University Press. doi:10.1093/acprof:oso/9780195313055.001.0001

Blum-Kulka, S. (1987). Indirectness and politeness in requests: Same or different? *Journal of Pragmatics*, *11*(2), 131–146. doi:10.1016/0378-2166(87)90192-5

Casey, G., & Evans, T. (2011). Designing for learning: Online social networks as a classroom environment. *International Review of Research in Open and Distance Learning*, *7*(12), 1–25. doi:10.19173/irrodl.v12i7.1011

Chan, J. F. (2005). *Email: A write it well guide--How to write and manage email in the workplace.* Oakland, CA: Write It Well.

Clark, R. C., & Mayer, R. E. (2008). *E-learning and the science of instruction.* San Francisco, CA: Jossey-Bass.

Claxton, R., Marks, S., Buranoksy, R., Rosielle, D., & Arnold, R. M. (2011). The educational impact of weekly emailed fast facts and concepts. *Journal of Palliative Medicine*, *14*(4), 475–481. doi:10.1089/jpm.2010.0418 PMID:21395446

Collins, M. (1998). The use of email and electronic bulletin boards in college-level biology. *Journal of Computers in Mathematics and Science Teaching*, *17*(1), 75–94.

Collison, G., Elbaum, B., Haavind, S., & Tinker, R. (2000). *Facilitating online learning: Effective strategies for moderators*. Madison, WI: Atwood Publishing.

Keller, E., & Fay, B. (2012). *The face-to-face book: Why real relationships matter in a digital marketplace*. New York, NY: Free Press.

Kelly, L., Duran, R. L., & Zolten, J. J. (2001). The effect of reticence on college students' use of electronic mail to communicate with faculty. *Communication Education*, *50*(2), 170–176. doi:10.1080/03634520109379242

Kitsantas, A., & Chow, A. (2007). College students' perceived threat and preference for seeking help in traditional, distributed, and distance learning environments. *Computers & Education*, *48*(3), 383–395. doi:10.1016/j.compedu.2005.01.008

LaRose, R., & Whitten, P. (2000). Re-thinking instructional immediacy for web courses: A social cognitive exploration. *Communication Education*, *49*(4), 320–338. doi:10.1080/03634520009379221

Leland, K., & Bailey, K. (2009). *Email in an instant: 60 Ways to communicate with style and impact*. Career Press, eBook.

Li, L., Finley, J., Pitts, J., & Guo, R. (2010). Which is a better choice for student-faculty interaction: Synchronous or asynchronous communication? *Journal of Technology Research*, *2*, 1–12.

Malley, S. B. (2006). Whose digital literacy it is, anyway? *Essential Teacher*, *3*(2), 50–52.

Marbach-Ad, G., & Sokolove, P. (2001). Creating direct channels of communication: Fostering interaction with email and in-class notes. *Journal of College Science Teaching*, *31*(3), 178–182.

McMillan, J., & Cheney, G. (1996). The student as consumer: The limitations of a metaphor. *Communication Education*, *45*(1), 1–15. doi:10.1080/03634529609379028

McSweeney, F. & Donnelly, R. (2009). *Applied E-learning and E-teaching in higher education*. Information Science Reference, eBook.

Mehrabian, A. (1981). *Silent messages: Implicit communication of emotions and attitudes* (2nd ed.). Belmont, CA: Wadsworth.

Raj, R. (2011). Evaluating the innovation of online learning systems in higher education. *International Journal of Management Cases*, *13*(4), 12–13. doi:10.5848/APBJ.2011.00106

Rockwell, S., Schauer, J., Fritz, S., & Marx, D. (1999). Incentives and obstacles influencing higher education faculty and administrators to teach via distance. *Online Journal of Distance Learning Administration*, *3*(2).

Steele, J. (2006). *Email: The manual: Everything you should know about email etiquette, policies and legal liability before you hit send.* Oak Park, IL: Marion Street Press, Inc.

Trenholm, S., & Jenson, A. (2004). *Interpersonal Communication* (5th ed.). New York, NY: Oxford University Press.

Trentin, G., & Repetto, M. (2011). *Faculty training for web enhanced learning*. eBook Collection (EBSCOhost).

Wainwright, M. (2005). *Emails 'Pose threat to IQ*. Guardian Unlimited.

Wray, M., Lowenthal, P., Bates, B., & Stevens, E. (2008). Investigating perceptions of teaching online & f2f. *Academic Exchange Quarterly*, *4*(12), 243–248.

KEY TERMS AND DEFINITIONS

E-Learning: Using electronic technology to obtain or facilitate information and instruction.

Emoji: A digital image used to express an idea, emotion, or item.

Emoticon: A combination of characters used to express emotion or expression.

Higher Education: Post-secondary education, beyond high school (secondary) level.

Instructional Immediacy: Reduced social distance between faculty and student due to an increased awareness of approachability, caring, and competence.

Netiquette: Online, or net etiquette.

Online Learning: A virtual learning platform where information and instruction is shared via the Internet and without a physical classroom meeting place.

Virtual Office Hours: A dedicated time for meeting online when a faculty member is available to students, either online via email, Skype, or another E-learning method.

Chapter 5
Guidelines for Working Collaboratively in Virtual Teams

Shelley Stewart
University of South Florida, USA

ABSTRACT

As virtual teams continue to become more prevalent, educational administrators, faculty, and other members of online communities must discover and employ guidelines for effectively collaborating in online contexts. Applying the same traditional team strategies to those working in dispersed groups of people may hinder communication and prevent optimal results. In today's world, teams need to execute and learn at the same time. It is time to re-define what constitutes a (virtual) team and consider new avenues for cooperating in an increasingly diverse, global, and continuously "plugged-in" society. A set of practical steps for why and how virtual teams can collaborate in digital environments is presented. Tips for implementing the steps are provided. An analysis of technological tools available for facilitating online team collaboration is also shared.

INTRODUCTION

Twenty-first century online educational contexts are inherently diverse, composed of students, instructors and administrators with various career goals, experiences and expertise, technical or otherwise. This being the case, organizational leaders must identify differences among the University's members and strategically plan for adequate, efficient communication in various formats facilitating collaboration among all members of the institution. This chapter will aid all stakeholders by presenting practical processes and tips for working collaboratively in virtual groups.

This chapter will provide guidelines that educational leaders, faculty, and students can follow to improve communication, manage conflict and work together productively in virtual settings, leveraging technical tools that are free, accessible and easy to use.

The aim is to advance communication and collaboration in online spaces by focusing on the ways group members can cooperate, fostering personal and professional growth for all.

DOI: 10.4018/978-1-5225-9814-5.ch005

BACKGROUND

Seventy percent of people globally work remotely at least once a week (IWG, 2018). Within the United States, whereas 20 percent of employees worked one (1) or more days per week virtually in 1996, by 2016, 60 percent of employees had the option to work one (1) or more days a week from home or other off-site location. More than 60 percent of organizations now offer telecommuting benefits, an increase of 14% as compared to 2012 (Society of Human Resource Management, SHRM 2016). Working productively in teams has been and will continue to be critical in many professions, including educational technology contexts.

Global virtual teams are becoming the new normal as people and projects continue to expand across borders, made possible by technological advances. Virtual teams present advantages such as the opportunity to capture multiple perspectives, harnessing top talent regardless of location and accelerating innovation while constructing new knowledge (Derven, 2016). Virtual teams are those made up of people in different physical locations (Ferrazzi, 2014). Virtual teams are also variously defined as geographically dispersed, electronically dependent, dynamic, or comprising diverse members working remotely (Gibbs & Gibson, 2006; Kirkman & Mathieu, 2005).

Virtual teams often operate apart from, around or in parallel to a more formal organization. Therefore, it is important to define and agree upon shared governance, decision frameworks and team protocols. Determining guidelines for the team, roles, responsibilities, sharing, access and storage of information, as well as technology selection is essential. Each virtual team will have its own unique culture. Setting guidelines for how, when and why the team operates helps form team cohesion and can accelerate progress (Derven, 2016).

MAIN FOCUS OF THE CHAPTER

Issues, Controversies, Problems

As (future) professionals, there is no doubt we will need to cooperate in a variety of groups and teams. It can be a positive, productive experience and/or result in conflict or inefficiencies. Despite the outcomes, the need for group collaboration will continue. "Two trends that are increasingly common in today's team-based settings include working on multiple teams simultaneously and communicating virtually" (Maynard, Mathieu, Rapp, & Gilson, 2012, p. 343).

A positive, productive experience may result from the variety of perspectives a team can tap into to innovate. Team members also bring unique skills and experiences to share and build upon. In addition, team participants that collaborate effectively create a synergy that can inspire future projects or other groups. On the other hand, one of the main problems with working in virtual groups is lack of communication. When the group has not formerly agreed as to when and how they will communicate it is likely someone will get left out or opts out of communication on their own accord. Another issue is roles and responsibilities. It is important to build in accountability measures to ensure contributions are balanced and add to the value of the team's project. Finally, "rules of engagement" are needed. If team members do not treat each other equitably or simply fail to engage, the team and its projects are in jeopardy.

Nevertheless, due to the increase in virtual communication technologies and the social dynamics of new generations of professionals, recommended guidelines for collaborating in virtual groups are appropriate. It is important not to disregard what we currently know about group interactions, rather to leverage prior knowledge and incorporate the use of new technological tools for optimizing the work of virtual groups (Maynard, Mathieu, Rapp, & Gilson, 2012; Cummings & Haas, 2012).

Solutions and Recommendations

The Benefits Derived From Collaborating Are Many

Each member brings a unique set of experiences and perspectives that informs the team as a whole. Various talents can be tapped for strength and productivity that benefit everyone, including the recipients of the product or service provided by the team. The distribution of workload among members allows for shared responsibility and increased efficiency. Each person on the team has the opportunity to hone the skills of their role or learn new ones from others.

These guidelines provide a framework for how virtual teams can work together successfully. They aid teams in working together to create a productive project, learn something new and think beyond themselves for the greater good. This model was developed as a potential process for facilitating teamwork in virtual settings to enable collaboration, "any-time, any-place".

The guidelines presented here are listed as a series of steps. Keep in mind that these stages are iterative and may occur more than once, or in a cyclical manner, as needed. Each step includes a rationale, answering the question of "why?" and "how" it can be accomplished, tools for implementation and tips for success. Tools listed here are free, open-source, easily accessible and user-friendly.

The basic steps for working collaboratively in virtual teams are:

1. Define the objectives/outcomes
2. Establish protocols
3. Create virtual work and storage space(s)
4. Project/team management
5. Progress checks / milestones
6. Evaluation
7. Completion and follow-up

The rationale and implementation (why and how) of each step is described. Recommendations for practically carrying out the steps are included. An analysis of technological tools that facilitate virtual, collaborative team work is also provided (See Table 7. Tools that facilitate working collaboratively online.

The following is a structure for how each step will be addressed:

Step #

Why – rationale
How – implementation
Tips – recommendations
Tools – technological options

Following the introductory format, each step is then described in detail.

Define the Team/Project Goals and Guidelines, Objective(s)/Outcome(s)

1. Why – mutual understanding, common goal
2. How – S.M.A.R.T.E.R., deliverable description
3. Tips – use action verbs, establish via group consensus
4. Tools – Google Doc, Evernote

First, define the objective(s) and outcome(s) of the team and project. The importance of establishing a common purpose or vision cannot be understated (Heath & Heath, 2017). Sixty-nine percent of the 379 human resource organizations polled by the Society of Human Resource Professionals in 2012 state that, "Setting goals for team initiatives and projects" is the most successful characteristic of virtual teams. Each member should have a mutual understanding of the ultimate goal and why it is important to achieve it. Reminder: objectives should be written with the S.M.A.R.T.E.R. framework in mind (Meyer, 2003; Doran, 1981):

- **S**pecific
- **M**easurable
- **A**ttainable
- **R**elevant
- **T**ime-bound
- **E**valuate
- **Re**-evaluate

For example, "Create a new website." is not a S.M.A.R.T.E.R. objective. An objective/outcome statement that is S.M.A.R.T.E.R. may be written as such, "Create a new website to market our online graduate certificate programs by the end of the year. The website will contain 4 areas: About, Contact, Programs and Register. Enrollment increase of 10% in 6 months and 25% in 1 year following the launch of the site is expected. Evaluate milestone status every 1 month." The use of action verbs, for instance, "create", "compose", "develop" and "produce" are recommended. To obtain maximum buy-in from team members (and all other stakeholders) gain group consensus on the objective(s)/outcome(s), prior to assigning the final task to the team.

Tools that facilitate development of objectives/outcomes in virtual environments include (text-based) are shown in List 1.

List 1. Tools that facilitate text-based development and storage

Google Apps (Docs): http://www.google.com/enterprise/apps/education/ EverNote: https://evernote.com/ Etherpad: http://etherpad.org/ Padlet: http://padlet.com/

Create Virtual Space(s)

1. **Why**: Information/data storage in a common area (prevents data loss/errors and controls versioning), provides equity among collaborators, assigns collaborators to specific roles and responsibilities, i.e. establishes and monitors accountability
2. **How**: Establish common tools to be used by collaborators, ensure access and training, if necessary
3. **Tips**: Gain consensus, consider technical comfort level of each team member
4. **Tools**: Big Blue Button, Google Hang-outs, Skype

Creating a common virtual space for organization and storage is essential for collaborative team work. This is important for data storage, sharing, accessibility and currency. The virtual space may include the use of more than 1 tool; depending on the variety of tasks the team must perform to achieve their goal(s). When deciding upon tools to facilitate collaborative group work online, consider the following factors/functionalities:

- App Available
- Asynchronous interaction
- Audio (speak and hear)
- Browser-based
- Cloud-based
- Cost
- Messaging
- Mobility
- Open-source
- Recording/saving
- Sharing
- Storage
- Synchronous interaction (real-time)
- Text
- Track changes (who contributed what and when)
- Usability
- Versioning
- Video

Again, gain consensus on the tools that will be used. Choose 1 or 2 main tools and only add another if necessary. In addition to selecting one of the tools for objective/outcome creation and data sharing/storage, consider another that facilitates verbal/visual communication as well. Tools that facilitate virtual interactions include those shown in List 2.

Establish Protocols

1. **Why**: Team agrees to standard operating procedures

List 2. Tools that facilitate virtual interactions

Big Blue Button: http://www.bigbluebutton.org/ (audio and presentations, i.e. virtual meetings) Canvas: http://www.instructure.com/ (learning management system with various integrated learning tools) Dropbox: https://www.dropbox.com/ (store and share) Google Apps (Drive): http://www.google.com/enterprise/apps/education/ (virtually unlimited storage, accessible from any web-browser) Google Hangouts Meet: https://gsuite.google.com/products/meet/ (host virtual meetings, chat face-to-face, global broadcasting) JoinMe: http://joinme.com (screen-sharing and tele-conferencing) Skype: http://www.skype.com/en/ (video and voice calls, file sharing, instant messaging, additional features are fee-based) Each of these tools is either open-source (universal access via free license) or offers the minimum of a free trial period.

2. **How**: Create/emulate processes for Netiquette, Conflict Resolution and Communication Plan and Project Plan
3. **Tips**: Consider obtaining input from team members and establishing consensus on the protocols and/or review institutional procedures to ensure team members are in agreement
4. **Tools**: Google Drive, Drop-box (See List 2)

Establishing protocols for team processes enables everyone to operate under the same conditions, avoiding inefficiencies and preserving data in common formats and storage areas. First, although it may seem mundane or obvious, it is critical to establish Netiquette guidelines or rules of behavior for communicating electronically. In instances where text is the sole form of communication, it is particularly important to convey concise, meaningful messages due in part to the absence of facial expressions and gestures. Also, communicating effectively via text avoids duplication of efforts. Clarity and brevity save time and frustration by preventing extraneous information that could muddle achievement of the team's goal. A sample of "Netiquette: The basics" is provided in Table 1.

Table 1. Netiquette: The basics

Netiquette Expectations	
Rules of behavior for the Internet and virtual communication. Please review these rules and conduct yourself accordingly.	
• Identify yourself clearly • Include a salutation • Use a professional signature line	• Include a (relevant) subject line • "Hey" or "Hi there!" does not convey significant meaning
• Acknowledge and return messages promptly • Be concise, get to the point and state if action is required	• Avoid sarcasm • Respect others' privacy by avoiding copying, quoting or forwarding people's emails
• Avoid excessive use of punctuation and CAPS • Not every statement needs 12 exclamation points or *lol* after it	• Use appropriate language, think, "Would I say this to someone's face?" • Use proper spelling/grammar
Courtesy is key Be kind	

Next, address conflict resolution. While the desire that teams run smoothly is preferable, problems can arise. Rather than stopping to develop a process to handle the issue on the spot, have a procedure in place. Again, everyone can use the same process, putting the project back on track. Table 2 provides strategies for effectively managing conflict and negotiating to a solution.

Now, develop a communication plan. It should include mode(s), frequency and project timeline (with iterative milestones). For instance, see Table 3.

Of 379 human resource organizations that use virtual teams, 63% report that, one of the most successful teamwork behaviors is developing plans for team initiatives and projects (Eversol-Minton, 2013). A project plan will include the communication plan as well as role descriptions/assignments (accountable party) and specific tasks/expectations. The project plan enables progress checking and manages scope creep. It also allows for assessment of issues, errors and revisions, early on in the project. See Table 4 for a sample segment of a team/project plan.

The roles and responsibilities of group members in your team may vary. In any case, define them up front. Be willing to shift roles/responsibilities as needed.

Store netiquette, conflict management strategies, communication plan and project plans in the designated virtual space.

Now that the netiquette, conflict management, communication plan and project plan have been established, and a virtual space is created, virtual team work can commence!

Table 2. Conflict resolution strategies

Conflict Resolution Strategies
• Designate one of the team members as a conflict moderator (each person can take a turn)
• Pause and reflect (examine biases, triggers or physical conditions that may be contributing to a misunderstanding)
• Clarify individual needs, re-identify or modify team objective/outcome
• Arrange to meet virtually in a mutually agreeable space/time
• Agree to actively listen, giving each member a voice. The conflict moderator should monitor for time and/or interruptions
• Remain flexible, entertaining all reasonable options, striving for "win-win-win" scenarios
• When a solution or compromise is reached, document it in writing and affirm that all team members agree to move forward

Table 3. Communication plan

Communication Plan		
Modes	**Frequency**	**Timeline**
Email (asynchronous) Google Doc (asynchronous) Skype (synchronous)	Informal Update 1 per week, all group members, formal documentation of progress and next steps, summarize any email communication Virtual gathering every 2 weeks, review Google doc, clarify, assign tasks	As needed Milestones: Start July 15 End December 15 Milestones: Kick-off July 1 End December 21

Table 4. Sample segment of a project plan

Project Plan		
Role	**Description/Tasks**	**Assigned**
Group Leader	Delegate, keep "pulse" of the group, report to supervisor	Jen
Communication Coordinator	Keep the lines of communication open, steady and flowing. Schedules virtual meetings, sends reminders	Ted
Compiler	Oversees timely data gathering and storage	Kim
Researcher	Locates and summarizes information relevant to the team's work, goals objectives and outcomes	Li

Project/Team Management

1. **Why**: Synergistic progress toward a common goal/completion of project
2. **How**: Follow communication plan, timeline & fulfill expectations
3. **Tips**: Adhere to plan vigilantly
4. **Tools**: At least one tool from List 1 and List 2

Using the selected tools for the team's virtual space and the stored netiquette, conflict management strategies, communication plan and project plan the team can begin its formal work; meeting the expected objectives and outcomes. When technological tools and protocols are developed and agreed upon prior to the commencement of the team's work, synergistic progress toward a common goal is anticipated. Throughout the collaborative phase of the team work, adhering to the established plans and protocols is strongly recommended. If upon interim evaluation, the plans, processes or tools need to change, make certain each group member understands the new addition and how it impacts the ultimate goal.

Progress Checks/Milestones

1. **Why**: Keep tabs on progress, informs the team members and supervisors, manages the scope
2. **How**: Review conflict management and communication protocols
3. **Tips**: Document everything!
4. **Tools**: Virtual space tool selections

Referring to the milestone date checks on the project plan, examine progress. Notate any conflicts and use the conflict resolution strategies to move past them. Also, consider what can be done about avoiding conflicts as the team's work continues.

The utility of the communication plan and tools to facilitate it should also be addressed. Determine if the plan's frequency and modes are adequate. Examine the timeline, is the project on track, if not, why? Has the scope remained stable? If not, what adjustments will need to be made? Will additional resources be necessary?

In addition, discuss challenges, unanticipated influences and potential changes. Of 379 human resource organizations that use virtual teams, 72% report that, "The most successful teamwork behavior is brainstorming solutions for problems or issues" (Eversol-Minton, 2013). Also, one of the four key reasons that make virtual teams successful is that they, "…support real-time problem-solving and are more flexible and responsive to changing demands (SHRM, 2018). A clear process for developing solutions to problems will ensure that everyone is operating under the same conditions, understands the next steps and overcomes obstacles to achieve the common goal/product.

Evaluation of Draft or Prototype, Re-evaluation and Revision

1. **Why**: Empowers team members to practice constructive criticism, keeps the project on track, brings issues to light-sooner, rather than later, prepares the final project for success upon submission
2. **How**: Provide an evaluation form, review protocols for constructive criticism, assign a specific role/team member to ensuring this step is well executed
3. **Tips**: Set a hard deadline for submission of evaluations, require not only criticism but solutions, ways to improve, engage all group members in reviewing formative feedback
4. **Tools**: Use virtual space and technological tools as described in lists 1 and 2

Evaluations allow the team members to celebrate successes and raise concerns. If concerns are addressed early in the team's work, there may be a more positive outcome, efficiency and satisfaction. Each team member should receive an evaluation form and/or and equitable opportunity to express themselves. See Table 5.

This document guides the reviewer through the evaluation and enables constructive criticism. Continuous improvement and suggestions from team members about how this can be accomplished are recommended. If the project is large, it may be wise to assign various parts of it to be evaluated by each team member in an iterative fashion. Make evaluation responsibilities clear, set deadlines and check-in on this micro-process along with the project evaluation overall.

Instruct all team members on how to offer, "caring criticism". There are several techniques that help facilitate the delivery of what might be perceived as negative feedback that can lead to improvement rather than hurt feelings or sour attitudes. See Table 6.

Similarly, the protocols for offering constructive criticism can be flipped for the recipient so that the advice supports positive team progress.

Table 5. Virtual team collaboration: Evaluation of progress

Tasks	Last updated: __/__/__	By: FirstName, LastName
Week __	Complete?	If no, list issues
		WHY? WHO is responsible? WHEN will it be complete? HOW (solution)?
Task 1	__Yes __No Date: __/__/__	
Task 2	__Yes __No Date: __/__/__	
Task 3	__Yes __No Date: __/__/__	
Task 4	__Yes __No Date: __/__/__	
Task 5	__Yes __No Date: __/__/__	

Table 6. Protocols for constructive criticism/solution generation

Protocols for Constructive Criticism/Solution Generation
• Use "I" language. For instance, "May I suggest trying methods X, Y, and Z" rather than, "You messed up!"
• Sandwich the criticism with positive feedback. "I like your introduction, it is concise and thorough. Let's see how we can capture the details in the next section and use that to write up a conclusion."
• Acknowledge the contribution and offer an alternative, "I see the direction you were going with this but let's frame it this way instead, and here's why . . ."
• Clarify intentions, assumptions and expectations. For example, "This appears contrite, was that your intent? Is there another way to say this?"
• Put the team and its goal before the critique. "We're all in this together and we want to meet our goal, let's examine my concern and move on."

Table 7. Reacting productively to criticism

Reacting Productively to Criticism
• Listen to each part of the feedback. Ask clarifying questions. Ask for suggestions. Solidify expectations.
• Remain neutral, no need to become defensive.
• Take a break. Remove yourself from the situation, team or criticism initially. Approach it again with a fresh attitude and/or more objective stance.
• Improve the project based on the feedback, re-submit it.
• Respectfully, thank the critic for their observations

Keep in mind that, "True collaboration is impossible when people don't trust one another to speak with candor. Solving problems requires that team members be unafraid to ask questions or propose wrong answers. It takes work to create a candid environment supported by respectful, honest relationships, but it's a challenge every member should embrace" (Ferrazzi, 2012).

As each member contributes his or her evaluation, ensure that the results/critique are stored and shared in the designated virtual space and arrange a review meeting. It is recommended that the review meeting be conducted in a synchronous virtual tool that includes real-time audio and preferably can be recorded (See Table 8). Agree on and prioritize the revisions that can be reasonably made based on the feedback. Set an amount of time or number of changes threshold that allows improvements to be made

Table 8. Virtual synchronous tools with real-time audio

Virtual Synchronous Tools With Real-Time Audio
• Big Blue Button (open-source)
• Adobe Connect
• BB Collaborate/Ultra (Blackboard product)(also records)
• Google Hang-outs Meet
• Join.me
• WebEx • Zoom

given the resource allocation. Assign specific revisions to individuals that will be held responsible for the changes. Document a rationale for why any suggestions were not implemented, if this is the case.

Completion and Wrap-Up

1. **Why**: Sense of accomplishment, allows team members to reflect on their work and prepare for future projects
2. **How**: As specified on communication and project plans
3. **Tips**: Remind team members of reflection and continuous improvement
4. **Tools**: Use virtual space and technological tools as described in Lists 1 and 2

Prepare the final version of the project. Adhere to the specified due date on the communication and project plans, storing and saving it in the virtual space. This allows team members to gain a sense of accomplishment by meeting the team's objective and to reflect on their work to inform future projects.

Generally speaking, after delivery, most groups will take a giant sigh of relief, disperse and scamper on to the next looming project. If at all possible, celebrate the team's efforts. In the virtual space, team members can leave messages of appreciation or complement one another on the positive aspects. These can build/increase morale. Consider designating a team member to briefly summarize the project and share the achievement of the team's goals with the supervising entity. Document lessons learned.

FUTURE RESEARCH DIRECTIONS

Twenty first century organizations operate in swiftly changing global environments that demand agility and require the use of sophisticated communication technologies (Cummings & Haas, 2012). "New ways of working are required in today's interconnected world, which reflects the changing realities of globalization, where collaboration and speed are paramount" (Derver, 2016). This indicates great opportunity for renewed and continuing research on collaboration and virtual teams. Indeed, the very definitions of these terms continue to evolve and are far from stable. Macro trends such as digitalization and globalization are changing the nature of collaboration by offering varied opportunities for building, structuring and spontaneously forming virtual teams. Virtual teams and collaborative activities within them will continue to advance rapidly. Future directions for those who study dispersed groups and offer guidelines for the successful work include re-defining the elements of what makes a team and remaining open to novel contexts. (Wageman, Gardner, & Mortensen, 2012, p. 301).

CONCLUSION

The earliest virtual teams were formed to facilitate innovation among top experts around the world who didn't have time to travel. Today, teams of physically dispersed employees are more often a necessity of doing "business" in a truly global and digitized world (Ferrazzi, 2014). Collaboration is an inherent component of productivity and innovation. Numerous telecommunication tools are accessible, free, easy to use and constantly evolving, allowing for ever more efficient and effective virtual teams. Hackman

(2012) proposes that 60 percent of the difference in how well a group eventually does is determined by the condition-setting of the *prework* done to ready the group for action. Due to the fact that what happens at the very beginning of the group's life--how it is launched—is highly consequential for what transpires subsequently, providing guidelines for successful virtual collaboration is critical.

REFERENCES

Cummings, J., & Haas, M. (2012). So many teams, so little time: Time allocation matters in geographically dispersed teams. *Journal of Organizational Behavior*, *33*(3), 316–341. doi:10.1002/job.777

Derver, M. (2016). Four drivers to enhance global virtual teams. *Industrial and Commercial Training*, *48*(1), 1–8. doi:10.1108/ICT-08-2015-0056

Doran, G. T. (1981). There's a S.M.A.R.T. way to write management's goals and objectives. *Management Review*, *70*(11), 35–36.

Ferrazzi, K. (2012). Candor, criticism and teamwork. *Harvard Business Review*. Retrieved from http://hbr.org/2012/01/candor-criticism-teamwork/ar/1

Ferrazzi, K. (2014). Getting virtual team right. *Harvard Business Review*. Retrieved from https://hbr.org/2014/12/getting-virtual-teams-right

Hackman, J. R. (2012). From causes to conditions in group research. *Journal of Organizational Behavior*, *33*(3), 428–444. doi:10.1002/job.1774

Heath, C., & Heath, D. (2017). *The power of moments: Why certain experiences have extraordinary impact*. New York, NY: Simon and Schuster.

Hirsh, A. (2017). How to use technology to support remote teams. Society for Human Resource Management. Retrieved from https://www.shrm.org/hr-today/news/hr-magazine/1017/pages/how-to-use-technology-to-support-remote-teams.aspx

IWG. (2018). Retrieved from https://www.cnbc.com/2018/05/30/70-percent-of-people-globally-work-remotely-at-least-once-a-week-iwg-study.html

Kirkman, B. L., & Mathieu, J. E. (2005). The dimensions and antecedents of team virtuality. *Journal of Management*, *31*(5), 700–718. doi:10.1177/0149206305279113

Martins, L. L., Gilson, L. L., & Maynard, M. T. (2004). Virtual teams: What do we know and where do we go from here? *Journal of Management*, *30*(6), 805–835. doi:10.1016/j.jm.2004.05.002

Meyer, P. J. (2003). *"What would you do if you knew you couldn't fail? Creating S.M.A.R.T. Goals". Attitude is everything: If you want to succeed above and beyond*. Meyer Resource Group.

Minton-Eversole, T. (2013). Society for Human Resource Management. Virtual teams used most by global organizations, survey says. Retrieved from http://www.shrm.org/hrdisciplines/orgempdev/articles/Pages/VirtualTeamsUsedMostbyGlobalOrganizations,SurveySays.aspx

Society for Human Resource Management. (2019). Retrieved from http://www.shrm.org/pages/default.aspx

Wageman, R., Gardner, H., & Mortensen, M. (2012). The changing ecology of teams: New directions for teams research. *Journal of Organizational Behavior, 33*(3), 301–305. doi:10.1002/job.1775

Wright, A. D. (2016). *Experts: Threefold increase in telecommuting is sign of the times.* Retrieved from https://www.shrm.org/resourcesandtools/hr-topics/technology/pages/threefold-increase-in-telecommuting-is-sign-of-the-times.aspx

ADDITIONAL READING

Are You an Inclusive Leader? available at: www.catalyst.org/knowledge/quiz-are-you-inclusive-leader [Google Scholar]

Bakken, R. Challenges to Managing Virtual Teams and How to Overcome Them. Retrieved February 20, 2019 from https://www.extension.harvard.edu/professional-development/blog/challenges-managing-virtual-teams-and-how-overcome-them

Berry, P. (2014). Communication tips for global virtual teams. Retrieved December 18, 2016 from https://hbr.org/2014/10/communication-tips-for-global-virtual-teams

Cheng, C., Chua, R. Y. J., Morris, M. W., & Lee, L. (2012). Finding the right mix: How the composition of self-managing multicultural teams' cultural value orientation influences performance over time. *Journal of Organizational Behavior, 33*(3), 389–411. doi:10.1002/job.1777

Higgins, M. C., Weiner, J., & Young, L. (2012). Implementation teams: A new lever for organizational change. *Journal of Organizational Behavior, 33*(3), 366–388. doi:10.1002/job.1773

Mortensen, M. (2011). Constructing the team: Inter-member compositional disagreement and its effects on team dynamics and performance. MIT-Sloan Working Paper Series. Cambridge, MA: MIT-Sloan School of Management.

Mortensen, M. (2015). A first time manager's guide to leading virtual teams. Harvard Business Review. Retrieved December 12, 2016 from https://hbr.org/2015/09/a-first-time-managers-guide-to-leading-virtual-teams

Schiller, S., & Mandviwalla, M. (2010). Virtual team research: An analysis of the theory use and framework for theory application. *Small Group Research, 38*(1), 12–59. doi:10.1177/1046496406297035

Shalev, K. (2019). Ideas for helping remote colleagues bond. Harvard Business Review. Retrieved January 12, 2019 from https://hbr.org/2019/02/ideas-for-helping-remote-colleagues-bond

Stewart, S. (2011). Groups 2.0: A model for facilitating group projects online using Web 2.0 technologies. Retrieved from https://sites.google.com/a/mail.usf.edu/group-projects-online/home

KEY TERMS AND DEFINITIONS

Asynchronous Learning: Learning occurring when learner and instructor or learner and learner are separated by time and distance.

Collaboration: Working with others to produce or create something.

Netiquette: Rules of behavior for the Internet and virtual communication.

Online Synchronous Learning: Online learning or meetings occurring in real time.

Team Research: The study of teams and their attributes.

Virtual Groups/Team: People that are geographically, organizationally and/or time dispersed workers brought together by information and telecommunication technologies to accomplish one or more organizational tasks.

Chapter 6
Transforming From the Classroom to an Online Nursing Educator
A Transformative Learning Experience for New Online Nursing Faculty

Denise Passmore
University of South Florida, USA

ABSTRACT

This chapter explores through phenomenological methodology the experiences of nursing faculty who transitioned from live to online teaching. These experiences are further examined through the theory of transformative learning to determine whether participants were able to transform their teaching identity from traditional classroom teacher (sage on the stage) to facilitators of learning. One-on-one interviews were conducted with 16 full-time nursing faculty at four state universities. Findings revealed that most faculty were originally hesitant to teach online and had multiple misconceptions regarding teaching methods and online student communication. With one exception, professional development for online teaching was limited. Most participants described transforming their teaching methods and philosophies as they gained more experience. Results implicate that faculty development should focus not only on educational principles and technology, but also on ways to connect with students and develop course content that helps maintain faculty identities.

INTRODUCTION

Dale was an experienced educator and a nursing scientist. She had just accepted a new position at a large state university and was summoned to the dean's office. "When the dean told me I'd be teaching online, my first concern was that I'd just gotten a mortgage and how was I going to pay for it now that I was losing my job." Fearing for her livelihood, she searched for online teaching development courses and enrolled in a costly program located across the country. A few weeks later she learned the reality

DOI: 10.4018/978-1-5225-9814-5.ch006

of her situation, no one at her new university knew how to teach online. Because she seemed to have some technical aptitude, the dean gave her the assignment. Eventually, she discovered that she preferred teaching online, being somewhat reclusive, she had the opportunity to interact with students in a way that suited her personality and provided her with more flexibility to do research.

Like Dale, many faculty, particularly those in a field such as nursing that is very "hands on", are initially uncomfortable with the online teaching process. Most faculty in today's environment were educated in traditional classrooms and have no personal experience with the online format. In this study, completed in 2009, only a few of those interviewed actually chose to teach online. Their first forays into the online classroom were often clumsy and unsuccessful. Additionally, they feared losing what they most valued in their teaching experience, communicating with their students.

In the rush to implement online education, adequate preparation of faculty is often overlooked or put aside until there is "more time." Not only must traditional faculty members continue to fully participate in the mission of their universities and colleges, which includes service and scholarship as well as teaching, but they must also teach in ways that are new to them – ways in which they have never been prepared pedagogically or technologically. Faculty, particularly nursing faculty, tend to be older, 60% are greater than age 50 (American Nurses Association (ANA), 2011), and received their own educations at a time when online education was unheard of or at the least was talked about in futuristic terms for somebody else, not us, not nurses. Now, many of these same nursing faculty find themselves in an environment where online education is a prevailing mode of education, either through fully online programs for licensed registered nurses (RNs) acquiring their baccalaureate degrees and graduate students, or at a minimum, to provide supplemental information to their students.

Growth in online nursing education has seen a sharp increase not only as a means to alleviate nursing shortages, but also to meet the Institute of Medicine's demand of providing a more highly educated nursing workforce to improve the safety and quality of patient care (Robert Wood Johnson Foundation and the Institute of Medicine, 2010). The growth of online nursing education has provided multiple opportunities for students and faculty members alike. As demand for more online classes increase, the need to ensure that online education is at least as effective as education delivered by "live" classes also becomes an issue. Therefore, it is imperative that faculty members who are moving to this teaching venue are aware of the inherent challenges and the needs that should be addressed to ensure quality of learning and adherence to accreditation standards. This chapter describes how a group of nursing faculty approached this transition and whether they were able to transform themselves from traditional classroom teachers to online facilitators of learning.

BACKGROUND

Despite some reluctance on the part of nursing faculty to move to online programs, comparisons between online and face-to-face learning have shown no significant differences in learning outcomes with the exception of highly technical clinical skills (Mccall et al., 2018). Learners and potential learners have come to value the convenience and flexibility of online education enabling them to continue their education regardless of locale or major life disruptions (Toufaily, Zalan, & Lee, 2018). With the inclusion of online courses, students can lower the time to graduation thereby reducing costs and enabling them to seek employment sooner (Galbraith & Mondal, 2018).

Online education has played an important role in supporting the mission of nursing education by reaching areas throughout the globe to provide educational opportunities and expanding baccalaureate programs to enable associate or diploma degreed RNs to further their education (Schnetter et al., 2014). Transitioning to a new style of teaching, as faculty move from traditional, lecture-oriented classes, can be a barrier to improved learning outcomes if the faculty lacks interest in utilization of learning methods and tools for online education (Mccall, Spencer, Owen, Roberts, & Heneghan, 2018). In an online environment, traditional approaches, such as lecture, are less successful than developing interactive sub-sections that utilize multiple online teaching tools, including case-based simulations, in improving learning outcomes and ensuring student satisfaction (McCall et al., 2018). Use of traditional didactic delivery, which includes lengthy static lectures and textbook readings with minimal instructor interaction often results in higher attrition (Stott & Mozer, 2016).

Teaching online requires an integrated knowledge of content, technology, and pedagogy in order to produce courses designed to be engaging, aligned with higher education standards and grounded in theory (Stott & Mozer, 2016). Developing online programs often necessitates faculty to rethink traditional methods of teaching and potentially reframe their philosophy of learning to ensure student-centered approaches to education (Schnetter et al., 2014). Developing and facilitating learner centered online approaches also requires more time on the part of the faculty which can discourage efforts to enhance the learning experience (Debiec, 2018).

Faculty, are facing new challenges in an era that has brought significant change and technological innovation to the classroom (Stott & Mozer, 2016). Focusing on increased demands of the online environment often leads to less time to explore all the various methods utilized in teaching online (Dumford & Miller, 2018). In many instances, adjuncts are utilized in teaching online courses and are not as involved as full-time faculty, due to employment outside the university setting, as well as constraints to use existing course content with little ability to enhance or personalize. Faculty are also concerned with the appropriate ways to develop courses when the students are relatively unknown (Smith & Crowe, 2017). According to a study of several private universities, preparation for online teaching is more frequently done through informal on-the-job training than other more formalized methods resulting in a significantly greater difference in feeling prepared to teach online between those with more formal preparation (Gurley, 2018).

Mentoring faculty new to online teaching creates a highly satisfactory experience to online educators, however, when available, some experienced classroom faculty may not feel the urgency to participate (Smith & Crowe, 2017). Faculty who are educated to teach online are more likely to approach the process as facilitators rather than employ traditional pedagogies (Gurley, 2018). Developing a core group of full-time online teaching faculty with dedicated leadership and preparation in online teaching was reported as a significantly successful model by one university (Beck et al., 2018). The model enables faculty to work from remote locations as well as providing nursing education in underserved areas. Faculty success in online teaching is often determined by the support of the institution and includes providing a supportive environment, specific institutional supports, such as faculty mentoring, and staffing support, including instructional designers and technology support (Mohr & Shelton, 2017).

Faculty described the ability to communicate effectively with students whom they never see face-to-face as another obstacle to online education. With the debut of social media, email, texting and other technological advances, faculty are afforded multiple means of communication that do not involve face time (Stott & Mozer, 2016). Evaluation of student contributions and provision of opportunities for student feedback, however, have been shown to motivate learners (McCall et al., 2018). Faculty presence within the online environment beyond static lectures and announcements is key to facilitating student engagement and supporting their learning experience (Schnetter et al., 2014; Stott & Mozer, 2016). Gurley (2018) demonstrated that faculty with formal training for online education communicated with students directly creating a more visible faculty presence, while those with on-the-job informal preparation were more likely to direct students to web-pages or You-tube videos.

Creating a sense of social presence in the online nursing classroom in order to address learner needs can be a considerable challenge (Beck et al., 2018). Sacred Heart University reports success through required meetings with faculty advisors, team projects, and connections through social media. Nurse educators report that student relationships in an online learning environment are important and includes being able to support student educational and professional needs (Smith & Crowe, 2017). Online courses are not reproductions of "brick-and-mortar" classes and can provide advantages beyond the classroom in building social presence and enabling students to facilitate course discussions through sharing of their knowledge and experiences (Lohr & Haley, 2018).

THEORETICAL FRAMEWORK

Unlike other adult learning theories, transformative learning emphasizes the cognitive processes of learning rather than the learner's characteristics. Adults must continually negotiate an environment defined by new and changing information (King, 2005; Mezirow, 2000). This theory attempts to define the process for assessing meaning of this new information in a relevant and rational manner and for subsequently developing a plan of action (Mezirow, 2000). Drawing from the work of Mezirow (1991), transformative learning occurs when adults experience a disorienting dilemma, such as in this example, the move from live to online teaching. All learning, according to Mezirow, is filtered through these meaning perspectives, which include our prejudices and misconceptions or lack of knowledge about a particular subject. Transformative learning, says Williams (2002), is not comfortable and requires us to readjust our meanings, which determine how we interpret what we think.

Most people, states Cranton (1994), have not examined their belief systems and even fewer look at all the meaning perspectives that form their beliefs. Mezirow states that only through critical reflection of previously held beliefs and assumptions will adults go through the process of building new roles and acquiring new skills that integrate into the individual's life as it was prior to the disorienting dilemma. Memory is key to the reflective process. Remembering is impacted by how well the new experience fits into an individual's meaning perspectives or whether the memory of the experience evokes anxiety. If the experience evokes anxiety, memories may be distorted and more difficult to assimilate. Reflective discourse can enable adults in the process of integrating new information and creating new meaning perspectives.

A potential for transformative learning requires preconditions such as setting aside bias and engaging in rational discussions of one's beliefs and theories. Without mature cognitive development, according to Merriam (2004), transformative learning cannot take place.

In order to develop a sense of themselves and become genuine educators, teachers must examine their assumptions about the role of traditional faculty members (Cranton, 2006). After self-awareness, being aware of individual students' learning is necessary (Cranton, 2006). This could be accomplished by the use of learning contracts in which students identify their own learning needs and goals (King, 2005). Students should have the opportunity to explore different frames of reference and new roles within a safe environment, utilizing the educator as a resource. Developing active learning experiences involving learners and addresses their needs and goals further the process by allowing learners to explore new perspectives (King).

In this chapter, we report on faculty members reflecting on their experiences in transitioning to the role of online instructor. Faculty members' knowledge of teaching and their perceptions of their role as teachers from a traditional cultural perspective (i.e., the sage on the stage) were examined to identify whether their self-concept has been altered in the transition allowing them to become instead facilitators of learning.

Nursing faculty face the same challenges as traditional faculty, but they must also maintain their nursing practices, make clinical visits, and provide service to the community. Online nursing programs are becoming increasingly popular in order to address the growing shortage of qualified nurses and to provide trained practitioners to serve in rural and other underserved communities. Preparing nursing faculty members for teaching online is vital to the success of these programs.

METHODS

A phenomenological method was used to explore the meaning of nursing faculty members' experiences around a specific phenomenon, online teaching. Phenomenology is a method of philosophical inquiry that enables researchers to examine the underlying beliefs and values of individuals within a field of practice (Merriam & Simpson, 2000). Moustakas (1994) states that "Phenomena are the building blocks of human science and the basis of all knowledge. Any phenomenon represents a suitable starting point for investigation" (p. 26).

Through one-on-one interviews, faculty members were asked to describe their experiences, lessons they learned, and their feelings about the role of the online educator. Mezirow (1991) states that research in transformative learning is difficult because the investigator does not have access to the meaning schemes or perspective of the participants. One of the methods recommended is the open-ended interview, which enables participants to convey additional information that may help the researcher when attempting to understand the participant's perspective.

Sample Selection

A purposeful criterion-based sample of individuals was included in this study. Criteria for inclusion were that participants teach in an online nursing program and began their teaching career in a live venue. Adjunct faculty were not included in this study, since they often do not receive the same type of institutional support and development as full-time faculty (Biro, 2005) and, therefore, may not have similar experiences. From three to five participants were recruited from four public university colleges of nursing that offered online as well as traditional nursing programs.

Data Collection

Data for this study was collected through semi-structured conversational interviews and a review of related materials, such as syllabi and topical outlines of courses, which further describe the experience of teaching online. Curriculum vitae were collected in order to assimilate demographic information and to maximize interview time. An open-ended interview guide was provided for each participant prior to the interview. The interview focused on the phenomenon, although the open-ended nature of the session enabled the participants to discuss related areas not specifically addressed by the researcher. Interview questions were as follows:

1. Tell me how you came to be a nurse educator and about your current teaching role.
2. What prompted you to begin teaching online?
3. Think back to when you got your first online teaching assignment. What were your assumptions and expectations about teaching online?
4. Please describe how you went about developing your first online class.
5. What role did your institution play in preparing you to teach online?
6. How do your initial assumptions compare to the actual experience of teaching online?
7. How do your methods for teaching online differ from those in your face-to-face courses?
8. What are the biggest differences you have found between teaching face-to-face classes and teaching online classes?
9. The traditional role of a faculty member is defined as "participation in teaching, research, and service." How has teaching online impacted that role?
10. Is there anything you would like to add that might help in understanding your experience in transitioning to online teaching?

Institutional review boards at each of the participating universities were contacted in order to ensure compliance. Interviews took approximately .5 to 1.5 hours, and, on a few occasions, additional follow-up questions were asked at the time of the interview or later, by email. All participants were emailed a transcription of the interview and were given the option of removing or clarifying information. No participants requested any changes be made.

Data Analysis

Each interview was transcribed and examined for potential themes pertinent to the research focus. Steps for analysis as identified by Moustakas (1994) are as follows and include descriptions of analyzing this data:

- *Search for statements in the interviews identifying how the participants are experiencing the phenomenon.* Transcribed interviews were uploaded into the Atlas.ti software system, and statements related to the phenomenon from each interview were highlighted and labeled with descriptors. Only statements that were directly related to the phenomenon were included.
- *Group statements by meaning and provide a textural description of the experience.* In this step themes were created under which to group statements from the interviews that were relevant to the phenomenon.
- *Construct a description of how the phenomenon was experienced.* A detailed description of each identified theme was constructed.
- *Construct an overall description of the meaning.* The themes identified for each participant were analyzed to depict a composite textural description of the group. From these textural descriptions followed a composite structural description.
- *After performing these steps for each of the participants, construct an overall composite of the data.* This step identifies a way of understanding how the participants experienced the phenom-

enon as a group. The textural and structural descriptions are synthesized to identify the meaning and essence of the experiences of all the participants.

In this study, the transcripts were analyzed for statements that revealed how faculty not only had accepted the move to online teaching, but found new ways to accommodate the challenges as well as acceptance in their role as faculty.

FINDINGS

For this study, 16 nursing faculty from four major state universities were interviewed. Interviews were conducted at the participant's location, typically in their offices or nearby conference rooms. Ages of the participants ranged from 45-62. Thirteen had doctorate degrees, and all had a least a master's degree in nursing and had been teaching at least 10 years in a nursing program. Eight of the faculty interviewed were located at satellite campuses. The interviews lasted from 30 minutes to 1.5 hours. The college's expectations for those teaching online were identical to faculty teaching face-to-face courses. They were all subject to the same evaluations, workload, and class sizes as in face-to-face courses. Table 1, provides a brief description of the faculty who participated in this study as well as whether they chose to teach online voluntarily or were required by administration to teach online.

Table 1. Participant description

Pseudonym	Year Graduated From Nursing School	Degrees	# Years Taught Online	Chose to Teach Online Voluntarily
Terry	1974	BSN, MSN, MEd	11	No
Leslie	1970	BS, MA, PhD	5	No
Pat	1972	BSN, MEd, MSN, PhD	7	No
Gerry	1988	BSN, MSN, PhD	5	Yes
Jesse	1970	BS, MA, MSN, EdD	2	No
Ronnie	1967	Diploma, BSN, MSN, DSN	5	No
Faye	1973	BSN, MSN, DSN	1	No
Joey	N/A	BSN, MSN, DSN	8	No
Casey	N/A	AS, BS, DN	5	No
Morgan	1970	BSN, MS, PhD	3	No
Stacey	1977	ASN, BSN, MSN MSN	1	Yes
Chris	1970	ASN, BSN, MSN	3	Yes
Ray	1978	BSN, MSN, PhD	6	Yes
Tony	1976	AA, BSN, MSN, PhD	5	No
Tyler	1964	AAS, BHS, MSN, PhD	4	No
Dale	1976	BSN, MSN, PhD	3	No

† Located at a satellite campus

Three major themes emerged from the data that are applicable to this study: 1) Getting Started; 2) Teaching Online; and 3) Communicating with Students. Getting started with online teaching was a challenge for each of the faculty and many found their early conceptions about what teaching online involved were almost immediately discovered to be inaccurate. Once faculty begin to feel more comfortable with the online medium, they found ways to teach online that reflected who they were as teachers as they learned to present content in innovative ways. Finally, fearing they would lose touch with their students, many found that communication in an online venue could be just as, if not more, effective than in a live classroom situation.

Getting Started

Faculty reported various levels of training and preparation when getting started to teach online. At one university, all faculty were required to attend a one-semester course to learn instructional design principles. Others asked for help from colleagues or signed up for workshops occasionally offered by the university. Ronnie was the first person within the college of nursing to teach online and had very little guidance or support. Her first impression of online courses was that the medium seemed flat and uninviting when she wanted it to be, instead, "interesting to me," assuming it would then be engaging to students, encouraging them to interact and learn the content. Her solution was to learn "how to do PowerPoint presentations and voice over … "it was a one-dimensional media so I had to do something with my assignments."

Terry assumed that teaching online would just involve "dumping my PowerPoint in the online class and that would be it that I didn't really need to make any changes. I already really had the course developed so this shouldn't be too much of a problem." Ray also thought that "I've taught this course for a couple of semesters, I've got all the PowerPoints, the quizzes, I'll just load it all on the night before the class." However, the transition was not as simple as she anticipated.

So I was sitting there loading it all on the night before the class and realized this PowerPoint makes absolutely no sense, unless I'm standing next to them talking about them. Because you have a slide that says 'what is a hypothesis.' Well in a classroom I put that slide up and I say ok what did you read about a hypothesis, and we talk about that and the slide makes lots of sense. But if all you're doing is sitting there with your computer screen and you see a slide that says what is a hypothesis ... this is not going to work. So it was a real quick how do you get that piece of the information that you sort of give to students in a classroom, that whole discussion interaction into this screen that's staring at them.

Some of the colleges utilized standards to provide guidelines that faculty could use in developing their courses. This was done both for ease of use and consistency throughout the program. Despite some of the advantages to the standards described by faculty members, Joey felt restricted by what could be done at her university when she began developing her online courses.

There were stricter guidelines on what could be put up, what couldn't, you know. How you could use stuff, that kind of thing. There were tools that the university provided, but you couldn't necessarily put something new up there and then require the students to do things on their end unless it was sanctioned by the college kind of thing. So there have been some limitations. And what I have found typically here

– what's done is you put up a PowerPoint and reading assignments and it's very droll and dry and not very productive. So I've become somewhat disillusioned with it over the years.

Several faculty expressed concern about online faculty who did not make use of resources available on campus. Casey believes that if faculty members were required to participate in online course development workshops and courses, they would improve the quality of the courses and enhance student learning. Dale is likewise alarmed by "experienced classroom faculty" who claim they "can teach online, but who then do not utilize resources available to help them improve. And I have found that [ability to teach online] not to be the case." Casey also feels that lacking background in educational principles is part of the problem with nurse educators whether their teaching is live or online. "Because we don't even have a very good theoretical background in that area [education], we stumble around like idiots for a few years until we figure it out." Lack of time to attend training or accessibility was reported by a number of faculty, so many relied on each other or tweaked existing classes handed down to them by their more experienced peers.

Many of the faculty identified their preference for a mentor who would guide them in teaching online rather than or as a supplement to attending classes and workshops. Tony believes that "people need a mentor. They need someone that has taught online before. I think it's a good idea to co-teach an online course with someone so you get a sense of how it's done." After going through a faculty development program Leslie remarked that "they had some experienced people [other faculty] and you could ask what did and didn't work." Now that Leslie and some of her colleagues have taught online for some time she stated that "we actually are mentors to everyone else coming in. So I always have a couple coming in talking about 'how'd you set yours up, why did you do it that way'." One experienced faculty, however, reported that the expectation that she would help guide and mentor others was a hindrance to her own work.

Teaching Online

Teaching in the online environment presented challenges to most nursing faculty in this study as they had to find new ways to present material they had been teaching for years in the classroom. When queried as to what tools they used to develop online content, PowerPoint was frequently referred to as a base for online content development. Leslie explained that "we do PowerPoints with voice over, which are the 'quote' lecture content, but the majority of the work is really within the assignment and reading material as well as [students] completing a project or an assignment." Gerry, however, was an exception among the faculty interviewed and reported not using PowerPoint or any other multi-media presentation tool. Gerry presents all content on PDFs because, "I have zero technology issues with PDFs. Everybody can open them; they can make them as big as they want to, they can print or save them. They can do whatever they want to with them."

Several faculty advised their colleagues to move beyond textual presentations of content and regurgitation of facts through online examinations. Jesse advises online faculty to "look for ways to optimize the experience … it shouldn't be an old-fashioned correspondence course." Assigning readings and multiple-choice tests to students does not provide a sufficient, satisfactory learning experience she explained. "You could've mailed it to them except you're giving it to them electronically. So it needs to be interactive. So you want to go out and start using some of that stuff that's out there." The importance of including interactivity in online courses became evident to Ray after teaching her first online class. "After I did it that first time, it's like, this is not the right way to do this. Let's go back and start over and develop content that's more interactive that keeps the students more engaged." Since that first time, Ray has incorporated activities that require students to "look for information in areas that they're interested in that might not necessarily be my topical area, but it's theirs. And therefore, it becomes more productive to the end user in terms of what they can do with it afterwards."

Some participants reported that they had already begun using methods other than lecture in their face-to-face classes and these methods translated more easily into the online environment. Casey explains "very early on I started to sort of modularize my teaching." These modules translated easily into the development of his online classes. To complement the modules, Casey started "taping every word that I say and posting it online" in order to "preserve classroom time for things like test reviews."

One issue that some faculty discussed was the tendency to assign too much interactive material to online students. It is easy, Leslie reports, "to send them to different web pages … and it becomes extremely time consuming for the students." Instead, Leslie tries to make the assignments manageable by focusing on fewer, more meaningful assignments.

To deal with skills that cannot be taught online, Casey offers a blended course to teach clinical procedures. "They have a number of modules that they have to complete. Then they take a test and, assuming they pass everything, they come up here [to campus], we put them up in a hotel at our expense using their online fee." On campus they learn to do "suture and splint and do biopsies and things." It gives faculty an opportunity to "make sure they're [students] actually real people that they're somewhat competent." During this time, faculty also tries to "have them do their check offs for their advanced health assessment course too." Thereby optimizing and limiting the amount of time students actually have to be on campus. Table 2 lists methods implemented by participants to make their online classes more interactive.

Participants had varied opinions on whether teaching online was significantly different or similar to teaching in face-to-face classes. Ray finds teaching online to be very different from teaching live classes. "Somebody asked me … could I teach research in the classroom [after having taught online for several years]. And I said no because I'd have to prep a whole new class. I can't just take my online stuff and walk into the classroom for three hours a week." Ray admits to using lecture as her primary method of teaching in live classes, while her online classes utilize discussion boards. Gerry also says that the "teaching methods are dramatically different from live" and that the spontaneity is missing from the online courses as well as the ability to use techniques, such as collaboration, that are successful in live classes. Other concerns expressed by Gerry relate to the inability to change methods of presenting content in the middle of an online lesson, unlike face-to-face classes, if students are having a difficult time understanding the material. Ronnie also believes that online teaching methods are different from which she uses in live classes, however, she found alternatives that she felt were successful in the online environment. "… and I couldn't do that [lecture] on the web so it forced me to be innovative. I think it was just a different way, not better or worse, it made the web three-dimensional." After teaching online, Morgan found that it had altered the way that she taught face-to-face and her earlier opinions on how to teach had been changed. Consequently, she has begun to use online teaching methods for her live classes. "It's changed my whole way that I think and approach students in the classroom."

Leslie contends that her teaching "method tends to be similar, whether live or online." As an example, Leslie talks about the importance of the discussion questions, which were used in her face-to-face classes to keep students engaged during three-hour lectures. These same discussion questions are used in her online classes to supplement the lecture notes and readings, believing that the questions were "engaging them into the class." Pat also uses "some of the same teaching methods online that I do with live, [these

Table 2. Online teaching methods

Class Discussions
• Students post written assignments on discussion boards so that other students, as well as faculty members, can read the essays and give feedback. In nursing this is especially relevant as some graduate nursing students may have more knowledge in a clinical specialty area than the faculty.
• Assign students to discussion groups according to their specialty area for peer support as they identify research topics.
• Post a current event weekly – a controversial current event related to healthcare – and pose probing questions about that event.
• Set up discussion boards to complement student clinical home visits. Focus on the cultural perspective or the values students brought into the relationship, versus the clients. It's not graded on spelling, and it doesn't have to be referenced, just provide a place for student to share their experiences.
• Assign students to read a book on a particular culture (such as *The Spirit Catches You and You Fall Down*, by Anne Fadiman) and discuss the book. Include pictures of the region and people.
Multimedia
• Incorporate video, audio, and Web links to support PowerPoints. Use authoring programs to record narration and to make file size manageable for student download.
• Incorporate audio files of the different sounds, such as heart murmurs recorded with an electronic stethoscope. Students can hear the murmur, and click on another audio file and hear the instructor talking about the murmur.
• Carry a digital camera to clinical practice and take photos of patients, not identifying kinds of pictures, and use those in class and work through cases.
Group Projects
• Do a group community cultural population assessment via PowerPoint with very specific instructions concerning what they need to demonstrate. Students look at *x* number of presentations and discuss what they've learned. Include a peer evaluation.
• Assign groups to a movie and popcorn. Each group chooses a movie that clearly depicts a cultural phenomenon and views it on their own via whatever multimedia system they have within their home. Then discusses it within their group.
Field Trips
• Assign students in women's health class to go to a local drug store and bring back information on three different contraceptive methods or devices sold over the counter. Students report on prices and analyze their experiences, answering the following questions: What did they encounter? What did people around them do? How did they feel looking at the contraceptives when other people were around?
• Assign students in women's health class to go to an agency that offers women's reproductive health services. It can be an abortion clinic, a fertility clinic, an ob/gyn, or the health department. They have to do an interview that is very descriptive to indicate they were actually there. How many parking spaces were there? What was across the street? How many trees did they see, and what kind were they? When they walked into the building, what color were the walls? How many chairs were in the waiting room? What was the name of their receptionist?
• Assign students to do a comparison of the medical staff organization chart to the nursing staff organization chart and draw some conclusions about the differences.
• Assign students to interview someone with a chronic disease, such as arthritis or diabetes and post the interview on the discussion board. Interview material should include: What's the impact on their subject's emotional life, their spiritual life, and their physical life? How much do they spend on medications?
Assessment
• Utilize case studies that apply what participants studied, to validate that they understand in regards to the general terms and principles from the readings.
• Present weekly quizzes that pertain to content that students are assigned to read.
Weekly Summaries/Directions
• Present a weekly video so that students see a visual of the instructor. Each week the videos introduce what to expect for the week. These are not pre-recorded, so if the instructor sees a lot of problems with a particular assignment, or a question on a case study or quiz that doesn't work very well, the video can describe the issue.
• Post a summary of the week and point out what was accomplished and where some ideas need to be enhanced.
PDFs
• Place all the content for each module in PDF form. There are no technology issues with PDFs. Everybody can open them, they can make them as big as they want to, and they can print or save them. Include alternate teaching examples, but essentially everything is in one format.
• Type out class lectures in a script, so that it is easy to present step by step. For example: here's a *t* test, here's regression, here's a chi square; walk through the process step by step. Turn it into a PDF and put it online for students to read.

include] having the most up-to-date information, providing the resources, making sure everything is pleasing whether it is [PowerPoint] slides or your pages here online."

Several participants concluded that when teaching online, the faculty role must be that of a facilitator of learning. Dale states that as an online educator "you must be a facilitator. You must see yourself that way or you won't do really well in that environment." Leslie also sees the online instructor role as being "more of a facilitator," particularly when teaching graduate students. "I'll help you learn. I try to emphasize to graduates that they are in charge of their learning." Pat stated that she saw herself "as being the facilitator and the person that could be the resource, and I tell them from the beginning you are really teaching the course to each other." Stacey also concurred that facilitation was an important factor in online teaching. "Facilitation versus the teaching moment is a biggie." Stacey reported learning not to react to everything that students placed on the discussion board, waiting instead to see comments from other students to determine whether they could identify resolutions among themselves. Tyler reports that adult nursing students all bring expertise to the course so "each of us is learning and teaching simultaneously." Tyler believes that this "egalitarian type of teaching method" can be done in either the face-to-face classroom or online."

Ray explains the significance of continuous learning because "things change so fast, in probably any profession, that you always have to be learning new things." Once nursing students graduate, she says, they will need to learn about new nursing techniques, new medications, and they will no longer have access to the university library or be able to refer to the text book, therefore, online learning helps them learn to decide "which ones [websites] are good sources that we [should] believe versus somebody deciding that 'we're' the expert on this topic." This type of learning, states Ray, "translates more to the rest of their life and their careers and their profession."

Communicating With Online Students

Communicating with students online is a concern for many faculty because, as Gerry says, "you can type an email and send it to everybody in the class … but evidently it has nine different interpretations." Gerry believes that this would not happen in a face-to-face class where "I look people in the eye and say has everyone looked at this and if you haven't you need to." Tyler also struggles with clarification of content in the online environment. "They kind of struggle with questions about what's really required and how much do I need to do and what's this paper really like." To address this, Tyler sets up an informal discussion board. "Students can get in there and ask questions of just anyone and the students can answer … So that's helped clarify with the syllabus questions and the assignment questions." Some faculty members felt that they were able to see whether students got the content online by ongoing dialogue through emails or discussion boards that connected them to the students' thought processes.

Ronnie tries to communicate regularly with students so that they will be mindful of the content. "If I don't hear from them in between assignments, I send them information that would be something from one of my distribution lists… to continuously engage them." Despite a belief that there is no substitute for face-to-face communication, Dale has created a variety of ways to circumvent the challenge, such as creating redundancy, by providing "opportunities for students to be able to ask questions every which way." Dale creates a discussion thread for every major assignment which includes documentation that defines success for that specific assignment. Multiple questions about an assignment indicate that instructions were not clear and need to be revised. Providing assignment feedback, states Chris, "is even more critical in an online class than it is in a face-to-face class because they know they're going to see you in a face-to-face class" and can ask specific questions regarding their assignments. To enhance connections with students and enable them to ask specific questions, Tony added virtual online office hours using Skype.

"How do you get to know your students when you can't see them?" is a concern expressed by many of the online faculty. Creating relationships with students in the online environment was deemed as impossible by some, while others reported creating even closer relationships and getting to know students even better than in face-to-face situations. These closer relationships in online classes were partially because of the numbers of students in large live classes which prohibit faculty from getting to know students individually. Tyler states that it is much easier to get to know students in an online class of 40 than in a live class of 60 to 90 students. "I get to know them by what they've said about themselves. And you can kind of follow … their threads [in online discussion boards] are a reflection of who they are." Ray reports knowing more about "online students then I do about my in-class students" Participants reported that online students are more forthcoming about their lives, and they see more discussion responses from more online students than they do in their face-to-face classes. Stacey has discovered that students "are not as cautious about what they say." Terry reported "many of them are very revealing in their postings and you do get to know them somewhat well." Dale also thinks "it's more effective. I've had more people reach out to me as an online educator to talk about career issues, career trajectories. I'm saddened to say I've even had people divulge some very serious personal problems."

Stacey, who admits to liking to talk and being in front of people, was dreading not having that connection with students. "However, it's not as bad as I thought it would be. Because they're nurses, maybe. They email me. They call me. We have a lot more interaction than I expected." Several faculty members described recognizing or being recognized in public venues by students they had never met face-to-face. Morgan describes making clinical visits to students who had been in her classes but whom she had never seen.

It was like we had known each other all along. It was really funny, because in every situation each one of them knew who I was. You know, I'd walk into the hospital or the clinic and they'd say, 'You're Dr. Morgan,' and it was really fun. We had a real great…I feel like I had a really good rapport with these students. And, some of them, I hadn't even seen their pictures, which was a very nice, very comfortable feeling.

Faculty, however, reported that this connectedness was not without its drawbacks. Tony states that, "there is a lot more time-intensive work to stay connected to students in an online format." Other faculty similarly reported the challenge in being available to their nursing students who work varying shifts and yet often expect immediate responses to their queries.

Discussion

Many faculty in this study demonstrated evidence in transforming from a traditional classroom-based teacher to a facilitator of learning. Transformative learning occurs when adults experience a disorienting dilemma that challenges one of their assumptions. In this study, almost all faculty members faced the experience of being told they were going to teach online. While many had not anticipated that it would make much difference in their roles as faculty members, they eventually discovered this was not the case. When asked to describe their experience, many found that their previous assumptions and beliefs about online education were challenged. "It's a different way of teaching and learning," reported Dale. Terry describes how when she looks back now, she is almost embarrassed at what her assumptions were about how to teach online. From these beginnings, most of the faculty learned that they had misconceptions about teaching online and only through faculty development and experience did they come to realize that traditional methods of teaching were not effective in online classes.

Another area that was transformative for faculty members was the discovery of the power of giving students the responsibility for their own learning and becoming facilitators rather than authority figures.

"It's more participative," stated Morgan, indicating the egalitarian nature of the online environment. That sentiment was echoed by other faculty members as well. "As an online instructor, I'm more of a facilitator… It puts students more in charge." One veteran online instructor reported that "I see myself as a facilitator of active learning…When you see it that way, you see that the students have that much more responsibility in their learning and you must create that environment and that community of learners." Faculty members described that after their first experiences teaching online they went back and started over in order to "develop content that's more interactive, that keeps the students more engaged."

Other participants also recognized the value in teaching online to foster lifelong self-directed learning in students.

I sometimes talked to students online about, you know its [online learning] lifelong learning, especially in the fields we're in, with nursing. The things we can teach a student today in whatever format in this building, when they graduate in six months and get out in practice, you know there's a new IV pump, there's a different medication. Things change so fast in probably any profession that you always have to be learning new things. You need those basics, but that's ongoing learning, and I think that's one thing you can do more so with the online course. Not relying on a textbook.

The traditional methods in which faculty were used to teaching and interacting were challenged. To survive in this new environment, they had to rethink their way of delivering content and communicating with students. Some of the participants not only accepted this new paradigm but also embraced it, enjoying the online innovations they developed and actually having new and, in some cases, better relationships with students. Many of the participants found themselves moving to a whole new construct regarding the role of faculty member and how they described their methods and values.

In this study, several faculty members showed evidence of transformative learning through the experience of teaching online. Though some had no expectations of what teaching online would be like, several had preconceived notions about the simplicity and ease of learning online, lack of communication, and lack of rigor that were, however, challenged by their experiences. Several participants reported that not only had they been changed by the experience in their approach to online education, but they had used the acquired knowledge to transform their face-to-face classes, as well. Their belief was that if active learning worked well online and created more independent thinkers who could be responsible for their own lifelong learning, this philosophy should also be applied to students who were in their face-to-face classes. A number of the faculty members described themselves as "facilitators of learning" and, while some contended that this had always been one of their principals, a few recognized that they had been changed by the online learning experience.

Not all faculty embraced online learning. One of these individuals had a strong dislike for online education and felt that faculty, particularly graduate faculty members, needed to be more involved in research than in the preparation it took to teach online. Two other individuals reported issues with difficult students in their online classes.

Other faculty members who reported transformative experiences were all over the spectrum as far as education, preparation, years of experience, and location. However, these participants did express a strong desire to make themselves available both physically and emotionally to students and to adapt their schedules to meet student needs. The personal philosophies, expectations, and intrinsic motivation of faculty members can impact the type of experience individuals have when teaching online and determine whether they will learn and transform or whether they will cling to their initial assumptions about online education regardless of their validity.

Solutions and Recommendations

In this study, nursing faculty members reported on their experiences in the online environment. Based on their successes and challenges, recommendations that could provide other faculty and administrators with knowledge and ideas for building successful online courses are presented here.

Faculty who are going to teach online need to have professional development and/or mentoring in order to successfully navigate the environment and effectively teach in the online classroom. As many nursing faculty (as well as other disciplines) do not have education backgrounds, they may need basics in educational theory and principles as well as technology and instructional design. Making them aware of on-campus or online resources can provide a valuable tool for those who are often isolated or rarely on campus due to clinical responsibilities or assignments at satellite campuses. Because of the rapid changes in technology and ongoing research in educational theory, it is imperative to provide opportunities for one-on-one training and assessment of faculty skills and knowledge on a regular basis. It is not likely that professionals who must keep up with the dynamic nature of their disciplines will also be able to remain knowledgeable regarding online course delivery, therefore, it is vital for administrators to ensure this is done on a university-wide basis, include this role as part of a faculty assignment, or employ an instructional designer to maintain online course effectiveness.

Mentors were mentioned by almost all faculty in this study as the most desirable method for getting acclimated to teaching online. Those who had them were highly pleased with the experience and those who did not usually resorted to requesting some type of informal mentoring from their peers. Faculty also needed efficient ways to contact other faculty for answers to questions or suggestions on how to present content. Bulletin boards or discussion groups that faculty could engage in with some instructional design presence as well is one way of being able to easily share knowledge, though most faculty preferred more one-on-one support. Collaboration with faculty members and instructional designers to design templates and standards for course development will reduce faculty time to develop courses and ensure continuity for students. Dietz-Uhler, Fisher, and Han (2008) showed that the use of standards improved student retention rates by 11%. Success was attributed to the fact that standards ensured that policies and expectations were clearly stated and that students were provided with rich interactive experiences.

Not all faculty should teach online. Forcing faculty members who have no desire, interest, or aptitude for teaching online is counter-productive to the mission of the school. Some faculty members in this study reported being very "anti-online" and, consequently, it is possible that students in these courses will not achieve the types of learning outcomes they might when faculty are committed to providing an exceptional learning experience. It is vital that those who do teach online need to be open to new ways of communicating and interacting with students.

FUTURE RESEARCH DIRECTIONS

Several topics that emerged from this study indicate a need for further research. Preparing doctoral students in nursing, as well as in other disciplines, to transform teaching methods to an online venue would be important in educating future generations. Looking at how mentors can be developed and utilized would enable institutions to formulate effective plans for mentoring programs. One school reported utilizing emeritus faculty to participate in online classes and provide mentoring support to faculty new to the environment. Research on mentoring could look at factors such as types of individuals who make the best mentors and whether the role could be filled in some other way than by increasing current faculty workloads.

The best, most effective methods of developing relationships with students without "burning out" faculty would be a topic for research that could greatly enhance the online teaching experience for faculty as well as students. Ensuring that students understand the content and how to do this most efficaciously, creating a unique faculty presence, and identifying student needs are all areas that faculty members in this study struggled with when teaching online. Finally, looking at how institutions can achieve academic rigor, faculty/student satisfaction, and adequate infrastructure in a cost-efficient manner should be further investigated, particularly by each discipline. If the purpose of online education is to provide a quality education to students who are unable to participate in traditional classes, then administration must also consider how to do this in a way that sufficiently supports faculty members without unduly burdening the students. In today's competitive market, very few institutions of higher learning can avoid delivering online education in order to attract students. Researching how to offer these programs more efficiently could enable schools to improve their offerings and ensure that students receive affordable, quality online education.

CONCLUSION

In this study, faculty members described their journey from live to online education. For most, it was a transformative experience that caused them to reflect on how they transformed themselves as teachers, not only in the online venue, but also how they taught in the traditional classroom. Instead of losing their identity and their ability to connect with students, they found ways to improve the process as they furthered their own academic philosophies. The most important lesson to take away from this is the need to include faculty voices in all aspects of preparing online programs. Faculty members' needs should be identified and acknowledged by administrators, faculty development groups, supporting staff, and technology departments. When online education is approached as a team effort, results can be more satisfying to faculty and students, and student learning outcomes can be addressed more effectively, ensuring that online education is at least as rigorous as face-to-face courses.

REFERENCES

American Nurses Association (ANA). (2011). *American nurses association fact sheet.* Retrieved from www.NursingWorld.org

Beck, M., Bradley, H. B., Cook, L. L., Leasca, J. B., Lampley, T., & Gatti-Petito, J. (2018). A paradigm shift from brick and mortar: Full-time nursing faculty off campus. *Nursing Education Perspectives, 39*(2), 107–109. doi:10.1097/01.nep.0000000000000211

Biro, S. C. (2005). *Adjunct faculty perceptions about their preparation, support, and value as online instructors.* (Ed.D. doctoral dissertation). Harrisburg, PA: Widener University. Retrieved from http://proquest.umi.com/pqdweb?did=1317311891&Fmt=7&clientId=65345&RQT=309&VName=PQD

Cranton, P. (2006). Fostering authentic relationships in the transformative classroom. *New Directions for Higher Education, 109*, 5–14.

Debiec, P. (2018). Effective learner-centered approach for teaching an introductory digital systems course. *IEEE Transactions on Education, 61*(1), 38–45. doi:10.1109/te.2017.2729498

Dietz-Uhler, B., Fisher, A., & Han, A. (2008). Designing online courses to promote student retention. *Journal of Educational Technology Systems, 36*(1), 105–112. doi:10.2190/ET.36.1.g

Dumford, A. D., & Miller, A. L. (2018). Online learning in higher education: Exploring advantages and disadvantages for engagement. *Journal of Computing in Higher Education, 30*(3), 452–465.

Galbraith, D., & Mondal, S. (2018). The road to graduation: On-line or classroom. *Research in Higher Education*, 35.

Gurley, L. E. (2018). Educators' preparation to teach, perceived teaching presence, and perceived teaching presence behaviors in blended and online learning environments. *Online Learning, 22*(2), 197–220. doi:10.24059/olj.v22i2.1255

King, K. (2005). *Bringing transformative learning to life*. Malabar, FL: Krieger.

Lohr, K. D., & Haley, K. J. (2018). Using biographical prompts to build community in an online graduate course an adult learning perspective. *Adult Learning, 29*(1), 11–19. doi:10.1177/1045159517735597

McCall, M., Spencer, E., Owen, H., Roberts, N., & Heneghan, C. (2018). Characteristics and efficacy of digital health education: An overview of systematic reviews. *Health Education Journal, 77*(5), 497–514.

Merriam, S. B., & Simpson, E. L. (2000). *A guide to research for educators and trainers of adults.* Malabar, FL: Krieger Publishing.

Mezirow, J. (1991). *Transformative dimensions of adult learning*. San Francisco, CA: Jossey-Bass.

Mezirow, J. (Ed.). (2000). *Learning as transformation: Critical perspectives on a theory in progress.* San Francisco, CA: Jossey-Bass.

Mohr, S. C., & Shelton, K. (2017). Best practices framework for online faculty professional development: A delphi study. *Online Learning, 21*(4), 123–140.

Moustakas, C. (1994). *Phenomenological research methods*. Thousand Oaks, CA: Sage.

Robert Wood Johnson Foundation and the Institute of Medicine. (2010). *The future of nursing: Leading change, advancing health. need publisher information or the website*. Author.

Schnetter, V. A., Lacy, D., Jones, M. M., Bakrim, K., Allen, P. E., & O'Neal, C. (2014). Course development for web-based nursing education programs. *Nurse Education in Practice, 14*(6), 635–640. doi:10.1016/j.nepr.2014.06.007

Smith, Y. M., & Crowe, A. R. (2017). Nurse educator perceptions of the importance of relationship in online teaching and learning. *Journal of Professional Nursing*, *33*(1), 11–19. doi:10.1016/j.profnurs.2016.06.004

Stott, A., & Mozer, M. (2016). Connecting learners online: Challenges and issues for nurse education—is there a way forward? *Nurse Education Today*, *39*, 152–154. doi:10.1016/j.nedt.2016.02.002

Toufaily, E., Zalan, T., & Lee, D. (2018). What do learners value in online education? An emerging market perspective. *E-Journal of Business Education & Scholarship of Teaching*, *12*(2), 24–39.

ADDITIONAL READING

Boz Yuksekdag, B. (2012). Interaction in Distance Nursing Education. *Turkish Online Journal Of Distance Education*, *13*(4), 245–255.

Corbett, A. (2012). Learning the lessons of moving education online. *Nursing Times*, *108*(16), 24–27. PMID:22667076

Dariel, O. P. D., Wharrad, H., & Windle, R. (2013). Exploring the underlying factors influencing e-learning adoption in nursing education. *Journal of Advanced Nursing*, *69*(6), 1289–1300. doi:10.1111/j.1365-2648.2012.06120.x PMID:22971122

Education Week (2011). *E-Learning 2011:* Crafting e-curriculum that inspires.

Fahy, P. J. (2008). Characteristics of interactive online learning media. In T. A. Anderson (Ed.), *The theory and practice of online learning* (2nd ed.). Edmonton, AB: AU Press, Athabasca University.

Gilmour, J. A., Huntington, A., Broadbent, R., Strong, A., & Hawkins, M. (2012). Nurses' use of online health information in medical wards. *Journal of Advanced Nursing*, *68*(6), 1349–1358. doi:10.1111/j.1365-2648.2011.05845.x PMID:21999429

Guise, V., Chambers, M., Conradi, E., Kavia, S., & Välimäki, M. (2012). Development, implementation and initial evaluation of narrative virtual patients for use in vocational mental health nurse training. *Nurse Education Today*, *32*(6), 683–689. doi:10.1016/j.nedt.2011.09.004 PMID:22056146

Hart, C. (2012). Technology and Nursing Education: Building an Online Toolkit. *Journal of Continuing Education in Nursing*, *43*(10), 441–442. doi:10.3928/00220124-20120925-95 PMID:23051778

Herrington, J., Herrington, A., Mantei, J., Olney, I., & Ferry, B. (Eds.). (2009). *New technologies, new pedagogies: Mobile learning in higher education.* Faculty of Education, University of Wollongong. Informal Learning. *Review of Educational Research*, *79*(2), 625–649.

Kirschner, F., Kester, L., & Corbalan, G. (2011). Cognitive load theory and multimedia learning, task characteristics and learning engagement: The current state of the art. *Computers in Human Behavior*, *27*(1), 1–4. doi:10.1016/j.chb.2010.05.003

Kuiper, R. (2012). EXPANDING the Repertoire of Teaching and Learning Strategies for Future Nurse Educators: Introducing Interpretive Pedagogies in an Online Graduate Nurse Education Course. *Nursing Education Perspectives, 33*(5), 342–345. doi:10.5480/1536-5026-33.5.342 PMID:23061195

Learning the Faculty Role: Using the Evolving Case Story of Professor Able in an Online Master of Nursing Education Program. (2013). *Journal of Nursing Education, 52*(2), 98-103. doi:10.3928/01484834-20130122-02 PMID:23330592

Little, B., Passmore, D., & Schullo, S. (2006). Using synchronous software in Web-based nursing courses. *CIN: Computers, Informatics. Nursing, 24*(6), 317–327.

Means, B., Toyama, Y., Murphy, R., Bkia, M., & Jones, K. (2010). *Evaluation of Evidence-Based Practices in Online Learning: A Meta-Analysis and Review of Online Learning Studies*. Washington, DC: U.S. Department of Education, Office of Planning, Evaluation, and Policy Development.

Merrill, M. D. (2009). Finding e3 (effective, efficient and engaging) Instruction. *Educational Technology, 49*(3), 15–26.

Reeve, K. L., Shumaker, C. J., Yearwood, E. L., Crowell, N. A., & Riley, J. B. (2013). Perceived stress and social support in undergraduate nursing students' educational experiences. *Nurse Education Today, 33*(4), 419–424. doi:10.1016/j.nedt.2012.11.009 PMID:23246284

Sailman, S. (2013). The virtual classroom: RN navigates road to successful online education. *Nurse. Com Nurseweek (West), 26*(2), 38.

Sherrod, B. (2013). Is online education right for you? *Nursing Management, 44*(4), 40–46. doi:10.1097/01.NUMA.0000428197.44883.69 PMID:23475272

Shishani, K., Stevens, K., Dotson, J., & Riebe, C. (2013). Improving nursing students' knowledge using online education and simulation to help smokers quit. *Nurse Education Today, 33*(3), 210–213. doi:10.1016/j.nedt.2012.03.002 PMID:22483161

Smith, C., Gillham, D., McCutcheon, H., & Ziaian, T. (2011). Scenariation: Scenario Generation for Online Teaching in Nursing and Health Sciences. *British Journal of Educational Technology, 42*(6), 962–972. doi:10.1111/j.1467-8535.2010.01105.x

Southern Regional Education Board (SREB) (2009). *Guidelines for Professional Development of Online Teachers.*

U.S. Department of Education, Office of Planning, Evaluation, and Policy Development, Evaluation of. (2010). Evidence-based practices in online learning: A meta-analysis and review of online learning studies. Washington, DC.

Walker, S., Dwyer, T., Moxham, L., Broadbent, M., & Sander, T. (2013). Facilitator versus preceptor: Which offers the best support to undergraduate nursing students? *Nurse Education Today, 33*(5), 530–535. doi:10.1016/j.nedt.2011.12.005 PMID:22244312

KEY TERMS AND DEFINITIONS

Discussion Boards: Discussion boards are tools within most learning management systems that enable students and faculty to post comments and facilitate an ongoing asynchronous discussion on a specific topic.

Facilitator of Learning: Faculty or teacher who uses active learning methods and encourages students to seek out valid information rather than rely on faculty for content and answers to questions.

Online Education: Web-based course work in which at least 75% of course content is delivered online.

Online Standards: In this chapter, standards refers to a set of elements including HTML, PowerPoint or other multimedia templates, course definitions and navigation elements used in designing content for an online course.

Registered Nurse (RN): A nurse who has graduated from an accredited college or university and has passed a professional licensing examination.

Technology Tools: In this chapter, technology tools refers to software, primarily, that can be used to develop or support online course content. This could include blogs, wikis, authoring tools such as Articulate or Captivate, and Web 2.0 tools available through the internet.

Transformative Learning: Process for assessing meaning of new information in a relevant and rational manner and subsequently developing a plan of action.

APPENDIX

Useful Websites

- **Design Principles Database (DPD):** http://www.edu-design-principles.org/dp/designHome.php
- **Instructional Design Learning Theories:** http://www.instructionaldesign.org/theories/index.html
- **Learning Theories:** http://www.emtech.net/learning_theories.htm
- **MERLOT (Multimedia Educational Resource for Learning and Online Teaching):** http://www.merlot.org/merlot/index.htm
- **Quality Matters:** https://www.qualitymatters.org/higher-education-program
- **The TLT Group:** http://www.tltgroup.org/
- **Web Design for Instruction: Research-Based Guidelines:** http://www.usask.ca/education/coursework/skaalid/

Chapter 7
Professional Development to Promote Online Communication, Collaboration and Learning Among Faculty:
A Community of Practice Approach

Mayela Coto
https://orcid.org/0000-0002-4558-3671
Universidad Nacional, Costa Rica

Lone Dirckinck-Holmfeld
Aalborg University, Denmark

ABSTRACT

Based on a critical re-reading of a study of a community of practice approach to professional development, this chapter uses Engeström's activity theory model to highlight the tensions that arise in a professional development program oriented to change teaching practice through the introduction of ICT and a student-centered pedagogical approach. Despite the community of practice potential, there are many tensions that inhibit this type of professional learning. These tensions can be summarized in four broad categories: institutional structures (division of work), the institutional culture (rules), levels of engagement (differentiations within the community), and faculty readiness (in the appropriation of tools and new pedagogy). By analyzing, in greater depth, the tensions, our goal is to reflect again in the design principles and to further elaborate on developing a professional development strategy based on a community of practice approach that can be used in broader contexts.

DOI: 10.4018/978-1-5225-9814-5.ch007

INTRODUCTION

To contribute to today's innovation-driven economy, universities must integrate new teaching and learning approaches that allow students to develop skills such as collaboration, problem solving, and critical and creative thinking (Adams et al., 2018). These challenges, together with the principles of long-life learning, online learning and blended learning, imply new demands for faculty, who must be prepared to face the growing expectations of being competent, both in terms of promoting the development of these new skills in the students as in the integration of content, pedagogy and technology (Crawford, 2008; Wall, 2013).

In general, the task of preparing faculty to meet these challenges relies in faculty professional development programs. Literature stresses that these programs must address changes in beliefs, knowledge, and habits of practice, in order to achieve changes in the quality of teaching and learning (Gibbs & Coffey, 2004; Light & Calkins, 2008; Ödalen, Brommesson, Erlingsson, Schaffer, & Fogelgren, 2019). Literature also shows that traditional professional development (event-based, one-hit training workshops) has been shown ineffective in supporting change in teaching practices. These shortcomings have provoked an interest towards community inspired models.

In the last decade, research has shown that communities of practice (Wenger, 1998) can be a catalyst to improving faculty' professional practice (Coto, 2010, 2014; Lantz-Andersson, Lundin, & Selwyn, 2018; Patton & Parker, 2017; Schlager & Fusco, 2004; Sherer, Shea, & Kristensen, 2003) . The notion of building learning communities has become a very valuable mean for engaging faculty in meaningful and effective professional learning (Barab, Kling, & Gray, 2004; Macià & García, 2016; MacPhail, Patton, Parker, & Tannehill, 2014; Patton & Parker, 2017; Wing Lai, Pratt, Anderson, & Stigter, 2006). In addition, the technological infrastructure currently available in many higher education institutions has the potential to create online and distributed learning environments that can facilitate and extend the professional development of teachers (Lock, 2006).

Despite its potential, there are many obstacles that inhibit this type of professional learning. Many of the faculty members do not have the knowledge, experience and skills necessary to work as productive members of a community of practice. They are very pressured by time, with the growing demand for teaching and research, and do not always receive incentives or support from the institution to participate in professional development activities (Coto, 2010, 2014; Powell & Bodur, 2019; Tsiotakis & Jimoyiannis, 2016). Further in a resource constraint setting, there may be additional challenges with respect to access to IT, Wi-Fi and Internet, and fewer experiences with the use of IT tools for teaching and learning.

This chapter is based on previous studies (Coto, 2010, 2014) that has its roots in the interlacing of two main theoretical areas: professional development (PD) in higher education and learning in communities of practice (CoP). In this chapter, and responding to a fifth phase of the design-based research methodology - Dissemination and adoption in broader contexts- (Coto, 2010; Reeves, 2006), we will revisit the data but this time we will use activity theory (Engeström, 1987; Engeström, 2001) to analyze the tensions and contradictions that have been identified in the first analysis of the data, in order to broaden the application of the design principles. As such we will be looking into "secondary contradictions emerging between constitutive components of an activity system" (Sannino & Engeström, 2018, p. 49).

THEORETICAL BACKGROUND

The professional development (PD) of teachers is a fundamental mechanism to improve teachers' competences, innovate teaching methods and promote new skills in students (González & Skultety, 2018; Light & Calkins, 2008; Prenger, Poortman, & Handelzalts, 2017; Wake, Dysthe, & Mjelstad, 2007; Zhang & Liu, 2019). The PD must be purposefully conceptualized, carefully implemented and used in a meaningful way to support teacher growth and change (Loughran, 2014). The rapid development of information technology has changed the form, the content, the resources and the environment in which the professional development of teachers is carried out (Unwin, 2015). Online learning has broken the boundaries of time and space, and teachers can access online learning activities anytime and anywhere, which has the potential to effectively resolve the conflict between their workload and their professional development processes (Chen, Chen, & Tsai, 2009; Ching & Hursh, 2014) and at the same time, can encourage them to learn new values and practices through participation in new forms of activity (Coto & Dirckinck-Holmfeld, 2008).

Communities of practice (CoP) are a specialized form of PD (MacPhail et al., 2014). They seek to break the walls of solitary and individualistic professional practice (Byrk, 2016) and create spaces where teachers learn from one another, promoting professional growth (Barab, Baek, Schatz, Scheckler, & Moore, 2008; Hadar & Brody, 2010; Schlager & Fusco, 2004). The CoPs are significant, have a purpose and revolve around authentic tasks (Lock, 2006; Patton & Parker, 2017; Wing Lai et al., 2006).

The CoP framework is based upon social or situated learning theory (Lave & Wenger, 1991). Wenger et al. (2002) define a community of practice along three dimensions: a domain of knowledge that creates a common ground and sense of common identity, a community of people who care about the domain and create the social structure that facilitates learning through interactions and relationships with others, and a shared practice that the community shares, develops, and maintains to be effective in its domain. Other researchers have proposed similar definitions for CoP. Barab et al. (2004) define communities of practice as "a persistent, sustained social network of individuals who share and develop an overlapping knowledge base, set of beliefs, values, history and experiences focused on a common practice and/or mutual enterprise" (p. 55).

When the members of a community do not necessarily share working contexts, nor are they geographically close, the communities of practice are called online or distributed communities (Wenger et al., 2002) which means that they depend on technology to connect the communities members, support work teams, build knowledge repositories, build a sense of community, encourage participation, foster identity and presence and offer online tutoring and instruction. Online and distributed communities are more challenging to keep alive. In addition, a distributed CoP usually needs a formalized structure to organize activities that would enable doing, becoming, experience and belonging for the members (Schlager & Fusco, 2004).

THE RESEARCH SETTING

The research scenario in the study was the National University (UNA) in Costa Rica, specifically the regional campuses. UNA is the second largest public university with around 20,000 students, 1800 academic staff and 1700 administrative staff. Besides the central campus in Heredia, UNA has several campuses throughout the country. Even though they are an important part of the university, many of the institutional efforts are placed on the central campus where most students and faculty staff are concentrated, thus the institutional initiatives usually take longer to reach the regional campus. The PD programs are not the exception.

At the regional campuses, many teaching staff is hired by short terms and part-time contracts. They carry out a variety of different tasks (academic, outreach, administrative) within the regional center, so time is a scarce resource for them. They usually do not have access to PD processes that take place mostly in the central campus.

The participants in the study were a group of 27 teachers from five geographically distributed campuses who have diverse fields of knowledge and diverse approaches to teaching and learning as results of their own professional experiences and context. Given the geographical distribution of the regional campuses, the study used networked technologies for two purposes: (1) contributing to the reduction of space and time barriers favoring the interaction among faculty; and (2) supporting a more sustainable and scalable teacher PD program within the institution (Schlager, Fusco, & Schank, 2002). The learning environment was designed as a framework for flexible and blended learning, rich in challenges and interactions around ICT and the philosophy and methodologies of problem and project-based learning (PBL), and teachers were considered as the main agents of their PD.

For a comprehensive presentation, design, analysis and results please look into Coto (2010). For this chapter, we use, in a partial way, a set of data from the original study, but we analyze it with a new theoretical lens (activity theory) in order get deeper insights into the dynamics of the findings, and to highlight the tensions that can hinder or act as springboards for a PD process. In our use of tensions, we use this in line with Engeström's use of disturbances and conflicts, but also his use of innovative attempts to change the activity (Engeström, 2001). In the graphic representations of the activity systems, we use a heart to symbolize the dynamics, while tensions such as disturbances and conflicts are symbolized using a kind of lightning or a cross.

THE RESEARCH APPROACH

Design-based research (DBR) is a methodology originated in the pragmatic paradigm. The Design-Based Research Collective (Design-Based Research Collective, 2003, p. 5) defines it as "an emerging paradigm for the study of learning in context through the systematic design and study of instructional strategies and tools". In achieving its aims of improving educational designs and advancing understanding of learning, DBR draws on the full range of social science research methods, combining a variety of quantitative and qualitative approaches (Barab & Squire, 2004; Sandoval & Bell, 2004).

The main sources of data for the study were online discussions, face-to-face meetings, and reflection workshops. The information was collected through questionnaires, interviews, workshops and participant observation. Given the strong online component of the intervention, over a period of ten months, online observation was carried out almost daily. All recorded sessions (face-to-face meetings, interviews, and workshops) were transcribed for data analysis. Online forum discussions were downloaded into text files. The textual data available for participant observation research include postings in discussion forums, e-mails, chat room interactions and produced artifacts. All the data gathered was analyzed through a recursive process to generate codes. Through the process of coding, collecting, grouping and organizing the data, several codes emerged that were grouped into networks or theme groups (all the details in Coto (2010)).

The DBR approach has a cyclical nature where each phase informs the next phase and, in turn, each phase can result in modifications of all the phases illustrating the iterative refinement nature of the approach. DBR runs through four phases: i. "Analysis of practical problems by researchers and practitioners"; ii. "Development of solutions with a theoretical framework"; iii. "Evaluation and testing of solutions in practice"; and iv. "Documentation and reflection to produce design principles", where researchers refine, add, and discard principles that comprise their understanding of the experience (Reeves, 2006). For this chapter, the authors expand the DBR model with a fifth phase called v. "Dissemination and adoption in broader contexts" that deals explicitly with analyzing whether the proposed design principles can effectively support teachers, from other contexts, in the process of transforming their teaching practices through the introduction of technology and PBL.

In order to broaden the application of the design principles, we analyze the tensions and contradictions that have been identified in the first analysis of the data, using Engeström activity theory (2001). The tensions and contradictions can be found: (1) within the elements (for example, tools, subjects); (2) between elements (e.g. a subject and a rule); (3) between a central activity at one point in time and a central activity later on; and (4) between activities (Engeström, 2014). To perform the analysis, the authors, separately, explored the data and drew the representation of the activity systems for each of the components. Then, they compared their findings and built a common understanding. This method increases the validation of the findings.

DESIGNING A PROFESSIONAL DEVELOPMENT PROCESS WITHIN THE FRAMEWORK OF A COMMUNITY OF PRACTICE

In this study, the design of a professional development environment entails the provision of facilities to enable and support the belonging of faculty staff to a distributed community of practice. The point of departure of the study is the premise that engagement in social practice is the fundamental process by which we learn and become who we are (Wenger, 1998), hence becoming a member of an emerging teaching focused on ICT collaborative pedagogies- community of practice should be both a process of identity construction, and a process of competence acquisition.

Participation in a community of practice involves action and connection, as Wenger stated, it "combines doing, talking, thinking, feeling and belonging" (1998, p. 56). In this regard, the participation of the faculty staff in the PD is seen as not just engagement in a set of activities, but as a process of being participant in a new teaching- learning practice and constructing an identity in relation to this practice.

The literature suggests that we cannot create a CoP for PD goals. However, Wenger (1998) argues that while you cannot design the learning you can *design for learning*. Wenger's conceptual architecture for learning provides a framework in which we can design a social learning space that affords the evolution of a CoP. This framework is expressed in terms of four basic dimensions that entail issues of meaning, time, space and power. Wenger captures these aspects with four dualities: reification and participation; designed and emergent; local and global; and identification and negotiability. In terms of the design of the PD program, the dualities are analytical tools that can give a better understanding of the process of design for a community.

- **Reification/Participation:** This duality creates two kinds of affordances for negotiating meaning as it concerns the need of creating a balance between resources for learning (reification) and the activities that make use of those resources (participation). In the context of the PD learning space, this dimension means bringing together a group of faculty staff through online and physical spaces and providing them with a balance between opportunities of participation and resources they will use in support of this participation. The negotiation of meaning evolves around core concepts, such as the introduction of technology in teaching practices, and student-centered pedagogical approaches (PBL).

- **Designed/Emergent:** Wenger (1998) emphasizes that "there is an inherent uncertainty between design and its realization in practice, since practice is not the result of design but rather a response to it" (p. 233). Within the study, a conscious effort was put into the design of tasks, spaces and organization that enables university teachers to engage in dialogues, discussions, project work and negotiations (Goodyear, Jones, Asensio, Hodgson, & Steeples, 2001). This duality involves allowing teachers to negotiate how they transform the design in ways that are meaningful to them; thus the ultimate goal of the design will be to create a space for continued negotiability among all the members of the community (Brosnan & Burgess, 2003).
- **Local/Global:** This duality refers to how a CoP relates with the rest of the world, through creating continuities across boundaries. The challenge in designing for a community with a focus on change is to create a balance between meeting the teachers' and immediate needs and a more global institutional change agenda (Barab et al., 2004). The core concepts and practices that must be negotiated need to have local significance to each teacher (and each regional campus) but at the same time be of global relevance to all teachers in the community and to the university community in general.
- **Identification and Negotiability:** The identification/negotiability duality refers to the degree to which members identify with the community and the extent to which they are empowered to shape the community, and as such it has an effect on the formation of the identity through the mix of participation and non-participation (Wenger, 1998). For the goals of PD programs this duality is very important. Teachers were invited to new practices; thus, they were able to decide whether to identify or not with the community practices and consequently whether to participate or not in it.

PRESENTATION OF FINDINGS

There were two types of data sets that contributed to this study. One set was comprised by the interviews and workshops which included spoken face-to-face discussion information, and the second set was drawn from observations, discussion forums and questionnaires, including only written information. This chapter presents the results related with the overall patterns of (A) participation, (B) engagement and identification with the community, and (C) learning.

Participation in the Community

The next sections will further analyze the issue of participation in three manifestations: online participation (including group work), face-to-face participation, and the development of the pedagogical intervention. This analysis will be using activity theory, and especially Engeström's graphical representation of the second generation of activity theory (Leontjew), as the lens.

Online Participation

Participation in online activities comprises participation in chats, blog reflection, discussion forums, and group work. This section examines each of them.

Chat Conversations

21 faculty members participated over time in 23 chat sessions. There was an average of five participants in each session, with a maximum number of participants of 14 and a minimum of two. The synchronous nature of the chat allowed direct interaction with everyone in the virtual room and the social space that was recreated were extremely valuable to the formation of a community identity. Participation in the chats was high at the beginning of the intervention, but then fell almost to a zero. Some of the reasons for the decline were: (1) the messy nature of the talks was overwhelming for some faculty who could not follow the flow of conversation; (2) some faculty, mainly from Coto Campus and the Marine Biological Station frequently experienced connection problems that hindered their participation; and (3) the chat sessions were transformed by some of the participants in a place in which to share all kinds of topics, such as weather, politics and national events. For other participants, those issues were irrelevant; therefore, they were unwilling to invest their time in this activity. These tensions and contradictions are illustrated in Figure 1.

Some of these tensions (the messy communication) are related to the tool (chat) or to the appropriation of the tool and the specific design of the chat-function in Moodle. Other tensions were related to the division of work, where especially the lack of a stable ICT infrastructure becomes a problem. This influences the balance and interactions between the participants in the community, making it especially difficult for the faculty staff from some of the regional campuses (Coto Campus and the Marine Biological Station) to participate actively. The third kind of tensions are related to the interpretation of social community. Though there was a shared understanding that core participation in a CoP both concerns social as academic communication as it has to do with identity transformation, it turned out that some

Figure 1. Online participation: Chat

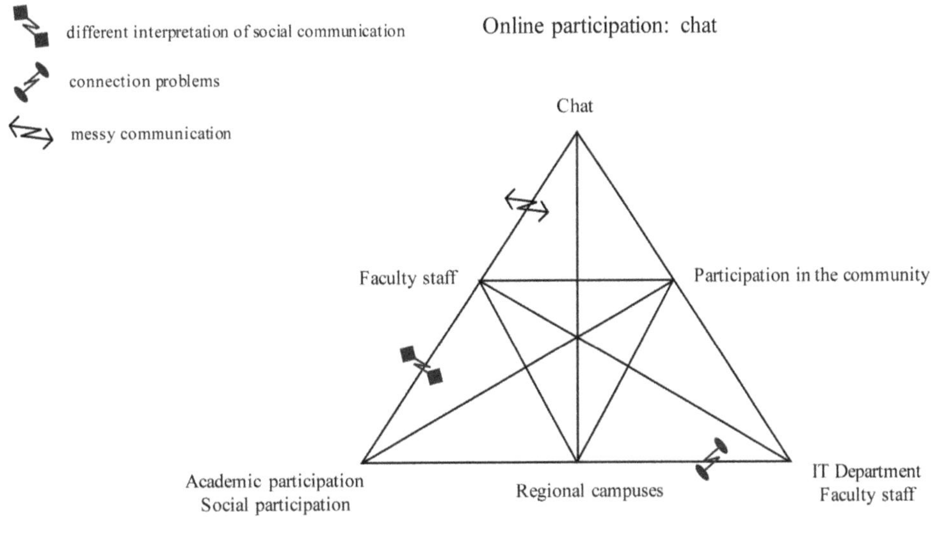

of the participants did not engage in the social communication. As these participants withdraw from participating in the chat it influences their participation in the community, and therefore the importance of the chat for community building.

Blog Reflection

The blog was conceived as a space of personal reflection on the learning process, as such its value as an activity was considered very high, both from the viewpoint of the learning experience at individual and community level. The personal blog was aimed at providing an ability to trace the individual learning through the entire process. However, the faculty was rarely willing to use the blogs. The entry of the blog with more participants (22) was regarding a personal presentation, and the entry with fewer participants (1) referred to blended learning. It does not mean that the faculty did not reflect on their learning process, just they were not engaged in keeping a personal blog. The process of reflection mainly took place in the co-located meetings and in the discussion forums that were considered meta-reflection spaces. The tensions in the use of blogs is illustrated in Figure 2:

We interpret the lack of use of the blog as primarily a tension between doing personal and community learning reflection in a semipublic and virtual space. Even the blog from a didactical design is expected to support the individual participants and the community to reflect and externalize the learning experience, it seems as this way of communicating was unfamiliar for most of the participants. When it comes to use the blog to present themselves, 22 participants responded to this task. This supports the interpretation that the staff were able to use the blog, however not for the intended external reflection.

Figure 2. Online participation: Blogs

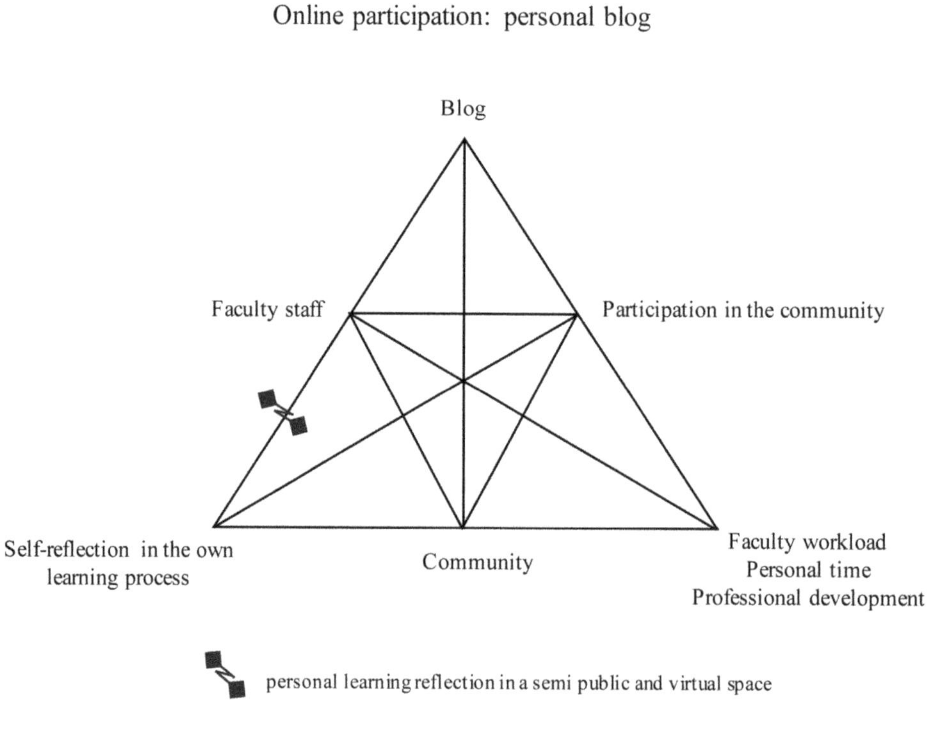

Discussion Forums

There were a total of 12 discussion forums. By nature, four of them were considered reflection forums, and the remaining eight targeted a specific subject domain, such as Project-based learning; UNA pedagogical model; Modalities of learning: challenges and limitations; and Design of educational materials. Each one of the twelve forums lasted between one and two weeks. It is worth noticing that peripheral participation in the online discussion forums was an activity that requires time. Table 1 shows the individual pattern of participation for each member in the discussion forums. It considers the "core" participation, meaning producing a post, and the "peripheral" participation, meaning reading but not writing. It is possible to deduce that all participants visited the community at some point and were able to see the discussions. There was a high diversity in participation, from almost null participation (P2 and

Table 1. Individual participation in the discussion forums

Faculty Members	Participation Over Time in the Discussion Forums *												Total Number of Postings
	#1	#2	#3	#4	#5	#6	#7	#8	#9	#10	#11	#12	
P1	1			1	1	1	0	1		0		1	25
P2	0						0		0				0
P3		1	1	1				1	1	0	1		13
P4			1						1			1	4
P5	1	0	0	1									2
P6	0	1	1	0					0		1		5
P7	1	1	0	1	1	1		0			1		16
P8	1	1	1	1	1	1	1	1	1	1	1	1	82
P9	0			1	1	1	0				1	1	24
P10	1	1	1	1			0	0			0		5
P11	1	0	1	1	1	1	1	1	0	1	1		21
P12	1						0		1	1	1	1	15
P13	1	0	0	0	0	1	0				1	1	7
P14	1	1	0	0		1	1	0	0	1	1	1	13
P15	0	0	1	1	1	0	0	1	0		1	1	11
P16	1	1	1	1	1	1		1	1		1	1	48
P17		1	1		1								8
P18	1		1	0	0	1							6
P19	0	0											0
P20	0	1	1	0									12
P21	1	1	1	1									10
P22	1	1	1	1			0				1	1	7

(Coto, 2014)
* For participants who were members of the community for more than three months
1 – active participation (writing a contribution)
0 – passive participation (just observing)

P19) to 100% participation (P8). It is also possible to appreciate that, in general, individual participation (marks with "1"), in online activities is higher than peripheral participation (marks with "0").

Research suggests that there are typically three distinct levels of participation in communities of practices: (1) The core group who participates intensely in the community and typically takes on leadership roles; (2) the active group who attends and participates regularly, and (3) the peripheral group who, while they are passive participants in the community, still learn from their level of involvement. Typically, this latter group represents most of the community (Lave & Wenger, 1991; Wenger et al., 2002).

Table 1 shows that three participants (P8, P11 and P16), stood out as successful and engaged community members. These faculty members were considered the core participants in this study. The active participation online is considered a good indicator to be considered in determining the category of "core group", because it was in the online environment where most discussion, negotiation of meanings and sharing took place. Regarding the active group who attended and participated regularly, seven faculty members can be considered to belong to this group: P1, P3, P7, P12, P14, P15, and P22. The last one can be considered a good example of an active participant. She began very enthusiastically in the community and took a leading role in her group. However, she felt and declared herself as not akin to online communication, and promptly she stopped her participation in the discussion forums. Despite this, she found her way within the community and became one of the most active participants in face-to-face meetings (Coto, 2014).

The last group, the peripheral one, is formed by members who even though they were peripheral participants in the community, still might learn from their level of involvement. Twelve participants belong to this group: P2, P4, P5, P6, P9, P10, P13, P17, P18, P19, P20 and P21, and they represent the biggest group within the community. From this group, there were four members who withdrew from the study in the early stages (May to June): P5, P17, P18, and P20, so they did not participate in the pedagogical innovation project. P18 is a case that may illustrate the process of a participant who had a peripheral participation while he was in the community and who finally decided to terminate his participation in it.

In general, the discussion fora worked well, and the participants were able to use them as intended (Figure 3).

Three groups of users evolved and could be identified (core group, active group, and peripheral group), however the analysis also reveals that this different levels of participation in the forum discussions may produce some tensions among the individuals. Some of the core participants, which took up the leadership in the forums expressed disappointment with the other participants not contributing enough. Our interpretation is, that participating in the online fora is one way of expressing membership and contributing to the building of the community, however the core members are also depending on the active members, and the peripheral members in order to stay "tuned". At the same time writing and contributing in foras were for the participants a new way of communication, which prerequisite not only the operational skills to use forums as well as a stable ICT infrastructure (which especially was missing in the Coto and Puntarenas campus), but also a readiness and competences to act in the online fora, and to express yourself about academic and social issues in a new mode of communication. The aim of using the communication fora was for the faculty staff to become familiar with and a necessary way of communicating and discussing among the participants, as they were distributed in space and time. Many of the participants were able to use the communication fora as a shared space for academic and social discussions, however it also produced (new) boundaries between the members of the community. One very clear example of these new boundaries was the participant (P22), who in the beginning was actively participating in the forums, but suddenly stopped. With regards to the online communication she

Figure 3. Online participation: Discussion forums

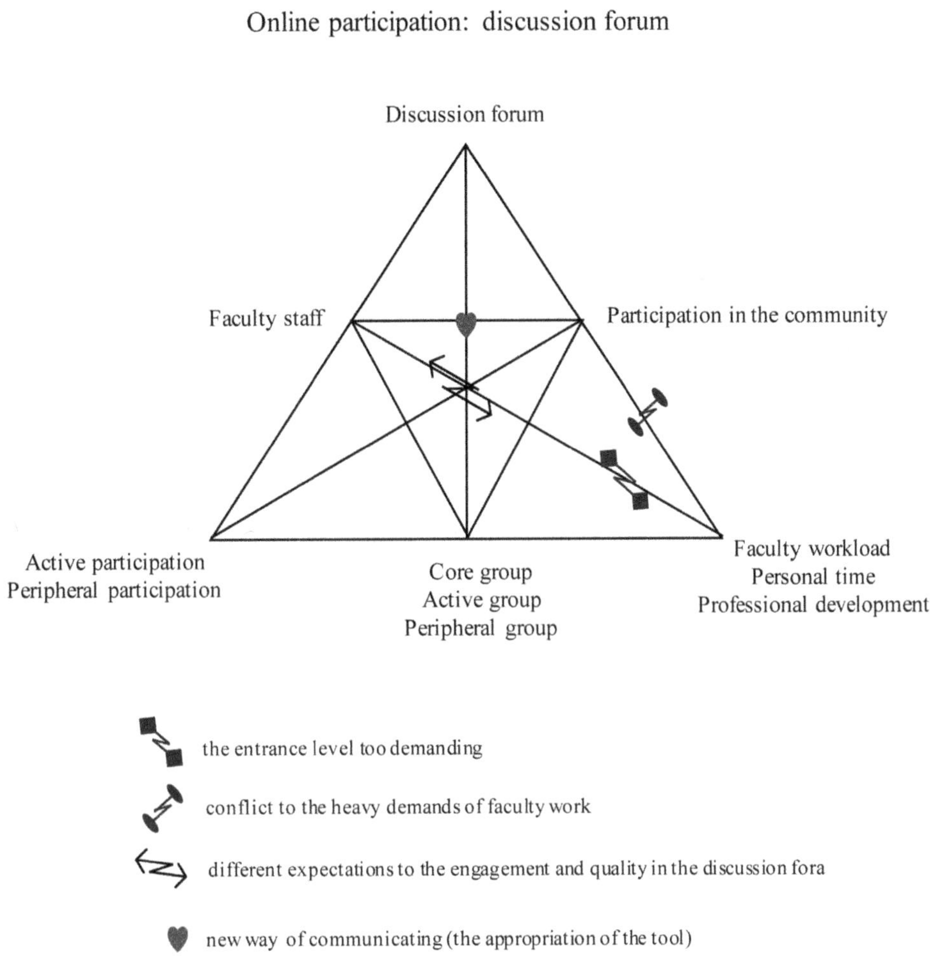

became a peripheral participant, however what we shall see later was, that she in the f2f communication took up the leadership, and in the overall CoP belong to the core group.

Four people, who had not participated in the forum discussions withdrew from the PD program. Especially P18 expressed that the entrance level (the ability to use the online communication for academic and social activities) was too demanding, and the overall PD process too demanding and abstract. He expressed that it was conflicting with his heavy demands of work as a faculty member.

Group Work

Group work was another activity designed to be carried out mainly in the online environment. The groups were established to create mutual dependencies between the participants and to support the individual construction of meanings through the construction of shared understanding, negotiation, confrontation and commitment (Dirckinck-Holmfeld, Jones, & Lindström, 2009). The groups were also organized inter-campuses to enable participants to truly experience by themselves the learning process using networked technologies. This decision was aligned with the principle of constructive activity (Gallant, 2000) which suggests that in order to increase the opportunities for change, faculty should experience the teaching and learning conditions they plan to create for their own students.

In addition, group work was considered fundamental for the design of the pedagogical intervention that the participants would implement with their students. The groups were envisioned as the places where members discuss, analyze and take decisions. However, there were a lot of organization and coordination problems, as well as misunderstandings and difficulties with setting up agreements. The activity in each group was very irregular, and even though the group members were visiting the group online space regularly, they were, in most cases, unable to make decisions, and consequently little progress happened. The tensions emerged in online group work is shown in Figure 4.

Community members argued lack of familiarity with the technology including lack of skills in asynchronous and synchronous communication and lack of skills in order to use the platform for group work. Moreover, they argued for lack of group culture including the practice of sharing, giving peer-support and lack of commitment to accomplish work. At the individual level, they also explained lack of motivation and time as reasons for why the distributed group work was not as productive as hoped for. Moreover, one argued, that it was a mistake to divide them into groups, when they were just becoming comfortable as a community. It was evident that working in virtual and distributed teams across the regional campuses required skills not inherent in the participants.

Figure 4. Group work: Online and distributed participation

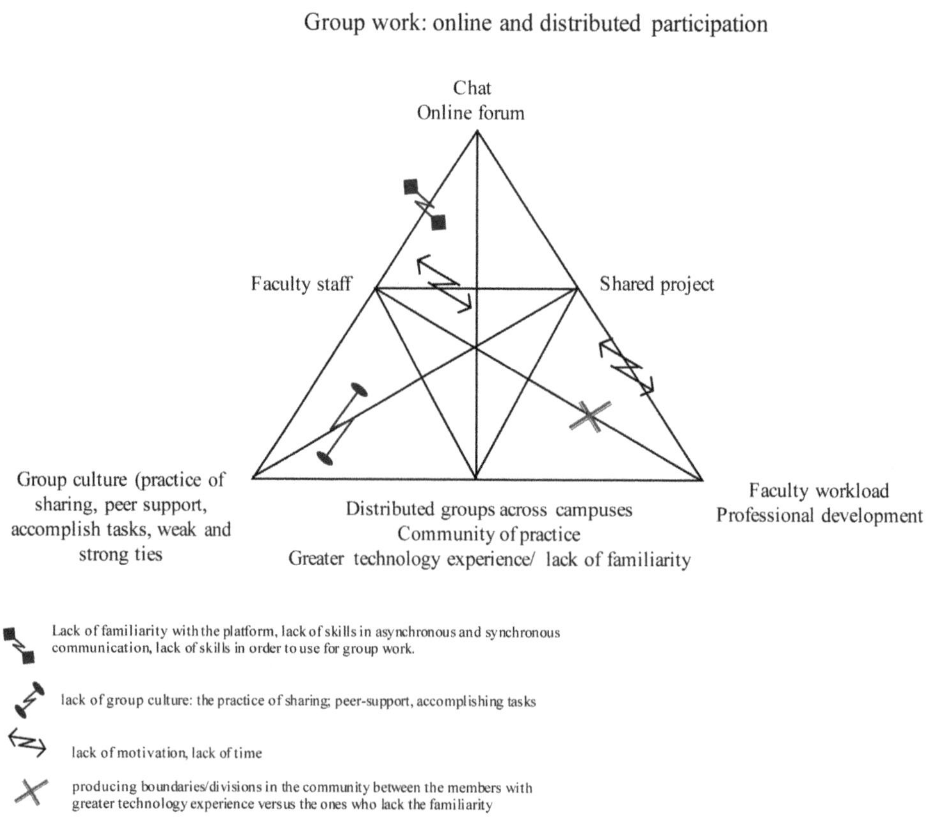

In general, the data for online participation suggests a general pattern of higher ability to participate to those members with greater technology experience and background. The inability for the groups to work in an effective way was a factor that negatively influenced academic participation and weakened the cohesion among members of the community and even led some faculty to leave the community.

Face-to-Face Modality Group Work

Once discovered that the online group work was not working as intended, the group work was moved to the local campuses in a face-to-face modality (see tensions in Figure 5). The intention of this change was to preserve the practice of sharing and peer-support beyond the online means. The new strategy worked well in three campuses: Nicoya, Liberia and Puntarenas. The participants supported each other in the process of designing and implementing the pedagogical intervention. In the other two campuses, Perez Zeledon and Coto Brus, the support that took place between the members of the group was quite low. Those who made progress in the program were working in rather individual ways.

Taking Nicoya's group as an example, it was clear that while the faculty members were not participating much online, they were gaining value from the community. They worked as a sub-community, where they read the suggested material, discussed it in their group, and used it in their classrooms to extend their teaching repertoire. So, the Nicoya's group work is an example of a practice based on shar-

Figure 5. Group work: Face to face participation

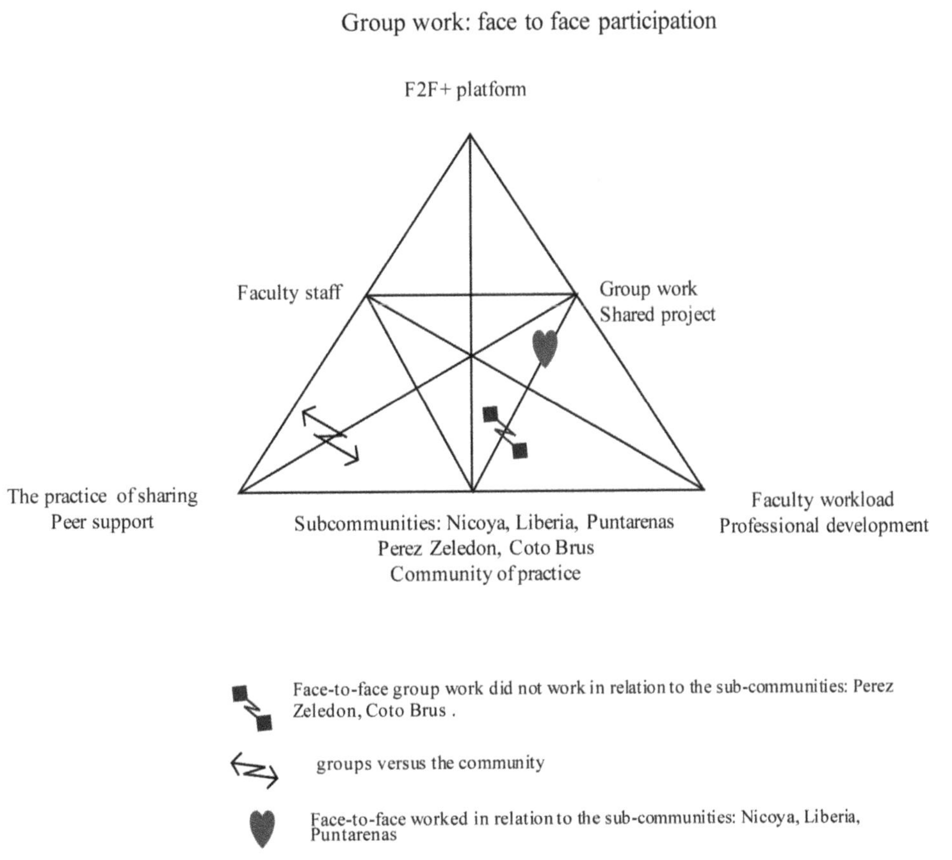

ing, caring and peer-support, while the groups in the two campuses, Perez Zeledon and Coto Brus not managed to get it to work - even after the groups were organized in a face-to-face modality.

This contradiction between the groups and the community may be explained by the concepts of weak and strong ties (Granovetter, 1983; Wang, Lu, Ester, Wang, & Chen, 2016). At the CoP level the faculty members are connected in somehow weaker ties than in the group work, where they become very depending on each other. And when it does not work due to the uncertain competences in distributed, online group working or as shared commitment in the f2f group work, the individual learner becomes isolated.

However, there is maybe a didactical design issue in the overall PD approach to consider, which may have reinforced this problem. With references to Dirckinck-Holmfeld, Jones, & Lindström (2009) there may be an ambiguity between the motive for the group work and the dependencies, which the groups may produce. When organizing for collaborative project groups as in PBL, the idea is that the participants share a project and a shared enterprise, however as the pedagogical intervention were not a shared project, it might - as also one of the participant express - be questioned if they really needed the local groups as they felt that they got more support from the community than from their local group. So, it might be worth considering the relations between the individual, the groups and the community and when and why to integrate groups. Especially forced distributed groups across regional campuses demands competences in online group work.

Face-to-Face Participation

Table 2 shows overall faculty participation in the six face-to-face meetings that took place during the intervention. Two of these meetings were global meetings in Heredia with all participants, and the other four were carried-out in each of the regional campuses.

The data shows that participation in face-to-face meetings was very regular which confirm the preferences of many community members for face-to-face communication. All in all, face-to-face communication in the seminars were perceived as very important for the academic and social discussions and reflections on the innovation of the teaching practices, and also to motivate the faculty members to engage in the community and to stay motivated. The participants in general like the f2f modalities based on a mix of presentations, design workshops and discussions as they provide a dynamic and "ready-at-hand" environment for discussions and learning, which was within the comfort-zone of the participants. Further, the attendance mirrors engagement, which makes it transparent for the community members to experience the community engagement.

Table 2. Participation in face-to-face meetings

Face-to-Face Meeting	Number of Participants
February	24
March	27
June	17
August	15
October	14
November	15

(Coto, 2014)

The tensions in the face-to-face participation and modality are illustrated in Figure 6.

In general, the regularity in the face-2-face activities underlines the need for a blended learning approach, However, there were tensions with respect to time and the faculty workload. A sub-group (P11, P14 and P16), always expressed a preference to communicate in an environment that encourages debate beyond the physical limitations. For these members, online communication offers the flexibility not previously available to carry out collaborative learning activities; however, the three of them were competent in using technology as a means of communication. The differences between online participation and face-to-face participation may be illustrated by P2. He participated in all face-to-face meetings but had not written a post in ten months (see Table 1).

In general, time was the most important factor that hinders participation. In most cases, there was always a tension between faculty workload at the university, personal time and time for PD. Daily activities at the university often interfered with the activities proposed in the community. Faculty members were struggling to bring the community into their daily routine. Normally, many of them did not have serious problems with attending face-to-face meetings but found that time for online participation was much more difficult for them.

Figure 6. Global face to face participation

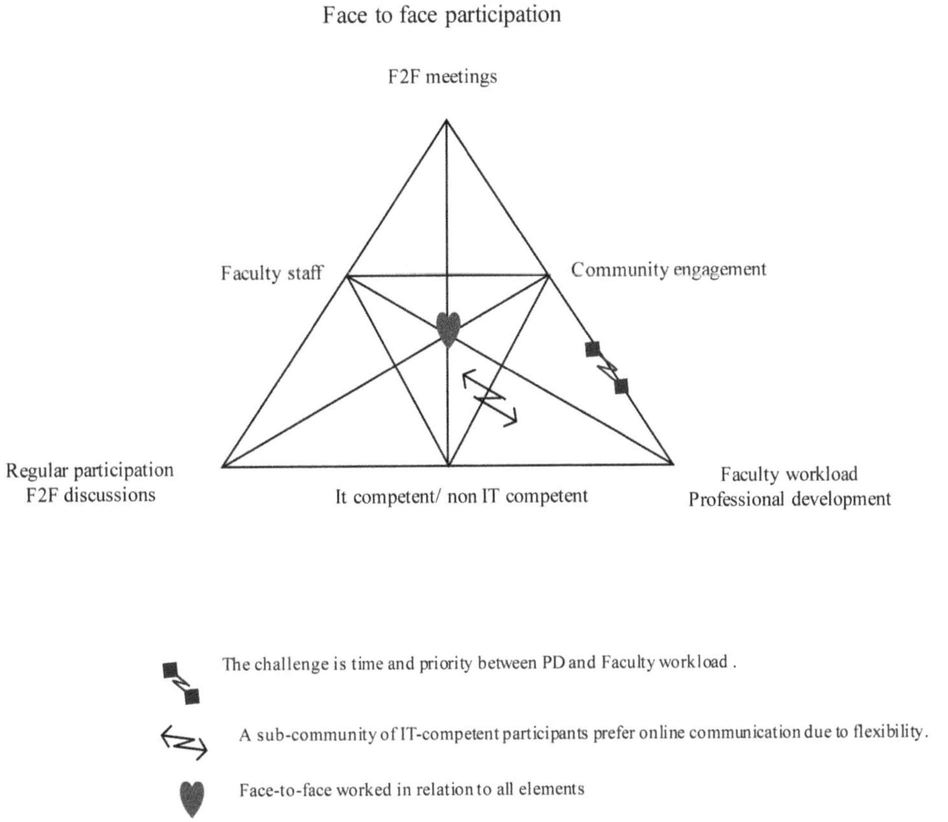

The Development of the Pedagogical Intervention

The literature points to the importance of providing opportunities to implement what is learned (Gallant, 2000; King, 2003; Lawler & King, 2001) and in DBR interventions are also a mean to create new knowledge and to learn from practice, as an intervention in practice always will reveal some unforeseen stepping stones. As a further strategy for integrating knowing, acting and being, each participant designed, implemented and evaluated a pedagogical intervention in their classrooms in order to enhance some aspect of their educational practice. The activity was highly situated and authentic, and 15 out of the 18 community members who completed the PD program, were able to go through the complete process. They pursued diverse goals in the design of their pedagogical interventions, such as motivating students (P14); making a more participatory course (P2 and P4); promoting reflection and analysis (P12); fostering collaborative work (P22); improving learning through the use of technological tools (P7 and P10); developing fundamental topics through the use of blogs (P1); and using technological tools to develop a project about local tourism (P3 and P6). The innovations were carried-out in courses from areas such as Education, Literature, Environmental studies, Tourism, Administration, Language, and Biology. The tensions emerged during this activity are illustrated in Figure 7.

Findings show that this was the activity as most of the faculty staff participated in. Despite of some problems related to time and perhaps energy constraints of busy professionals, this approach was highly successful in creating practical relevance for their learning. By being capable of making changes [with diverse levels of complexity] in their teaching, the community members felt empowered in their practice,

Figure 7. Pedagogical intervention

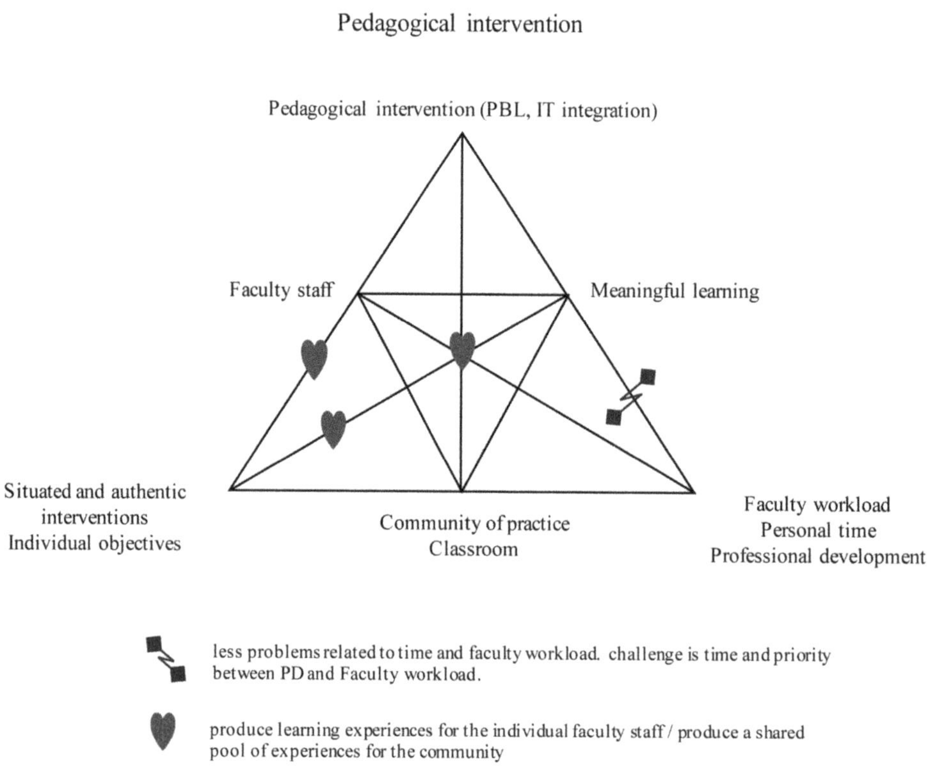

role and future perspectives. Further, for the community, the interventions served as a pool of practical experiences which it was meaningful to engage in and connect to.

Engagement and Identification With the Community

Engagement defines who belongs to the CoP (Wenger, 1998). Through the engagement in discussions and collaborative work, faculty members were confronted with the necessity to negotiate their current multiple practices and experiences. The new theoretical knowledge and practical training in ICT and PBL gave them methodological skills which had an impact on their professional practice. However, each participant found a unique place and identity within the community, and it was framed by their engagement and identification with the community. Table 3 indicates the faculty members' perceptions about their engagement with the community.

The data comes from the final questionnaire and was answered by twelve participants. The community has a defined area of knowledge and practice (ICT+PBL) that shapes the domain and establishes the common ground which gives members the motivation to meet, discuss and share. From the data it can be concluded that 75% of faculty showed interest in the topics that were discussed and thus in the domain of the community. It also can be seen that only 50% of the members stated that they participated regularly in the diverse proposed activities. This is important, because participation in a CoP requires regular interactions to contribute to the development of the domain and the practice.

In connection with the exchange of experiences and sharing of resources, the data show that 75% of the them were willing to share stories, experiences and ways of solving problems, but only 58% of them participated in resource sharing. One possible explanation for this situation is that it in this context it usually requires less time for faculty to share their stories and everyday experiences than to find additional resources. Furthermore, sharing of resources usually requires more technological skills. Maybe the sharing of stories is also more meaningful to the community and more ready-to-hand, than the focus on sharing of additional resources.

The final item in the Table 3 indicates how faculty themselves valued their responsibility and commitment to the learning activities. The data show that only 58% of them said they had assumed responsibility for participation in learning activities. However, this value is strongly influenced by the feelings of members about their general lack of online participation, since as discussed above, the average rate of participation in the face-to-face activities was high, plus 15 of 18 faculty members were able to design,

Table 3. Engagement with the community

	Totally Agree	Agree	Disagree	Totally Disagree	NR
Interest and positive attitude toward the topics	41.67	33.33	8.33	8.33	8.33
Participation in activities has been constant	8.33	41.67	25.00	16.67	8.33
Sharing of experiences, histories and ways to solve problems with other members	8.33	66.67	8.33	8.33	8.33
Exchanging of resources with the other members	16.67	41.67	16.67	16.67	8.33
Responsibility and commitment with the learning activities	16.67	41.67	25.00	8.33	8.33

(Coto, 2014)

implement and evaluate an educational intervention in their classrooms. This situation reflects how they created a strong link between participation in the online website and their participation and commitment as members of the community. Because members did not participate online as much as they would have liked, their perception of commitment to the community was weakened.

The tensions that arise in the process of engagement to the community are illustrated in Figure 8.

In general, commitment was an issue that generated some controversy. Some members believed that a strong and steady commitment is necessary for PD to be effective and for the community to be productive. Others felt that the way to make a commitment should be flexible, so people need to be able to contribute when they can and as they can. The former was critical of those who did not contribute regularly and thoroughly. These issues of commitment are characteristic of a CoP. If a community is seen as voluntary, which Wenger express in many of his writings, the organic development of the community will show if the strongly committed or the ones, which find commitment to be more flexible will emerge as the core members. However, as a PD strategy, we will recommend making the requirements for commitments even more explicit, for the participants to be confronted with this even before entering the community. Double standards may create confusion and frustration in the community.

Wenger (1998) points out that an important condition to be able to negotiate meaning is identification. As such, identification influences learning and on the formation of the identity through the mix of participation and peripheral-participation. Table 4 indicates the self-perception of participants regarding their identification with the community. The data come from the final questionnaire and was answered by twelve participants.

The tensions regarding the identification to the community are illustrated in Figure 9.

From the data, it appears that 83% of the members felt that they were part of the community. Because it was a distributed community, it is important to consider that the inability to negotiate meanings can create an identity of nonparticipation and marginality, and this may be the case for some participants. Regarding trust and the value of contributions, 83% of faculty believed that the community offered a

Figure 8. Community engagement

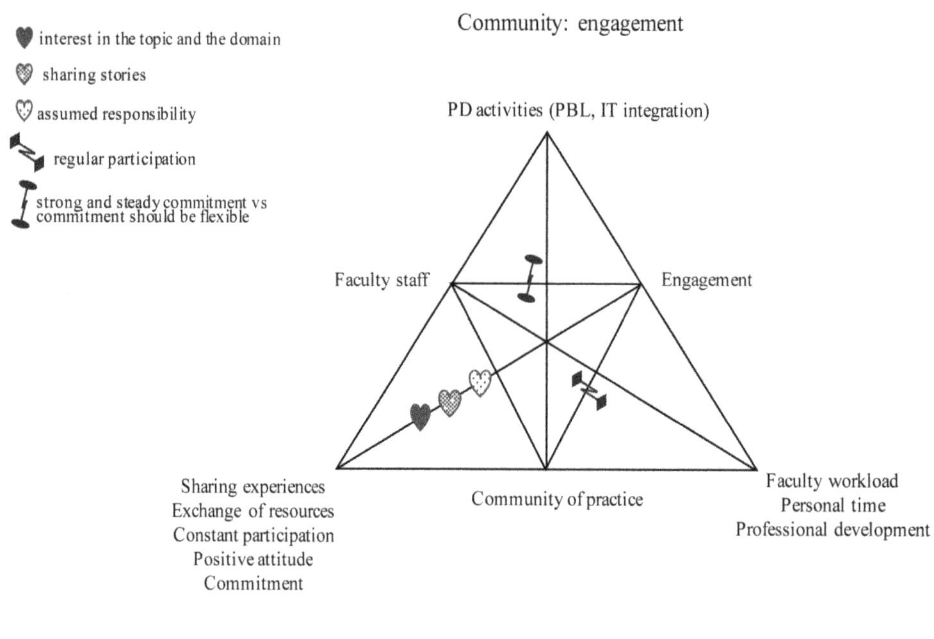

Table 4. Identification with the community

	Totally Agree	Agree	Disagree	Totally Disagree	NR
Feel part of the community	58.33	25.00	16.67	0.00	0.00
The community offers a safe and trust space to express freely	50.00	33.33	0.00	8.33	8.33
My contribution is important and valued by other members of the community	58.33	16.67	8.33	8.33	8.33
Positively value shared learning with community members	75.00	8.33	8.33	0.00	8.33
Belonging to the community allows to improve professional practice	66.67	25.00	8.33	0.00	0.00

(Coto, 2014)

safe and trusty space to express freely. This *trust* could be seen in the open and free way in which they presented their thoughts, questions, and doubts in the learning activities. It is important to note that, in some cases, there was an existing degree of trust among the participants of the local campus and participation in the community promoted the consolidation of this trust.

Despite the faculty feeling free to express themselves, only 75% of them reported that their contributions were valued by the other members. This situation can be associated with lack of reciprocity. A community thrives on reciprocity, "on giving back", and in widespread participation in community building efforts (McDonald et al., 2003). When faculty members participated in a discussion and received no response from the other members, they felt that their contributions were not valuable enough for the others to bother to participate. For active participants, fairness dictates that one needs to give back something of comparable value. The lack of reciprocity had a negative effect on motivation and social engagement and, to some degree, devalued the learning process, clearly affecting the cohesion of the community.

As non-participation discouraged some academics to participate, the daily and active participation of other academics also discouraged participation. P8 was the academic with highest participation in

Figure 9. Community identification

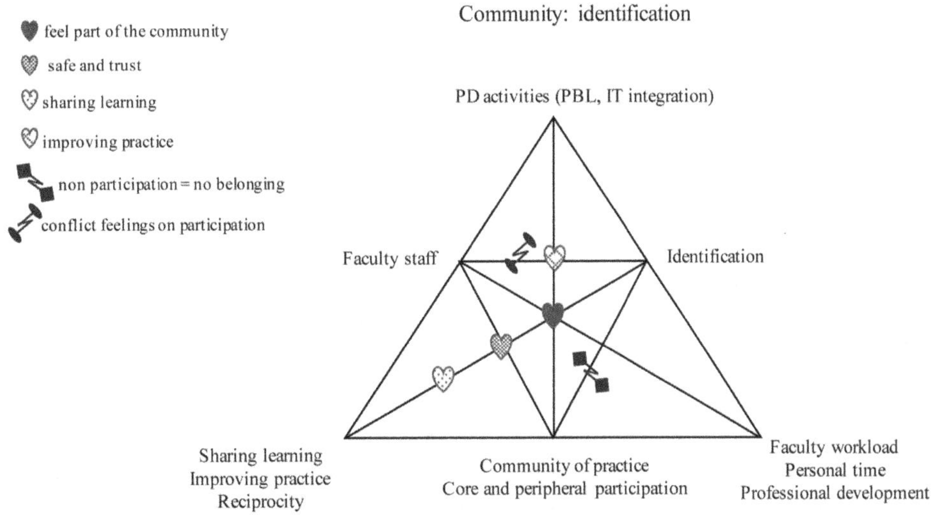

the community. He attended all the face-to-face meetings and participated in online discussions almost daily. Furthermore, he made many contributions to the community, such as complementary readings, supporting references, and conceptual maps. This very central participation provoked conflictive feelings in some participants.

Given the geographical distance among campuses, the establishment of relationships among participants was complex. However, despite the difficulties, 83% of the participants appreciated the interaction and the shared learning with colleagues. This could be noticed in some of the answers to the question "What we did well as a community?", where 8 out of 14 academics mentioned aspects such as sharing and support of each other; sharing new experiences; sharing ideas; and sharing practices. About 92% of faculty asserted that belonging to the community allowed them to improve their professional practice. The community favored the development of expertise, which in turn was transferred to the classroom and influenced teaching and learning processes. Through the design, implementation, evaluation and communication of findings about their pedagogical innovations, the participants provided strong evidence of how learning in the community had an impact on their professional practice.

Learning Into a Community of Practice

A central conviction in communities of practice, is that learning is a social process that involves building connections: connections between what is being learned and what is important to the learner, connections between what is being learned and those situations in which it is applied, and connections among the learner and other learners with similar goals (Barab et al., 2004; Hadar & Brody, 2010; Prenger et al., 2017). The community was an opportunity to learn with and from colleagues and there was a growing understanding of the acquisition of new knowledge, skills and competences. The members were engaging in opportunities to learn, share and engage in professional discussions with their colleagues. These opportunities were identified as valuable and, in some cases, as crucial for faculty who work in remote locations and who do not have many opportunities to participate in professional learning activities.

In some sub-communities, especially Liberia and Nicoya, the participants have benefitted from working closer to their colleagues, they learned to work as a community, they engaged in supporting each other and in sharing expectations and experiences.

Literature also suggests (Layne, Froyd, Simpson, Caso, & Merton, 2004; Loughran, 2014; Zhang & Liu, 2019) that providing faculty with opportunities to explore, discuss and reflect about their teaching conceptions and practice, enabled them to become less resistant towards different pedagogical approaches. The participants in this study were required to think and act, in some depth, about their teaching over a 10 months' time frame. This is a much longer period than the regular PD processes, and it is considered, as also identified by Gallant (2000) that this longer period of engagement contributed to creating continuity in their learning through an ongoing, and incremental process. Table 5 shows how participants experienced the PD process, in terms of their learning.

Learning is a process that changes people. The central issue in learning is becoming a practitioner, not learning about practice (Wenger, 1998). A key outcome of learning, in the context of social learning, is a way of being, of being a type of person in a specific practice context, it is a process of reconstructing identity (Kirkup, 2002; Warhurst, 2006). Through their participation in the community of practice, sharing experiences and negotiating meaning as they were developing new skills to integrate technology into their teaching, and for incorporating new pedagogical approaches,, the community members gradually shifted from the periphery of the practice to the establishment of an identity in the core of the community.

Table 5. Learning in the PD process

	Totally Agree	Agree	Disagree	Totally Disagree	NR
The PD process allows me to develop skills to integrate technology into my teaching practice	41.7	50.0	8.3	0	0
The PD process allows me to develop skills for incorporating new pedagogical approaches in my teaching practice	75.0	8.3	16.7	0	0
What I have learned is applicable to my academic work	83.3	0	16.7	0	0
The development of the pedagogical innovation allows me to apply what I learn in the PD process	66.7	25.0	8.3	0	0

(Coto, 2014)

Being part of "something bigger" was a strong motivation for most faculty, they feel connected to others and feel that they are contributing to improve teaching practice at institutional level. However, a few of the participants disagree on the learning experience regarding new pedagogical approaches and the application to their academic work. There may be several explanations. However, one explanation may be that the focus on the online tools took up too much attention and the design for community engagement were so demanding related to their other academic obligations, that it was not efficient for them with respect to these dimensions. Figure 10 shows the tensions that emerged in the PD process

In summary, the community framework provided the participants with the necessary social interaction environment for collegial learning and dialogue. Their interaction allowed different perspectives on topics and issues and they found it interesting and supportive to interact in the group. In most cases, it appeared that their thinking and practice changed. Hence, even though the participants faced obstacles, they learned as a response to participating in the community, what can be considered as significant and meaningful learning for the development of their competence. Further they became capable of setting

Figure 10. Community learning

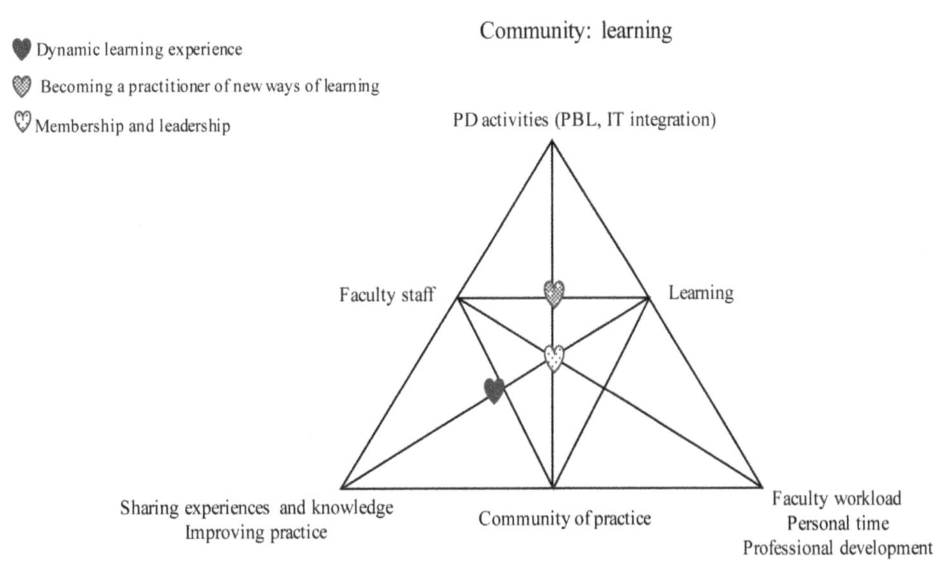

new pedagogical objectives and integrating PBL and ICT for student learning, and to carry out actions and operations to make it happen (Kaptelinin & A. Nardi, 2006). They succeeded in creating interventions in the classroom engaging the students in new ways of teaching and learning, and mastering ICT to a certain operative level to be able to communicate in online fora, using chat etc. As such the communities of practice approach is not only a productive PD approach, however, may influence the teaching and learning beyond the teachers CoP.

DISCUSSION OF THE FINDINGS: CHALLENGES AND TENSIONS

The PD model proposed in this study represented a multiple challenge for the participants. They were asked to do things that most of them were not used to doing. First, they had to revisit their beliefs and values about teaching; second, they had to engage in student-centered approaches (PBL), third, they had to work collaboratively; and fourth, most of this collaborative work took place via online technology. In navigating through all these challenges, the participants experienced problems. These tensions can be summarized in four broad categories: institutional structures (division of work), the institutional culture (rules), levels of engagement (differentiations within the community), and faculty' readiness (in the appropriation of tools and new pedagogy).

Institutional Structures (Division of Work)

Within the institutional structures, this study identified the following obstacles: lack of time and access to technology. Most of the participants in this study felt that their workload was so demanding that they could not do what they had to do in the community within reasonable time. Despite the efforts to make the PD program more manageable, the issues of time and workload remained a problem for many participants. The research literature (Chen et al., 2009; Ching & Hursh, 2014; Lock, 2006; Tsiotakis & Jimoyiannis, 2016) and the results of this study suggest that the establishment of extra and necessary time for continuous PD in a CoP approach is very difficult.

In a resource constraint setting, the lack of access to adequate technological resources is also another factor that affected the PD. 96% of the participants had computers at home, but only 65% of them had Internet access at home, so they depended on institutional facilities to participate in online activities. However, while the access to technology and the internet was fairly stable in some campuses, in other campuses, the participants experienced continuous problems with the access to the Internet. This influenced not only the individual faculty staff, but also the dynamic in the community, as access to the internet becomes a new boundary. A distributed learning CoP is deeply depending on stable and strong internet connectivity.

Institutional Culture (Rules)

The institutional culture in which the community is embedded can act as an obstacle to community development (Lock, 2006). In this study and despite the participants' motivation, the insular way in which many faculty members used to work affected the transition to a collaborative environment. It became evident that cross-institutional group work was difficult, and, to some extent, it diminished rather than strengthened the community cohesion. Another consequence of this trend towards individualism is that the faculty members do not have references to compare their experiences. They rarely know what happens in the classrooms of other colleagues. This study proposes that references are essential to convert abstract ideas about the quality of teaching in specific actions. To some extent, the community approach proposed by this study contributes to diminishing the problem of lack of references and examples of good practice.

These perspectives add complexity to designing for a community, because in order to be alive, a community needs the development of relationships, active participation and productive interactions among members. In line with Preece et al. (2004) the study found that for faculty to work in a collaborative way, a redefinition of the institutional culture is needed. The project demonstrated that faculty finds it very valuable and meaningful to learn new skills by participating in a community of practice. However, for this to become an institutional strategy, this approach should be backed up and reified in the rules and policies of the institution. How can the institution value and facilitate a community orientation? How to develop policies and incentives to support a community of practice approach. For the transition to occur, it is vital that the faculty receive support and incentives from the institution (MacPhail et al., 2014; Patton & Parker, 2017; Warhurst, 2006).

Levels of Engagement

Another tension that was identified by the study as an obstacle for the PD process was the levels of engagement in the learning activities. This study has found that the ways in which the faculty participated and the level of sophistication of their contribution varied considerably from one to another. The core members tended to be the ones who were fully engaged in their PD, despite other work activities. The other participants showed difficulty maintaining a regular participation, so, in some cases they failed to become active members of the community. Those who felt less comfortable with technology also found that the time needed to resolve technical issues was disappointing, which contributed to their peripheral position in the process.

There were also differences in the responses of the members to the learning activities, especially in the discussion forums. The core and most active participants tended to write longer and more complex ideas, while less-active and peripheral members wrote shorter and simpler contributions, although there were exceptions. Although these differences were acceptable within the spirit of communities of practice, findings show that this can be problematic in the context of faculty PD processes. The complex and extensive contributions of some members tended to create feelings of insecurity and inadequacy in some of the less active participants. This contrast in the levels of participation must be handled sensitively in order to avoid serious damage to community cohesion.

Although peripheral participation is considered legitimate (Lave & Wenger, 1991; Palloff & Pratt, 2005; Wenger, 1998), and to some extent, it was agreed among UNA participants that it was valid for them to interact at different levels, depending on particular circumstances, in the dynamics of building a community, the lack of participation did have some effect. In the community, continuously passive participants were viewed as non-contributors and became a source of frustration for the visibly active participants. The community as a unit needed active participants to add value for all members in order to support learning, engagement, and the long-term sustainability of the community. In an online community, engagement as active participation is easier to recognize as the online communication traces the engagement, and this may establish new boundaries in the community. In the institutional strategy for supporting COPs this issue of levels of engagements must be addressed.

Faculty' Readiness

The findings show that face-to-face sessions of any sort were found very valuable by the participants in building relationships as well as in working through technical issues. Many of the participants had a lack of confidence in the use of technology, and this situation could even be worst in a resource constraint setting. The study addressed this gap through the initial training and ongoing support of the facilitator. However, for some faculty, the learning curve was so long and so frustrating that they gave up the community after two or three months of belonging to it.

Several authors (Ching & Hursh, 2014; Eib, 2002; Killion, 2000; Salmon, 2004; Unwin, 2015), argue that in designing distributed communities of practice, it cannot be assumed that the faculty staff are familiar with online participation. From the quality dialogues that took place in the workshops it was evident that it was necessary to foster a culture of online communication and learning among participants. Some of them did not feel fully comfortable with online communication. The behavior of those members in the online part of the PD program was an indicator that additional conditions were necessary before they were able to significantly interact online. In order to participate effectively in an online environment, the faculty need to be self-motivated, self-confident, have the required technological and communicative skills, and not least a supportive and efficient virtual infrastructure However, we also need to acknowledge, that what it means to be self-confident vary among the participants. The institutions must therefore consider how to support faculty to become self-confident in these new forms of communication and learning.

REFLECTIONS ON THE DESIGN OF THE PROFESSIONAL DEVELOPMENT PROGRAM

In the following, we present and discuss the principles around the four dualities and the tensions that emerged in the findings.

Duality: Participation and Reification

From the analysis it could be seen that the structures of participation chosen in the design were both an incentive and a hindrance to participation. All participants acknowledge the importance of face-to-face activities, even for many of them it was time-consuming to attend, while some of the participants expressed a need for more training especially on how to use the virtual learning environment. Among factors that diminished online participation were time, technical competences and the lack of a culture of online learning and communication, as well as a low bandwidth in some locations. However, what was stressed again and again was the institutional reification and lack of time allocated for really engaging in the TPD and the community building.

The most important and challenging reification made by the participants was to design a pedagogical innovation. This reification was a central facility for supporting engagement, imagination and alignment (Wenger, 1998). It allowed them to create alternative teaching/learning scenarios, envisioning new trajectories and, in many cases, pushing their own boundaries. The reification of the members' learning processes in an educational project seems highly satisfactory. This process required the full commitment of the participants and the integration of their own knowledge and experiences, and in that sense, as has also been identified by Ollila and Simpson (2004) they gained more opportunities for PD than in other less demanding activities - such as readings. However, the first organization of the interventions in groups across the regional campuses was an example of reification, which hinders participation. And for some members it needed a lot of repair work to get them back to the community approach.

Duality: Designed and Emergent

During the intervention, there was a constant interplay between the theoretical ideas and the practical requirements for designing a situation viable in the UNA context. Furthermore, the chosen method for this investigation –design-based research- supports the recursive movement between the theoretical ideas and the practical requirements. Dealing with institutional resources (mainly the facilitator's availability of time) as well as with the participants' schedules, needs, expectations and their competences (technical and cultural) to communicate through technology, drove us to refine the design and revisit our understanding of the underlying theories. So, one learning to draw is the need to plan for a continuous adjustment of the initial design, which naturally comes from the transformation of the learning environment as it was experimented for the faculty within the institutional context.

Duality: Local and Global

PD must be aligned with the institutional mission and should promote institution-wide dialogues (Sorcinelli, Austin, Eddy, & Beach, 2006). A CoP relates with the rest of the world, through creating continuities across boundaries. The design in this study encouraged the exchange of knowledge and experiences among participants at two levels: locally in the same campus and globally with faculty from other regional campuses at UNA. It is very distinct that the exchange of knowledgeability among members that came from different local communities promoted learning not only at the individual level but also for the whole community. The pedagogical innovations designed, implemented and evaluated by the participants (in diverse contexts, condition, targets group, and areas of knowledge) were a boundary object that created continuities across boundaries and allowed the expanding of knowledge. They also enforced UNA's policies about the use of ICT in teaching and about a pedagogical model focused in a student-centered and lifelong learning approach, and therefore in fact not only aligned to the institutional mission (Sorcinelli et al., 2006), but also pushed for a possible direction.

The local and global duality can also be a duality between the ongoing practice and global views on the new methodologies and theories. For sure the pedagogical design based on the principles of CoP, PBL and blended learning *"disturbed"* the local practices, however overall seen, the community approach supported a respectful, trustful and caring environment which supported the individual faculty staff to engage, learn and belong in a situated manner possible for him/her with respect to other obligations, skills and engagement.

Duality: Identification and Negotiability

The initial source of participants' identification with the community was the domain of the community itself. All faculty staff that accepted the invitation to be part of the community was eager to innovate their practice. In this respect, the community offered an opportunity to envision possible futures trajectories within the university. As well, the cultivation of the distributed CoP as part of a model for PD was conceived as a strategic and innovative initiative within the university. For the participants, this was important, the members were proud of belonging to the community; they considered themselves as pioneers and leaders who were contributing to changing institutional teaching practices.

Ollila and Simpson (2004)) state that the connection between PD, identification and negotiability is strong. According to them, the members identify more with the community when they have more opportunities to negotiate its practice. However, not all participants had the same levels of participation in the renegotiation process. Poor or little participation in the online activities provoked the perception of an inability to contribute to the community, and consequently their feelings of ownership over the community's enterprise were weak. In conclusion, the community members assumed different levels of participation, the participants closer to the core of the community were able to identify with and develop a feeling of belonging to the community to a greater extent that those with a peripheral role. However, maybe an important reflection is, what makes members to core members of the community are not necessary equivalent with how well they handled the digital tools and the online communication, however a more subtle, dynamic and complex negotiation going on in the community also reflecting the individuals identification, engagement and belonging to the community.

Overall, the design principles behind the four dualities were productive, however a redesign may consider how to design for a greater flexibility and belonging in the "big group", and in the smaller working groups (project groups). Following the principles of community of practice, we should avoid forced working groups, however, develop flexible ways of establishing working groups based on the organic dynamics among the participants. The findings value face-to-face modality groups, however when the it-infrastructure becomes more elaborated in all campuses, it might support new working groups constellations. However, there is no doubt in the findings, that some face-to-face activities are urgent for a community of practice. Further, the findings support that the primary focus should still be on the "big group" in order to provide for an overall alive community (Wenger et al., 2002), where the negotiation of meaning and identity work can take place.

CONCLUSION

The central postulate of this study was that a CoP approach offers potential as an option for effective faculty PD. The community created the social context for collegial learning and dialogue in which faculty constructed an identity in relation to a new practice. It contributes to expanding professional and personal networks, fostering a culture of sharing among faculty and reducing isolation. It also provided a safe place to make mistakes, to experiment, and to explore, discuss, reflect and re-conceptualize their conceptions and values about teaching practice. It offered faculty learning opportunities of doing, belonging and becoming, transforming the process of learning in a process of identity formation and not just an accumulation of skills and information.

From the findings, it can be concluded that the impact of community membership on faculty members' learning was complex and provoked many tensions. It was different for each participant depending on their levels of participation, engagement, identification and empowerment to negotiate and shape the practice. However, in general, belonging to the community helped the faculty develop a sense of expertise as they participated in peer-to-peer learning. Learning and change did take place and faculty members became more knowledgeable of their practice and gained an impact on the institutional practices. Overall, the theory of communities of practice and the way Coto (2010) has conceptualized and applied the theories of social and situated learning in a specific context have provided detailed insights and understandings into how professional teacher development and learning is a participatory process that involves more than acquiring skills and detached knowledge. As such the findings support the research which stresses that PD programs must address changes in beliefs, knowledge, and habits of practice, in order to achieve changes in the quality of teaching and learning (Gibbs & Coffey, 2004; Hadar & Brody, 2010; Light & Calkins, 2008; MacPhail et al., 2014; Patton & Parker, 2017; Prenger et al., 2017; Smyth, 2003). And further, that COPs provide a safe and trustworthy base for dealing with the interwoven dimensions of theory and practice through socially mediated reflections and constructions.

Further, the findings support that a community of practice model may help to overcome the shortcomings of the traditional PD strategies of event-based, one-hit training workshops, and transmission from experts (sometimes consultants) to faculty as described by Lock (2006) and Schlager & Fusco (2004). A community model is favoring several principles:

- A long-term engagement and a gradual development and transformation of the learning culture;
- Interwoven training, learning, application and not least ownership
- Acquiring new skills through a process of identity building
- Building on each other member as experts and mutual participation
- Developing digital scholarship through identification and negotiability
- Learning from outside and linking to the global communities through theories and experts, however reflecting and localizing these inputs in their context;

The study confirms the community of practice as a strong and productive approach to PD, which integrate PD as continuing learning in the everyday practice of a community. To sustain the model, institutions should reflect and develop strategies on how to facilitate for PD as a community of practice. These strategies should reflect on the four dualities as discussed above:

- Participation and reification
- Designed and emergent
- Local and global
- Identification and negotiability

The four pairs of dualities are linked and interdependent. In order to apply this approach in other contexts, the designers and initiators must reflect upon the dualities and if they can be deployed and appropriated within the culture of the given institution in a balanced and dynamic manner. Can and will the institution support this dynamic and emerging approach of participation and reification, designed and emerging?, how to balance the design to achieve the professional development goals while it is embedded in the informal and voluntary nature of participation in a community?, should a professional development model let members define the power and direction of the community, or should we design more structured ways of organization and learning for the sake of the professional development goals?. And do the participants agree to contribute to and to engage in the collaborative participation in a community, and are they willing to contribute to and give to the community along with learning from peers based on principles of mutual learning, trust, identification and engagement? And, are they willing (both peers, facilitators and the institution) to allow and support for the different levels of engagement that the participants showed in this study?. Do they allow members to engage in the learning activities in very different levels without diminishing the learning outcomes for the whole community? And, whether it is possible to offer different learning pathways for participants without diminishing the sense of shared community.

On a more tangible level, the designers of the PD program and the institution must reflect upon the conditions for the faculty staff for participating and engaging in the program. How to compensate for them, so they get time to engage with the community? How to ensure that all in the community have a fair access to the use of digital tools and the internet? And finally, how to make it possible to provide extra resources and situated help to the ones who are not used to working in an online and technology rich environment? If these conditions can be met, the CoP approach might be a promising approach to teacher professional learning as it provides for "the experience of doing, becoming, and belonging".

REFERENCES

Adams, S., Brown, M., Dahlstrom, E., Davies, A., DePaul, K., Diaz, V., & Pomerantz, J. (2018). *NMC Horizon Report: 2018 Higher Education Edition*. Louisville, CO: EDUCAUSE.

Barab, S., & Squire, K. (2004). Design-Based Research: Putting a Stake in the Ground. *Journal of the Learning Sciences*, *13*(1), 1–14. doi:10.120715327809jls1301_1

Barab, S. A., Baek, E., Schatz, S., Scheckler, R., & Moore, J. (2008). Illuminating the Braids of Change in a Web-Supported Community: A Design Experiment by Another Name. In A. Kelly, R. Lesh, & J. Baek (Eds.), Handbook of Design Research Methods in Education: Innovations in Science, Technology, Engineering, and Mathematics Learning and Teaching. London, UK: Routledge.

Barab, S. A., Kling, R., & Gray, J. H. (2004). *Designing for virtual communities in the service of learning*. New York, NY: Cambridge University Press. doi:10.1017/CBO9780511805080

Brosnan, K., & Burgess, R. (2003). Web based continuing professional development - a learning architecture approach. *Journal of Workplace Learning*, *15*(1), 24–33. doi:10.1108/13665620310458794

Byrk, A. (2016). Accelerating how we learn to improve. *Educational Researcher*, *44*(9), 467–477. doi:10.3102/0013189X15621543

Chen, Y., Chen, N.-S., & Tsai, C.-C. (2009). The use of online synchronous discussion for web-based professional development for teachers. *Learning with ICT: New Perspectives on Help Seeking and Information Searching*, *53*(4), 1155–1166. doi:10.1016/j.compedu.2009.05.026

Ching, C. C., & Hursh, A. W. (2014). Peer modeling and innovation adoption among teachers in online professional development. *Computers & Education*, *73*, 72–82. doi:10.1016/j.compedu.2013.12.011

Coto, M. (2010). *Designing for Change in University Teaching Practices. The case of UNAgora: A community of Practice Approach to Facilitate University Teacher Professional Development in ICT and Project-Oriented Problem Pedagogy.* (Doctoral dissertation). Aalborg Universitet, Institut for Kommunikation, Aalborg, Denmark.

Coto, M. (2014). A Distributed Community of Practice to Facilitate Communication, Collaboration, and Learning among Faculty. In C. N. Stevenson, & J. C. Bauer (Eds.), *Building Online Communities in Higher Education Institutions: Creating Collaborative Experience* (pp. 327–368). doi:10.4018/978-1-4666-5178-4.ch018

Coto, M., & Dirckinck-Holmfeld, L. (2008). Facilitating Communities of Practice in Teacher Professional Development. In Proceedings of the 6th International Conference on Networked Learning. Greece: Lancaster University. Retrieved from http://www.networkedlearningconference.org.uk/abstracts/Coto.htm

Crawford, K. (2008). Continuing professional development in higher education: The academic perspective. *The International Journal for Academic Development*, *13*(2), 141–146. doi:10.1080/13601440802076657

Design-Based Research Collective. (2003). Design-Based Research: An Emerging Paradigm for Educational Inquiry. *Educational Researcher*, *32*(1), 5–8. doi:10.3102/0013189X032001005

Dirckinck-Holmfeld, L., Jones, C., & Lindström, B. (2009). Analysing Networked Learning Practices in Higher Education and Continuing Professional Development. Rotterdam, The Netherlands: Sense Publishers.

Eib, B. J. (2002). Online learning and professional development. *Principal Leadership*, *3*, 61–64.

Engeström, Y. (1987). Learning by Expanding - an activity theoretical approach to developmental research. Helsinki, Finland: Orienta-konsultit. Retrieved from http://communication.ucsd.edu/MCA/Paper/Engestrom/expanding/toc.htm

Engeström, Y. (2001). Expansive Learning at Work: Toward an activity theoretical reconceptualization. *Journal of Education and Work*, *14*(1), 133–156. doi:10.1080/13639080020028747

Engeström, Y. (2014). Learning by expanding. Cambridge, UK: Cambridge University Press. doi:10.1017/CBO9781139814744

Gallant, G. (2000). Professional development for Web-based teaching: Overcoming innocence and resistance. In E. J. Burge (Ed.), *New directions for adult and continuing education* (pp. 69–78). San Francisco, CA: Jossey-Bass. doi:10.1002/ace.8807

Gibbs, G., & Coffey, M. (2004). The impact of training on university teachers on their teaching skills, their approach to teaching and the approach to learning of their students, 5 (1) 87-100. *Active Learning in Higher Education*, *5*, 87–100. doi:10.1177/1469787404040463

González, G., & Skultety, L. (2018). Teacher learning in a combined professional development intervention. *Teaching and Teacher Education*, *71*, 341–354. doi:10.1016/j.tate.2018.02.003

Goodyear, P. Jones, C., Asensio, M., Hodgson, V., & Steeples, C. (2001). Effective networked learning in higher education: notes and guidelines. Lancaster, UK: Centre for Studies in Advanced Learning Technology. Lancaster University.

Granovetter, M. (1983). *The strength of weak ties: A network theory revisited.*

Hadar, L., & Brody, D. (2010). From isolation to symphonic harmony: Building a professional development community among teacher educators. *Teaching and Teacher Education*, *26*(8), 1641–1651. doi:10.1016/j.tate.2010.06.015

Kaptelinin, V., & Nardi, A. B. (2006). Acting with Technology: Activity Theory and Interaction Design. In First Monday, 12, p. 345). doi:10.5210/fm.v12i4.1772

Killion, J. (2000). Logon to learn: To reap benefits of online staff development, ask the right questions. *Journal of Staff Development*, 48–53.

King, K. P. (2003). Learning the New Technologies: Strategies for Success. *New Directions for Adult and Continuing Education*, *98*(98), 49–57. doi:10.1002/ace.99

Kirkup, G. (2002). Identity, community and distributed learning. In M. R. Lear, & K. Nicholl (Eds.), *Distributed learning: Social and cultural approaches to practice* (pp. 182–195). London, UK: Routledge-Falmer.

Lantz-Andersson, A., Lundin, M., & Selwyn, N. (2018). Twenty years of online teacher communities: A systematic review of formally-organized and informally-developed professional learning groups. *Teaching and Teacher Education*, *75*, 302–315. doi:10.1016/j.tate.2018.07.008

Lave, J., & Wenger, E. (1991). *Situated learning: legitimate peripheral participation*. Retrieved from http://www.loc.gov/catdir/description/cam024/91010450.html http://www.loc.gov/catdir/enhancements/fy0702/91010450-t.html

Lawler, P. A., & King, K. P. (2001). *Refocusing faculty development: The view from an adult learning perspective*. Presented at the Pennsylvania Adult and Continuing Education Research Conference

Layne, J., Froyd, J., Simpson, N., Caso, R., & Merton, P. (2004). *Understanding and improving faculty professional development in teaching*. Presented at the 34th ASEE/IEEE Frontiers in Education Conference. 10.1109/FIE.2004.1408683

Light, G., & Calkins, S. (2008). The experience of faculty development: Patterns of variation in conceptions of teaching. *The International Journal for Academic Development*, *13*(1), 27–40. doi:10.1080/13601440701860227

Lock, J. V. (2006). A new image: Online Communities to Facilitate Teacher Professional Development. *Journal of Technology and Teacher Education*, *14*, 663–678.

Loughran, J. (2014). Professionally Developing as a Teacher Educator. *Journal of Teacher Education*, *65*(4), 271–283. doi:10.1177/0022487114533386

MacDonald, J., Atkin, W., Daugherity, F., Fox, H., MacGillivray, A., Reeves- Lipscomb, D., & Uthailertaroon, P. (2003). *Let's get more positive about the term "lurker."*

Macià, M., & García, I. (2016). Informal online communities and networks as a source of teacher professional development: A review. *Teaching and Teacher Education*, *55*, 291–307. doi:10.1016/j.tate.2016.01.021

MacPhail, A., Patton, K., Parker, M., & Tannehill, D. (2014). Leading by Example: Teacher Educators' Professional Learning Through Communities of Practice. *Quest*, *66*(1), 39–56. doi:10.1080/00336297.2013.826139

Ödalen, J., Brommesson, D., Erlingsson, G. Ó., Schaffer, J. K., & Fogelgren, M. (2019). Teaching university teachers to become better teachers: The effects of pedagogical training courses at six Swedish universities. *Higher Education Research & Development*, *38*(2), 339–353. doi:10.1080/07294360.2018.1512955

Ollila, M., & Simpson, A. (2004). Dimensions of Design: A Comparison of Professional Development in Two On-Line Learning Communities. *Proceedings of the IEEE International Conference on Advanced Learning Technologies*, 271–275. 10.1109/ICALT.2004.1357417

Palloff, R., & Pratt, K. (2005). *Online learning communities revisited.* Presented at the 21st Annual Conference on Distance Teaching and Learning.

Patton, K., & Parker, M. (2017). Teacher education communities of practice: More than a culture of collaboration. *Teaching and Teacher Education*, *67*, 351–360. doi:10.1016/j.tate.2017.06.013

Powell, C. G., & Bodur, Y. (2019). Teachers' perceptions of an online professional development experience: Implications for a design and implementation framework. *Teaching and Teacher Education*, *77*, 19–30. doi:10.1016/j.tate.2018.09.004

Preece, J., Nonnecke, B., & Andrews, D. (2004). The top 5 reasons for lurking: Improving community experiences for everyone. *Computers in Human Behavior*, *20*(2), 201–223. doi:10.1016/j.chb.2003.10.015

Prenger, R., Poortman, C. L., & Handelzalts, A. (2017). Factors influencing teachers' professional development in networked professional learning communities. *Teaching and Teacher Education*, *68*, 77–90. doi:10.1016/j.tate.2017.08.014

Reeves, T. C. (2006). Design Research from a Technology Perspective. In J. van den Akker, K. Gravemeijer, S. McKenney, & N. Nieveen (Eds.), *Educational Design Research* (pp. 52–66). London, UK: Routledge.

Salmon, G. (2004). E-moderating. The key to teaching and learning online (2nd ed.). Abingdon-on-Thames, UK: Routledge Falmer. doi:10.4324/9780203465424

Sandoval, W., & Bell, P. (2004). Design-Based Research Methods for Studying Learning in Context: Introduction. *Educational Psychologist*, *39*(4), 199–201. doi:10.120715326985ep3904_1

Sannino, A., & Engeström, Y. (2018). Cultural-historical activity theory. *Cultural-historical Psychology*, *14*(3), 43–56. doi:10.17759/chp.2018140305

Schlager, M. S., & Fusco, J. (2004). Teacher professional development, technology, and communities of practice: Are we putting the cart before the horse? In S. Barab, R. Klin, & J. Gray (Eds.), *Designing for Virtual Communities in the Service of Learning*. Cambridge, MA: Cambridge University Press. doi:10.1017/CBO9780511805080.009

Schlager, M. S., Fusco, J., & Schank, P. (2002). Evolution of an On-line Education Community of Practice. In K. A. Renninger, & W. Shumar (Eds.), Building virtual communities: Learning and change in cyberspace (pp. 129–158). New York, NY: Cambridge University Press. doi:10.1017/CBO9780511606373.010

Sherer, P. D., Shea, T. P., & Kristensen, E. (2003). Online Communities of Practice: A Catalyst for Faculty Development. *Innovative Higher Education*, *27*(3), 183–194. doi:10.1023/A:1022355226924

Smyth, R. (2003). Concepts of Change: Enhancing the Practice of Academic Staff Development in Higher Education. *The International Journal for Academic Development*, *8*(1-2), 51–60. doi:10.1080/1360144042000277937

Sorcinelli, M. D., Austin, A. E., Eddy, P. L., & Beach, A. L. (2006). Creating the Future of Faculty Development: Learning From the Past, Understanding the Future. Bolton, MA: Anker Publishing Co.

Tsiotakis, P., & Jimoyiannis, A. (2016). Critical factors towards analysing teachers' presence in on-line learning communities. *The Internet and Higher Education*, *28*, 45–58. doi:10.1016/j.iheduc.2015.09.002

Unwin, A. (2015). Developing new teacher inquiry and criticality: The role of online discussions. *British Journal of Educational Technology*, *46*(6), 1214–1222. doi:10.1111/bjet.12194

Wake, J. D., Dysthe, O., & Mjelstad, S. (2007). New and Changing Teacher Roles in Higher Education in a Digital Age. *Journal of Educational Technology & Society*, *10*, 40–51.

Wall, J. (2013). *A Framework for Academic Professional Development in Higher Education*.

Wang, X., Lu, W., Ester, M., Wang, C., & Chen, C. (2016). Social Recommendation with Strong and Weak Ties. *Proceedings of the 25th ACM International on Conference on Information and Knowledge Management*, 5–14. 10.1145/2983323.2983701

Warhurst, R. P. (2006). "We Really Felt Part of Something": Participatory learning among peers within a university teaching-development community of practice. *The International Journal for Academic Development*, *11*(2), 111–122. doi:10.1080/13601440600924462

Wenger, E. (1998). *Communities of practice : learning, meaning, and identity*. Retrieved from http://www.loc.gov/catdir/description/cam029/98202423.html http://www.loc.gov/catdir/toc/cam026/98202423.html

Wenger, E., McDermott, R. A., & Snyder, W. (2002). *Cultivating communities of practice : a guide to managing knowledge*. Retrieved from http://edrev.asu.edu/reviews/rev405.htm

Wing Lai, K., Pratt, K., Anderson, M., & Stigter, J. (2006). *Literature Review and Synthesis: Online Communities of Practice*. Dunedin, New Zealand: Faculty of Education, University of Otago.

Zhang, S., & Liu, Q. (2019). Investigating the relationships among teachers' motivational beliefs, motivational regulation, and their learning engagement in online professional learning communities. *Computers & Education*, *134*, 145–155. doi:10.1016/j.compedu.2019.02.013

ADDITIONAL READING

Booth, S. E. (2012). Cultivating knowledge sharing and trust in online communities for educators. *Journal of Educational Computing Research*, *47*(1), 1–31. doi:10.2190/EC.47.1.a

Britt, V. G., & Paulus, T. (2016). Beyond the four walls of my building: A case study of #edchat as a community of practice. *American Journal of Distance Education*, *30*(1), 48–59. doi:10.1080/08923647.2016.1119609

Brown, R., & Munger, K. (2010). Learning together in cyberspace: Collaborative dialogue in a virtual network of educators. *Journal of Technology and Teacher Education*, *18*(4), 541–571.

Coutinho, C. P., & Lisboa, E. S. (2013). Social networks as spaces for informal teacher professional development: Challenges and opportunities. *International Journal of Web Based Communities*, *9*(2), 199–211. doi:10.1504/IJWBC.2013.053244

El-Hani, C. N., & Greca, I. M. (2013). ComPratica: A virtual community of practice for promoting biology teachers' professional development in Brazil. *Research in Science Education*, *43*(4), 1327–1359. doi:10.100711165-012-9306-1

Goodyear, V. A., Casey, A., & Kirk, D. (2014). Tweet me, message me, like me: Using social media to facilitate pedagogical change within an emerging community of practice. Sport, Education and Society, 19(7), 927e943. . doi:10.1080/13573322.2013.858624

Mackey, J., & Evans, T. (2011). Interconnecting networks of practice for professional learning. *The International Review of Research in Open and Distributed Learning*, *12*(3), 1–18. doi:10.19173/irrodl.v12i3.873

Smith, S. U., Hayes, S., & Shea, P. (2017). A critical review of the use of Wenger's Community of Practice (CoP) theoretical framework in online and blended learning research, 2000-2014. *Online Learning*, *21*(1), 209–237. doi:10.24059/olj.v21i1.963

Tseng, F.-C., & Kuo, F.-Y. (2014). A study of social participation and knowledge sharing in the teachers' online professional community of practice. *Computers & Education*, *72*, 37–47. doi:10.1016/j.compedu.2013.10.005

KEY TERMS AND DEFINITIONS

Communities of Practice: A group of people who share an interest and are willing to invest time and effort to learn and to share experiences and ways to improve their practice.

Distributed Community of Practice: A community of practice that uses online means and face-to-face meetings for communication.

Dualities: A pair of elements that are present in different degrees, it could be understood as a creative tension between the elements. In terms of design for learning, a duality can provide room for innovation and change.

Faculty Professional Development: A process through which faculty receive formal and informal training.

Identity Formation: In the context of a community of practice, identity formation is an integrated component of learning. It is constructed through processes of engagement in practice and negotiation of meaning.

Online Participation: Includes participation in activities that take place through online means, such as chats, blog reflection, discussion forums, and group work.

Chapter 8
Online Teaching and Learning in Higher Education Settings:
Focus on Team Effectiveness

Mette L. Baran
Cardinal Stritch University, USA

Janice E. Jones
Cardinal Stritch University, USA

ABSTRACT

This chapter intends to answer the question, "What are some guidelines for working effectively in virtual teams?" To further advance existing literature, the authors utilized a qualitative phenomenological approach with a randomly-sampled group of seven students who had completed master's-level education courses that were conducted in an online format at a private Midwestern University. Students were halfway through their course completion at the time of data collection. In addition, a random sample of one program administrator and four faculty members were interviewed. Specifically, students who enrolled in online Master's in Education courses are required to work in study teams to complete a certain portion of the course work. Study teams can often be difficult to navigate in person and with the added dimension that a virtual experience brings to developing trusting, successful working relationships, different working guidelines are needed. Findings revealed that managerial and social aspects of online learning and teaching were critical for online students' success.

DOI: 10.4018/978-1-5225-9814-5.ch008

INTRODUCTION

"The single most important factor, the substrate, which will determine the success (or failure), of any organization in the 21st Century: TRUST." – Warren Bennis

Adult learners once considered a non-traditional population in higher education have established a firm normalcy. The research of Knowles (1980) proposes that adult learners are motivated by learning experiences that are directly applicable to their lives, tend to be self-directed, and want to feel that they have a definite sense of purpose in a learning experience. These foundational elements of adult learning are well-documented and understood by successful adult learning practitioners. The authors use Chao's (2009) definition of an adult learner as someone who "is a self-directed person, 24 years of age and above whose engagement and readiness to learn is based on the immediate applicability to the development tasks of his/her social role incorporating his/her reservoir of experience" (p. 906).

What is lesser known is how adult learners thrive in an online learning environment. As online learning expanded in higher education, much of the research emphasis focused on the undergraduate experience, as well as the experience of students who re typically not considered adult learners (students ranging in age from 18-22). Early research into the experiences of adult learners in online environment found less than promising results. Adult students tended to be less academically successful in online learning, were retained at a lower rate than their non-adult peers and found online learning to be a less attractive learning option.

The authors investigate how these adult online students finding success? What strategies are instructors using to offer students the best chance at success in this learning environment?

For the sake of this chapter, the term "adult learning environment" will reference any adult learning experience purposely designed to occur in the face-to-face classroom environment, a blended format with instructor providing instruction prior to the classroom experience (e.g. flipped teaching model), or a synchronous or asynchronous online format as frequently found in distance learning. The adult learning environment term seeks to encompass the number of learning modalities adults engage in today.

The new normal in business and education today is using technology to aid colleagues and students communicating and working together collaborative in virtual teams to complete tasks. Over 80% of all businesses today utilize virtual collaboration as they compete in a fast-paced global marketplace. Virtual meeting and team collaboration thus become more evident and imperative. In 2006, more than half of all higher education organizations offer online courses (Hoffman, 2006). This landscape has changed dramatically over the last decade. Allen and Seaman (2016) noted that as online learning has proliferated, so has its success among adult students. The 2015 Babson Survey of Online Learning reports a 3.9% increase in the number of distance education students, a slight increase over the 3.7% increase in 2014. In 2015, there were 5.8 million distance education students accounting for 28% of all enrolled students. Of this total, 2.85 million were taking all their coursework toward a degree at a distance; while 2.97 million were taking some, but not all their courses at a distance (p. 4).

Indeed, the online format is one of the most popular formats for adult learners, ranking third in preference for students at private institutions. According the 2015 *Noel-Levitz Adult Learner Marketing and Recruitment Practices Benchmarking Report* Among private institutions with adult programs, online or blended formats are in place at over 60% percent of those institutions. Further, The Western Interstate

Commission for Higher Education Cooperative for Educational Technologies (WCET) reflects that 28% of all college students now take at least one distance education course, and that 14% of all higher education students took all their courses exclusively at a distance (Poulin & Straut, 2015). They further note that 28% of students enrolled in at least one of their courses via distance education in the fall of 2014.

These reports show that distance education enrollments continue to grow, even in the face of declining overall higher education enrollments. Public institutions continue to enroll the largest portion of distance education students, with 72.7% of undergraduate and 38.7% of graduate-level distance students. While all types of institutions offer online learning, "Public institutions represented nearly three quarters of all fall 2014 enrollments (72%) (Allen & Seaman, 2016, p. 8).

Higher education institutions must become mindful of designing online degree programs that aid the communication and collaboration between students and assist in the virtual maneuver of the online learning experience as online learning allows for rich student interactions. They also need to teach students how to learn online (Pallof & Pratt, 2001). Furthermore, course designers need to pay attention to the importance of social constructivism in online learning. Learning is a social activity. Meaning is constructed through interaction and communications with others, so collaboration is needed to build knowledge in online learning communities. Students, faculty, and program administrators are grappling with learning teams in the online environment. As online course developers try to replicate the best practices of traditional classrooms, the asynchronous technology of the Internet has added great capability while also increasing the confusion that distance in space and time can add to the learning process.

This chapter will address what is needed to create successful virtual teams. More importantly, this chapter will address this from the unique vantage points of the three constituents, that of: the student, administration, and faculty. Utilizing a qualitative research approach allows the voice of the participant to be heard; sharing stories of successes and struggles though in-depth interviews. Addressing this issue from the three stake holders added a richness and depth to the chapter and the resulting literature base. First the authors discuss the overview of the program where this research study was conducted. Detailed discussion of Professional Learning Theory and Communities of Practice in Higher Education, Online Learning Community, Adult Learning Theory, Effective Virtual Teams, Trust and Key Components of Trust, Achieving Trusting Relationships in Virtual Teams, Ethnocentrism, and The Role of the Instructor in Virtual Teams, then follow.

BACKGROUND

Overview of Program

The educational program where the study was conducted is a Master's in Education Program (MEL). Students are appointed to teams based on various assignments. Each student will be assigned to a minimum of two teams per course and this is interchangeable from course to course. Students have no control over who their team members will be, and each assignment only lasts for a maximum of two weeks. This means that students need to be able to connect quickly and learn to collaborate and communicate in an efficient way in order to complete small group assignments. These typically consist of an assignment that requires a shared response for assessment by the instructor. Typically, these are case studies that require a common analysis and shared oral and/or written response. Teams of students work together and complete these projects using typical course management tools such as an electronic discussion forum and email messages or telephone conferencing. The learning environment is strictly online. Students use printed textbooks and each course has its own website. There is a full-time administrator of the online program as well as a web page coordinator. Instructors are either part-or full time, many teach the courses that they designed.

REVIEW OF THE LITERATURE

Professional Learning Communities

While Professional Learning Communities (PLCs) were first developed and researched in the K12 educational systems, the concept can be applied to ensure adults. The focus of PLCs on the three principles of learning, collaboration, and results (DuFour & Eaker, 1998; DuFour, Eaker, & Dufour, 2005) relate directly to the essential elements of adult learning as defined in by Malcom Knowles' principles of andragogy, or adult learning theory: self-concept, adult learning experience, readiness, orientation, and motivation (Knowles, 1980). Just as classrooms of adult learners today need new ways of engaging students through effective instructional practices that activate learning, PLCs' are designed to engage participants in the work that will lead to organizational successes. Teaching principles designed by instructors must be carefully planned and delivered in order to lead to successful learning by adults. Whatever the level of PLC dimensions in an organization, the use of PLCs in the adult learning environment is a system thinking approach towards teaching and learning that recognizes the interconnectedness of the experiences of individuals in groups and organizations and how this influences future experiences for participants.

The PLC principles of learning, collaboration, and results fit well with not only what adult learners bring to the classroom but also what the adult learners can carry back to their organizations in terms of creating learning communities. Like organizations, adult learning environments that use PLCs must be places where all learners' "commitment and capacity" must be present. This further assumes the change in the role of the instructor from the "grand strategist" to a facilitator of the learning process. This shift of the instructor's role, as also described in other parts of this chapter in terms of establishing trust is part of a change process that has been influencing adult learning throughout the last part of the twentieth century and well into this century.

Learning Communities in Higher Education

The theory of PLCs also connects to the work of thinkers such as Dewey, Thorndike, Bobbit, and Tyler. These theorists shaped the learning environments through the nineteenth and twentieth century and their work connect with Knowles' principles of andragogy. For example, the experiential learning theory and behavioral learning theory of these thinkers exists in the tenants of PLCs, including the idea of a community of learners. These communities in the adult learning environment, are arguably appealing to the adult learning seeking new knowledge and skills based upon the principles espoused by Knowles of prior experience, problem solving, and motivation. The emergence of learning communities is indeed an interesting and recent pedagogical development in higher education.

The researchers define learning communities as, "Professional educators working collectively and purposefully to create and sustain a culture of learning for all students and adults" (Hipp & Huffman, 2010, p. 12). Additionally, various strategies have been developed to foster learning communities in an online setting. The objectives of lude communicating effectively, strengthening social ties, collaborating in small teams, establishing social networks, and collaborating in knowledge construction (Chang, Chen & Li, 2006; Jones & Issroff, 2005; Wang & Poole, 2004; Yang, Wang, Shen, & Han, 2007). However, online behaviors and roles that are fundamental to the functioning of online learning communities, however, have seldom been compared (Yang et al., 2007).

Online Learning Community

Students often do not control their access to other members of an online class, as that is typically an instructor's decision. However, when a course instructor chooses to organize class activities so online students can interact, then the Online learning communities (OLCs) are like traditional learning communities in many ways. Some of the greatest differences in communication (most often conducted via written word rather than via spoken words, the often-asynchronous nature of the collaboration, and access to the instructor. Hetland, Skogstad, Hetland, and Mikkelsen (2011) identify five central dimensions of a learning climate in their study of the relationship between leadership and learning in a work setting that are present in this organization to greater or lesser degree; the dimensions are "sufficient time to learn and perform, autonomy and responsibility, team style, opportunities to develop, and guidelines on how to do the job" (p. 15).

Motivating the Adult Learner (Adult Learning Theory)

Educators teaching adult learners need to know the concepts of the adult learning theory and be able to incorporate them into their teaching style. Malcolm Knowles (1913-1997) was an American educator who theorized adult education. He brought the term andragogy into use as a term associated with adult education. According Malcolm Knowles, andragogy is the art and science of adult learning, thus andragogy refers to any form of adult learning. (Kearsley, 2010). The term is like pedagogy, which involved teaching children. In Greek, the terms mean man-leading in comparison to child-leading, respectively. The German educator, Alexander Kapp, is attributed to be the first to use the term, andragogy in 1833.

Knowles (1984) gave adult learners 5 characteristics:

1. **Self-Concept**: As a person matures his self-concept moves from one of being a dependent personality toward one of being a self-directed human being
2. **Experience**: As a person matures, he accumulates a growing reservoir of experience that becomes an increasing resource for learning.
3. **Readiness to Learn**: As a person matures his readiness to learn becomes oriented increasingly to the developmental tasks of his social roles.
4. **Orientation to Learning**: As a person matures his time perspective changes from one of postponed application of knowledge to immediacy of application, and accordingly his orientation toward learning shifts from one of subject-centeredness to one of problem centeredness.
5. **Motivation to Learn**: As a person matures the motivation to learn is internal. (p. 12).

Also, according to Knowles (1984) there are four principles that are applied to adult learning:

1. Adults need to be involved in the planning and evaluation of their instruction.
2. Experience (including mistakes) provides the basis for learning activities.
3. Adults are most interested in learning subjects that have immediate relevance to their job or personal life.
4. Adult learning is problem-centered rather than content-oriented. (Kearsley, 2010)

Educators need to become *facilitators* of adult education, helping the adult learner to set and achieve goals and guide them in choosing the subjects and courses needed to fulfill these goals. They need to keep in mind that the adult learner needs to know why the course is important to their learning and life situation. The adult learner brings into the continuing educational arena a rich array of experiences that will affect the learning styles and assimilation of knowledge. Adult learners need to be able to apply the knowledge into their life situations.

Knowles (1984) opened the doors of inquiry and the study of adult education focusing on five crucial assumptions about the adult learner:

Self-direction:

In its broadest meaning, 'self-directed learning' describes, according to Malcolm Knowles (1975) a process:

... in which individuals take the initiative, with or without the help of others, in diagnosing their learning needs, formulating learning goals, identifying human and material resources for learning, choosing and implementing appropriate learning strategies, and evaluating learning outcomes (p. 18).

Knowles (1975) puts forward three immediate reasons for self-directed learning. First, he argues that there is convincing evidence that people who take the initiative in learning (proactive learners) learn more things, and learn better, than do people who sit at the feet of teachers passively waiting to be taught (reactive learners). 'They enter into learning more purposefully and with greater motivation. They also tend to retain and make use of what they learn better and longer than do the reactive learners.' (p. 14)

A second immediate reason is that self-directed learning is more in tune with our natural processes of psychological development. 'An essential aspect of maturing is developing the ability to take increasing responsibility for our own lives – to become increasingly self-directed' (Knowles, 1975, p. 15).

A third immediate reason is that many of the new developments in education put a heavy responsibility on the learners to take a good deal of initiative in their own learning. 'Students entering into these programs without having learned the skills of self-directed inquiry will experience anxiety, frustration, and often failure, and so will their teachers (Knowles, 1975, p. 15).

Knowles' (1980) theory of andragogy is an attempt to develop a theory specifically for adult learning based on the theories of andragogy which is adult learning and pedagogy which is childhood learning. It is widely accepted that adults and children learn differently and have different instructional needs and requirements. Andragogy honors adults as self-directed learners who desire a climate of mutual respect and trust when they are under instruction. Facilitation of adult learning involves the opportunity for the learners to diagnose gaps in existing knowledge or skills and to identify opportunities to close these gaps. Adults appreciate the opportunity to define their own instructional goals that are defined by fully articulated performance criteria. This changes the role of the instructor from "being the expert with perhaps the sole or major responsibility for being the information source to that of facilitator, coach, or mentor – one who provides leadership and wisdom in guiding student learning" (Berge, 2008, p. 409).

Andragogy, according to Conner (1997-2004) involves five assertions: 1) Letting learners know why something is important to learn, 2) showing learners how to direct themselves through information, 3) relating the topic to the learner's experiences. In addition, 4) people will not learn until they are ready and motivated to learn. 5) This requires helping overcome inhibitions, behaviors, and beliefs about learning (para. 12).

Rachal (2002) urged that there is often a disconnect between the adult learners' needs and teaching practice:

Andragogy calls for learner control, measures of knowledge acquisition based upon performance standards, and the voluntary involvement of students in the learning activity. Most of these conditions do not exist in the university. One of the primary tenets of andragogy is that learning is pursued for its intrinsic value. Finally, andragogy calls for the measurement of satisfaction and for learner determined outcome measures. Neither of these conditions is readily found in higher education where faculty set the learning objectives and where satisfaction is not the primary determinant of future course offerings. (pp. 210-227)

Thoms (2001) characterized adult learners as having set habits and strong taste, a great deal of pride, a rational framework (values, attitudes, etc.) by which they make decisions and have developed group behavior consistent with their needs and have a strong need to apply what is learned and apply it now. Chao's (2009) description of learning is adopted as the operational definition for this paper: "learning as any process leading to a change in efficiency or use of conscious and unconscious cognitive processes that lead to a permanent capacity change not solely caused by biological maturation or ageing"

Taking into consideration these characteristics and assumptions of the adult learners, the underpinnings of andragogy teaches us that the adult learners' motivation to learn must be different from those of children. Both intrinsic and extrinsic factors affect motivation which change during the different stages/needs in their lives, add to the complexity. Motivation to learn would differ based on their individual experience, aptitude, and attitude. This would include individual characteristics of the learner, the perceived value of the learning task, and how much experience the adult learner had with the topic. Dymock (2007) argues that additional motivational factors such as social relationships, external expectations, social welfare, professional advancement, escape/stimulation and cognitive interest dynamically changes based on one's self direction, experience, readiness to learn and immediacy of application aside from which stages of life/needs they are in. Yak explains that the life stage/needs of an adult learner also determine his/her value system be it existence, relatedness, or growth needs. The life stage/needs also significant influence the adult learner's decision to participate in learning as it affects one or even all the 3 dimensions of learning (cognition, emotion, or environment). The adult learners' reason and purpose for learning creates the motivation to engage in learning therefore one must understand why and what is the reason and purpose for engaging in adult learning.

Rachal (2002) examined andragogy as a means of educating adults:

When it comes to adults, the foundation of higher education must assume that the adult learner has primary responsibility for their own motivation. This is not to suggest that the external environment cannot be facilitative, only that it does not encourage responsibility. Andragogy also calls for learner control, measures of knowledge acquisition based upon performance standards, and the voluntary involvement of students in the learning activity. Most of these conditions do not exist in the university. One of the primary tenets of andragogy is that learning is pursued for its intrinsic value. Finally, andragogy calls for the measurement of satisfaction and for learner determined outcome measures. Neither of these conditions is readily found in higher education where faculty set the learning objectives and where satisfaction is not the primary determinant of future course offerings. (pp. 210-227)

Conner (1997-2004) argued that Andragogy is:

The art and science of helping adults learn. In the andragogical model there are five assertions: 1) Letting learners know why something is important to learn, 2) showing learners how to direct themselves through information, 3) relating the topic to the learner's experiences. In addition, 4) people will not learn until they are ready and motivated to learn. 5) This requires helping overcome inhibitions, behaviors, and beliefs about learning. (para. 12).

Leaders are telling us that the future of work is that of collaboration. So, if we are to succeed in this collaborative, global economy where more and more of us are working in virtual teams, trust becomes ever more vital so that we can all win. And right now, the uncertainty around us is compounded by constant organizational change and a fragile and battered economy. Distrust leads to dysfunctional relationships slowing down every interaction with direct economic impact

Review of Research on Effective Virtual Teams

Successful outcomes of virtual learning depend on a shared culture that facilitates the making of knowledge and the contributions of all team members. Frontier (2012) argues that students learn three ways; experience, be told, and watch. Experiential learning involves doing by learner either through direct or indirect experiences. Hearing and seeing are more passive but important methodologies to deliver instruction and training. All learning involves at least one of these techniques. Effective learning in most cases involves all three ways. Creating opportunities for all three ways of learning is critical to virtual learners' success. Study teams can often be difficult to navigate in person and with the added dimension that a virtual experience brings to developing trusting, successful working relationships, different working guidelines are needed. Everyone on a virtual team must be a leader willing to drive their part of the process. Virtual teams don't work very well if the team members can't self- manage the process and their own time. It is important that those who design the learning team and procedures delegate enough authority so that virtual team members can proceed without having to need approval for every step.

Goold, Augar, and Farmer (2006) found that, even though, on average, students enjoyed working in teams in a classroom setting, most were less enthusiastic with working in a group in an online environment. Yoon (2006) examined online student team behaviors in seven virtual teams, categorizing the behaviors into three domains - Work, Social, and Management. In reviewing student behaviors over time, Yoon found that most interactions in early weeks of a team project were aimed at social behaviors (42.6%), which he speculated "might indicate that virtual learning team members try hard to enhance the social presence in an online environment before focusing on work.

Cooperation and motivation to participate are two crucial indices for distinguishing between the achievement of online groups (Guzdial & Turns, 2000; Lin et al., 2007). Ligoria (2001) proposed that when communities are organized into groups consisting of members with different abilities, the overall purpose of the community must be kept in mind along with a sense of collaboration. However, a virtual team can also face challenges and issues that must be addressed for a successful team operation (Liu, Magjuka, Bonk, & Lee, 2007). Such an environment can create difficulties for effective communication and collaboration (Montoya-Weiss, Massey, & Song, 2001). Thus, it has been suggested that virtual teams may have to make extra efforts in communication and collaboration for a successful operation. Lin et al. (2007) found that while over 50% of participants in the superior group habitually cooperated; few participants in the inferior group did so. They also indicated that participants in the superior group were more enthusiastic about sharing knowledge than those in the inferior group. Similarly, Ligoria (2001) proposed that when communities are organized into groups consisting of members with different abilities, the overall purpose of the community must be kept in mind along with a sense of collaboration. According to Ligorio (2001), the collaborative dimension of knowledge building comprises the community of the team.

Trust

Although some claim that working in virtual teams can produce additional challenges owing to the absence of social cues that can transfer interpersonal affections, including trust, research suggests that such absence does not necessarily hinder development of trust in virtual teams but may merely prolong the process of trust building (Walther,1996; Henttonen & Blomqvist, 2005). Learning is about developing a sense of trust (Weidman & Bishop, 2009). Trust is the primary building foundation of all successful relationships, both personal and business. No relationship can exist for even a short period of time if trust is not present. Hence, building trust among online learners is vital for their long-lasting, satisfying, rewarding, and successful relationships. In addition, relationships drive performance.

Studies also suggest that trust can play the same important roles in the functioning of virtual teams as in traditional teams (Morris, Marshall, & Kelleyrainer, 2002; Henttonen & Blomqvist, 2005). A synthesis of existing research suggests that development of trust is associated with continuous interactions and communications and repeated interpersonal exchange (Wilson, Straus, & McEvily, 2006; Crossman & Lee-Kelley, 2004).

As in traditional teams, social communications (greetings, exchanges of personal information) can play an important role in developing trust in virtual teams (Henttonen & Blomqvist, 2005). Contemporary theory of ''swift trust'' (Jarvenpaa & Leidner, 1999) posits that highly active, proactive, and enthusiastic actions can strengthen trust.

As in traditional teams, social interactions are important for team effectiveness. In virtual team, trust is perhaps more critical than ever as trust development, generally believed to be a pre-requirement for team effectiveness, may be undermined based on the lack of human touch (Grossman & Lee-Kelley, 2004). Much research supports the positive effect of trust on team outcomes. For instance, trust can enhance collaboration among team members (Serva & Fuller, 2004). Kiffin-Petersen (2004) noted that trust influences team effectiveness related to problem solving, decision making and communication. Students need to build the emotional bridges of trust and relationships with each other (Liu, Magjuka, Bonk, & Lee, 2007) to create a stronger, more effective learning community.

For the purposes of this paper, trust is viewed as the honest and caring way faculty and students relate to each other to cultivate strong interpersonal relationships which leads to enhanced motivation towards learning. If trust can serve as a commitment and high performance how does it impact student learning and performance? We know that when trust thrives in organizations, the literature supports that good things happen. One can then expect the same to happen to students. They should become more motivated if they trust their instructions and hence accelerate their learning. Trust acts a as a catalyst for learning (Kahane, 2006). Just as trust is a fundamental necessity for organizational success can one expect the same positive outcomes in a classroom setting? Furthermore, when faculty and students trust each other, does it lead to more engagement and motivation? Stephen Covey notes that, "Financial success comes from success in the marketplace, and success in the marketplace comes from success in the workplace. The heart and soul of all of this is trust." It appears that trust transcends all organizational contexts and leads to the same positive outcomes.

Research on teacher -student relationships in secondary school settings support the notion that when trust flourish student learning outcomes are positively impacted (Byrk & Schneider, 2004; Tschannen-Moran, 2004). Trust is the bond that encourages social networks, which may lead to improved teacher-student relationships and student outcomes (Dabney, 2008; Durnford, 2010). When teachers and student work together to set mutually agreeable goals, suggestions from student are actively sought, and students are part of a positive work group, then then the basis for enhanced motivation are met (Vecchio & Appelbaum, 1995). Trust is based on interpersonal dependence and involves an individual and group willingness to be vulnerable to another party based on the confidence that the party is benevolent, reliable, competent honest and open (Cummins & Bromiley, 1996; Hoy & Tshannen-Moran, 2003). The more interaction the parties have over time, the more their willingness to trust one another is based upon the other party's actions and their perceptions of one another's intentions, competence, and integrity (Bryk & Schneider, 2003).

Key Components of Trust

In general terms, trusting relationships involve risk, reliability, vulnerability, and expectation (Hoy & Tschannen-Moran, 2003; Young, 1998). If there is nothing at stake, or if one party does not require anything of the other, trust is not an issue. In higher educational setting settings, however, risk and expectations abound. Faculty and students alike are constantly put in positions in which they are not only expected to perform certain duties but in which their well-being depends upon others fulfilling certain obligations, as well. As researchers Bryk and Schneider (2003) explain each party in a relationship maintains an understanding of his or her role's obligations and holds some expectations about the obligations of the other parties.

As with the connection between increased educator trust and student achievement, the relationship between trust and collaboration is not one of simple cause and effect. Instead, trust and collaboration are mutually reinforcing: the more parties work together, the greater opportunity they must get to know one another and build trust. At the same time, as Tschannen-Moran's (2001) study indicates, the level of trust already present in the relationship influences parties' willingness and ability to work together.

A more precise definition of trust, drawn from Tschannen-Moran and Hoy's (1998) comprehensive review of the literature includes five key components commonly used to measure trustworthiness:

- **Benevolence**: Having confidence that another party has your best interests at heart and will protect your interests is a key ingredient of trust.
- **Reliability**: Reliability refers to the extent to which you can depend upon another party to come through for you, to act consistently, and to follow through. 3
- **Competence**: Like reliability, competence has to do with belief in another party's ability to perform the tasks required by his or her position. For example, if a principal means well but lacks necessary leadership skills, he or she is not likely to be trusted to do the job.
- **Honesty**: A person's integrity, character, and authenticity are all dimensions of trust. The degree to which a person can be counted on to represent situations fairly makes a huge difference in whether he or she is trusted by others in the school community.
- **Openness**: Judgments about openness have to do with how freely another party shares information with others. Guarded communication, for instance, provokes distrust because people wonder what is being withheld and why. Openness is crucial to the development of trust between supervisors and subordinates, particularly in times of increased vulnerability for staff.

Achieving Trusting Relationships in Virtual Teams

In traditional working teams, team members rely on eye contact, body language and past performance to help develop trusting, working relationships. Goleman (1995) suggests that there are four clusters of important competencies that make up such Emotional Intelligence: self-awareness, self-management, social awareness, and relationship management. To be successful in a virtual team, good self-managers take responsibility for their actions, seek high performance achievement and self-improvement. In addition, they strive to be conscientious, organized, and careful about their work, to be punctual, self-disciplined, and helpful. Ground rules, boundaries, check in opportunities for progress and improvement and feedback are topics that will be covered by the authors in the literature review portion of the chapter. The qualitative research results will undoubtedly bring the perspective of the administration, the faculty, and the student to the forefront of this chapter on guidelines for working in virtual teams.

Ethnocentrism

We live in an increasingly multicultural society and "ethnocentrism" is a commonly used word in circles where ethnicity, inter-ethnic relations, and similar social issues are of concern. The usual definition of the term is "thinking one's own group's ways are superior to others" or "judging other groups as inferior to one's own". "Ethnic" refers to *cultural heritage*, and "centrism" refers to the central starting point... so "ethnocentrism" refers to judging other groups from one's own cultural point of view (Barger, 2008). Working collegially together in groups, then, may be difficult when members may be from highly diverse backgrounds.

In addition, faculty members often expect students to work efficiently together in groups without providing added resources or assistance. This is challenging to achieve even in traditional classroom environments. Online students have a greater challenge in making sure that their team members work together proficiently, and course instructors may need to provide more assistance to their online students to make sure that teams work well together.

The Role of the Online Instructor

Teaching presence is critical to facilitating relevant online learning that achieves defined outcomes. However, the traditional role as teacher is modified. Salmon, 2004, notes that the teacher becomes just one resource of many as the control of learning is shared with the student. The online teacher is expected to adopt a more facilitative approach in creating a learner-centered environment. Berge (2008)) breaks down the online instructor roles into four categories: pedagogical, social, managerial, and technical. Some of these functions overlap or can be placed in more than one category and not all these need to be carried out by the same person. However, Berge points out that it is "the instructor's job to make sure that all the roles are successful (p. 409). Paulsen (1995) divide the educational moderator's role into three major responsibilities – organizational, social, and intellectual. Further substantiating research was done by Rossman (1999) in an empirical study which supports these classification systems. Through an analysis of over 3,000 student course evaluations from 154 university courses, Rossman found that student comments and complaints clustered into three major groupings which correspond to the three categories of cognitive, social and teaching presence.

METHODOLOGY

The present qualitative phenomenological study was conducted at a private institution of higher education in a Midwestern state in the United States. The specific program reviewed was a master's in educational leadership program, currently in its first year of existence. Creswell (1998) suggested that the process of collecting data for a phenomenological study requires a small group of people. The focus is finding common shared experiences of graduate students working collaboratively together in virtual teams.

The purpose of this research study is to add to the existing body of knowledge by examining best practices for organizing effective virtual learning teams and the organization of those teams as determined by students, faculty, and administrators. All students, $n = 14$, from the first program cohort were asked to participate in the study. The students were currently in the 6th course of the program or about halfway through. All students were part time students enrolling in one course at the time. In addition, one program administrator and 4 randomly selected faculty members were interviewed one-on-one. The following questions were asked to each student participant during in-depth interviews. The faculty and administrative members answered questions 4, 5, 6, and 7 only.

Interview Questions:

1. How do you and fellow cohort members generally work together in teams?
2. How important is developing trusting relationships with team members for the team's success?
3. How do you best develop trust among team members?
4. What are the key variables in your opinion for achieving successful team outcomes in the virtual learning environment?
5. What guidelines, if any, does the team need to establish for successful learning outcomes?
6. How should teams be structured?
7. When building online learning communities, how can faculty and students help in designing an online learning community?

This qualitative phenomenological research study discovered and explored the phenomena as lived and experienced by the participants design was used as a method to explore and/or describe a social human problem (Creswell, 1998). A phenomenological inquiry or qualitative research uses a naturalistic approach that seeks to understand phenomena in context-specific settings. The main aim of using this research method is discovering the meaning beliefs, experiences, perceptions, and attitudes of students, administrators, and faculty as part of being participants in this online learning community.

In order to discover and gain better understanding of human experiences, in-depth un-structured open-ended interview questions are recommended (Creswell, 1998). In the process of data analysis, a qualitative research uses inductive data analysis process, and the final report is provided in a descriptive form, which incorporates expressive participants' voices, beliefs, and perceptions in themes and text (Eisner, 1991). A qualitative method allows researchers to identify the structural meanings of experiences while at the same time uncovering the themes and contexts that account for the lived experience of the participants studied.

The sample included 14 cohort members who were current students halfway through their Master of Educational Leadership (MEL) studies. The participants were invited via email to be interviewed by the researchers. A total of 7 (50%) students expressed a willingness to participate in the study. The researchers arranged for a time and place to conduct the one-on-one interviews. In addition, one program administrator and 4 faculty members were interviewed. By utilizing this triangulation technique, the researchers were able to obtain information that shredded a detail portrait of the phenomenon studied.

The open-ended, structured interviews were used as the primary strategy for data collection. Using open-ended questions allows individual variations to unfold. The interview guide was used, but there were no predetermined answers. In this case, semi-structured interviews allowed a researcher to probe and explore more information.

Findings Pertaining to Students

The data were organized into the following themes:

1. Challenges Impacting the Success of Online Working Teams
2. Factors that impact the success of online teams
3. The Role of Trust in Successful Online Teams
4. Guidelines for Developing Successful Online Teams
5. Structural Factors to consider for Successful Online Teams
6. Factors to consider for Higher Educational Institutions for creating Successful Online Learning Communities

Tables 1- 6 outline the data findings.

Findings Pertaining to the Administrator and Faculty

The researchers conducted in-depth interviews with the program administrator and a total of 4 faculty members who regularly teach online courses.

The data were organized into the following themes:

Table 1. Challenges impacting the success of online working teams

Categories and Theme	Quotes
• Scheduling • Finding time for the work • Changing team membership • Unfamiliarity	"Scheduling is difficult especially with kids, work, and time differences" "Team work is very difficult online" "It is difficult having groups that are always changing. I do not feel that I really know the other student in the cohort or their professional backgrounds" "A component lacking in this cohort in my opinion based on the fact that most members do not know one another"

Table 2. Factors that impact the success of online teams

Categories and Theme	Quotes
• Organization & Time Management • Team Leadership • Accountability • Strong Communication • Trust • Humor	"We determine timelines and guidelines through brainstorming in a discussion board or through email" "Organization and communication. I believe have been key in successful team outcomes in the online programs" "Making sure you get your work done on time" "Typically, one person takes the lead, there is some collaboration, but one person does the majority of the work" "Be accountable, do what you say you are going to do and be respectful of people's ideas and time" "Strong communication is important" "Team members stepped up and filled in if the need was there" "I believe that trust is built through open and honest, frequent communication" "Everyone has to do their part and be respectful and open to the point of view of everyone" "Fortunately, most team members are motivated, and everyone does their part to complete task" "One team member in particular I have grown to trust with asking questions, venting about our day, and being able to incorporate some humor!"

Table 3. The role of trust in successful online teams

Categories and Theme	Quotes Related to
• Trusting relationships is Important	"We depend on each other to learn and for grades. Trusting relationships are very important" "I feel that I can trust team members to complete work and do so successfully since we are working toward a common goal" "Trust is very important as we are "spending" a lot of time together in the program" "It is very important because personal information about us, our school and our district are shared"

Table 4. Guidelines for developing successful online teams

Categories and Theme	Quotes
• Respect • Timelines • Norms	"I feel that respect is a major factor. To respect everyone and his or her thoughts and ideas" "I really wish that there were more norms established about communication. Frequently, within group assignments I have no idea when the other members will be checking in and the communication is often disjointed. When I was in the first online cohort whenever group work was assigned my group established chat times to lay out individual tasks and a timeline. I think that this should be a norm for group work" "The team needs to set a timeline, communicate which responsibilities they will be taking on and then stick to the plan" "Respectful dialogue that allows us to honestly state what we are doing and gain insights from others"

Table 5. Structural factors to consider for successful online teams

Categories and Theme	Quotes
• Interchangeable Teams • Self-organized Teams and Pre-Selected Teams	"I like the change in groups from activity to activity, so you get to work with all members" "Self- organized or pre- chosen has both been successful" "Teams should be structured either in a self-organized fashion or by considering people's strengths. I have been on teams with people who do not participate at all and do not respond to the group and with people who do all the work before the team has a chance to collaborate. This does not lead to effective teamwork"

1. Key variables for achieving successful team outcomes in the virtual learning environment?
2. Guidelines needed for successful learning outcomes?
3. Structuring of effective online teams
4. Stakeholder role in building effective online learning communities

SOLUTIONS AND RECOMMENDATIONS

The decision to introduce online learning in Higher Education may seem to be a logical next step for many Higher Education institutions; however, there are many facets to consider when developing virtual programs. A larger set of conditions need to be considered. This study focused on the organization of virtual teams and some key guidelines that need to be present. As discussed, the four categories of skills

Table 6. Factors to consider for higher educational institutions for creating successful online learning communities

Categories and Theme	Quotes
• Faculty Sympathetic to Student Work/Life Balances • Faculty Flexibility • Communication Norms • Flexibility with Alternative Communication Sources • Synchronized Sessions	"Being flexible and understanding to other's lives. Sometimes it is very challenging to balance school, online learning, and families" "Faculty has to be flexible. There are assignments due almost every day and work and life can get in the way" "Students can provide honest feedback about courses" "Both faculty and students have to be open and willing to try new things" "More norms on frequency of communication" "Team discussion boards have been the primary source of collaboration thus far, not the most effective for group work in my opinion. I like the idea of utilizing the Angel chat rooms, Skype, etc." "The many portals of communication, resources, rubrics, calendars, etc. have been really helpful. There are many places that I can look for answers when I am confused. I think initiating team activities with a synchronous blackboard session would help the process. Also, a log or some way of showing who has done what (maybe a self-reflection) would help hold everyone accountable" "Encourage dialogue and reinforce promptness. There are times when personal issues arise that cause delays in responding and participating. It is essential that the other team members are made aware of when a team member is off line for a period. There were times early on where a few of our cohort members had difficulties and we were not aware. It became difficult for us to know if we should wait or continue the work without them" "It might be helpful to have blackboard sessions for teams to meet at the start of a project. That way, students could get the work organized and then finish the process through email and phone calls"

Table 7. Key variables for achieving successful team outcomes in the virtual learning environment?

Categories and Theme	Quotes
• Team Interaction • Utilizing Various Communication Tools • Frequent Communication	"The first step is to actually ensure that there will be some team interaction" "I have found requiring daily interactions with course material and student posting to one another for assignment completion is a key to success" "One of the most fruitful activities I have seen is to have them participate in discussion boards where there is a non-threatening question in which everyone can share their ideas. As more ideas are shared, they get to know each other's personality via words" "The faculty member needs to act like a facilitator ensuring frequent communication between students as well as students and faculty member" "Explicit in assignment directions it is helpful to provide the number of times they are to post to one another and the purpose of the post"

Table 8. Guidelines needed for successful learning outcomes?

Categories and Theme	Quotes
• Norms	"The establishment of team norms is essential. At a minimum these norms might include confidentiality, respectful disagreement, and a commitment to contribute to the online discussions. The biggest threat to learning outcomes in the online environment is the possibility of someone being offended and checking out. Establishing the ground rules from the outset lessens this possibility" "Establishing group norms is essential for any type of work group be it face to face or online. Allowing the group members to share their preferences for when to meet, what to set for deadlines, decision making process, how to resolve conflicts, best format they work in (email, skype…) and to discuss/problem solve any potential barriers to successful completion of assignment/project"

Table 9. Structuring of effective online teams

Categories and Theme	Quotes
• Peer Reviewed Assignments • Interchangeable Team Membership	"In one of my online courses there were several assignments that required pairs of students to do a peer review of a classmate's work" "I intentionally change the pairs each time to give them a different teammate. They liked having interactions with different students, and as is natural found people they gravitated to after a while. At that point, they looked forward to the opportunity to work with their "favorite" classmates" "Changing groups membership throughout the course is another best practice so students get a sense of all their fellow course mates" "If the online cohort extends over several months, I believe it is critical to mix up groups and even strategically place people in groups so as to challenge them" "I believe there are a number of factors can fall in to the structuring of teams. If possible, at the start of a course do some type of survey to have students discover their work style and preference. True Colors is a great tool and can help the instructor determine how to organize teams, so people work with a variety of work styles and gain an understanding of group process. So, considering diversity, work preference and even location in case some may want to meet in person" "One assignment was to debate why staff development was necessary and why it is unnecessary. I placed the biggest advocate for staff development in the why it is unnecessary group to stretch her thinking. She did a great job in the debate and it opened her eyes to the blindspot in her leadership. So, instructor knowledge of student is key too"

Table 10. Stakeholder role in building effective online learning communities

Categories and Theme	Quotes
• Consistent Presence • Frequent Interactions between Stakeholders • Faculty Feedback	"Faculty and students' biggest role are to be involved and have a consistent presence" "The more interaction the faculty member has with the students, and the students with each other, the stronger the learning community. If students do not interact with faculty, or with each other, they feel isolated and the learning community never materializes" "I have found the daily interactions around the required posts accentuate the depth and richness of the community. Initially the required posting tied to the rubric force the interactions but as time goes on people are truly engaging and creating an authentically responsive learning community" "Having instructor presence is key and having the instructor share stories and examples allows for greater sense of community. Feedback, feedback and feedback! The early in the course feedback is received and expected the better. I want my students to have a clear understanding that they are important to me and that their individual learning is equal to how they are helping others learn in the class"

– pedagogical, social, managerial and technical - of an online instructor were noted by Berge (2008) as being critical to ensure the successful learning outcomes for students. The findings of this research study aligned with these principles.

The authors noted that students did not mention issues such as space and time distance, or even psychological distance that often arise in the discussion of online learning environments. Nor technical problems were brought forward as may have been expected. However, two areas that were mentioned was managerial (their time, organization, norms, and commitment) and social (communication and relationship building). Similarly, the administration and faculty noted managerial (interchangeable team membership, peer reviewed assignments, and feedback) and social (online presence, communication, and stakeholder interactions) as important areas. This last finding was also noted in a research study by Misanchuk and Anderson (2001), who stressed the importance of interactions and suggest interactions could be encouraged at different levels, such as communication and cooperation levels.

In addition, the element of trust is significant in virtual teams. All student participants noted this. According to one student: "It is very important because personal information about us, our school and our district is shared." It is critical that course designers and faculty take this into consideration in ensuring that frequent student interactions and social activities are built into the course. The distributed nature of the participants makes for some challenges that otherwise may have been addressed face-to face. This may often be exaggerated if members of the team have not established a trust-based relationship. When individuals are separated, they are less likely to establish the one-to-one relationships upon which trust is often built (Chinowsky & Rojas, 2003). Therefore, assignments and the structural design of the programs need to be paid attention to. The online faculty teaching in the MEL programs currently incorporates a minimum of 3 synchronized sessions per course in order to allow for added social interactions.

Pawar and Sharifi (1997) urged that, albeit geographically separated, the need for virtual teams to establish initial relationships is critical and that they require initial face-to-face meetings to develop a sense of ''team'' for their members. This theory is also supported by findings in the U.S. Department of Education meta-analysis study report released in September 2010. This meta-analysis of 50 studies, 43 of which were focused on adult learners rather than elementary or secondary students, found that "instruction combining online, and face-to-face elements had a larger advantage relative to purely face-to-face instruction than did purely online instruction" (Means, Toyama, Murphy, Bakia, & Jones, 2010, p. 15).

The establishment of clear guidelines for and directions as well as clear expectations for each team member is critical. One student urged, "Be accountable, do what you say you are going to do and be respectful of people's ideas and time." Course designers and faculty must be as clear as possible communicating assignment expectations and goals at each stage of the process. Just as with traditional classes, the online instructor must be clear about course requirements (Palloff & Pratt, 2001) and communicate high expectations (Coghlan, 2002).

CONCLUSION

This study noted the many successes institutions of Higher Education are experiencing by offering more and more courses online. However, as stressed by the researchers, several non-technical guidelines must be considered in order to ensure that the promise of online learning communities does not turn into non-effective virtual instruction. The successful implementation of a virtual team requires an organization to address issues from a diverse set of influences. Findings from this study focused on the managerial and social nature of virtual learning and instruction. Students implied the importance of establishing trusting relationships and the establishment of clear guidelines for task completion and expectations from team members. Administrator and faculty participants noted the importance of building in social interactions through peer reviewed assignments, interchangeable team membership, online presence, and frequent feedback. Higher education institutions must demonstrate that they are reliable providers of good quality education regardless of the delivery model and they must respond to the increasing demand for meaningful and relevant teaching. Students as well as employers and policy makers want to assure that education will prepare students for rewarding employment and for professional growth over a lifespan.

REFERENCES

Allen, I., & Seaman, J. (2016). Online report card: Tracking online education in the United States. ERIC Document. ERIC Number: ED572777.

Barger, K. (2008, July). *Ethnocentrism.* Retrieved from http://www.iupui.edu/~anthkb/ethnocen.htm

Berge, Z. (2008). Changing instructor's roles in virtual worlds. *Quarterly Review of Distance Education*, *9*(4), 407–414.

Byrk, A. S., & Schneider, B. (2004). *Trust in schools.* New York, NY: Russell Sage Foundation.

Chang, C. K., Chen, G. D., & Li, L. Y. (2006). Constructing a community of practice to improve coursework activity. *Computers & Education*, *50*(1), 235–247. doi:10.1016/j.compedu.2006.05.003

Chao, R., Jr. (2009). Understanding the Adult Learners Motivation and Barriers to Learning. Retrieved from https://www.academia.edu/1267765/

Chinowsky, P. S., & Rojas, E. M. (2003, July). Virtual Teams: Guide to Successful Implementation. *Journal of Management Engineering*, *19*(3), 98–106. doi:10.1061/(ASCE)0742-597X(2003)19:3(98)

Coghlan, M. (2002, September). *Facilitating online learning.* Retrieved from http://users.chariot.net.au/~michaelc/olfc.html

Conner, M. L. (1997-2004). *Andragogy and Pedagogy.* Ageless Learner. Retrieved from http://ageless-learner.com/intros/andragogy.html

Creswell, W. (1998). *Qualitative inquiry and research design; choosing among five traditions.* Thousand Oaks, CA: Sage.

Crossman, A., & Lee-Kelley, L. (2004). Trust, commitment and team working: The paradox of virtual organizations. *Global Networks*, *4*(4), 375–390. doi:10.1111/j.1471-0374.2004.00099.x

Cummings, L. L., & Bromiley, P. (1996). The Organizational Trust Inventory (OTI): Development and validation. In R. Kramer, & T. Tyler (Eds.), *Trust in organizations* (pp. 302–330). Thousand Oaks, CA: Sage. doi:10.4135/9781452243610.n15

Dabney, J. (2008). *Show me that you care: the presence of relational trust between a principal and teachers in an urban school.* Columbus, OH: Ohio State University.

DuFour, R., & Eaker, R. (1998). *Professional Learning communities at work: Best practices for enhancing student achievement.* Alexandria, VA: Association for Supervision and Curriculum Development.

DuFour, R., Eaker, R., & Eaker, R. (2005). *On common ground: The power of Professional Learning Communities.* Bloomington, IN: Solution Tree.

Durnford, V. (2010). *An examination of teacher-student trust in middle school classrooms.* Amherst, MA: University of Massachusetts.

Dymock, D. (2007). *Engaging Adult Learners.* Canberra, Australia: Adult Learning Australia.

Eisner, E. W. (1991). *The enlightened eye: Qualitative inquiry and the enhancement of educational practice.* New York, NY: Macmillan Publishing Company.

Frontier, T. (2012, June 15). *Windows on intelligence.* Presented at Summer Institute 2012 of Cardinal Stritch University, Milwaukee, WI.

Goleman, D. (1995). *Emotional Intelligence Why It Can Matter More Than IQ.* New York, NY: Bantam Books.

Goold, A., Augar, N., & Farmer, J. (2006). Virtual teams: Exploring the student experience. *Journal of Information Technology Education*, *5*, 477–490. doi:10.28945/260

Guzdial, M., & Turns, J. (2000). Effective discussion though a computer-mediated anchored forum. *Journal of the Learning Sciences*, *9*(4), 437–469. doi:10.1207/S15327809JLS0904_3

Henttonen, K., & Blomqvist, K. (2005). Managing distance in a global virtual team: The evolution of trust through technology-mediated relational communication. *Strategic Change*, *14*(2), 107–119. doi:10.1002/jsc.714

Hetland, H., Skogstad, A., Hetland, J., & Mikkelsen, A. (2011). Leadership and learning climate in a work setting. *European Psychologist*, *16*(3), 163–176. doi:10.1027/1016-9040/a000037

Hipp, K. K., & Huffman, J. B. (2010). *Demystifying professional learning communities: School leadership at its best.* Lanham, MD: Rowan & Littlefield Education.

Hoy, W. K., & Tschannen-Moran, M. (2003). The conceptualization and measurement of faculty trust in schools: The omnibus T-Scale. In W. K. Hoy, & C. G. Miskel (Eds.), *Studies in Leading and Organizing Schools* (pp. 181–208). Greenwich, CT: Information Age Publishing.

Jarvenpaa, S., & Leidner, D. (1999). Communication and trust in global virtual teams. *Organization Science, 10*(6), 791–815. doi:10.1287/orsc.10.6.791

Jones, A., & Issroff, K. (2005). Learning technologies: Affective and social issues in computer-supported collaborative learning. *Computers & Education, 44*(4), 395–408. doi:10.1016/j.compedu.2004.04.004

Kiffin-Petersen, S. A. (2004). Trust: A neglected variable in team effectiveness research. *Journal of the Australian and New Zealand Academy of Management, 10*(1), 38–53.

Knowles, M. (1984). *The Adult Learner: A Neglected Species* (3rd ed.). Houston, TX: Gulf Publishing.

Knowles, M. S. (1975). *Self-directed learning.* Chicago, IL: Follet.

Knowles, M. S. (1980). *The modern practice of adult education: From pedagogy to andragogy. Englewood Cliffs.* Cambridge, UK: Prentice Hall.

Ligoria, M. B. (2001). Integrating communication formats: Synchronous versus asynchronous and text-based versus visual. *Computers & Education, 37*(2), 103–125. doi:10.1016/S0360-1315(01)00039-2

Lin, F., Lin, S., & Huang, T. (2007). Knowledge sharing and creation in a teachers' professional virtual community. *Computers & Education, 50*(3), 742–756. doi:10.1016/j.compedu.2006.07.009

Liu, X., Magjuka, R. J., Bonk, C. J., & Lee, S. (2007). Does sense of community matter? An examination of participants' perceptions of building learning communities in online courses. *The Quarterly Review of Distance Education, 8*(1), 9–24.

Means, B., Toyama, Y., Murphy, R., Bakia, M., & Jones, K. (2010). *Evaluation of Evidence-based practices in online learning: A meta-analysis and review of online learning studies.* Washington, DC: U. S. Department of Education.

Misanchuk, M., & Anderson, T. (2001). Building community in an online learning environment: Communication, cooperation and collaboration. Proceedings of the *Sixth Annual Mid-South Instructional Technology Conference*, Murfreesboro, TN, Middle Tennessee State University. Retrieved from http://kevinmcmanamon.files.wordpress.com/2012/01/building-community-in-an-online-learning-environment.pdf

Montoya-Weiss, M. M., Massey, A. P., & Song, M. (2001). Getting it together: Temporal coordination and conflict management in global virtual teams. *Academy of Management Journal, 44*(6), 1251–1262.

Morris, S. A., Marshall, T., & Kelleyrainer, R. (2002). Impact of user satisfaction and trust on virtual team members. *Information Resources Management Journal, 15*(2), 2–30. doi:10.4018/irmj.2002040103

Pallof, R., & Pratt, K. (2001). *Lessons from the cyberspace classroom: The realities of online teaching.* San Francisco, CA: Jossey-Bass.

Paulsen, M. (1995). Moderating educational computer conferences. In A. Berge, & M. Collins (Eds.), *Computer-mediated communication and the on-line classroom in distance education*. Cresskill, NJ: Hampton Press.

Pawar, K. S., & Sharifi, S. (1997). Physical or virtual team collocation: Does it matter? *International Journal of Production Economics*, *52*(3), 283–290. doi:10.1016/S0925-5273(97)89241-9

Poulin, R., & Straut, T. (2016). WCET Distance Education Enrollment Report. Retrieved from https://files.eric.ed.gov/fulltext/ED570525.pdf

Rossman, M. (1999).. . *Journal of Asynchronous Learning Networks*, *3*(2). Retrieved from http://www.aln.org/alnweb/journal/Vol3_issue 2/Rossman.htm

Salmon, G. (2004). *E-moderating: the key to teaching and learning online*. London, UK: Kogan Page. doi:10.4324/9780203465424

Serva, M., & Fuller, M. (2004). Aligning what we do and what we measure in business schools: Incorporating active learning and effective media use in the assessment of instruction. *Journal of Management Education*, *28*(1), 19–38. doi:10.1177/1052562903252648

Tschannen-Moran, M. (2001). Collaboration and the need for trust. *Journal of Educational Administration*, *39*(4), 308–331. doi:10.1108/EUM0000000005493

Tschannen-Moran, M. (2004). *Trust Matters*. San Francisco, CA: Jossey-Bass.

Tschannen-Moran, M., & Hoy, W. K. (1998). Trust in schools: A conceptual and empirical analysis. *Journal of Educational Administration*, *36*(4), 334–352. doi:10.1108/09578239810211518

Walther, J. B. (1996). Computer-mediated communication: Impersonal, interpersonal, and hyperpersonal interaction. *Communication Research*, *23*(1), 3–43. doi:10.1177/009365096023001001

Wang, M. J., & Poole, M. (2004). Nurturing a dynamic online learning community among teens. *International Journal of Learning*, *9*, 859–870.

Weidman, R., & Bishop, M. (2009). Using the jigsaw model to facilitate cooperative learning in an online course. *Quarterly Review of Distance Education, 10*(1), 51-64, 89-91.

Wilson, J. M., Straus, S. G., & McEvily, B. (2006). All in due time: The development of trust in computer-mediated and face-to-face teams. *Organizational Behavior and Human Decision Processes*, *99*(1), 16–33. doi:10.1016/j.obhdp.2005.08.001

Yang, F., Wang, M., Shen, R., & Han, P. (2007). Community-organizing agent: An artificial intelligent system for building learning communities among large numbers of learners. *Computers & Education*, *49*(2), 131–147. doi:10.1016/j.compedu.2005.04.019

Yoon, S. W. (2006). Two group development patterns of virtual learning teams: Linear progression and adaptive progression. *Quarterly Review of Distance Education*, *7*(4), 297–312.

Young, M. D. (1998, April). *Importance of trust in increasing parental involvement and student achievement in Mexican American communities*. Paper presented at the annual meeting of the American Educational Research Association, San Diego, CA. (ERIC Document Reproduction Service No. ED423587).

KEY WORDS AND DEFINITIONS

Adult Learning Theory (Andragogy): A theory specifically for adult learning based on the theories of andragogy (which is adult learning) and pedagogy (which is childhood learning) (Knowles, 1980).

Emotional Intelligence: Consist of four clusters of important competencies - self-awareness, self-management, social awareness, and relationship management (Goleman, 1995).

Ethnocentrism: The usual definition of the term is "thinking one's own group's ways are superior to others" or "judging other groups as inferior to one's own". "Ethnic" refers to *cultural heritage*, and "centrism" refers to the central starting point... so "ethnocentrism" refers to judging other groups from one's own cultural point of view (Barger, 2008).

Learning: Students three ways; experience, be told, and watch. Experiential learning involves doing by learner either through direct or indirect experiences. (Frontier, 2012).

Learning Climate: Consists of five central dimensions -"sufficient time to learn and perform, autonomy and responsibility, team style, opportunities to develop, and guidelines on how to do the job" (Hetland, Skogstad, Hetland, & Mikkelsen, 2011, p. 15).

Learning Communities: "Professional educators working collectively and purposefully to create and sustain a culture of learning for all students and adults" (Hipp & Huffman, 2010, p. 12).

Professional Learning Community: The focus of PLCs on the three principles of learning, collaboration, and results (DuFour & Eaker, 1998; DuFour, Eaker, & Dufour, 2005).

Chapter 9
Maintaining Relationships Through Social Media and the Way Forward

Richard H. Afedzie
Pentecost University College, Ghana

Stanford Nartey
Pentecost University College, Ghana

James Aller
Georgia Southwestern State University, USA

ABSTRACT

This paper examines the influence of social media in our global political, social, and business landscape. It underscores the argument that the value of social media in our 21st century social and business life-styles cannot be overlooked. It explores some of the ways in which social media has shaped and positively maintained friendship, dating, and family relationships. It also highlights some of the growing challenges and emerging moral risks associated with unregulated social media prevalence in the society and offers ways to minimize threats posed by unfettered social media use in the society.

INTRODUCTION

Background of Social Media Communication

The concept of social media has assumed greater influence and legitimacy in our 21st century global communication. It has become ubiquitous in our everyday communication, business interactions and an important aspect of our everyday life. The advancement of social media has created a new paradigm that influences every aspect of society from communication with each other, dating, spiritual, retail, education, appointments, and nearly every aspect of one's life has been affected by social media. The growth of social media across the global socio-political and business landscape has influenced every aspect of

DOI: 10.4018/978-1-5225-9814-5.ch009

our dating and relationship lifestyle. In fact, it has facilitated instant communication and exchange of information globally. Specifically, it has facilitated easier access to information and enhanced communication across a broader spectrum of our socio-cultural lifestyle. It is a form of online communication platform that facilitates common interactions among diverse groups of individuals and communities (Kunz & Hackworth, 2011). Beyond the sharing of information and communication online, social media has a far-reaching impact on our 21st century society because of the increasing trend at which relationships are developed and formed. The interactions that occur on social media is primarily the result of the relationships that exist among families, friends, and work colleagues.

The capacity to foster online communication that goes beyond geographical boundaries is a major driver of social media's defining influence on relationships among individuals and communities. Social media interaction has been argued to be the most common and fastest means to developing and fostering long - distance relationships, which often overlook the cultural and geographical barriers. Over the past decade, most social relationships in the realm of politics, business and personal interactions have often been channelled by means of a social media communication (Colliander & Dahlen, 2011).

Since the launch of Facebook and Twitter in the first decade of the 21st century, there has been a steady increase in new social media sites such as Foursquare, Spotify, Tumblr, Instagram, snapchat, twitter, LinkedIn, Pinterest, Vine and WhatsApp. Current social media sites have been created to meet the need of online dating and making friends based on an individual's social and career interest. "Social media has come to deeply penetrate our lives: Facebook, YouTube, Twitter and many other platforms define many of our daily habits of communication and creative production" (Van Dijck, 2013). Van Dijck argues that "culture of connectivity" and terms like "friending", "trending" and "sharing" have taken on different meanings in our social media culture.

How Social Media Has Positively Influenced the Society

This chapter argues that social media communication has created a world of instant information dissemination and progressively contributed to deepening intercultural understanding, dialogue, and relationship on a global scope. It is an undeniable fact that social media interaction is the driving force in our rapid social, economic, technological and religious changes. It has offered individual citizens, marginalized groups and local communities the authority to assemble, relate constructively to each other and make free speech a collaborative global media networking. This process has truly encouraged active citizen participations in their civil responsibilities and the democratic processes of their countries. Furthermore, users' ability to actively participate and respond instantaneously to occurring events signify a future where culture differences are respected, because it drives users' initiatives to consider other worldviews. The presence of social media has also created avenues for family members to share their special occasions, joy, success stories, annual life events on common social media platforms and networking. Specifically, the ability of social media to enhance delivery of information and promote effective communication is supported by the need for relationships among individuals.

Notably, social media has also become a tool for fostering relationships and mobilizing political uprising in many countries across many parts of the world (Wiest, 2011). Through social media networking, citizens across different parts of the globe have organised protests against unpopular economic policies. Presently in many sub-Saharan countries, citizens have mobilized themselves through a common bond of relationship to protect high cost of living and political suppression of civil liberties by their government. For example, through Facebook messages, some political activists in numerous Middle Eastern countries including Syria and Iraq were able to organise and mobilize protests during the Arab Spring in 2011. Further examples include the current protests going on in Sudan and Algeria that have led to the removal of both presidents who have ruled their countries for more than thirty (30) years. These protests were organized through social media platforms such as Facebook and WhatsApp and started in March 2019 and are still ongoing as today (1st July, 2019). Ultimately, social media has fostered the creation of both political and social groups across different cultural boundaries.

Benefits of Social Media

The premise of this chapter is that social media mode of communication is the bedrock sustaining most global business and socio-economic relationships. In many instances, social media networking sites have helped individuals with severe medical conditions receive emotional support from people with similar medical conditions (Lim & Putnam, 2010). The presence of social media has encouraged individuals in geographically isolated communities to pursue education and learn vocational skills in an online format.

Consumers of a specific product are able to interact with one another primarily because of the existence of social media. Members in an organisation are also able to convene meetings and interact with one another promptly by using social media networking such as texts, tweets, pokes, chats and emails. In many instances, potential job seekers looking for new employment opportunities, and entrepreneurs seeking for venture capital are often successful because of online communication and social media interaction. Through social media, such as Facebook and LinkedIn, individuals can reconnect to old friends, classmates and advertise their career experiences on the social networking platforms. Many professional interests groups have linked up and forged common bonds of understanding through social media networking. For example, LinkedIn offer a social networking platform for people to manage their relationship with professional business partners and colleagues.

The widespread adoption of social media has prompted many organisations to shift their marketing efforts from mass media broadcast to relationship oriented social media marketing campaign. In our 21st century marketing landscape, social media outreach for consumers utilize professional marketing strategy on how consumers foster relationship to solicit information about a service and product (Mefolere, 2015). Consumer-to-consumer advertising about a product and service has also grown increasingly with the proliferation of social media networking. In essence, social media has become an easy and convenient way to market goods and services. Social media platforms never close their doors and users don't have to struggle with parking spaces, traffic situations and trekking through many stores to find the goods and services they want. They can browse the internet from the comfort of their offices and homes without tying their time to salespeople (Kotler & Armstrong, 2016).

Maintaining Relationship Through Social Media

Kincaid and Rogers (1981) affirmed that network communication produces decisions that are culturally sensitive. In 1981, they had little insight as to the growth of social media that was right around the corner. Now, those network communications are influenced by not only a family or small network of friends but potentially thousands that have no involvement or responsibility to an outcome. Historically, group communications have played critical roles in society. Family and close networks determined or at least influenced social behaviors and reproductive behaviors (Kincaid, 1981). Participation in the social media platforms has made the world more connected. One needs not look beyond the use of twitter or Facebook to see a visual representation of that communication.

Changing the Management of Threat Assessment Through Social Media

On April 19th, 1995, Oklahoma City bombing of the Federal building happened by what was categorized as a domestic terrorist. It was the worst domestic attack on US soil at that time. The local news was live in a matter of less than 10 minutes. At the time, it was considered a game changer in terms of a news outlet's ability to bring the public news in a few seconds. Sutton, Palen, and Shklovski, (2007) stated that community information resources and other back channel communications activity enabled by social media are gaining prominence in the disaster area, despite concern by officials about the legitimacy of information shared through such means". "Crisis informatics takes a broad view of disaster activity – one that considers the trajectories of change and information pathways that are emerging because of new media and capabilities across the entire social space (Palen & Liu, 2007)

In 2009, a human resource director for a big box retail chain in Texas, underscored the relative value of the social media on the US business landscape by asserting that: "I was contacted by a store in Galveston, Texas and informed that the store had been hit by a tornado. There was significant damage and the scene was being searched for injuries. Knowing that the local authorities were already aware, I contacted the corporate office and sent a message to the "threat assessment" department. The department informed me that they were already aware, had video footage of the store and already had a plane enroute to the location. They were aware from social media postings of customers. That was all in a period of less than five minutes." (Palen, Vieweg, Sutton, Liu, & Hughes, 2010).

Challenges Associated With Social Media

Social media has made direct targeting possible. This has led to intimate relationship building where both positive and negative behaviours and practices are taught and learned. Social media has the power to educate, entertain, inform and inflame passion just as the traditional media, however, it has also been associated with negative social influence in the society. Indoctrination into various groups such as the Islamic State in Iraq and Syria (ISIS), which is terrorising citizens of these countries is one such example of how social media is utilized in fomenting chaos and disorder. Other negative influences include teaching people how to commit suicide through a one-to-one interactive basis. For instance, on Monday, Jan. 28, 2019, BBC news reported about a British teenager who had committed suicide through the help of influences on Instagram. In many of these instances, agents of suicide videos are able to figure out their victims' emotional challenges and coach them to do what they would under normal circumstances not do. Further, many young men rescued from Islamic State of Iraq and Syria (ISIS) revealed that they were lured into joining the deadly group through social media platforms and videos watched on YouTube. They got indoctrinated in the process. Two recent examples are a lady of American decent who got married to one of the members of the Islamic group and had a child with him now wanting to reunite with her family after the husband was killed, and another British young man currently in prison custody in Syria pleadding to be allowed back into the UK. Both victims confessed on BBC News in June 2019 that they were indoctrinated and have regretted their actions.

For all the positive impacts of social media, it has created other ethical challenges and some of those tend to exploit mental health. Individuals that are potentially struggling with day- to-day psychological challenges feel the added pressures to portray their lives with false impressions about their predicaments because of the social impact of the social media. To many of these individuals, writing and posting for many is an outlet for connections, healing, productivity and coping with stress. That same platform leads to increased feelings of isolation, cyber bulling and reduced self-esteem in other cases (Aboujaoude, Savage, Starcevic, & Salame, 2015). There appears to be a significant struggle to manage the negative effects of the platform without infringing on the positive areas for others. These boundaries are evolving and societal pressure along with the corporate entities that benefit from the platform carry the burden of identifying those boundaries.

The scope of influence and reach of social media has given rise to the emergence of anti-social practices and ethical lapses in many social media platforms and communication blogs. Bad actors have hidden behind the façade of anonymity to abuse the privileges of transparency and privacy of other users. The right to log on the various social media websites has also given self-entitlement to many users to live by their own ethical values and morals, which has created myriad of ethical problems for many businesses and audiences. Another intriguing area of social media is online dating which has made it possible for people to look beyond their immediate environments and surroundings for a mate. With this benefit also comes many possible risks and deceptions which go beyond the scope of this work. Social media has also been a negative influence for many employees, as many times employees look through a person's Facebook. This is directly linked to moral issues which are debatable and result in judgement calls that may not be appropriate. Another interesting issue is that of videos being posted to social media, especially those of racial profiling. This has caused both divisions and unifying effects in our culture. Posted videos on Facebook and whatsApp for instance have ranged from the good, the bad and the ugly. As such, the introduction of regulation by the various social media providers is key to promoting ethical behaviour among users.

Challenges such as fraud, fake news, shady deals, privacy invasion, security (Al-Mashaqbeh, 2015), deception (Kasturi & Vardhan, 2014), lies and half-truths, bad influence, addiction (Singh, Chopra, & Kaur, 2015) and many more are concerns associated with social media. Mgbeahurike, (2015) noted that half-truths and fake news travel faster and cause huge damages within seconds via social media. Fraudulent schemes include situations where people are deceptively made to donate monies presumed to be for the support of worthy causes that only end up in the pockets of fraudsters. To minimise online abuses, governments have investigated social media organisations and imposed fines. Typical examples include Facebook and Cambridge Analytica in 2018, which were culprits for not securing the personal information of Facebook users. Social media platform developers who think they are just platform developers who can get away with what is posted on the platforms should rethink because more and more responsibility is now placed at their doorsteps (Newman, Levy, & Nielsen, 2015) and this trend is likely to increase in the future. For instance, the US government passed a law to protect children who go online. This law is the Children's Online Privacy Protection Act (COPA) which requires website operators targeting children to post privacy policies on their sites to notify their parents about what specific information they collect about the children and how that information is going to be used. The parents must give their full consent before this information is gathered on children, especially those under 13 years of age. Under the Act, Xang.com was fined \$1m for breaching the Act on some 1.7 million minors (Reilly, 2014; Wolford, 2013). Website operators must also increase self-regulation to avoid these fines. Some have in fact taken initiatives to operationalize self-regulation. For example, TRUSTe, a non-profit organisation works with Microsoft to conduct audits of organisations' security privacy measures to help browsers browse safely. TRUSTe, it is believed has the perception that when there is openness and mutual trust, the internet will be a safe place for all browsers where comfort, and diversity will be upheld. The company thus lends its Trademark stamp of approval to websites that meet its security and privacy standards (TRUSTe, 2014).

Laws must be passed to make it compulsory for every web developer to belong to an association where their practices will be supervised by the government. For instance, the Direct Marketing Association (DMA) is building consumer confidence in direct online shopping. It launched a privacy promise to American consumers which requires all members to adhere to consumer privacy rules that have been carefully crafted to protect online consumers. This includes the requirement to notify consumers on the use and renting, selling and exchange of their personal data to others. They are also required to allow clients to opt out of any further transfer of their data or solicitation by third parties. They must also respect the views of their clients who will not want to receive calls and mails from web marketers (Farnham, 2014). Organisations who flouted this law and bombarded potential customers with many such intrusive calls have received fines in the United Kingdom and other European countries. Kotler & Armstrong (2016) noted that most of the firms that have signed up to this association belong to the Fortune 100 companies.

Web developers must also be able to build software into their systems that will detect fake news and trace them to the source. Such persons who post unwholesome information or activities online should be fined, named and shamed or even banned entirely from using various websites to serve as a deterrent to others. For example, paedophiles, child pornographers and scammers should be easily traceable and when caught should be made to face the above consequences. Policing online privacy is thus the right thing to do.

Social media owners should encourage users to abide by the same values that respects the privacy, confidentially and trust of others. Users breaching the rights of others by anonymously publishing their personal information and disregarding the sensitivity of others should be shamed and generally called out by all users. The attitude of shaming and calling out unethical behaviour can draw attention to users to shirk such unethical behaviour.

There should also be a stated rule to remove and disable users who violate the interests of others by posting immoral contents on the social media website. Outlining this policy measure would strengthen common moral values among users, improve usability and ethical behaviour on the social media platforms. Users embracing common values such as responsibility, accountability and consideration of others would ensure trust and enhance ethical behaviour on the social media platform. In this respect, personal self-regulation would be regarded as an ethical model for all users.

Agreeing to a statement of moral approbation and self-regulation by users should be a cardinal moral principle to all users. This principle will drive a sense of self-respect and a sense of moral approval among users. This concept of self-respect and moral approval aligns with the theory of moral approbation which states that an individual is likely to behave morally because of participation in a social group. In socialisation, an actor reflects on the behaviour of individuals before a moral decision is acted upon. The wish for approbation will guide a person to respect other individuals near them in a group, because other perspectives of his behaviour is vital to him (Trevino, 1986). However, when one reads Facebook or tweets from even those who are supposed to lead our countries, one might argue that we do not practice moral approbation on social media as we do when not relating to others virtually. For instance, we have been divided into the extreme left and right to a great extent. This is deeply accentuated when we tweet back and forth or make comments on Facebook. Creating an ethical environment, self-regulation and instituting a strict code of ethics for social media websites is paramount to managing an ethically responsible social media platform for all users.

REFERENCES

Aboujaoude, E., Savage, M. W., Starcevic, V., & Salame, W. O. (2015). Cyberbullying: Review of an old problem gone viral. *The Journal of Adolescent Health, 57*(1), 10–18. doi:10.1016/j.jadohealth.2015.04.011 PMID:26095405

Al-Mashaqbeh, I. F. (2015). Social media practice: The challenges of using Facebook in higher education. *Malaysian Journal of Distance Education, 17*(2), 37–50. doi:10.21315/mjde2015.17.2.3

Colliander, J., & Dahlen, M. (2011). Following the fashionable friend: The power of social media weighing publicity effectiveness of blogs versus online magazines. *Journal of Advertising Research, 51*(3), 313–320. doi:10.2501/JAR-51-1-313-320

Donegan, R. (2012). Bullying and cyberbullying: History, statistics, law, prevention and analysis. *The Elon Journal of Undergraduate Research in Communications, 3*(1), 33–42.

Everett, M. R., & Kincaid, L. D. (1982). Communication networks: Towards a new paradigm for research. *Social Forces, 61*(1), 325–327. doi:10.2307/2578109

Farnham, A. (2014). Fighting telemarketers: When do-not-call list fails, these strategies work, *ABC News,* Jan. 21. Retrieved from http:// abcnews.go.com/Business/best-ways-turn-tables-telemarketers/story?id=21534413; and www.donotcall.gov

Kasturi, S. K., & Vardhan, P. B. (2014). Social media: Key issues and new challenges - A study of Nalgonda district, *Global Media Journal, Summer Issue, 5*(1), 1–12.

Kotler, P., & Armstrong, G. (2016). *Principles of marketing, 16th Global Edition*. San Francisco, CA: Pearson Publication.

Kunz, M. B., & Hackworth, B. A. (2011). Are consumers following retailers to social networks. *Academy of Marketing Studies Journal, 15*(1), 1–23.

Lim, C., & Putnam, R. D. (2010). Religion, social networks, and life satisfaction. *American Sociological Review, 75*(6), 914–933. doi:10.1177/0003122410386686

Mefolere, K. F. (2015). WhatsApp and information sharing: Prospects and challenges. *International Journal of Social Science and Humanities Research, 4*(1), 615–625.

Mgbeahurike, O. (2015). Social media: To build and to destroy. *Archcardinal's Blog on Economic and Burning Issues in Nigeria*. Retrieved from https: archardinal.wordspress.com/2015/06/05/socialmedia-to-build-and-to-destroy/

Newman, N., Levy, D. A. L., & Nielsen, R. K. (2015). Reuters institute digital news 2015: tracking the Future of News. Reuters Institute for the Study of Journalism. Oxford, UK: University of Oxford. doi:10.2139srn.2619576

Palen, L., & Liu, S. B. (2007, April). Citizen communications in crisis: Anticipating a future of ICT-supported public participation. In *Proceedings of the SIGCHI conference on Human factors in computing systems* (pp. 727-736). New York, NY: ACM. 10.1145/1240624.1240736

Palen, L., Vieweg, S., Sutton, J., Liu, S. B., & Hughes, A. (2007). Crisis informatics: Studying crisis in a networked world. In *Third International Conference on e-Social Science* (7-9).

Palen, L., Vieweg, S., Sutton, J., Liu, S. B., & Hughes, A. (Oct. 2010). Crisis informatics: studying crisis in a networked world. In *Third International Conference on e-Social Science* (pp. 7-9).

Reilly, R. B. (2014). Feds to mobile marketers: stop targeting kids, or else, *Venture Beat,* March 27. Retrieved from http://venturebeat. com/2014/03/27/feds-to-mobile-marketers-stop- targeting-kidsor-else-exclusive/.

Singh, N., Chopra, N., & Kaur, J. (2015). A study to analyse relationship between psychological behavioural factors on WhatsApp addiction among youth in Jalandhar District in Punjab. *Global Advanced Research Journal of Management and Business Studies*, *5*(4), 203–207.

Trevino, L. K. (1986). Ethical decision making in organizations: A person-situation interactionist model. *Academy of Management Review*, *11*(3), 601–617. doi:10.5465/amr.1986.4306235

TRUSTe. (2014). 2014 TRUSTe US Consumer Confidence Index, *TRUSTe.* Retrieved from www.truste. com/us-consumerconfidence- index-2014/

TRUSTe. (2014). 2014 TRUSTe US Consumer Confidence Index. Retrieved from www.truste.com/ us-consconsumerconfidence- index-2014/

Van Dijck, J. (2013). *The culture of connectivity: A critical history of social media.* Oxford, UK: Oxford University Press. doi:10.1093/acprof:oso/9780199970773.001.0001

Wiest, E. A. (2011). Social media in the Egyptian revolution. *International Journal of Communication*, *23*(4), 2–3.

Wolford, J. (2013). Facebook still has a big problem with underage users, and they know it, *WebProNews*, Jan. 24. Retrieved from www.webpronews.com/facebook-still-has-a-big-problemwith- underage-users-and-they-know-it-2013-01

KEY TERMS AND DEFINITIONS

Social media: It is a platform for disseminating information. It is usually collaborative computer-mediated technologies that enable making and sharing of information, ideas and other modes of communications through virtual communities and networks.

Online Communication: It indicates the forms in which individuals can interact with one another over a computer network such as the internet. These forms may include e-mail and chat rooms.

Social Media Platforms: This refers to an internet-based technology that facilitates the growth, placement and management of social media services. It offers the capability to set up social media websites and services with full social media network usability.

Social Networking: It is specifically the use of reserved websites and functions to communicate with other users, or to local people with common interests to one's own.

Geographical Barriers: It is primarily the natural occurring development or body of water that separates and detaches as area from others. General geographical barriers are oceans, rivers, lakes, mountains, canyons and islands.

Chapter 10
Effectively Utilizing a Socially Mediated Network:
Facilitating Meaningful Collaboration Among Pre-Service Student-Teachers and University EFL Students

Dustin De Felice
Michigan State University, USA

Wesley A. Curtis
University of South Carolina, USA

Luz María Ortiz Alcocer
Universidad de Quintana Roo, Mexico

ABSTRACT

Cooperative learning has evolved over the years to include web-mediated elements within traditional and virtual classrooms. In this chapter, authors discuss a collaboration that used computer-supported collaborative learning through an online socially-mediated network. This collaboration served as a bridge between two universities from different countries. Not only did this collaboration link the students from each university together, but it provided language learners and pre-service student-teachers with the ability to benefit from the unique connection between them (i.e. students needing to learn language and teachers needing to practice teaching a language). Authors discuss the collaboration, the framework, and the format of this cooperative learning project. Much of this discussion is rooted in the experiences of some of the students who participated in its evolution with the intent to provide a direction for implementing such a type of collaboration in other institutions.

DOI: 10.4018/978-1-5225-9814-5.ch010

INTRODUCTION

What do trilingual Mexican university students in a rural area have in common with pre-service student-teachers at an urban university in the United States? Both groups utilized a socially-mediated network to create a learning space designed to facilitate the attainment of their academic goals. The students in Mexico needed to practice and develop their English language skills (especially in developing cultural competence and conversational abilities), while the U.S. students needed to interact with and develop strategies for teaching English language learners. As this particular case highlights, collaborations can easily exist in virtual spaces through any number of available platforms.

Collaborations can also serve as a bridge between universities from around the world. While there are many types of virtual outlets, the availability of socially-mediated networks have made collaborations an integral part of daily life for many (e.g., Facebook, Instagram, LinkedIn, Snapchat, Twitter, VK, WeChat, etc.). Students, faculty, and administrators often turn to socially-mediated networks in their personal and professional lives for many reasons (Sykes, Holden, & Knight, 2019). As Langhorst (2009) noted, people tend to gravitate toward virtual networks. In this way, a socially-mediated network could be an appropriate choice as a bridge between universities because many educators and learners appear to have a preference for such collaboration simply because of its virtual nature. These virtual networks can also serve to link language learners while allowing for the practice of language skills (De Felice, 2012, 2013). Additionally, these virtual networks provide an opportunity to have meaningful and more authentic experiences for students from rural areas who are learning a foreign language they cannot or only infrequently encounter in their local communities.

The underlying assumption for creating a university-bridged collaboration is that such an arrangement would support the educators' and students' needs while providing an inexpensive, yet expansive learning space. Taking advantage of various platforms, applications, and programs, these collaborative environments can be structured to include any number of components that take into account the needs of today's language classroom (Ioannou & Stylianou-Georgiou, 2012; Rojano-Caceres, Ramos-Quintana, & Vargas-Cerdán, 2012). First, students can be engaged in learning while being around the platforms within a face-to-face environment (many times, educators can work with their students in laboratories or classrooms at their universities). Second, educators and students can work in/through their network while being at a distance from each other. In this manner, the platform can act as a mediator for connecting the geographically distinct entities and may serve as an anchor for this type of cooperative environment. Third, given the advances in software development, the platform can act as a 'member' in a cooperative group. This membership can be in the form of a quiz maker, an application where the learner interacts with a specific component or a space for uploading content, among others. Lastly, the collaboration can serve higher purposes for the educators and language learners, especially in terms of learning a language (De Felice, 2012).

BACKGROUND

Socially-Mediated Networks

The use of socially-mediated networks can enhance instruction, establish deeper relationships with students, and/or substitute for a learning management system (Carter, Foulger, & Ewbank, 2008; Cruickshank,

Chen, & Warren, 2012; Reinhardt & Thorne, 2019). All three of these advantages are important considerations for many language learning classrooms. Educators can enhance instruction by using networks to include highly fluent speakers from target countries, give students more time with the language in an immersive environment and place learning responsibilities onto the student (where creative content is not only accepted, but encouraged in the form of blogs, podcasts, videos, presentations, etc.). When the educator serves as a participant-observer within the network, he or she may be able to develop deeper relationships with students because participation is expected of all community members. Lastly, many learning management systems have one major disadvantage inherent in their design. Most systems do not allow the language of instruction to be different from that of the university at-large.

Although the tools and platforms themselves are an important piece in creating that expansive learning space, the pedagogical and instructional design choices are just as important. The use of cooperative learning strategies is a natural fit for socially-mediated networks and the underlying context for this chapter. In the next section, the theory behind cooperative learning and how it benefits from computer support is discussed.

Cooperative Learning

In this section, the focus is on cooperative learning (CL), its meaning, the reasons for using CL, and the ways CL may be used. In using CL, educators are able to increase opportunities for student interaction, for ownership in projects, and for creating lasting relationships within a group framework. Cooperative learning is sometimes confused with collaborative learning, which is another approach to structured group work. However, there are slightly different meanings between these two terms. In cooperative learning, group members share the workload. For example, group members write four separate sections of a paper independently and the four sections are combined into one product. In collaborative learning, group members develop shared meanings about their work. For instance, group members produce four sections of a paper and make them into a single and unified group paper (Johnson & Johnson, 2008). Despite the differences, the term "cooperation" is often used to refer to either "cooperation-based" activities or "collaboration-based" activities in cooperative learning research.

There are three types of cooperative learning (Johnson & Johnson, 2008), which are commonly used in standard classrooms. However, these approaches are also being used in combination with instructional technology in many contexts. In the first approach, called formal cooperative learning, students work from one class period to several weeks to achieve shared learning goals and jointly complete specific tasks and assignments (e.g., problem solving, writing a report, or having a dialogue about assigned text materials). A second approach, called informal cooperative learning, has students work to achieve a joint learning goal in temporary, ad hoc groups that last from a few minutes to one class period (e.g., students engage in 3 to 5 minute focused discussions before and after a lecture and 2 to 3 minute turn-to-your-partner discussions). A third type, cooperative based groups focus on long-term, heterogeneous units that share similar characteristics. These groups share stable membership with participants who have primary responsibilities for providing support, encouragement, and assistance to make academic progress and develop cognitively and socially in healthy ways. The use of cooperative learning in a traditional classroom has been successful for many educators and the potential for success exists for moving this approach online through computer support.

Computer-Supported Cooperative Learning

As many distance learning educators use synchronous platforms like Skype to take advantage of many-to-many interaction in a live format, they are able to incorporate the following features into their teaching: classroom/conference replication, content development/inclusion, rich media support, management and usability, and technological considerations in accessibility and security. Often these approaches are made up of a combination of applications that allow for the transfer of files or the inclusion of multimedia content. Some researchers refer to the next stage in this process as Mobile-assisted language learning (MALL) where mobile applications are used to support these learners' interactions (Plonsky & Ziegler, 2016; Sykes et al., 2019). By combining cooperative learning and these types of technologies, advantageous outcomes are possible. Cooperative learning in standard classrooms can have powerful effects on abundant cognitive and affective outcomes such as academic achievement, cognitive development, intergroup relations, motivation and anxiety (Cruickshank et al., 2012; Ioannou & Stylianou-Georgiou, 2012). In addition to traditional cooperative learning, there has been a growing interest in the potential of Web-mediated tools as facilitators for students' learning. These two trends emerge in computer-supported cooperative learning (CSCL), which seeks to combine classroom-based cooperative learning with computer technology. However, is effectiveness the same for an online environment and will those same benefits transfer to that arena?

In order for computer-supported cooperative learning environments to succeed, educators must be familiar with two areas. First, educators must be familiar with the nature of cooperative learning and what makes it both different from competitive learning and individualistic learning. Second, the results of using CSCL require educators to operate under a different assumption when evaluating the end products. In fact, the end product is not as vital as the discussion and negotiation that occurs between the students while they are interacting and sharing in the learning process. Further, educators must focus on the students' abilities to develop critical thinking skills and they must measure their students' understanding of the subject area (Persico, Pozzi, & Sarti, 2009). CSCL is also a method for attempting to have students receive instruction that is uniquely tailored to meet their needs, abilities and motivations (Johnson & Johnson, 2008).

In addition to understanding the types of and the basic elements in cooperative learning, there are also concerns for working with groups. For instance, ensuring groups made up of diverse individuals with a variety of learning preferences is a preferred way to organize student interactions as long as students who are at risk academically are not isolated (Felder & Brent, 2001). In attempting to avoid dysfunctional teams, one strategy involves letting interpersonal problems surface naturally, and then equipping the students with strategies for dealing with them. This step begins with putting the class into small groups and giving them a few minutes to brainstorm ways of dealing with group problems. Once the group has completed a list of ideas, they work to reach a consensus on best strategies for solving their problems. Another possible concern is the student who does not fully participate in the group (Rienties et al., 2012; Rosen, Carrier, & Cheever, 2013). These types of challenges may involve the instructor who is in a position to penalize the non-participating team member. Another strategy for working through this challenge would be to institute a peer rating system to adjust the team assignment grade separately for each team member (Felder & Brent, 2001). For any issue related to grading student work, it is important for instructors to create a policy or practice early on in a cooperative learning environment so that students are aware of their responsibilities.

One way of maximizing the interaction between the students is to construct learning communities with cooperative learning at its core. Classroom-based learning communities exist in forms that include the entire classroom within one interaction, as seen in the example of an elementary school classroom where the teacher and students are engaged daily in activities and practices as a whole (Saville, Lawrence, & Jakobsen, 2012). These learning communities can also occur within a classroom where groups of students work to complete either problem-based activities or engage in activities designed to bring forth a collective effort for understanding the course content. In this collaboration, the educators needed to rethink this classroom-based learning community (Sykes et al., 2019) because the students and instructors were not located in the same geographic area. However, the students in Mexico and the United States were both integral in completing the classroom-based tasks. This experience was focused on a learning community and based on experiential learning. The students in Mexico needed to construct and complete assignments that were intended to improve their English language abilities while explaining or describing issues and traditions in their culture. Using this student-created work as a base, the pre-service student-teachers in the United States needed to evaluate and critique contributions of their Mexican counterparts. By partaking in these activities, the pre-service student-teachers were engaging in real-world tasks that would aid them in becoming teachers for developing language learners.

EXPERIENCES IN CREATING, COLLABORATING, AND CONTINUING A SOCIALLY MEDIATED NETWORK BASED ON CSCL

Using CSCL through a socially-mediated network, a collaboration project between two university classes was set up. There were a number of areas where the classroom activities overlapped and where the students had various professional and academic goals that could not be reached through traditional means within the two universities. One educator worked in a rural area in Mexico where the students did not have enough direct contact with English language and US culture. The other educator worked in an urban university where it was not easy to connect pre-service student-teachers to English language learners. For the remainder of this chapter, the discussion is focused on the experiences with creating the network and continuing the project across semesters. There is also a discussion on the experiences of three students in Mexico who participated in the collaboration, because their opinions, descriptions, and observations led to many changes and improvements to the overall endeavor.

Creation of a Private Socially-Mediated Network

When the collaboration initially began, the educators discussed at length the type of software, application, or program that could house such a dynamic and interactive endeavor. These educators investigated using the university-available systems to create the collaboration without much success. While the tools available at each university were excellent in connecting students within the university, there were no easy ways to connect students across university systems. Given the popularity of Facebook, there was some initial interest in using it as the basis for the collaboration. Facebook offers a number of ways to create groups that include various levels of privacy/security (Reinhardt & Thorne, 2019). While this type of space was a viable option, the recent number of platform and privacy changes made this choice problematic for a secure and private educational space. There was also interest in using a more flexible virtual space since the collaborative objectives required a series of applications/tools within the platform.

Additionally, many individuals choose to not engage in socially-mediated networks like Facebook or prefer their personal spaces separated from their academic or professional lives. One last difficulty with using Facebook is that it is not as highly customizable as other platforms.

Many socially-mediated networks include features not present in the networks with greatest market share in the Western hemisphere. Alternative platforms for setting up a group space include Vine, Yahoo! Groups, LinkedIn, WhatsApp, WeChat, Line, and Wordpress among others (see Roseth, Akcaoglu, & Zellner, 2013 for a description of combining multiple applications in a classroom situation). Since the capacities, tools, and requirements vary for each of these online sources, the needs of the collaboration should be matched with the best possible outcome. In this particular collaboration, we needed a virtual space that fit the following criteria: customizable, private and affordable. After reviewing numerous options, a Ning-supported platform was chosen where the educators were able to create a private, invitation-only space that was customizable and affordable. The Ning platform offered an additional benefit, which was that students were able to log into the interaction through their own socially-mediated networks (e.g., Facebook, Twitter, LinkedIn, etc.). While there are various pricing options (from $25USD a month), the basic package was chosen because it offered sufficient membership numbers, expansive Web space and the ability to incorporate html code for some specific tools/applications.

Implementation of Collaboration Between Universities

In terms of the collaboration itself, the platform was initially set up as a space where partnerships (assigned by the educators) could interact. With this model, the educators hoped to see students developing a solid relationship whereby the pre-service student-teacher could support the English language learner in his/her language development. This approach envisioned the platform as a conduit for interaction with minimal instructor intervention.

Experiences With Socially-Mediated Networks

Over five semesters, students from a university in Yucatan, Mexico interacted with university students in Florida, United States. Around 500 students collaborated through a Ning-enhanced platform where their experiences, comments, and questions led to multiple changes, revisions, and improvements. The analysis of the use of words, quality of interaction, technology limitations, and language challenges were focused on the students in Mexico who were pursuing a bachelor's degree in language and culture. Their native language was Yucatec Maya, but they were also fluent speakers of Spanish and were learning English in the university. Their proficiency levels with English varied, but most were enrolled in their third or fourth semester of English language instruction. Each of them described their interactions as having positive, yet frustrating qualities. They found that being able to teach their own culture was an exciting and likeable experience overall and being connected to students who were interested in learning about their native language and culture was also very motivating. Lastly, they welcomed the opportunity to learn about the Florida students' culture while practicing their English because it was a very practical experience that differed from their normal classroom interactions. The connection made the language learning experience very hands-on and encouraged them to use their new English language skills for real-world applications.

There were many students in the collaboration, but the initial focus was on the experiences of three: Kanik, Siis, and Ts'íikil. Kanik was a pseudonym for a student who was in her early twenties pursuing a bachelor's degree with plans to teach young children in her future. Her pseudonym means *Learn* in Yucatec Maya and reflected her commitment to education. Siis means *Cool* in Yucatec Maya and it was a pseudonym for another student who was pursuing the same degree as Kanik. He was focused on projects meant to disseminate his language and culture through various forms of media (radio, Websites, television, etc.). His pseudonym referred to his calm, confident manner during the interactions. Lastly, Ts'íikil (Yucatec Maya word for *Courage)* was a student in his early twenties. Much like Kanik and Siis, Ts'íikil was enrolled in the same university program. He was a very productive member within the collaboration and he was very interested in learning about the pre-service student-teachers from the United States. Like many young people in college, he was not sure what his future plans would be, but he felt English was an important skill that he needed for whatever direction he went in. His pseudonym referred to his introverted personality. He was also anxious about his English ability, but courageously worked diligently to improve himself through the interaction.

Interaction Qualities

The interactions occurred through a Ning platform where there was an interchange of experiences based on culture and language. These students used a Ning portal to complete various tasks through postings, blog listings, chat rooms, and audio recordings that were assigned by their instructors. This multimodal approach was set up to create an interactional space. During the interaction, the students gained knowledge about each culture through a series of activities and projects that required interacting through the network (Abrams, 2019; Reinhardt & Thorne, 2019). While the intention was to develop intercultural competence, many times that meant discussing surface-level cultural issues like clothing, food, or customs (mostly in differentiating the Mayan students from those of Mexicans in general). This focus on Mayan culture was a favorite for all three students, though such interactions did create some unexpected consequences.

Because of how important their approach to culture was, the students encountered a number of frustrations in their interactions. In many areas in the network, the students found their virtual classmates in Florida did not seem to be interested enough in some of their postings. They were disappointed that there was not much interaction in the form of questions, comments, or on the content of their postings. In some cases, this frustration was related to the way the comment feature worked. The asynchronous nature of this feature led many students to avoid answering questions or replying to comments because there was not an immediate reaction required. In other cases, the amount of time it took for a response to appear often led to fewer comments or questions following any of the original posts. A different consequence occurred when multiple comments were found. The flow of conversation was often interrupted by the addition of multiple comments. The messiness of the comment format was challenging for many students in the network.

By focusing on culture, the students became confident in explaining their traditions, customs, rituals, and experiences. Ts'íikil also spent time teaching some of his language directly. He taught some basic words and phrases. His discussions of language were directly linked to his Mayan culture. Much of this work was done through the blogging tool in the network. As noted in Ducate and Lomicka (2008), the use of microblogs (i.e., blogs contained within a network) allows students to focus on content while working to improve their writing abilities. In addition, the public nature of the blog postings meant students were exposed to more examples of writing that may have contained creative, experimental, and interesting content. All of this writing existed in a relaxed environment and gave the students the opportunity to foster ownership in their work.

The interaction was almost exclusively in English and these students posted material, texts, and recordings at varying times throughout the semester-long experience. As the work was mostly asynchronous, much of the work involved written tasks, including the creation of blogs, comments or, at times, synchronous chatting. When chatting occurred, the participants felt their experience intensify and it gave them the opportunity to practice their English language skills in real-time (Rubio, Thomas, & Li, 2018). Kanik talked about practicing her English when chatting, and she found the complexity of her interactions exacerbated by the need to simultaneously figure out how to use the network and interact with the students in Florida (Abrams, 2019). This synchronous interaction put pressure on the students because there was very little time to think, plan, or edit messages sent (Alvarez-Torres, 2001). All of the students would comment on this difference and they would mention they preferred posting material asynchronously because they had time to think, plan, or edit messages. Thus, this preference for less intense interactions appears to stem from, in part, the reduction of affective stimuli afforded by asynchronicity (Ortega, 2017). Unfortunately, these types of deeper experiences were not utilized with much frequency because they relied on random encounters between members on the site. In many cases, synchronous chat was not feasible due to differences in student schedules and time zones.

Siis described much of his time in the network as productive and fruitful. He liked the opportunity to practice his English in a virtual space because he considers himself a shy individual. The asynchronous nature of his work meant he was able to spend extra time on his postings, which lessened his feelings of insecurity. He also found the focus on culture refreshing. He was able to compare his work with that of the students in Florida and discover similarities and differences between them. He found that aspect of the interaction a very powerful learning tool. While there were many areas within the network, most of the students spent their time on the "My Page" section. This page included a space for a user's picture, a list of tools for email messaging or user options, an activity feed and a list of content (e.g., the number of entries in the blog, comments posted by the member, etc.). Since users were able to post a picture under their name, many students chose a picture of themselves doing some of their favorite activities at home or at school, while others chose a picture that represented them (e.g., a picture of a flower, a pet or something similar, etc.).

Technology Limitations Through Challenges and Barriers

Some aspects of the interaction were not positive and these frustrations and difficulties were related to the level of comfort that each student had with technology (Abrams, 2019). Other complications were related to physical aspects of the virtual setting. Because most of the students from Mexico did not have a strong background in technology, they needed to utilize much of their time learning how to use the platform. This limitation led to using others, including the supervising professor in Mexico, as resources for helping learn how to interact in the portal. Lastly, all of the interactions, whether asynchronous or synchronous, required the use of the Internet. The on-campus connection speed was slow and at times difficult to work with, which led to a lower level of engagement.

For all three Mayan students, technology skills were an issue during the collaboration. Kanik, in particular, discussed her limited background with computers. While she was comfortable using a smartphone and could use email, word processing programs, and Internet browsers, she was unfamiliar with the tools in the network. Many times, she frequently needed to rely on other students in the collaboration or her supervisor to help her complete the various tasks during the semester. While this reliance on others may be viewed as a limitation, under a cooperative learning model it is considered a benefit because she developed new skills through her interactions with others.

One key component to most socially-mediated networks involves the presence of a chat tool, which can turn any collaboration into a synchronous platform. Alvarez-Torres (2001) noted the pressures with real time means there is little time to think, plan, or edit any message sent. This type of interaction mirrors an interaction in person and can be an important component to incorporate into any collaboration. For example, Ts'íikil often sought assistance from the students in Florida through the use of the chat function in the platform. He discussed these interactions because it was helpful to receive assistance from another student, and it was an opportunity for him to practice his written conversational language. While he found these interactions challenging, he would often try to set up times to meet with others in the platform because of the language growth he felt was occurring (Rubio et al., 2018). Kanik and Ts'íikil's experiences represent the type of supportive growth that enables learning to occur in varied ways and may lead to developing deeper connections to technology and the people involved in the collaboration.

Finally, the current integration of software applications into suites is creating new sets of tools that require more skill sets for participants (Bloch, 2008a). Specific to language classrooms, there are a number of implied needs that require interactions using the four traditional skills (i.e., listening, reading, speaking, and writing). Godwin-Jones (2005) and Chen, Belkada, and Okamoto (2004) discuss a number of virtual environments where the use of multiple channels allows for learning to occur within all four of those traditional skill-sets. These advances bring about more issues for their use in classroom settings and are referred to as "technological literacy" (Bloch, 2008b). In some respects, traditional asynchronous tools (e.g., Google documents) become synchronous in nature due to software functions allowing multi-user and real-time editing capabilities, which some of the students utilized to complete various classroom tasks (Simpson, 2005). Microblogs are another example of collaborative tasks employed in the study that were drawn from research literature (see Ducate & Lomicka, 2008). These blogs are shared within the network and give students the opportunity to upload, edit, or comment on the various entries. These networks that allow for real-time editing in both small and large groups are changing the manner in which language learning can occur.

As many of the students discussed that they already had limited abilities with socially-mediated networks, their difficulty with 'technological literacy' (Bloch, 2008b) would be exacerbated by the network itself. Because the network featured a number of tools integrated into a common platform supported by English language menus, buttons, and tools, the Mexican students found navigating the system more difficult. While the platform allowed for additional languages, one language needed to be set as the default language (in this case English as the participants in Florida did not speak Spanish). There are difficulties inherent in using multiple modalities in a virtual environment. For example, the complexity increases when more than one tool is used to communicate (a necessity in a language learning situation). This complexity can also be increased because a common language may need to be chosen across the network (for example, if Spanish/Yucatec Maya-speaking students are learning English, the network's built-in interface language may need to be in Spanish while the interactions would be in English). In many cases, these students were familiar with the features of the network due to their use of other socially-mediated networks like Facebook (with a Spanish language interface), but often they were not able to transfer their technology literacy until they became familiar with the terms, menus and options in English.

One of the biggest challenges for all three Mayan students was centered on infrastructure. Their campus is located in a rural area of Mexico and the connection speeds were considerably slower during various points of the day or the connection was only sporadically available. The slow connection speed was especially apparent when they attempted to upload photographs, recordings, graphics, or other multimedia files. In many cases, the students would need to upload their content at Internet cafes in the community where the speed and stability were more consistent. Other times, the network itself was unable to handle larger file sizes and students needed to upload their content onto other providers (e.g., YouTube for videos as one example) and provide an embedded link to ensure their content appeared in their blogs or posts in the platform. In addition to upload difficulties, there were other challenges because of the slow download speeds. As more content was uploaded into the network, the time required for a page to download became longer and, often, interrupted with the downloading of the Webpage itself. In such instances, the full page was unable to load or timed out, which left the students with no way to interact with the network when the dropdown menus, tools or tabs were unable to load. While the internet connection was not ideal on campus, it was the main source of access for these students since many of them do not have connections in their homes. Additionally, students only had access to computers during their time on campus when they were not in class. As most students traveled long distances to attend classes at the university, there was not always sufficient time to devote to activities in the platform. Upon further reflection, the students in Mexico found another challenge much more difficult to overcome. In the next section, Siis, Kanik, and Ts'íikil talked openly about their difficulty with sharing their culture using English.

Developing the Collaboration: From Changes to Rethinking Its Beginnings

Upon reflection, the students involved in the collaboration saw themselves as beginning educators with multiple roles and tasks to accomplish. Any work students completed in the platform was carried out in addition to their coursework and other daily activities, such as part-time jobs. Another important consideration in their experience was the fact that the collaboration was temporal in nature. Most students completed their experience within a semester before moving onto other coursework or projects. In that sense, their time was spent on using the collaboration for gaining experience for their future careers rather than on developing more familiarity with the network. Kanik, Siis, and Ts'íikil gave us very detailed explanations of their interactions and one constant theme was that they felt a little overwhelmed with the technology portion of the collaboration. Since they were told to use the platform, they were not able to suggest another option that might have provided them with more familiarity and/or control over their work. In many respects, a different platform may have worked better given the technology difficulties. In some cases, more explanations/options, such as mobile messaging applications, may have mitigated the Internet connection difficulty. For example, spending some class time discussing ways of making file sizes smaller (through compression or file zipping) may have helped with the delays in uploading/downloading materials.

In reality, many participants reported that many of the partnerships bypassed the platform in favor of using email and/or another social media like Facebook. Additionally, there were a number of unintended and unplanned difficulties with the partnership model. For example, when students bypassed the platform, instructors no longer had access to the students' progress. The instructors could contact students directly for more information, but this step was an additional task that added to the administrative responsibilities. More importantly, the assumption was that the assigned partnerships would function for both participants. Of course, there were many instances of incompatible personalities and/or other difficulties (often related to expectations of email replies) as well as issues of attrition. Lastly, the most fundamental difficulty with basing the collaboration on this partnership model occurred in the lack of equal participant numbers. In any given semester, the course enrollments differed so much that there were not enough participants to complete the expected number of partnerships. Given these difficulties, a number of changes were made to approach the collaboration in a completely different way after the first two semesters.

Technology wasn't the only limitation/challenge to the students' experiences. Due to the nature of the interactions, the collaboration at times became more of a storage space than a collaborative environment. With mostly asynchronous interactions, the students did not gain as much experience with direct contact as originally planned. In fact, the instructors ended up relying on blogs, comment walls, and emails for the bulk of student work because they were unable to incorporate more synchronous interactions into the collaboration. As the collaboration evolved over the semesters, a number of students commented on the reliance on text based work over other media. As many of the students were frequent Facebook users, they occasionally talked about the need for more pictures, videos, and graphics within the collaboration. This inclusion of pictures was important for the overall network and the Mexican students felt it would have contributed an additional element to their cultural explanations. For example, when the students had trouble explaining a particular Mayan tradition, they felt the addition of a picture would ensure that students understood their description. In terms of videos, the Mexican students were interested in more practice with their speaking and conversation as well.

Once those needs were identified, the instructors created a number of spaces dedicated to pictures, videos and related links. The front page of the interaction was changed to include an area where students could send photographs that were posted on a daily basis. These photographs gave the students more control over the look of the collaboration, and it allowed them to indirectly teach more about themselves and their interests. The instructors also created another page that was strictly for videos. Students had the option of uploading videos (or links to videos) into this area. A number of class assignments were also incorporated where the students were asked to create videos for the collaboration. The students in Florida, for example, created videos based on the themes in the Mexican students' coursework. One example included a short video or a presentation that included photographs of the U.S.-based students' neighborhoods. These videos/presentations contained a short quiz and the students in Florida were responsible for creating materials using principles they were learning in their pedagogy courses. In addition to these structured spaces, separate pages were created where anyone could post photographs or videos that were not directly tied to a specific assignment or course-related activity.

Lastly, there were a number of suggested improvements that dealt with the collaboration activities. Ts'íikil was very interested in improving the CSCL activities because he often wanted to share more about his language as well as his culture. He felt strongly about the connection between language and culture and he wanted to spend more time developing lessons or posts about basic Yucatec Maya. Many times, he was able to discuss specific terms or vocabulary items, but he wanted more time with whole language activities like dialogs or role-playing situations. The collaboration ended before his suggestion was implemented and the instructors reflected on his information rather deeply because such a focus would have given the students in the U.S. the opportunity to be language learners. This focus may have subsequently contributed to their development of empathy toward their Mexican counterparts, because they would have been immersed in language and culture learning as well.

Obviously, there are a plethora of ways in which a collaboration can occur. In this particular case, a chance connection was made at a conference in Mexico where the instructors decided to work to create an online collaboration that could benefit their students. This connection occurred during the question portion of a presentation and led to numerous conversations through email to get the collaboration established. Such a random occurrence might not be the best way to secure a connection. Another disadvantage to such an arrangement is that without direct institutional support, knowledge, or expertise, the collaboration itself is only as stable as the instructors who volunteer to make it work. For example, the collaborations led to more development, more reflection, and more administration. As Russell and Curtis (2013) have noted, facilitating online language learning takes far more time than preparation for traditional face-to-face classes. All of these developments were handled in conjunction with daily job requirements and, at times, work on the collaboration was stalled due to semester-specific activities (e.g., testing, grading and/or registration). Lastly, a collaboration is limited by the continued support of the individual instructors. In this case, both instructors moved to other positions, and the collaboration could no longer exist in its earlier form without *a priori* succession planning. This development is important because the courses, students and programs at each university could have continued to benefit from the collaboration if a different approach had been implemented.

FUTURE RESEARCH DIRECTIONS

The collaboration had its share of successes and challenges, but the overall future direction for using CSCL may rely less on traditional desktop and laptop solutions. Instead, the current ubiquity of smartphones calls for a new paradigm for creating a network. As the collaboration came to an end, the instructors were already navigating different kinds of challenges and problems that were directly linked to students attempting to enter the collaboration through a handheld device. Many times, students were unable to view the drop-down menus, toolbars or hyperlinks because of the small screen size of their device. In other cases, the students were unable to log into the network because their smartphone did not allow for direct connections to traditional Web-based pages. The instructors also encountered more challenges when they began to incorporate more video, photographs and other multimedia files because some handheld devices did not support the necessary applications or plug-ins for viewing such files. Over the course of the collaboration, they revisited their own assumptions as instructors, and they started to leave more specific instructions that included references to what systems and applications they would recommend that students use to access a specific activity or area within the collaboration.

As noted earlier, some participants in the CSCL were beset by issues related to connectivity and lack of technology resources. Additionally, lack of familiarity with the Ning platform utilized, as well insufficient time made developing step-by-step technology training modules for each feature of the site unfeasible. Therefore, for educators and researchers considering undertaking a CSCL project, the recommendation is that a pre-project survey be conducted among likely or confirmed participants to ascertain which platforms might be most suitable for the proposed project. Motivation and attitude(s) toward language learning have long been identified as important factors in second language acquisition (see Zheng, Liang, Li, & Tsai, 2018), and thus, utilizing participants' preferred application or platform for CSCL delivery could potentially enhance learning outcomes. Future CSCL studies will want to explore the impact of platform on participants' enthusiasm and any potential correlation with learning outcome attainment. Other factors CSCL developers and researchers should take into consideration are access, accessibility, familiarity, pedagogical flexibility and cost. Many of these considerations may now be addressed through the selection of a robust mobile application.

Mobile-assisted language learning (MALL) provides a means for anytime, anywhere education (Wagner, 2005). As mentioned above, the ubiquity of mobile phones and cellular signals offers the potential for educational access in some of the Earth's remotest populated areas (Fotouhi-Ghazvini, Earnshaw, & Haji-Esmaeili, 2009). While media and technologies traditionally employed in instructional delivery (including post, broadcast television, cable, and fiber optic wiring) may not be available to students living off campus in rural areas, mobile devices —especially cellular phones— are often already at hand. Thus, mobile-learning (ML) is no longer considered to be a plausible possibility for the future, but rather, it is a staple in the stable of pedagogical conduits for 'millennials' (Kárpáti, 2009).

Despite the increasingly ubiquitous presence of mobile devices capable of being exploited for pedagogical purposes, there are a number of factors that should be taken into consideration when determining whether or not to take the M-learning route to facilitate CSCL projects (which the authors call MSCL rather than more commonly-used MCSCL). Data plan limitations are one example. As indicated above, cellular users whose data plans might constrain their usage could be adversely impacted by tasks requiring significant data usage, as this would come at increased personal expense. Some service providers, such as Telcel in Mexico, do not currently charge users for messaging via Facebook or WhatsApp. Any future collaboration should assess the availability and use of such applications in contexts in which a combination of access, speed, distance, cost, and pedagogical concerns must be balanced. Likewise, many people will find the cost of sufficiently fast and up-to-date mobile devices prohibitive. Thus, educators should make the equipment needed for any MSCL projects mandatory and the instructors should obtain and maintain a limited number of loaner devices to ensure that no students are disenfranchised by such requirements.

As noted above, the ubiquitous adoption of mobile devices worldwide signals the arrival of a powerful educational platform for historically disenfranchised learners in areas unreached by other types of infrastructure (Shurville & Browne, 2006). As such, any future collaborative projects among language learners and pre-service student-teachers should explore these options (Arnold & Ducate, 2015). However, before moving forward with changes like those suggested above, there is one more research activity from the experiences with the collaboration that should be explored. The focus on the experiences of Kanik, Siis, and Ts'íikil was because of their unique characteristics in that they were highly successful, motivated, and reflective. Looking back on the overall collaboration, there were a small number of students who were not successful. Many times, these students left the collaboration as a result of external factors, but they should be interviewed to learn more about their reasons for withdrawing from the course in the event that it was not related to a personal reason.

CONCLUSION

Upon reflection, the collaboration gave more than 500 students the opportunity to interact and learn from each other in a virtual space. For the students in Mexico, their coursework was given added weight because they were producing material in English that highly fluent speakers (in many cases native speakers) were reading, reviewing and revising. Students in the United States were able to work with an English language learner for the duration of a semester. These pre-service student-teachers were able to practice their teaching skills while learning about the challenges and difficulties facing language learners writ large, and they were, therefore, able to develop empathy for individuals involved in learning a language. For everyone involved in the collaboration, it served as a platform for practicing and honing various skills (from teaching to language learning). Since many of the students (both from Mexico and the United States) planned on becoming teachers upon completion of their degrees, this collaboration served as a type of virtual internship early in their careers as educators. Lastly, the platform served as an opportunity to become acquainted with a person outside of their traditional networks and, with the cultural focus, many students reported learning as much about themselves as they did about others.

One final note of import for this project exists in the precarious situation for indigenous languages in Mexico and the students who speak them. Being speakers of Yucatec Maya means their language is currently in danger of disappearing within a few generations. These students are extremely proud of their language and heritage, and they were thrilled to be able to share their language and culture with outsiders. In fact, Ts'íikil's family and friends were surprised to find out about his experiences with this collaboration. They felt such an effort would be good for his future and encouraged his continued pursuit of such types of educational opportunities. As Siis spent more time with the collaboration, he started to share more about his traditions and customs in a variety of ways because he was interested in transmitting his culture and language to as many people as he could. He saw this collaboration as an extension of his work in other areas, which was focused on disseminating knowledge of his culture to other parts of the world. He firmly believed that if his people did not take advantage of opportunities to spread knowledge about their language and culture, they may disappear. He also believed that everyone has a responsibility to nurture, maintain, and share their own culture while engaging in learning about other cultures. Kanik felt she contributed to the growth and development of others. She was proud to discuss her culture openly and to let the U.S.-based students know that she is as proud of her Mayan ancestors as she is of her current day Mayan-Mexican heritage. She would tell the students in Florida that even though many people believe her culture is in danger of vanishing, she focused on the way it is currently transforming and evolving into something new and different.

As indicated earlier, there is much research on the advantageous outcomes of using CSCL and this collaboration supports the claims of previous research. The students in Mexico felt the collaboration led them to experience higher achievement in their English coursework. Moreover, the addition of technology led to greater productivity and learning opportunities. Many times, they were able to generate more creative ideas and discussions because their interactions were with highly fluent speakers who were interested in understanding the culture of students in Mexico and had an interest in their success as language learners. Lastly, the students discussed their greater facility in transferring technology skills developed via the collaboration into their coursework-at-large. This transfer included a feeling of having more control of their learning and the development of greater relationships and social presence in virtual spaces. In the end, this unique collaboration resulted in a positive and satisfying experience for most participants (including for the moderators). Siis commented on his experience teaching culture that "everyone can teach his own culture. All people are able to do this, but if you don't believe it, you can't do it." Even with all the technology, culture, and language challenges, Siis remained positive and confident about his goals and his future plans, which is an attitude many should plan to adopt in any future MSCL/CSCL projects.

REFERENCES

Abrams, Z. (2019). Interpersonal Communication in Intracultural CMC. In N. Arnold, & L. Ducate (Eds.), *Engaging language learners through CALL. From theory and research to informed practice*. Sheffield, UK: Equinox Publishing.

Alvarez-Torres, M. J. (2001). On “chatting” in the foreign language classroom. *The Clearing House: A Journal of Educational Strategies, Issues and Ideas*, *74*(6), 313–316. doi:10.1080/00098650109599216

Arnold, N., & Ducate, L. (2015). Contextualized views of practices and competencies in CALL teacher education research. *Language Learning & Technology*, *19*(1). Retrieved from http://www.lltjournal.org/item/2880

Bloch, J. (2008a). Integrating the computer and internet. In *Technologies in Second Language Composition Classroom*. Ann Arbor, MI: University of Michigan Press.

Bloch, J. (2008b). Issues in using technology in the L2 composition classroom. In *Technologies in Second Language Composition Classroom*. Ann Arbor, MI: University of Michigan Press.

Carter, H. L., Foulger, T. S., & Ewbank, A. D. (2008). Have you Googled your teacher lately? Teachers’ use of social networking sites. *Phi Delta Kappan*, *89*(9), 681–685. doi:10.1177/003172170808900916

Chen, J., Belkada, S., & Okamoto, T. (2004). How a Web-based course facilitates acquisition of English for academic purposes. *Language Learning & Technology*, *8*(2).

Cruickshank, K., Chen, H., & Warren, S. (2012). Increasing international and domestic student interaction through group work: A case study from the humanities. *Higher Education Research & Development*, *31*(6), 797–810. doi:10.1080/07294360.2012.669748

De Felice, D. (2012). Nahuatl as a classical, foreign, and additional language: A phenomenological study. *Qualitative Report*, *7*(78), 1–23. Retrieved from http://www.nova.edu/ssss/QR/QR17/defelice.pdf

De Felice, D. (2013). *A phenomenological study of teaching endangered languages online: Perspectives from Nahua and Mayan educators*. Retrieved from ProQuest Dissertations and Theses. (1317032973)

Ducate, L. C., & Lomicka, L. L. (2008). Adventures in the blogosphere: From blog readers to blog writers. *Computer Assisted Language Learning*, *21*(1).

Felder, R. M., & Brent, R. (2001). Effective strategies for cooperative learning. *Cooperation & Collaboration in College Teaching*, *19*(2), 69–75.

Fotouhi-Ghazvini, F., Earnshaw, R. A., & Haji-Esmaeili, L. (2009, September). Mobile assisted language learning in a developing country context. In *2009 International Conference on CyberWorlds* (pp. 391-397), Bradford, UK. Piscataway, NJ: IEEE. 10.1109/CW.2009.28

Godwin-Jones, R. (2005). Emerging technologies: Messaging, gaming, peer-to-peer sharing: Language learning strategies & Tools for the millennial generation. *Language Learning & Technology*, *9*(1), 17–22.

Ioannou, A., & Stylianou-Georgiou, A. (2012). Mashing-up wikis and forums: A case study of collaborative problem-based activity. *Educational Media International*, *49*(4), 303–316. doi:10.1080/09523987.2012.741201

Johnson, D. W., & Johnson, R. T. (2008). Cooperation and the use of technology. In J. M. Spector, M. D. Merrill, J. V. Merrienboer, & M. P. Driscoll (Eds.), *Handbook of research on educational communications and technology* (pp. 401–418). New York, NY: Routledge.

Kárpáti, A. (2009). Web 2 technologies for net native language learners: A "social CALL". *ReCALL*, *21*(2), 139–156. doi:10.1017/S0958344009000160

Langhorst, E. (2009). You are here. No budget for travel? Try video chat. *School Library Journal*, *55*(6).

Ortega, L. (2017). New CALL-SLA research interfaces for the 21st century: Towards equitable multilingualism. *CALICO Journal*, *34*(3), 285–316. doi:10.1558/cj.33855

Persico, D., Pozzi, F., & Sarti, L. (2009). Design patterns for monitoring and evaluating CSCL processes. *Computers in Human Behavior*, *25*(5), 1020–1027. doi:10.1016/j.chb.2009.01.003

Plonsky, L., & Ziegler, N. (2016). CALL-SLA interface: Insights from a second-order synthesis. *Language Learning & Technology*, *20*(2), 17–37. Retrieved from http://llt.msu.edu/issues/june2016/plonskyziegler.pdf

Reinhardt, J., & Thorne, S. L. (2019). Digital literacies as emergent multifarious repertoires. In N. Arnold, & L. Ducate (Eds.), *Engaging language learners through CALL. From theory and research to informed practice*. Sheffield, UK: Equinox Publishing.

Rienties, B., Giesbers, B., Tempelaar, D., Lygo-Baker, S., Segers, M., & Gijselaers, W. (2012). The role of scaffolding and motivation in CSCL. *Computers & Education*, *59*(3), 893–906. doi:10.1016/j.compedu.2012.04.010

Rojano-Caceres, J. R., Ramos-Quintana, F., & Vargas-Cerdán, M. D. (2012). On fostering a co-creative process within a CSCL framework. *Creative Education*, *3*(4), 383–391. doi:10.4236/ce.2012.34061

Rosen, L. D., Carrier, L. M., & Cheever, N. A. (2013). Facebook and texting made me do it: Media-induced task-switching while studying. *Computers in Human Behavior*, *29*(3), 948–958. doi:10.1016/j.chb.2012.12.001

Roseth, C., Akcaoglu, M., & Zellner, A. (2013). Blending synchronous face-to-face and computer-supported cooperative learning in a hybrid doctoral seminar. *TechTrends*, *57*(3), 54–59. doi:10.100711528-013-0663-z

Rubio, F., Thomas, J. M., & Li, Q. (2018). The role of teaching presence and student participation in Spanish blended courses. *Computer Assisted Language Learning*, *31*(3), 226–250. doi:10.1080/09588221.2017.1372481

Russell, V., & Curtis, W. (2013). Comparing a large- and small-scale online language class: An examination of teacher and learner perceptions. *The Internet and Higher Education*, *16*, 1–13. doi:10.1016/j.iheduc.2012.07.002

Saville, B. K., Lawrence, N. K., & Jakobsen, K. V. (2012). Creating learning communities in the classroom. *New Directions for Teaching and Learning*, *2012*(132), 57–69. doi:10.1002/tl.20036

Shurville, S., & Browne, T. (2006). ICT-driven change in higher education: Learning from e-learning. *Journal of Organisational Transformation & Social Change*, *3*(1), 245–250.

Simpson, J. (2005). Learning electronic literacy skills in an online language learning community. *Computer Assisted Language Learning*, *18*(4), 327–345. doi:10.1080/09588220500335463

Sykes, J. M., Holden, C. L., & Knight, S. W. P. (2019). Communities: Exploring digital games and social networking. Interpersonal Communication in Intracultural CMC. In N. Arnold, & L. Ducate (Eds.), *Engaging language learners through CALL. From theory and research to informed practice*. Sheffield, UK: Equinox Publishing.

Wagner, E. D. (2005). Enabling mobile learning. *EDUCAUSE Review*, *40*(3), 41–42.

Zheng, C., Liang, J., Li, M., & Tsai, C. (2018). The relationship between English language learners' motivation and online self-regulation: A structural equation modelling approach. *System*, *76*, 144–157. doi:10.1016/j.system.2018.05.003

ADDITIONAL READING

Arnold, N., & Ducate, L. (2019). *Engaging language learners through CALL. From theory and research to informed practice*. Sheffield, UK: Equinox Publishing.

Berge, Z. L., & Collins, M. (2006). *Resources for moderators and facilitators of online discussion*. Retrieved from http://emoderators.com/moderators-homepage/

Chapelle, C. A., & Douglas, D. (2006). The technology thread. In *Assessing language through computer technology*. Cambridge: Cambridge University Press. doi:10.1017/CBO9780511733116.002

De Almeida Soares, D. (2008). Understanding class blogs as a tool for language development. *Language Teaching Research*, *12*(4), 517–533. doi:10.1177/1362168808097165

Johnson, E. M. (2002). The role of computer-supported discussion for language teacher education: What do the students say? *CALICO Journal*, *20*(1), 59–79. doi:10.1558/cj.v20i1.59-79

Johnson, R. T., Johnson, D. W., & Stanne, M. B. (1986). Comparison of computer-assisted cooperative, competitive, and individualistic learning. *American Educational Research Journal*, *23*(3), 382–392. doi:10.3102/00028312023003382

Ng, C., Yeung, A. S., & Hon, R. Y. H. (2006). Does online language learning diminish interaction between student and teacher? *Educational Media International*, *43*(3), 219–232. doi:10.1080/09523980600641429

Pérez, C. (2009). Indigenous languages: Nahuatl, Quechua, & Maya. *Multicultural Education*, *17*(1), 22–26.

KEY TERMS AND DEFINITIONS

Asynchronous Interactions: These interactions are characterized by working at any time and/or place on activities, tasks, or contributions. In a sense, these interactions are the opposite of synchronous interactions in that they can occur at the participant's convenience and do not require the active participation of another member (just the tools themselves). Types of asynchronous interactions include blogs, discussion boards, comment walls, audio-drop boxes, etc.

Collaborative Learning: This term refers to classroom work, assignments, or tasks that require students to work to create one unified project. In other words, the students submit an assignment that was jointly created into a final end result. This type of learning is usually part of structured group work and differs from cooperative learning, though both terms have been used interchangeably in research and in the field.

Computer-Supported Cooperative Learning (CSCL): Using cooperative learning as a foundation, CSCL refers to building, constructing, or sharing knowledge through social interaction that is supported by technology (whether in the form of computers or through virtual applications, platforms, or tools). This type of learning can utilize any number of formats and be completed synchronously or asynchronously.

Cooperative Learning (CL): Much like collaborative learning, CL focuses on students working in groups to complete activities, tasks, or assignments. These groups are structured so that each student is responsible for a specific portion of the activity. The final outcome of this approach allows the students to benefit from multiple perspectives, resources, and skills.

Pre-Service Student-Teachers: These university students are enrolled in education programs and major in various specific degrees (from early childhood to secondary education). Upon completion of their degrees they will most likely enter a classroom as a teacher holding a specific teaching license. Pre-Service Student-Teacher as a term is used to distinguish these students from the children/adults who are their students in the field. This distinction is important during the time these pre-service student-teachers begin their internship where they are no longer students, but they are also not yet recognized as a teachers in their own right.

Socially Mediated Network: This term refers to online communities that are housed in virtual spaces where a number of Web tools are combined within one site. The features of a socially-mediated network include the ability to construct profiles, view other users' profiles and posts, interact with other users and modify or add to the site content. The typical Web tools in such a network are a blend of synchronous and asynchronous components that are combined in a multimodal framework. These networks are often referred to as social networking sites in some research areas.

Synchronous Interactions: These interactions are characterized by working at the same time (though not necessarily the same place) on activities, tasks, or contributions. In a sense, these interactions are the opposite of asynchronous interactions in that they must occur with the active participation of another member. Types of synchronous interactions include chatting, instant messaging, direct calling, virtual classrooms, etc.

Chapter 11
Utilizing Social Networking Sites for Communication in Higher Education

Jodi Whitehurst
Arkansas State University – Beebe, USA

Jim Vander Putten
University of Arkansas at Little Rock, USA

ABSTRACT

This chapter first analyzes the need for communication and collaboration tools to connect units of higher education. It then examines a popular social networking site, Facebook, as a possible platform of communication. This chapter also discusses findings from a phenomenological study that explored rhetorical roles employed by participants on Facebook and then connects findings to current research concerning communication and collaboration in higher education. Data indicated that messages on Facebook were used for cooperation and coordination, but not necessarily collaboration. It also indicated that while participants were audience-minded, they were not necessarily audience-aware, and participants used audience shaping as a coping mechanism. Finally, composers' inclinations to exercise authority over their personal, representational space (Facebook wall) led the researchers to conclude that use of Facebook in higher education may best be achieved by creating a Facebook page or group for specific communicative purposes.

INTRODUCTION

Over the past decade institutions of higher education have encountered various internal and external challenges. From a decline in completion rates, to a decline in funding, to a decline in trust and support, the American university has confronted (and continues to confront) multiple crises. One indicator of an institution's resilience while managing challenges is the quality of its communication (Boyer, 2016). At the same time, colleges and universities have become complex webs of administrators, faculty members, support staff, and students. Such organizational structures hinder communication and ultimately the

DOI: 10.4018/978-1-5225-9814-5.ch011

flow of ideas. Now, more than ever, it is integral for professionals in higher education to find creative ways to foster a culture of communication and collaboration in order to withstand the challenges ahead.

In the last decade, professionals have studied social networking sites as possible platforms for communication and collaboration in higher education. However, these studies have often been narrow in scope, typically focusing on specific course disciplines, such as Cain and Policastri's (2011) study of Facebook use in a pharmacy management, leadership, and business course; LaRue's (2011) study using Facebook as course management software in a nursing informatics course; and Estus' (2010) study utilizing Facebook in a geriatrics pharmacotherapy class. Studies like these are useful for understanding the use of a particular social networking site within a specific discipline. However, they do not indicate how these platforms might be used on a broader scale. To understand the nature of communication on social networking sites and how they might be utilized in higher education, it is useful to study the rhetorical situation on these platforms (Olson, 2001).

To illustrate the differences in the rhetorical situation while using a social networking platform, first consider communication and collaboration as it occurs in a face-to-face setting. Typically, the number of participants is limited to a physical space—in a room and in a geographic region. They are limited by time since collaboration must take place synchronously. They are limited by the visual tools available (i.e. pictures, videos, and links). In face-to-face situations, the audience members often listen passively until his or her turn to speak. In contrast, communication through a social networking site imposes no restrictions through physical space, time, or time zones since collaboration can take place asynchronously. Also, numerous tools are available for illustration and reference for all collaborators. The audience is rarely passively reading; they are responding in multiple rhetorical forms.

This illustration demonstrates some of the ways in which roles of composers and audience members in collaboration naturally change in a social networking platform, like Facebook. The roles re-shape the context of the communication act (Olson, 2001). Gaining a better understanding of rhetorical roles of communicators and collaborators on social networking sites could offer insights into how these digital platforms might be used effectively across units of higher education.

For the last decade colleges and universities have been utilizing social media. For example, Barnes and Lescault's (2012) edition of their annual national study of college and university social media adoption included interviews with 456 institutional representatives at an array of different institutional types. Data analyses indicated that nearly 100% of colleges and universities surveyed used some form of social media in 2010-2011, and this increased from 61% in 2007-2008. Findings from longitudinal data analyses suggested that institutional usage continues to rise for the most popular tools, but adoption of others has leveled off or fallen. Ninety-eight percent of colleges and universities reported having a Facebook page in 2010-2011. This is more than a 10% increase from the previous year, and it is more than a 60% increase since 2008-2009. While digital platforms like Facebook are being utilized in higher education, they are typically only used to recruit and research prospective students (Barnes & Lescault, 2012).

For many years, Facebook has been one of the most commonly used social networking sites for American internet users. In a Pew Research Center survey by Smith and Anderson (2018) involving 2,002 American adults, Facebook and YouTube were the most commonly used social networking sites. Sixty-eight percent of respondents used Facebook, more than Twitter (45%), Instagram (35%), Pinterest (29%), and Snapchat (27%). However, the number of Facebook users is leveling off while other social networking sites continue to rise, and Facebook, which has dominated social media usage, has now been surpassed by YouTube (73%).

There is evidence that professionals in higher education are participating on Facebook. Data from a Pew Research Center survey by Parker, Lenhart, and Moore (2011) including college presidents at 1,055 two-year and four-year institutions indicated that college presidents were "major adopters" of technology (p. 7). It also indicated that 50% of those college presidents surveyed used Facebook. In addition to this, survey data from a Faculty Focus (2011) study of faculty Facebook use including nearly 900 faculty members indicated that the majority were utilizing Facebook. Of those respondents, nearly 85% of faculty members had Facebook accounts. Almost all respondents to a 2015 Educause survey of more than 13,000 faculty reported owning laptops, tablets, and/or smartphones. This can facilitate the adoption of instructional technology for the purposes of using Facebook. However, about half of survey respondents believed additional technology training was necessary, including training on social media, to increase instructional effectiveness. These studies and others like them have indicated that increasing numbers of professionals in higher education are selecting to participate on Facebook. Some have even incorporated Facebook into the higher education classroom, and while it remains a contentious subject, there is evidence that it could increase student engagement and learning. In a study conducted by Akcaoglu and Bowman (2016) involving 87 students from 15 institutions, students who used Facebook for class perceived greater value in the course content and experienced higher levels of student engagement. Most recently, Sheeran and Cummings (2018) investigated levels of student engagement in courses with official and unofficial Facebook groups. The study used within and between group analyses of 471 participants to study levels of student engagement (in terms of relationships with faculty members, relationships with peers, behavioral engagement, cognitive engagement, and sense of belonging). Those students in the courses with official Facebook groups reported significantly higher levels of relationships with peers compared to those in the unofficial Facebook group. Furthermore, both groups reported having a higher sense of belonging. There is clear evidence that administrators and faculty are utilizing Facebook in higher education.

Studying Communication in Digital Environments Using Rhetoric

Every type of communication—including the messages composed on Facebook—takes place in the context of a rhetorical situation. A rhetorical situation is traditionally understood to include interactions between an author, an audience, and a message (Welch, 1990). Historically, rhetoric implied oral communication, but when focus shifted from oral communication to written communication, the rhetoric was reshaped (Ede & Lunsford, 1984). A similar re-creation of rhetoric is taking place as interfaces have shifted from paper to screen (Lunsford, 2006).

Contemporary rhetoric has focused less on the simple, traditional concepts of author, audience, and message and more on a rhetoric that is disciplinary in nature; that is to say that contemporary rhetoric is thought to construct and regulate within specific discourse communities or platforms. Some examples of this splintering of rhetoric include You's (2005) rhetorical analysis of Chinese textbooks to understand ideologies in the People's Republic of China, Hoang's (2009) identification of a "rhetoric of injury" in the 2002 interracial conflict at a public California university, Cushman's (2008) analysis of political identities among Native scholars, and Trabold's (2009) analysis of a resistance rhetoric of South African anti-apartheid journalists. Each of these rhetorical analyses examined communication within separate contexts to gain insight into the rhetorical situations.

One field of particular interest to many contemporary rhetoricians is that of digital rhetoric, which represents a convergence of multiple disciplines (Yancey, 2009). Digital rhetoric is concerned with examining how rhetoric functions within digital environments, like the popular social networking site, Facebook.

In This Chapter

In this chapter the authors will begin by discussing the major expansions in higher education which have led to a greater need for digital spaces to aid in communication and collaboration; the growth of digital platforms (including Facebook) as a means of connecting; the justification for studying Facebook communication through the rhetorical lens; the methods, analyses, and findings of a qualitative study of the rhetorical situation on Facebook; and conclusions concerning Facebook as a platform for communication and collaboration in higher education.

BACKGROUND

The "Multiversity" and the "Metaversity"

It is difficult to unravel and roll out the details of what led to the complex, multi-functional American university. As E. D. Duryea (2000) observed, "...complex institutions such as universities do not appear full-blown at a particular point in time. They evolve through that complicated process by which men and cultures mingle over a history fraught with traditions and happenstance" (p. 3). The modern research university grew into a multi-purposed, multi-governed, multi-structured entity. No one articulated this better than Kerr (1963), former University of California president, who described the contemporary American university at an unprecedented time of growth. He described the American university as a "multiversity," needing to balance teaching and research roles, create a curriculum of generalization and specialization, attend to individual students in an immense student body, and, most relevant to this book chapter, generate contact "broader than the one-way route across the lectern or through the television screen" (Kerr, 1963, p. 119).

Institutions of higher education have continued to expand in the 21st century and have precipitated an even greater need for channels of communication. One indication of expansion is student enrollment. The National Center for Education Statistics (NCES, 2018), the primary federal entity for collecting and analyzing education data in the United States, reported a 41% increase in enrollment at degree-granting institutions between 2000 and 2016. In Fall 2016, total undergraduate enrollment in degree-granting postsecondary institutions was 16.9 million students, which is an increase of 28% from 2000. According to a 2011 NCES report, colleges have also become more diverse. Between 2000 and 2010, the enrollment of students ages 25 and older increased 42%, and the number of women increased by sixty-two percent (NCES, 2011). In addition, Hispanic, Asian/Pacific Islander, and Black minority groups all increased in enrollment growth (NCES, 2011). Colleges and universities in the United States have not only been serving increasing numbers of students but increasingly diverse populations. This growth in enrollment has produced a need for greater numbers of faculty, staff, and administrators. Furthermore, it has necessitated a platform for communication to connect them.

Another indication of expansion in higher education can be found in the increased number of campuses. Many institutions support some form of extended campus networks (Fonseca & Bird, 2007). These intended supplements or complements to the primary institutions vary in purposes, but the primary reasons are often to generate additional revenue or to reach underserved populations (Fonseca & Bird, 2007). Extended campuses also vary in distances from their main campuses (Baron-Nixon, 2007). For example, Drexel University, based in Pennsylvania, also has campuses in New Jersey and California. Duke University, with multiple schools and institutes in North Carolina, also opened a campus in China. While this trend has served important purposes, the physical spreading of campuses has created another hindrance to open communication in higher education.

Those examples of higher education expansion mentioned up to this point still bear a resemblance—albeit to a greater degree— to the complex features of Kerr's (1963) depictions of the multiversity. However, over the last decade the expansion of higher education has stretched in new directions— passed what can be recognized through Kerr's descriptions of the growing complexities of the university— toward digital spaces. While complications that resemble the multiversity continue, there now also exists a digital dimension of higher education expansion. This digital expansion involves people interacting in virtual digital environments, a phenomenon referred to by Collins (2008) as a "metaverse." The metaverse term—or perhaps it should be "metaversity" for the purposes of this discussion—was used by Collins (2008) to refer mostly to Second Life, a virtual 3-D digital world. However, the term, defined as the "convergence of virtually-enhanced physical reality and physically persistent virtual space," could easily apply to many digital spaces now utilized by institutions of higher education (Collins, 2008, p. 52).

Higher learning in online environments is a prime example of the metaversity. The number of classes taking place completely online has increased exponentially in the last decade. A study by Seaman, Allen, and Seaman (2018) of Babson Survey Research Group based on data from more than 4,700 colleges and universities indicated that in the 2016 Fall semester, 31.6% of college students took at least one online class. The Babson Survey Research Group has studied online learning for fourteen consecutive years and has reported growth every year (2018). Sloan Consortium (2012), a professional leadership organization in online learning, conducted a 10-year study based on responses from chief academic officers at more than 2,800 colleges and universities in the United States from 2002 to 2012. In this time, the number of online learners increased from 570,000 to 6.7 million. In the same report, a survey of chief academic officers indicated that 69.1% of chief academic officers stated that online learning was critical to their long-term strategy.

In addition to creating a virtual learning place for more students, learning in digital spaces creates a virtual work environment for more faculty members. Professionals in higher education are becoming more geographically dispersed. In these situations, there is no longer a "water cooler effect," where employees build relationships through chance encounters; there is no shared physical space to collaborate on joint projects; and there is no communication to organize and coordinate day-to-day operations. Studies on collaboration suggest that collaborators experience increased and more meaningful knowledge production, improved learning outcomes, and an overall improved environment (Kezar & Lester, 2009). There is also evidence that the Generation X faculty (those born between 1965 and 1981) thrive in environments with continuous opportunities for feedback (Bova & Kroth, 2001); professional relationships; and webs of support that are non-hierarchical, collaborative, and cross-cultural (Sorcinelli &Yun, 2007). As higher education culture changes, it is necessary to locate new channels of communication and collaboration, like digital spaces that allow for connectivity between geographically dispersed administrators, faculty, staff, and students.

The Growth of Digital Networks as Communication Platforms

The term "Web 2.0" was conceived by Dale Dougherty—author, editor, publisher, and co-founder of O'Reilly Media— in 2004 and popularized by MediaLive International and O'Reilly Media (Madden & Fox, 2006). It was a comprehensive term to be used by marketers, analysts, and other professionals in the field of technology to refer to emerging features of the participatory web (Madden & Fox, 2006). Since its inception, Web 2.0 has had multiple definitions. The majority of these definitions involve a listing of interactive capabilities, such as O'Reilly's definition, which includes "utilizing collective intelligence, providing network-enabled interactive services, giving users control over their own data" (Madden & Fox, 2006, p. 1). Concept words that aptly encompass these multiple definitions include: interactivity, networked, and user-generated.

O'Reilly Media sponsored a conference back in 2005 to characterize the paradigm shift taking place since the initiation of Web 2.0. They characterized the transformation as being a shift from static, isolated repositories of information (Web 1.0) to dynamic, user-driven, participatory sites (Web 2.0) (Singel, 2005). Ross Mayfield, CEO of a California-based company that creates Wiki software, portrayed the transformation as Web 1.0 being commerce-focused and Web 2.0 being people-focused (Singel, 2005). However it is defined, Web 2.0 is a socially networked digital space that brings people together in user-driven participatory forums.

In discussing Web 2.0, it is also necessary to consider the mobile computing devices that have enabled this pervasive connectivity. Mobile computing systems include devices that can be moved without inhibiting their computing capabilities. Distinguishing features of mobile computing devices includes their small size, wireless networked connectivity, and power sources that enable mobility (B'Far, 2005). Some popular examples of mobile computing devices include laptops, smartphones, tablets, and e-readers.

Data from a 2018 survey conducted by researchers at the Educause Center for Applied Research including 64,536 undergraduate students at 130 institutions indicated that 95% of students owned smartphones and 91% of students owned laptop computers (Galanek, Gierdowski, & Brooks, 2018). The report indicated that "practically every student has access to at least one of the technologies students identify as among the most important for their academic success" (Galanek, Gierdowski, & Brooks, 2018, p. 7). Laptops, hybrids, desktops, and smartphones were rated as "very important" or "extremely important" to student success. However, the importance of these devices differs considerably by student demographics. Women, students of color, students with disabilities, first-generation students, students who are independent (with or without dependents of their own), and students who reported being from disadvantaged socioeconomic backgrounds see their devices as significantly more important to their success than their peers. While demographics do impact the perceived academic need for these devices, nearly all students rated them as important to their academic success (Galanek, Gierdowski, & Brooks, 2018). It is clear that mobile devices are already an important part of communication in higher education.

The development of Web 2.0 along with the advances in mobile computing devices has caused an unprecedented degree of connectivity. One of the most popular facets of Web 2.0 is social networking sites. Boyd and Ellison (2006) defined social networking sites as "web-based services that allow individuals to (1) construct a public or semi-public profile within a bounded system, (2) articulate a list of other users with whom they share a connection, and (3) view and traverse their list of connections and those made by others within the system" (p. 211). Since their introduction, social networking sites (SNSs) have attracted millions of users. After joining, these users are typically prompted to design personal profiles and to locate others with whom they share some association. Common terms used to identify these connections include "contacts," "fans," "followers," or "friends." This public display of connections has been a distinguishing characteristic of SNSs. Acknowledging these connections enables users to link to other personal profiles and navigate through connections of connections (Boyd & Ellison, 2006). The majority of SNSs also have some form of messaging tool that enables users to leave private messages for people with whom they have an established connection. Other than creating personal profiles, establishing connections within the network, and private messaging, features for SNSs vary greatly (Boyd & Ellison, 2006).

Studies have indicated a steady increase in social media use by adults. A Pew Research Center survey reported by Smith and Anderson (2018) of 2,002 adult internet users indicated that 69% of online adults use some type of social networking site. A comparison of past data analyses suggested a trend of increasing social media usage among online adults from 8% in 2005 to 29% in 2008 to 65% in 2011, and finally 69% in 2018 (Madden & Zickuhr, 2011; Smith & Anderson, 2018). Data further indicated that the majority of SNS users—roughly two-thirds— reported that they make social media platforms a part of their everyday lives.

Social networking sites gained real popularity in 2002 and 2003 with the launch of sites like Friendster, LinkedIn, and MySpace. While MySpace attracted significant media attention in the United States and around the world, many other social networking sites developed in niche communities (Boyd & Ellison, 2008). Friendster gained users in the Pacific Islands. Orkut became the premier social networking site in Brazil and India. Mixi was widely adopted in Japan, and Bebo became common in the United Kingdom, New Zealand, and Australia (Boyd & Ellison, 2008). However, no social networking site matched the number of users participating on the social networking site, Facebook.

Facebook launched in 2004 as a Harvard-only social networking site. It quickly expanded to include all interested users (Cassidy, 2006). In 2012, Facebook was the second most accessed website in the United States, and it was the most accessed social networking website in the world (Most Popular Websites, 2011). As of 2011, there were 500 million active Facebook users, and 48% of those checked Facebook every morning (Hepburn, 2011). In 2010, a 20-minute span of time meant that 1,000,000 links were shared; 1,323,000 photos were tagged; 1,484,000 invitations were sent out; 1,587,000 walls were posted; 2,716,000 photos were uploaded; 4,632,000 messages were sent; and 10,208,000 comments were made (Hepburn, 2010). More recently, a Pew Research Center survey reported by Smith and Anderson (2018) of 2,002 adult internet users indicated that 68% of adults in America use Facebook. With the exception of YouTube (73%), Facebook is the most widely-used social networking site.

Facebook is also a commonly used social networking site on college campuses. For example, evidence suggests that more and more administrators are using Facebook. Data from a Pew Research Center survey by Parker, Lenhart, and Moore (2011) of college presidents at 1,055 two-year and four-year institutions indicated that college presidents were "major adopters" of technology (p. 7). It also indicated that 50% of those college presidents surveyed used Facebook (Parker, Lenhart, & Moore, 2011). In addition to this, survey data from a Faculty Focus (2011) study of faculty Facebook use including nearly 900 faculty members indicated that the majority were utilizing Facebook as well. Of those respondents, nearly 85% of faculty members had Facebook accounts (Faculty Focus, 2011). Also, Sapkota and Vander Putten (2018) completed a qualitative study to investigate business communications faculty members' perceptions of using social media in the college classroom. Faculty accepted social media as an important business tool, but curricular adoption was inconsistent because of varying levels of faculty knowledge of social media.

The development of Web 2.0 in conjunction with mobile computing devices has produced widespread digital interconnectivity. At the hub of this phenomenon are hundreds of social networking sites that the majority of American online adults access daily. One of the most commonly used SNS in the United States and on college campuses is Facebook.

Studying Facebook Communication Through the Rhetorical Lens

As a part of the old Trivium, rhetoric has had a long and celebrated history. Through the course of time, it has been defined in numerous ways. For this reason, rhetoric has been somewhat perplexing to those outside of the discipline. For the purposes of this study, rhetoric will be defined very broadly, as Lunsford (as cited in Howard, 2010) defined it, as "the art, practice, and theory of human communication" (p. 172). Because the purpose of this study was to gain an understanding of communication as it occurs on Facebook, rhetoric was the selected means of analysis.

Another rationale for selecting rhetoric to analyze communication on Facebook is its inherent relationship with technology. *Techne*, a key concept in classical rhetoric, refers to the art of bringing form to material in order to achieve some purpose. *Techne* rhetoric, like digital technologies, combines technical knowledge with an artistic awareness in order to achieve a desired rhetorical purpose (Porter, 2009). As Yancey stated in an interview with D. A. Hart (personal communication, March 19, 2011) and other professionals have echoed, "...the technology that you use is rhetorical—it's appropriate to the purpose..." Since Facebook is a digital platform that involves technical knowledge to integrate digital technologies (for example, video and text) to achieve a purpose, it was appropriate to use the rhetorical lens to study communication.

While this study examines the communication situation through rhetoric, traditional rhetorical heuristics were not used in data analysis. Rhetoric has typically relied on traditional heuristics, such as the five cannons of rhetoric—invention, arrangement, style, memory, and delivery—or the rhetorical appeals—logos (message logic), pathos (reader emotion), and ethos (writer credibility). However, since the focus of discourse shifted from oral speech to written communication, from written communication to static screens, and from static screens to interactive digital communication interfaces; scholars within the field of rhetoric and composition have questioned whether these traditional heuristics still apply to 21st century digital discourse (Lunsford, 2006).

The evolution of the canons of rhetoric from oral communication to interactive digital communication can best be illustrated by discussing delivery. Delivery, the fifth of the five canons of rhetoric, traditionally involved *how* something was said whether than *what* was said. It was concerned with voice and gestures during oral speaking. However, delivery—historically associated with the human body—took a subordinate (if any) position when discourse moved from oral communication to written communication (Lunsford, 2006). As discourse then shifted to static screens and again to interactive digital technologies, rhetoricians recovered the canon of delivery for digital rhetoric. As Kathleen Welch (1990) argued, "The fifth canon is now the most powerful canon of the five" (p.26). While digital delivery is still concerned with *how* something is said, it has evolved into a consideration of how composers select interactive technologies to deliver their messages.

This evolution of rhetoric has sparked the creation of new loosely-bound heuristics to describe the canons in digital situations. For example, Porter (2009) framed five contexts for digital delivery, including body/identity, which involved online representations of the body; distribution/circulation, which was concerned with technological options for circulating digital information; access/accessibility, which represented audience connectedness to information on the Web; interaction, which referred to the range of types of interactions; and economics, which involved copyright and ethical use of information. Porter

(2009) described these topics as "categories that operate heuristically and productively across multiple situations to prompt rhetorical decisions" (p. 208). While Porter and others caused professionals to consider how the canons of rhetoric could be redefined in new digitally-defined systems, these heuristics have not typically been developed or tested through research. It is also unknown whether one heuristic could classify any one canon across multiple digital platforms.

Most relevant to this study, it has been recognized that digital rhetoric could also alter the traditional discursive roles in communication. Lunsford (2006) recognized this when she stated, "It is as though our old reliable rhetorical triangle of writer, reader, and message is transforming itself before our eyes, moving from three discrete angles to a shimmering, humming, dynamic set of performative relationships" (p. 170). It is obvious that professionals in rhetoric and composition are probing the traditional rhetorical constructs to determine whether they apply when transplanted to digital communication. For this reason, this study employed a phenomenological approach, resisting the tendency to classify data into traditional rhetorical heuristics.

MAIN FOCUS OF THE CHAPTER

Methods

In the spring of 2011, a phenomenological study was conducted to explore the rhetorical roles that Facebook users employ as composers and audience members while communicating through this digital platform. The goal was to gain a broad understanding of the communication acts taking place on Facebook. The central research question guiding this study was: what is the essence of the rhetorical situation in communication on Facebook? Issue sub-questions included:

1. What types of messages are being composed on Facebook?
2. What considerations are made when shaping content on Facebook?
3. In what ways do audience members respond to messages on Facebook, and what considerations do they make when responding?

Participants

Six face-to-face interviews were conducted to explore themes involving the rhetorical composer and audience roles on Facebook. The interviewees were divided into three age groups with one male and one female represented in each group. Group one consisted of two participants in the 18 to 24-year-old bracket; group two contained two participants falling in the 25-35 year span; and group three consisted of two participants in the 36 and older grouping. Previous studies support differences in the ways men and women and various age groups utilize Facebook. For example, a Pew Research Center study by Hampton, Goulet, Rainie, and Purcell (2011) involving 1,787 internet users indicated that Facebook participation varied based on age and gender. More specifically, data suggested that "women and the young drive Facebook usage" (p. 14). This data indicated that 18% of women reported updating their status daily compared to only 11% of men, suggesting that women participate on Facebook more frequently than men. Furthermore, those Facebook users over the age of 35 who participated in the survey were least likely to have updated their statuses, indicating that older age groups participated less than younger age groups. Therefore, for the purposes of this study, maximal variation sampling (for age and gender) was used so that a full range of acts of various composers and audience members could be included in the data. The goal was not to further study the characteristics of these age and gender groups but to obtain a typical sampling, to use a broad scope, and to include an open range of composer and audience activities.

At the onset of the study, one priority was to obtain participants who were not acquaintances since it is arguable that interviewees could alter their answers based on their relationship and knowledge of the interviewer. The majority of the interviewees—two in group one and two in group three—were obtained through a gatekeeper. This gatekeeper provided e-mail addresses for her acquaintances and co-workers, and invitations to participate in the study were sent out through this medium. Of the eight invitations sent out, four agreed to become participants in the study.

All six interviewees were asked the same questions pertaining to their Facebook use, and all responses were audio recorded. The interviews ranged from about 20 to 30 minutes long, depending upon the length of answers. No interviews were limited by outside time constraints, and the interview protocol was comprised of five questions:

1. Describe the kinds of posts or messages you generally put on Facebook. Feel free to use examples if it is helpful.
2. How do you decide whether to post something on Facebook? Describe an example of a time when you chose to put something on Facebook and a time when you chose not to put something on Facebook (maybe you even deleted it) and why.
3. When you are composing on Facebook, how do you usually decide whether to use pictures, symbols, or text? Again, please describe examples.
4. How do you decide to respond to some posts and not to respond to others? You can use examples if it is helpful.
5. In what ways do you think that using Facebook has benefitted you? What evidence do you have of this benefit? Give an example of how it has benefitted you.

Data Analysis

The data analysis procedure followed the five-phase cycle as described by Yin (2011). The first phase involved compiling verbatim transcripts of all answers to interview questions that pertained to composer and audience. The second phase, disassembling, included uploading the data into NVivo9 qualitative data analysis software and coding emerging constructs. During the third phase, reassembling, the themes were organized, and a table was generated. Interpretation of the data was the fourth phase, which will be reported in the "Results and Discussion" section of this chapter. Finally, Yin's (2011) fifth phase of data analysis, concluding, will address the application of these results to communication and collaboration in higher education.

During the second phase of data analysis, two initial themes emerged. Interview data was coded in two categories: (a) composer considering audience and (b) audience considering message. To better understand these initial category codes, consider the following quote from the male in group two:

I don't use symbols like the smiley face. That seems too immature, like something a teenager would do. I don't use LOL. I just spell out 'I'm laughing out loud.' I also know that everyone does not know all the symbols. I don't know the symbols. I just found out what OMG means. Sometimes I get confused when they write in code or symbols.

The first half of this quote— "I don't use symbols like the smiley face. That seems too immature, like something a teenager would do. I don't use LOL. I just spell out 'I'm laughing out loud.' I also know that everyone does not know all the symbols."—was coded as (a) composer considering audience because the participant was discussing ways he considered his audience while composing. The second part of the quote— "I don't know the symbols. I just found out what OMG means. Sometimes I get confused when they write in code or symbols."—was coded as (b) audience considering message since the participant was referring to his response to messages he read on Facebook.

During this initial coding, it became obvious that at times the line between composer and audience roles blurred. This often occurred during real-time chat. To account for this additional theme, a third category was then created for (c) composer-audience role. To better understand this category, consider a statement from the male in group two: "Other times, like when a sports game is on, you get on there and everybody is talking about what they're seeing while it's going on." In this instance, the participant is not clearly defined as composer or audience; he is both.

During the coding of these primary categories— (a) composer considering audience, (b) audience considering message, and (c) composer-audience—varying characteristics in each category emerged. For example, when participants mentioned "liking" certain posts (referring to the action of clicking the "like" option under Facebook posts), it was coded as (b) audience considering message. At the same time, when participants discussed reading and viewing messages as audience members, it was also coded (b) audience considering message. However, these are very different actions. Therefore, sub-categories were developed for each of the three categories to account for these differences. For the purpose of clarification, these differing characteristics within each major category will be referred to as "characters." All categories were further delineated into the emerging characters under each major category.

Therefore, the data analysis unfolded, beginning from two broad categories— (a) composer considering audience and (b) audience considering message. The inability to separate some acts into these two initial categories formed a third category—(c) composer-audience role. Then distinct sub-categories or "characters" emerged within each of the three categories.

Composer Considering Audience Category

The (a) composer considering audience category was divided into three characters: linear posts, wall design, and audience shaping. The linear posts character included all composing that proceeded down the page in a linear direction. This type of composing involved all text, pictures, media, etc. Two typical examples of linear posts mentioned during interviews were status updates and picture posting. The second character, wall design, included more multi-dimensional, recursive composing, such as photo albums, reported interests, and other representational information that stayed attached to the composer's wall or profile. The final character under (a) composer considering audience that was also the most unexpected was audience shaping. Due to the large pool of readers on Facebook, composers often shaped or specified their audiences using tools like messaging and groups. To understand the type of comment coded as audience shaping, consider the following comment from the male in the age 18-24 group: "Anything that I think should be private, I do direct messaging or chatting." Comments like this one implied a different sort of audience mindfulness, one in which the composer shaped the audience to fit the message as opposed to the traditional shaping of a message to fit the audience.

Audience Considering Message Category

The second category was (b) audience considering message. The characters that surfaced during coding included: passive audience and active audience. The passive audience role included only reading and viewing composing done by others. In other words, this was the undetected audience. A quote from the female in group one, the 18-24 age group, that was coded in this category was, "Facebook provides the opportunity to see what everybody is doing without getting involved. So, indirectly you can know what people are doing, but you don't have to communicate with them about it." This audience role differed from the active audience role. The active audience was detected by answers to posts, replies to messages, and similar feedback activities. The active audience role involved responses that could be detected by other users while the passive audience role only involved comments that referred to viewing and reading.

Composer-Audience Category

The final category was (c) composer-audience role, and it had two characters, which were titled real-time communication and space keeping. The first character, real-time communication, involved activities, like the chat tool, that did not obviously shift between composer and audience roles. One previously mentioned quote from the male in the 25-35 age group best characterizes this role: "Other times, like when a sports game is on, you get on there and everybody is talking about what they're seeing while it's going on." In this instance, the participant assumed the audience and composer roles during real-time conversation. Not only was he a member of a community audience, he was also a member of a sports audience. At the time he was receiving text and viewing a game, he was also composing. Reading, viewing, and composing was all happening simultaneously.

The second character involved in the (c) composer-audience role was space keeping. Space keeping involved activity concerned with protecting a participant's personal wall from unwanted composing. The following quote from the male in the 25-35 age group provides an example of space keeping:

I have received inappropriate posts from people. I took them off my friends list because they were posting inappropriate pictures. I decided that I didn't want my wife, pastor, or employer to see it... Companies and employers now look at your Facebook page...One lady at work got fired for inappropriate pictures of herself. They are really patrolling that to see what lifestyle their employees really live and how they're being represented. Sometimes personal lifestyle affects your work. Everyone can see how you're representing the company.

This Facebook user (and others) viewed the inappropriate composing from others on his wall as a negative representation of him. He, therefore, became the audience (reader and viewer) and composer (editor) of his space. Hence, the role of composer and audience was filled relatively at the same time.

RESULTS AND DISCUSSION

Coding through NVivo9 revealed that the (a) composer considering audience role was the role most discussed by participants when asked about their Facebook use. The unexpected category—(c) composer-audience role—was only mentioned two percent of the time. Linear post references accounted for the majority of the (a) composer considering audience category while the active audience character accounted for most of the (b) audience considering message category. The space keeper character accounted for most of the (c) composer-audience category references. It is important to note that the number of references to these roles does not necessarily imply a connection to the importance of the roles or the frequency of the roles used on Facebook. It is merely another way to describe the data. A thorough description of data is an important means of interpreting qualitative data (Yin, 2011). The remainder of this section will address the three issue sub-questions contributing to the main research question for this study and connect the results to a discussion of communication and collaboration on Facebook.

Types of Messages Being Composed on Facebook

The comments concerning messages composed on Facebook were primarily in the (a) composer considering audience category. The linear posts character accounted for the majority of the types of messages in this category. The term "linear posts" could be misleading, because the term seems to imply messages involving simple text that moves down the screen (like a page), involving a simple top-to-bottom and left-to-right message. This could not be further from the truth. Consider the following quote from the male in group one that was coded as a linear post:

Most of my wall posts are links. I'll copy and paste and comment about the link. I sometimes comment on somebody's wall just to add humor. I put links though if I find items someone may like—music, funny videos—I put it on my wall.

Eleven of the thirty-seven references in the linear posts character involved non-text composing. However, these were coded "linear composing" because the text, links, pictures, videos, and other multimedia were positioned in a linear direction moving down the user's Facebook wall.

Many of the references to messages on Facebook involved simple text composed by the participants or personal photos with text. For example, the male in group three stated, "I mostly just use text. My wife and daughter use a lot of pictures though. She [wife] even adds on my Facebook, but I mostly just use text." The type of message referred to by this participant is read on the screen in a traditional way, top-to-bottom and left-to-right. However, some of the references to messages on Facebook involved a sort of multimedia arrangement that included arranging pictures, videos, and links designed by other people and text composed by the participants. For example, the quote mentioned earlier from the male in group one referred to the action of copying and pasting in a link and adding his own composing with the link. In instances such as these, messages were more like multimedia collages that reflected arrangements of collective composing.

Most relevant to this book chapter, comments from participants suggested that many Facebook messages were used for cooperation and coordination but not necessarily for collaboration. As Kezar and Lester (2009) noted, collaboration must involve joint goals and a reliance on others to accomplish those goals. They also added that for collaboration to take place, participants must have shared rules, norms, and structures (Kezar & Lester, 2009). Bailey and Koney (2000) defined collaboration as parties who "work collectively through common strategies" and "relinquish some degree of autonomy toward the realization of a jointly determined purpose" (p. 6). Data in this study did not indicate this degree of alliance between participants. This does not necessarily imply that Facebook cannot be used as a tool for structured collaboration, but analyses did not indicate that it was a part of the unstructured communication naturally taking place on Facebook among the participants in this study.

While interview data concerning messages on Facebook did not suggest that collaboration was a major part of communication acts, it did suggest that messages on Facebook were commonly used for cooperation and coordination. Cooperation, which involves shared information and joint support, is particularly evident in the interview data (Bailey & Koney, 2000). For example, the male in group three stated, "I had a friend looking for information on a flower shop in [city name]. I responded and provided all [of the] information for a flower shop." The male in group one stated, "Facebook is a benefit if I need some immediate information about a paper or a test or dates. I can go online now and just have 80 friends sitting there on Facebook..." Likewise, the male in group two commented, "Posts I respond to are often questions to give information." Comments like these indicated that messages on Facebook were often used for cooperation.

Data also indicated that messages involving information sharing were often simple self-reporting. For example, the male in group two stated, "I'm remodeling my kitchen, and I posted pictures to share my work to show the difference." He also stated, "I've put a picture of my kid sitting on our dog and funny comments about my kid." The female in group one said, "Last night I was bored at work, and I just updated my status with 'Cleaned up my apartment a little bit today. Now I'm at work trying to be productive." Likewise, the female in group two stated, "My posts are about my day...or if there was a major event or vacation going on." Five of the six participants indicated that Facebook had benefitted them by keeping them connected through information sharing messages like these.

Messages involving coordination, which involves shared tasks and compatible goals, was also evident in the interview data (Bailey & Koney, 2000). For example, the male in group three stated, "I have a long-distant friend whose son was in town. We got in contact through Facebook, and when his son came to town, I was able to help him." Likewise, the male in group two stated, "I use it [Facebook] sometimes with certain people when I draw house prints for work. They'll send me their information on Facebook. Then I send back plans through e-mail." This comment indicated a shared task and a shared goal. However, it was not necessarily collaborative action, which would require a reliance on collaborators, shared power, and shared responsibility (Kezar & Lester, 2009; Bailey & Koney, 2000).

Considerations by Composers When Shaping Content on Facebook

Of the three main categories—(a) composer considering audience, (b) audience considering message, and (c) composer-audience—the (a) composer considering audience had the most references. Data from this study indicated that although composers were very audience-minded, they were not necessarily audience aware. The vast audience on Facebook made it very difficult and almost impossible to craft audience-aware messages. All participants at some point in the interview indicated extreme caution when composing. For example, the female in group three stated, "On special events I put pictures up. I don't put up exclusive pictures that don't include all friends. I don't want other people to feel excluded...I don't like to offend people." The male in group two stated, "It is usually humor that offends people... There are a lot of my friends who are not offended by that type of humor, but there are some who might get offended by it so I don't even post." Some participants, like the male in group one, chose to deal with challenges in determining audience through audience shaping. He stated, "I'm careful about what I post and what others' pictures and comments are posted on my wall as well. Anything that I think should be private, I do direct messaging or chatting." As illustrated in this quote, instead of shaping his message to fit the audience, this participant used Facebook tools to shape or limit the audience receiving the message. This type of audience shaping defies the traditional dynamics of a rhetorical situation by giving the composer unprecedented control over the audience.

Another character that involved composers shaping content was space keeping, which was classified in the (c) composer-audience category. Space keeping involved all activity concerned with protecting a participant's personal wall from unwanted composing. Several comments by participants referred to the Facebook wall as being a space that represented them, although much of the composing was done by other people. For example, consider a quote by the male participant in group two: "I have received inappropriate posts from people. I took them off my friends list because they were posting inappropriate pictures. I decided that I didn't want my wife, pastor, or employer to see it." Quotes like this one suggested that composers viewed their wall as a representational space, and they exercised authority over the composing there. It also indicated the degree to which the composer and audience roles can become blurred.

To illustrate this connectivity, think of this in terms of writing on paper. Consider a group of composers writing on their own papers. Every time the composers write on their own papers, they must also go to the papers of every other participant to write the same thing. In this situation, which of the participants is the audience and which of the participants is the composer? When participants look at their papers, are they the composers of the document or the audience members? The answer is both. In the case of composing on Facebook, data suggested that the participants in this study redeemed that personal space by editing or deleting the composing of others.

The space keeping character illustrates the extent in which Facebook is a collectively constructed space. Data indicated that composing was often a shared act, and in personal spaces (like the Facebook wall) the composing of others was viewed as a collective representation of the owner of that space. However, it also demonstrated study participants' unwillingness to completely give authority of their space (Facebook wall) to the group.

Many scholars in the field of rhetoric and writing have contended that digital writing shifts the authority of writing from single composers to collective composers. Data from this study indicated that while participants did not exercise a great degree of power over their personal composing, they did exercise power over their personal spaces. When composers did exercise power over their composing, they did this through audience shaping—selecting which audience members received their messages. This finding is relevant to the discussion of utilizing Facebook for communication and collaboration. It is possible that composers may not feel the same responsibility to protect their representational space if a shared space was established, like a Facebook group or a Facebook page designed for specific communicative or collaborative purposes.

Types of Responses and Considerations by Audience Members

Data concerning responses by audience members mainly occurred in the (b) audience considering message category. The majority of these comments pertained to the active audience character. Participant statements were coded in the active audience character when they referred to responding in ways that could be detected by other Facebook users. However, it is important to note that the responses were active in more than one way. Active responding involved "liking" a post, responding with text, or responding with multi-media. Consider this quote from the male in group two: "I sent information to a friend who asked a question about how to watch a sports game on a website. I sent a link to give her the information, and she was really grateful." This quote implied a very active style of responding in which the audience member was able to produce real results for the composer. Another way audience members actively responded to composing was to "like" a comment. This type of response operated as simple affirmation for the composer. For example, the female in group one stated, "There are some times I will 'like' an inspirational quote. I won't comment on them, but I will 'like' them." In this instance, this Facebook participant viewed the "like" option as a lesser form of audience feedback than commenting. This is another Facebook option that very obviously altered the rhetorical audience role. Audience members were able to provide feedback that required very minimal effort.

The passive audience character, or the undetected audience, allowed participants to read and view without interference. Take into account this quote by the female in group one: "I do go Facebook creeping. It's profile creeping. You look at other status updates. If you're a creeper that means you look at other profiles." This same participant later stated, "Facebook provides the opportunity to see what everyone is doing without getting involved. So, indirectly you can know what people are doing, but you don't have to communicate with them about it."

This type of passive audience role has also been referred to as surveillance. This term was first used by Lampe, Ellison, and Steinfield (2006). In a very influential study, Lampe, Ellison, and Steinfeld (2006) conducted two surveys of first-year students at Michigan State University. Data from this study indicated that Facebook allowed members to maintain relationships just by "allowing users to track other members of their community" (Lampe, Ellison, & Steinfeld, 2006, p. 167). While most discussions concerning surveillance tend to be negative, data from this study of rhetorical roles on Facebook indicated that surveillance offered a relationship maintenance component that participants viewed as valuable. For example, consider the quote from the female in group two: "It [Facebook] keeps me in the loop more than I can be. I'm able to see photos and growth without being directly in the vicinity." The male in group three stated, "I use it [Facebook] for a long-distance brother… I learned information—that he got married—on Facebook. We were able to meet his wife on Facebook." Likewise, the male in group two said, "I have [a] long distance family [member] that I didn't speak to. Now we're in constant contact. I get to see pictures of his kids or family." Comments like these suggested that being audience members on Facebook allowed participants to maintain relationships by reading and viewing information about members of their community.

A point particularly notable to this discussion of communication and collaboration on Facebook is that relationship maintenance is an integral part of collaboration. As Gajda (2004) noted, "Collaboration depends upon positive personal relations and effective emotional connections between partners" (p. 69). The literature concerning collaboration indicates that the foundation for partnerships is an ongoing interpersonal connection (Gajda, 2004; Bailey & Koney, 2000; Austin, 2000). It is possible that Facebook might be used to reinforce relationships that could lead to collaborations.

FUTURE RESEARCH DIRECTIONS

This chapter adds to the objectives of this book by providing stakeholders in higher education information concerning the types of communication taking place on Facebook. Data from this study indicated that Facebook was already being utilized for cooperation and coordination, two features that could have strong positive impacts on units of higher education. For example, this could be used to better serve students by eliminating the need to go between multiple offices to obtain solutions to problems. Coordinating efforts could also lead to greater efficiency through sharing information resources. Future research specifically addressing the uses of Facebook to aid in cooperation and coordination between units of higher education is needed.

This study explored the communication situations naturally taking place on Facebook. While data did not indicate that collaboration took place, more research is needed to address collaboration using Facebook in a formalized collaborative situation. Collaborators managed by external structures could greatly affect the potential for collaboration using this digital platform. Finally, a conceptual model reflecting the rhetorical situation on Facebook could be a useful tool to guide future research across multiple units and disciplines in higher education.

CONCLUSION

It is important to understand that most of the collaboration literature is conceptualized as developing through various degrees or strengths of partnerships. For example, Bailey and Koney (2000) conceptualized alliances as developing through a four-level continuum: cooperation, coordination, collaboration, and coadunation. At the beginning of the continuum, cooperation involves shared information and joint support, and at the end of the continuum, coadunation involves an integrated structure in which individual members surrender their autonomy. These varying degrees of partnerships are often referred to as alliances (Gajda, 2004). Therefore, it is important when considering platforms for collaboration not to dismiss those that support a lesser degree of alliance, which could progress into collaboration.

This point is particularly relevant in the context of this study, which indicated that messages on Facebook did not suggest collaborative alliances but did suggest cooperation and coordination. As alliances increase from cooperation toward collaboration, they increase in their extent of interdependence and in their need for formalization (Gajda, 2004; Bailey & Koney, 2000). Formalization is the extent in which members are managed by external structures, like policies or procedures (Bailey & Koney, 2000). This study focused on understanding the essence of the unstructured communication acts already taking place on Facebook and how stakeholders in higher education might utilize this to improve communication and collaboration in higher education. Therefore, the absence of formalization within the design of this study possibly limited the likelihood of locating collaborative alliances.

This study also suggested that composers on Facebook took part in collective composing but still exercised power or control over their personal representational spaces (Facebook wall). Literature concerning alliances suggests that as alliances progress through the continuum toward collaboration, collaborators must also relinquish greater degrees of autonomy or individual power (Bailey & Koney, 2000). For this reason, the personal space on Facebook could prove to be a hindrance to collaboration. This might be avoided by creating a shared space, like a Facebook page or group for particular collaborative purposes.

Finally, this study indicated that audience members on Facebook used this platform for maintaining relationships. This could pose a threat to professionals who desire to separate their public and private lives. However, the literature concerning alliances suggests that maintaining relationships is integral for sustaining partnerships (Austin, 2000; Gajda, 2004). As Austin (2000) noted, collaborators must "connect personally and emotionally" to maintain successful alliances (p. 173). Findings from this study indicated that Facebook could be a valuable communication tool to navigate the growing complexities of American colleges and universities.

REFERENCES

Airey, J. (2011). The disciplinary literacy discussion matrix: A heuristic tool for initiating collaboration in higher education. *Across the Disciplines: A Journal of Language, Learning, and Academic Writing*. Retrieved from http://wac.colostate.edu/atd/ clil/airey.cfm

Akcaoglu, M., & Bowman, N. D. (2016). Using instructor-led Facebook groups to enhance students perceptions of course content. *Computers in Human Behavior*, *65*, 582–590. doi:10.1016/j.chb.2016.05.029

Austen, J. (2000). *The collaboration challenge: How nonprofits and business succeed through strategic alliances*. San Francisco, CA: Jossey-Bass.

B'Far, R. (2005). Mobile computing principles: Designing and developing mobile applications with UML and XML. Cambridge, UK: Cambridge University Press.

Bailey, D., & Koney, K. M. (2000). *Strategic alliances among health and human services organizations: From affiliations to consolidations* [ABRIDGED]. Thousand Oaks, CA: Sage. doi:10.4135/9781483328546

Barnes, N., & Lescault, A. (2012). Social media adoption soars as higher-ed experiments and reevaluates its use of new communications tools. Retrieved from http://www.umassd.edu/cmr/studiesandresearch/socialmediaadoptionsoars/

Baron-Nixon, L. (2007). *Connecting non full-time faculty to institutional mission*. Sterling, VA: Stylus.

Bova, B., & Kroth, M. (2001). Workplace learning and generation X. *Journal of Workplace Learning*, *13*(2), 57–65. doi:10.1108/13665620110383645

Boyd, D. M., & Ellison, N. B. (2008). Social networking sites: Definition, history, and scholarship. *Journal of Computer-Mediated Communication*, *13*(1), 210–230. doi:10.1111/j.1083-6101.2007.00393.x

Boyer, R. (2016, July 16). Great colleges to work for 2016. *The Chronicle of Higher Education*. Retrieved from https://www.chronicle.com/specialreport/Great-Colleges-to-Work-For/47

Cain, J., & Policastri, A. (2011). Using Facebook as an informal learning environment. *American Journal of Pharmaceutical Education*, *75*(10), 1–8. doi:10.5688/ajpe7510207 PMID:22345726

Cassidy, J. (2006). Me media: How hanging out on the internet became big business. *The New Yorker*, *82*(13), 50.

Collins, C. (2008, Sept. 15). Looking to the future: Higher education in the metaverse. *Educause Review*. Retrieved from http://www.educause.edu/ero/article/looking-futurehigher-education-metaverse

Cushman, E. (2008). Toward a rhetoric of self-representation: Identity politics in Indian country and rhetoric and composition. *College Composition and Communication*, *60*(2), 321–365.

Dahlstrom, E. (2012). *ECAR study of undergraduate students and Information technology, 2012*. Retrieved from http://net.educause.edu/ir/library/pdf/ERS1208/ERS1208.pdf

Duggan, M., & Brenner, J. (2012). *The demographics of social media users-2012*. Retrieved from http://pewinternet.org/~/media//Files/Reports/2013/ PIP_SocialMediaUsers.pdf

Duryea, E. D. (2000). Evolution of the university. In M. C. Brown (Ed.), *Organization and governance in higher education* (5th ed.). Boston, MA: Pearson Custom Publishing.

Ede, L., & Lunsford, A. (1984). Audience addressed/Audience invoked. In V. Villanueva (Ed.), *Cross talk in comp theory: A reader* (2nd ed., pp. 77–95). Urbana, IL: NCTE.

Estus, E. L. (2010). Using Facebook within a geriatric pharmacotherapy course. *American Journal of Pharmaceutical Education*, *74*(8), 145. doi:10.5688/aj7408145 PMID:21179256

Faculty Focus. (2011). *Social media usage trends among higher education faculty*. Retrieved from http://www.facultyfocus.com/free-reports/social-media-usage-trends-among-higher education-faculty/

Fonseca, J. W., & Bird, C. P. (2007, October). Under the radar: Branch campuses take off. *University Business Solutions for Higher Education Management*. Retrieved from http://www.universitybusiness.com/article/under-radar-branch-campuses-take

Gajda, R. (2004). Utilizing collaboration theory to evaluate strategic alliances. *The American Journal of Evaluation*, *25*(1), 65–77. doi:10.1177/109821400402500105

Galanek, J., Gierdowski, D. C., & Brooks, D. C. (2018). *ECAR Study of Undergraduate Students and Information Technology, 2018*. Retrieved from https://library.educause.edu/ resources/2018/10/2018-students-and-technology-research-study

Hampton, K., Goulet, L., Rainie, L., & Purcell, K. (2011). *Social networking sites and our lives: How people's trust, personal relationships, and civic and political involvement are connected to their use of social networking sites and other technologies*. Retrieved from http://pewinternet.org/Reports/2011/Technology-and-social-networks.aspx

Hepburn, A. (2010, March 22). Facebook: Facts and figures for 2010 [Web log post]. *Digital Buzz*. Retrieved from http://digitalbuzzblog.com/facebook-facts-figures-2010

Hepburn, A. (2011, Jan. 18). Facebook statistics: Stats and facts for 2011 [Web log post]. *Digital Buzz*. Retrieved from http://digitalbuzzblog.com/facebook-statistics-stats-facts-2011

Hoang, H. (2009). Campus racial politics and a "rhetoric of injury.". *College Composition and Communication*, *61*(1), 188.

Howard, G. T. (2010). *Dictionary of rhetorical terms*. Bloomington, IN: Xlibrus Publishing.

Kerr, C. (1963). *The uses of the university*. Cambridge, MA: Harvard University Press.

Kezar, A., & Lester, J. (2009). *Organizing higher education for collaboration*. San Francisco, CA: Jossey-Bass.

Lampe, C., Ellison, N., & Steinfeld, C. (2006). In P. Hinds, & D. Martin (Eds.), A Face(book) in the crowd: Social searching vs. social browsing. *Proceedings of the 2006 20th anniversary conference on Computer supported cooperative work* (pp. 167-170). New York, NY: Association for Computing Machinery.

LaRue, E. M. (2012). Using Facebook as a course management software: A case study. *Teaching and Learning in Nursing*, *7*(1), 17–22. doi:10.1016/j.teln.2011.07.004

Lunsford, A. (2006). Writing, technologies, and the fifth canon. *Computers and Composition*, *23*(2), 169–177. doi:10.1016/j.compcom.2006.02.002

Madden, M., & Fox, S. (2006). Riding the waves of "Web 2.0:" More than a buzzword but still not easily defined. Retrieved from http://www.pewinternet.org/ Reports/2006/Riding-theWaves-of-Web-20.aspx

Madden, M., & Zickuhr, K. (2011). *65% of online adults use social networking sites.* Retrieved from http://pewinternet.org/~/media//Files/Reports/2011/PIP SNSUpdate-2011.pdf

Most Popular Websites. (2011). *Most popular websites on the internet.* Retrieved from http://mostpopularwebsites.net/

National Center for Education Statistics, Institution of Education Sciences. (2011). *Digest of education statistics, 2011.* Retrieved from http://nces.ed.gov/fastfacts/display.asp?id=98

National Center for Education Statistics, Institution of Education Sciences. (2018). *The Condition of Education, 2018.* Retrieved from https://nces.ed.gov/pubs2018/2018144.pdf

Olson, D. (2001). *The world on paper.* New York, NY: Cambridge University Press.

Parker, K., Lenhart, A., & Moore, K. (2011). *The digital revolution and higher education: College presidents, public differ on value of online learning.* Retrieved from http://www.pewinternet.org/~/ media// Files/Reports/2011/PIP-Online Learning.pdf

Porter, J. (2009). Recovering delivery for digital rhetoric. *Computers and Composition, 26*(4), 207–224. doi:10.1016/j.compcom.2009.09.004

Richardson, J. T. (1999). Centralizing governance isn't simply wrong; it's bad business, too. *Chronicle of Higher Education.* Retrieved from http://chronicle.com/article/Centralizing Governance-Isnt/8672

Sapkota, K., & Vander Putten, J. (2018). Social media acceptance and usage by business communications faculty. *Business and Professional Communication Quarterly, 81*(3), 328–350. doi:10.1177/2329490618777818

Seaman, J. E., Allen, I. E., & Seaman, J. (2018). *Grade Increase: Tracking Distance Education in the United States.* Retrieved from https://www.onlinelearningsurvey.com/highered.html

Sexton, J., & Bollinger, L. C. (2002). Fostering collaboration in higher education. *Bulletin - American Academy of Arts and Sciences, 55*(3), 59–68. doi:10.2307/3824212

Sheeran, N., & Cummings, D. J. (2018). An examination of the relationship between Facebook groups attached to the university courses and student engagement. *Higher Education, 76*(6), 937–955. doi:10.100710734-018-0253-2

Singel, R. (2005, Oct. 6) Are you ready for Web 2.0? *Wired.* Retrieved from http://www. wired.com/ science/discoveries/news/2005/10/69114

Sloan Consortium. (2012). *Changing course: Ten years of tracking online education in the United States.* Retrieved from http://sloanconsortium.org/publications/survey /changing_course_2012

Smith, A., & Anderson, M. (2018). *Social Media Use in 2018: A majority of Americans use Facebook and YouTube, but young adults are especially heavy users of Snapchat and Instagram.* Retrieved from http://www.pewinternet.org/2018/ 03/01/social-media-use-in2018/

Sorcinelli, M. D., & Yun, J. (2007). From mentor to mentoring networks: Mentoring in the new academy. *Change, 39*(6), 58–61. doi:10.3200/CHNG.39.6.58-C4

Thelin, J. (2004). *A history of American higher education*. Baltimore, MD: The Johns Hopkins University Press.

Trabold, B. (2009). Walking the cliff's edge: The new nation's rhetoric of resistance in apartheid South Africa [Excerpt]. *College Composition and Communication*, *61*(2), 372.

Welch, K. (1990). Electrifying classical rhetoric: Ancient media, modern technology, and contemporary composition. *Journal of Advanced Composition*, *10*(1), 22–38.

Yancey, K. B. (2009). *Writing in the 21st Century*. Urbana, IL: National Council of Teachers of English.

Yin, R. K. (2011). *Qualitative research from start to finish*. New York, NY: Guilford Press.

You, X. (2005). Ideology, textbooks, and the rhetoric of production in China. *College Composition and Communication*, *56*(4), 632–653.

Chapter 12
Technology and Culturally Competent Strategies for the Online Classroom

Justina Elise Kwapy
Grand Canyon University, USA

ABSTRACT

The last decade has brought an increase in online courses in the educational setting. One-quarter of American college students are in an online degree program, and 32% have taken at least one online course. While students, higher universities, and faculty are enjoying the convenience and flexibility of online learning environments, there is an increasing concern over the support in distance education, teaching methods, and a social disconnectedness of students from the course. This chapter explores how technology can support a successful online learning experience and impede the dissatisfaction and higher dropout rates among students in distance learning programs. Higher institution's online faculty are now faced with the task of creating a virtual community of learners, meeting both the academic and social needs of students.

INTRODUCTION

Online programs offer students an opportunity to further their education at their convenience, with the flexibility of learning, despite family, work and other personal obligations. Higher education faculty are no longer only required to teach in the traditional brick and mortar style, but also teach in the virtual learning environment. Teaching methods must now include building a sense of community in their classrooms that mirror those of the traditional classroom, but also giving students the connectedness and sense of belonging that make them successful, motivated, and ready to learn. McMillan and Chavis (1986) define a sense of community as "a feeling that members have of belonging, a feeling that members matter to one another and to the group, and shared faith that members' needs will be met through their commitment to be together". Personalized instruction is now an essential element of an online instructor's teaching practices and pedagogy (Popescu, 2010). It is expected that an online community

DOI: 10.4018/978-1-5225-9814-5.ch012

establishes this connectedness of instructor and students. Community can be defined by the relationships and interactions between students and instructor. Research suggests that once a reliable technology system is in place, the design of the course and pedagogy utilized can play more of a significant role in facilitating community building than the actual e-learning platform (Rovai, 2002a, 2002c). Promoting interaction among community members through collaboration provides opportunities for members to learn from each other, contribute to each other's learning, and recognize and accept the differences and perspectives of each learner. Collaboration has been determined to be one of the most crucial elements of successfully integrating technology in the online classroom.

Giving instructors and students the tools to be successful in the online learning environment is essential for success. Instructors can facilitate this sense of community through careful planning, support and intentional tasks and activities that support the best practices of community building through the use of technology and a social presence that motivates and encourages student connectedness, both individually and in a group. Factors that can contribute to online attrition includes high college costs, poor program fit, and lack of technical support for online students (Angelino, Williams, & Natvig, 2007; Patterson & McFadden, 2009; Rovai, 2003).

BACKGROUND

More than four and a half million students were enrolled in at least one online course in 2009 (Allen & Seaman, 2010). The Distance Education Enrollment Report 2017, conducted by the new Digital Learning Compass organization, reveals the number of higher education students taking at least one distance education course in 2015 now tops six million.

Although online courses offer convenience, the social interactions found in the classroom between the professor and students continue to be an area of uneasiness due to the high attrition rates in online programs (Angelino, Williams, & Natvig, 2007). A prime concern for administrators of online degree programs and operative faculty training is an empirically-informed understanding of intentional and effective instructional practices that create meaningful, community-building interaction between students and instructors. Evidence demonstrates that a student's sense of community in an online learning environment contributes to the learner's gains, engagement and overall satisfactions with the online course.

An academic learning community is present through the connectedness of the learners and faculty. In an online learning environment, learners have little connection to the physical university. School spirit, cohesiveness and connection to the university must be demonstrated through the use of technology (Rovai, 2003). Without the sense of a learning community present, learners can experience a sense of isolation and disconnectedness from the online class and university, and ultimately, from their learning and success.

SOCIAL PRESENCE

Research demonstrates that a social presence is essential in promoting student success in the online classroom (Swan & Shih, 2005). Swan & Shih suggest that social presence exists through the sharing of learners' experiences, collaboration and meaningful connections that result in an increased and effective learning experience. Social presence emerges when instructors support students in engaging in genuine dialogue that supports.

The instructor's role of facilitating the online course plays a significant role in the frequency of students' active interactions in an online course (Garrison, 2001; Raovai, 2007; Yuan & Kim, 2014). According to Garrison et al. (2010), students are more likely to feel a sense of community in their online course when the discussions encourage participation. The asynchronous platform that exists in the online learning environment can serve as a challenge for instructors in meeting the social needs of learners. Strategies that employ existing technology can contribute to the lack of face-to-face interactions of a traditional school. Instructors must utilize teaching methods that create a social presence in the online learning environment, and promote collaboration among the entire learning community.

Connectedness to other learners and faculty is an important characteristic of a successful learning community. Connectedness facilitates higher achievement (Rovai, 2003); however, many learners do not establish relationships with others outside of the online classroom. A study was conducted to address the perceived connectedness to other learners, faculty, the school and the university. Responses demonstrated that 68% of learners indicated some degree of connectedness to other learners and 59% indicated some connectedness to their school. Connectedness to their university was at 58%. More than 40% of learners felt no connection to their school or university. These numbers indicate ramifications of retention and referrals of new learners to the school. The study demonstrated that support staff was also integral to their overall satisfaction with the school. These support staff include technical support and academic support services. A supportive, encouraging and knowledgeable technical staff is essential for putting students at ease with the use of technology and encouraging them to increase their technological skills. Social network features such as profiles, groups, and chat functions can promote a more personalized interaction among the members of an online community.

TECHNOLOGY AND COMMUNITY BUILDING

The accessibility and effective use of technology in the online learning environment is essential. Access to technology by both the instructor and learners carries the potential to support the development of a learning community where students can learn, socialize, access support and gain meaningful experiences from their online course.

Integrating technology in the classroom provides instructors the opportunity to support the various learning styles in their classrooms while stimulating student engagement and learning. According to Wang, Shannon, and Rodd (2013), online education offers many options of course delivery without students being present. Instructors can use technology to incorporate innovative strategies that increase student motivation and learning.

Technology can increase the growth of and aid the development of a learning community. Both asynchronous and synchronous discussions can promote sharing information, ideas and mentoring among learners and faculty. Communities of learners will not only develop because of the technology present, but rather the role the technology plays in creating meaningful collaboration where learners feel safe, open and welcome to participate.

Research suggests a positive relationship between teaching practices with student achievement, satisfaction, performance, assessments, and learner preferences (Dennen et al., 2007; Gaytan & McEwen, 2007; Lin & Overbaugh, 2007). However, traditionally trained professors, who may not be well versed in online education research theory or practice, may not know the importance of building learning communities and the impact that it has upon learning (Liu, Magjuka, Bonk, & Lee, 2007). Furthermore, Durrington,

Berryhill, & Swafford (2006) report some online teachers lack sufficient knowledge of using technology to increase student sense of community, specifically with interactions between students and instructor.

A national study also found that professors integration of technology generally to be low (Smith & Caruso, 2010). The findings indicate a slow adoption process of technology tools and resources by higher education faculty. The low usage of integration of technology in the higher education environment may not be too surprising when referring to the "technology acceptance" theory. For example, Gibson et al. (2008) indicated that higher education faculty acceptance of technology was not related so much as to ease of use, but to its usefulness. Instructors are ignoring a powerful tool by not increasing their use of technology in the online classroom.

INSTRUCTOR'S ROLE IN COMMUNITY BUILDING

One of the pertinent issues facing online faculty is to understand what our students expectations are concerning our roles and responsibilities within the classroom setting. Although many instructors may understand the traditional face-to-face classroom paradigm, the online environment can present new challenges and opportunities not evident in a traditional classroom. The traditional classroom setting typically involves a lecture that is dominated by the instructor. Students often still expect this model and are accustomed to it. Instructors also tend to be comfortable with this model. The online environment, however, places new demands on instructors as students' expectations can differ.

Craig, Goold, Coldwell, and Mustard (2008) conducted a survey of online students to determine their expectations of online instructors' roles and responsibilities. The findings from the study are as follows: 92 percent indicated that instructors should provide useful feedback; 84 percent indicated instructors should provide guidance in discussion forums; 75 percent wanted instructors to challenge them about issues; 74 percent of students indicated they wanted stimulating experiences; and 73 percent wanted their instructor to provide more overall challenging experiences.

An instructor's teaching style, methods and overall presence are found to be associated with a student's sense of learning community. Instructors must take on a leadership, yet facilitator role in the online classroom. Not only do online instructors need to take on a leadership role for nurturing students' academic learning, but also lead in a social role to engage and challenge students in a community of learners.

In the online learning environment, creating a sense of community is not a simple task. There are no pep rallies, marching bands or football teams. There are no offices or lounges in which to connect informally. Learners in the online learning environment often progress through their coursework with little or no human contact. Staff members working from their home offices typically work in isolation, detached from family, colleagues, and the institution. As described by Maslow (1954), most online learners and instructors will succumb to the basic human need of belonging.

Ouzts (2006) found students that reported low sense of community identified minimal interaction with peers and dissatisfaction with the instructor and overall course. Online instructional practices may serve as an importance in student satisfaction and sense of community. Teacher communication was rated the highest of importance by students in measuring perceptions of quality instruction (Craig, Goold, Coldwell, & Mustard, 2008; Dennen et al., 2007; Gayton & McEwen, 2007). Dennen et al. (2007) identified that online instructors may not have the understanding of how to communicate with students in an online course in a way that is done so in the traditional classroom to build a sense of community.

Online learning allows the instructor and students to connect to the course from any location in the world at any given time. However, the important component of traditional courses that needs to be implemented into the online course is communication building through a community of learners. Online instructors are given the additional task of social context within the online course in creating and facilitating an online sense of community. Developed models of online teaching roles identify specific roles of the instructor which include the socialization aspect of creating a community of learners (Craig et al., 2008; Ice et al. 2007). Research has found that there are different strategies an online instructor can implement in the course design to help students gain a sense of belonging, which eliminates the feelings of isolation, creates a sense of community, and student satisfaction.

Dennen et al. (2007) found that instructors' perception of students' beliefs of their actions was identified to have a strong correlation to student satisfaction, in addition, communication and interaction which falls under the categories pedagogical and social, as described by Bawane and Spencer (2009). Although communication has been identified as an important practice of the online teacher as perceived by students, the use of synchronous tools in the online learning environment, synchronous communication was not rated as high as feedback and immediacy asynchronously (Dennen et al., 2007).

Continuous instructor communication was identified as an indicator of measurement for a quality online course (Gayton & McEwen, 2007). Online students do not have face-to-face contact with peers and the instructor as found in traditional classroom settings. Therefore, online instructors face the challenge of building a sense of community within the virtual classroom using tools and strategies to eliminate student perceptions of isolation. According to Dickey (2004), learning is impacted by student perceptions of isolation. Because an online professor does not normally have direct verbal contact with an entire group of students in a classroom, the professor implements communication and collaboration strategies through asynchronous feedback with students through posted messages, directions, and contact through email. The online instructor becomes a facilitator of a course and implements multiple strategies for communicating course requirements and text-based discussions.

In another study, Ice, Curtis, Phillips, and Wells (2007) identified an online teaching model of four main pedagogical roles of an online professor: profession-inspirer, feedback-giver, interaction-facilitator, and social rapport builder. These defined functions serve as a model in understanding the different strategies online professors implement in the virtual learning environment. The online instructor forms a community of learners through facilitation of discussions that promote learning and understanding of the course objectives and provides continuous feedback to guide inquiry and provoke learning (Ice et al., 2007).

The sense of community in the online environment involves the understanding of student perceptions of feelings in the nontraditional classroom with focus on students' sense of belonging, interaction, isolation, class climate, and sense of individual importance (Rovai, Wighting, & Liu, 2005).

Misanchuk and Anderson (2001) suggest strategies that promote successful online learning through increasing the levels of communication and interactions with others. This can be achieved through non-instructional activities such as posting personal profiles and interests and participating in dialogue in online café's and chat rooms that foster off-topic discussions. Utilizing strategies that encourage learners to participate in in-depth discussions, problem-solving and peer review also stimulate increasing levels of interactions with others in the online learning environment. Instructors need to be proactive in their classrooms by bringing in new ideas, outside sources, and real-world examples to make the material more meaningful for students.

Instructional practices in the online environment have been a focus to develop an understanding of teacher and online students' perceptions' of effective online teaching practices (Dennen, Darabi, & Smith, 2007; Gaytan & McEwan, 2007; Young, 2006). There is a positive correlation between teacher presence in the online classroom and student motivation and success. Teacher presence in an online course includes interaction in the online learning environment where the student perceives the instructor as visible, active, and involved in the course and learning environment. Durrington et al. (2006) defined multiple strategies to increase instructor interaction in an online course such as immediacy, detailed feedback on discussion postings, and community building. The promotion of instructor immediacy and presence in an online course and its relation to student satisfaction, motivation, and cognitive learning consists of the online faculty member integrating various teaching and learning strategies that enhance the virtual presence of the instructor and the interaction between students in the class and with each other. Craig (2008) found student perceptions' of faculty roles placed at high importance, along with meaningful feedback on course work and instructor guidance in the online discussions. The top-rated faculty roles as perceived by students included providing meaningful feedback and guidance in student discussion boards as the two highest perceived roles of the online instructor (Craig, 2008). Student perceptions of online teacher roles as it relates to student achievement and satisfaction were related to teacher correspondence and immediacy (Dennen et al., 2007), which confirms previous research identification of meaningful responses to student inquiries and coursework (Craig, 2008).

As a result of these findings, higher education institutions that offer online programs should investigate ways to increase quality community-building, and communication between learners, peers and instructors. Innovations in this endeavor can have an effect on the high rate of attrition found in online learning (Allen & Seaman, 2010).

SOCIAL CONNECTION AND COMMUNITY BUILDING

A study adopted from the Inclusion of Self in Other (IOS) questionnaire developed by Aron et al. (1992) measured perceived connectedness to four aspects of a university: other learners, faculty, school, and the university. Respondents were asked how they perceived their relationship with other learners, faculty, school and university. In comments related to their responses to connectedness to other learners, the primary theme was that there was no relationship with other learners outside of class. One respondent commented that "while in contact with other learners, there is no relationship beyond a professional association and academic discussion."

Social ability represents the extent to which learners utilize the resources of the social context to achieve important goals (Laffey, Lin, & Lin, 2006). The fit among learners and the instructor in the course can affect the depth of the social ability. Both the instructor and the learners must be knowledgeable of the tools available to them. Learners who exhibit more social ability in the classroom tend to be more apt to communicate openly and frequently with the instructor and other learners. A learner's written skills can affect this. Written communication plays a large role in the success of a student's success in the online learning environment. Students who are able to post messages using a supportive and connected voice were found to have a stronger sense of community and were more successful in the course. Communication, sharing opinions, expressing thoughts and providing support to each other in the written form all influence the social nature of online learning.

Along with a sense of community, previous research suggests that social ability is a key determinant of how students experience online learning. Lin et al. (2006) demonstrated that social ability played a large predictor for online students' satisfaction and was critical for moving students into a central role in the online community. Students' participation and interactions with others is also determined by their knowledge and how well the online tools scaffold their social needs and achievement of learning goals.

In the online learning environment, the use of technology tools is necessary for both social and academic learning. Schwier (2002) stated that the accessibility and use of technology tools for online learning is critical in building and facilitating a virtual learning community due to the use of technological tools that provide a space for students to gather and communicate.

Social media has had a profound effect on how we communicate with one another. The amount of connectivity brought about by this new modality of communication has had and will continue to have a significant influence on society in many different ways. Social media has permeated nearly every segment of society, including education. Many of our students come to our courses with an abundance of knowledge of social media, and the issue online instructors face is how to use this technological knowledge to increase the connections in the classroom, and improve the educational process. Since students arrive in our classrooms with existing technological knowledge, instructors can minimize the learning curve associated with online learning. Many students have had experience with the concept of peer-to-peer learning. This exchange of ideas and thoughts is a positive force in the online classroom, where collaboration plays an integral role in facilitating higher levels of interaction.

Social media also presents challenges toward effective learning. The anonymity of this modality allows individuals to post thoughts without accountability. Instructors must also model and provide guidance within the online classroom on how to extend and expand upon their initial posts. There is also the need to correct spelling and grammar mistakes that are often present and acceptable within social media, and encourage our students to speak and write with more academic writing in mind. It is essential that instructors utilize our students' social media skills toward creating an environment in which we improve the connectivity of higher-order and problem-solving thinking processes.

The importance of social interactions on online learning has evolved into a major area of research.

The study of social interactions in the online learning environment includes exploration of teaching practices and relationships between course design, delivery, instruction, and interaction and the effects on sense of community and student retention (Angelino et al., 2007; Drouin, 2008; Outzs, 2006; Young, 2006). Social interaction and the understanding of how learners gain knowledge are found in the social constructivism theory (Vygotsky, 1978). Social constructivism in education bases learning on social interaction with peers and instructors to build upon current knowledge in a welcoming environment that encourages exploratory interactions and engagement in new ideas.

Social presence and interaction between instructor and students have offered a unique look into online learning affected by the growth in online enrollment in higher education institutions. The study of online learning and teacher practices has generated further investigation as to understanding online presence, such as interaction with students by the instructor and practices to build such interaction and its correlation to student satisfaction and academic achievement (Durrington et al., 2006; O'Leary & Quinland, 2007; Shea & Bidjerano, 2008; Sher, 2009).

COLLABORATIVE LEARNING AND COMMUNITY BUILDING

Online communities cannot develop on their own without careful planning, continued support, and intentional tasks and activities. They can provide an ideal learning environment where interaction among students plays a large role in the learning process. Facilitation of online teams can also increase community. Without cross-teams, students will unlikely feel a connection to other learners, except those in their assigned team. Although students are usually assigned to one team throughout a course, other strategies such as class-wide discussions or ad hoc groups should be used to connect students with other class members other than those in their group.

In a collaborative learning environment, knowledge is shared among learners as they work towards common learning goals. Learners are not passive receptacles but are active in their process of acquiring knowledge as they participate in discussions, search for information, and exchange opinions with their peers. Knowledge is co-created and shared among peers, not owned by one particular learner after obtaining it from the course materials or instructor. The learning process creates a bond between and among learners as their knowledge construction depends on each other's contribution to the discussion. Hence, collaborative learning processes assist students to develop higher order thinking skills and achieve richer knowledge generation through shared goals, shared exploration, and a shared process of meaning making (Brookfield, 1995; Christiensen & Dirkinick-Holmfeld, 1996; Jonassen, Davidson, Collins, Campbell, & Haag, 1995; Palloff & Pratt, 2005).

Many online courses have incorporated group learning as part of the course requirements, whereas others have veered away from utilizing group work in their courses. Placing students in working groups can create a set of problems that often take away from the learning success of students. There are seven most commonly found problems that can be existent in group learning:

Problem 1: Student antipathy toward group work.
Problem 2: The way the groups are selected.
Problem 3: Lack of collaborative and group-work skills among members.
Problem 4: Students who do not carry their weight.
Problem 5: Inequality of student abilities.
Problem 6: Non-active group members.
Problem 7: Assessing students individually within a group.

Discussions and dialogue with students around the benefits of group work can help overcome some of the resistance students may have toward group work. Group work in the online learning environment can have benefits such as:

- Developing rapport with other learners.
- Develop negotiating skills for working with others.
- Develop and sustain the motivation and commitment for working with others.
- Developing teamwork expertise.

Selecting online groups can be a challenge for online instructors and affect the success of the individuals in the group. Some instructors may randomly select groups based on age, gender, geographic location, or even month of birth. There is some evidence that heterogeneous groups can be advantageous due to the various perspectives that are brought to the group (Kagan, 1997; Johnson & Johnson, 1989). Others select groups based on student backgrounds, personalities and interests.

Students may lack the necessary skills to work effectively in a group. Instructors must be aware of these deficient skills and spend the time to introduce new students to skills such as team-building, effective communication, netiquette, presentation skills and responsibilities to other group members.

When students encounter others who are not willing to pull their weight in the group, pressure from the instructor may be necessary. A signed group agreement outlining group norms from each group member and setting expectations of norms at the beginning of the class can help, along with regular reminders from the group leader on deadlines and role and responsibilities.

Inequalities of student abilities can be evident in most groups. Utilizing learner strengths and weaknesses in group members can better even out this imbalance of skills. Group members should also be willing to express to groups members their areas of strength from the beginning, so they are not assigned an area that is an area of weakness later on.

Disappearing or inactive group members can have a detrimental effect on the success of the group. When a group member drops the course or is inactive, the instructor should step in right away and reassign roles. Regular monitoring of groups by the instructor is necessary for early intervention of group members that are not active or present in the group.

Assessment of group members both individually and collaboratively is essential. Self-assessment of individual group members, peer and group assessment techniques can be beneficial for both students and the instructor. Students can learn from assessment of themselves and their group members. It is important that the instructor drives the assessment process for students, so it is done in a professional and constructive manner.

The dissatisfaction and reluctance that students may express over mandatory participation in group projects often results from a sense of not having full control over the quality of the project and the subsequent grade assigned, particularly when someone in the group has less than satisfactory performance. This is a good reason for instructors not to place as much emphasis on grading much as helping students to learn the skills of collaboration, including how to deal effectively with group members who are unable or unwilling to participate fully in the group process. If the right environment is created, both high-performing and low-performing students are able to reflect on and articulate their opinions about their experience and the outcomes of their learning. That being said, it is important to acknowledge the extra time and special skills required of instructors to ensure the effectiveness of small group learning experiences. Research appears to confirm that small group collaboration online needs careful management by the instructor (cf. Swan, Shen, & Hiltz, 2006, p. 51).

Online communities cannot develop on their own without careful planning, continued support, and intentional tasks and activities. Instructors must value the role of the online community in student success and with their overall satisfaction with the course.

EFFECTIVE FACILITATION AND COMMUNITY BUILDING

Uncertainty exists in new learning environments as to what strategies work in the online learning environment and why (Shea, 2006). Online instructors face the task of meeting the needs of a variety of learning styles, lack of experience with technology, and student motivational factors (Smaldino, Lowther, & Russell, 2012).

Wilson et al. (2004) stated that it is important for online instructors to model community participation skills and values, including turn-taking, netiquette, thoughtful responses to peer's posts, and organization and facilitation of community events and chat. Many online instructors admitted that they felt they lacked the adequate skills necessary to facilitate an interactive classroom and create a sense of community. Students learning at a distance can possess feelings of disconnect from the institution they attend. Without a clear design, frequent interaction with instructors, and active discussions with peers, student satisfaction or sense of belonging is significantly lower (Swan, 2002).

Faculty should become not just effective facilitators, but effective online cheerleaders for students. Faculty must enter the online classroom and gain student attention, motivation and diligence. There are several steps that are necessary. First, the faculty member should have prepared beforehand clear and specific course policies, faculty contact information, course announcements and grading rubrics. Providing additional and specific instruction for more complex assignments is necessary for better understanding of individual assignments. During the class, instructors can use email, classroom messages, Questions for Instructor forum, Twitter, Facebook, personal websites, course announcements and phone calls to motivate student attention and diligence. It is important to utilize one or more methods of communication in order to ensure effective and productive contact with all students.

Another practice that can further increase motivation among students includes empathizing with students. Instructors should let students know that they understand the commitments and sacrifices that go along with life-long learning. Being available, approachable and timely in responses and feedback are practices that online instructors must employ. Online courses should have the structure, transparency, and potential for communication in order to affect student satisfaction (Swan, 2002).

An appropriately structured online classroom can create a better learning environment. Discussion forums are paramount to learning and the student must be expected to participate regularly in each week's discussion questions. There are varieties of strategies an online instructor can implement in order to close the gap on proximity, build rapport with students, and meet the student's individualized needs.

- Provide intriguing and interesting titles and posts.
- Provide a current event post linked to the week's topics.
- Incorporate outside websites, You Tube videos or illustrations that better explain the weekly topics and objectives.
- Pose a thought-provoking question based on the weekly topics and objectives that has a life-application to it.
- Use the weekly discussions as an avenue to assess student learning.
- Encourage student to relate weekly topics to personal experiences.

The discussion forum is the core of the online class. It is where the majority of the students gathers, share ideas and collaborate with their fellow students and instructor. Instructors should view the discussion forum as the central focus of the course and employ strategies that encourage and motivate all students to be active leaders in the forum.

CULTURALLY COMPETENT TEACHING STRATEGIES

Much of the language we use comes from cultural aspects of our lives-many words which are impossible to translate because of its cultural meaning. It is important that educators deepen their understanding of the impact of social and cultural factors on language learning through culturally responsive teaching practices. Employing competent teaching and learning strategies through the use of conceptual and critical thinking skills is essential. Cultural influences can influence instructional approaches in the teaching and learning process. Students must investigate, question and reflect on their biases from a nonjudgmental perspective. Instructors should encourage students to admit and explore their own personal biases. This self-reflection gives students the opportunities to investigate their own biases use the knowledge gained to expand their views of others and their environment. Breaking down the stereotypes that often exist among our classrooms can affect the tone and climate of the online classroom.

In order to create a "safe space" in our classrooms for our students to learn, we must allow students to explore what having a "safe space" means personally to them. A great way to achieve this is by having students describe or write about what the terms "safe" and "space" mean to them personally, and what do they look like. This gives the instructor a better view on their students' perspectives and how to proceed with possible biases. Instructors can also place students in teams and have each team engage in active discussion around what their definition of a "safe place" looks and feels like.

Instructors can support the existence of a "safe space" to learn by creating a classroom climate where all students feel they belong and taking risks is encouraged and embraced. Only when students are able to address their fears are they able to have a sense of belonging in the course, and as a result, experience the "safe space" in which to learn.

Aydin and Ceci (2013) found language and culture influenced the susceptibility, as many individuals might not understand what the speaker actually meant by what they said and may use their own biases to understand it. Sensitivity to the cultural differences requires instructors to engage students in self-awareness activities that promote reflection on their cultural assumptions. Providing students with culturally responsive methods of learning and opportunities to learn more about the differences of their classmates promotes self-reflection of their own assumptions and beliefs and encourages mutual respect between the instructor and students, and students and peers. Effective instructors not only learn from but learn about their students. Effective cultural competent teaching practices recognizes the result of intercultural communication as a means of promoting learning for all.

Active listening is a key component of promoting culturally competent teaching and language for all. Culturally competent instructors lead the class in structured activities around traditions, religion, independence, education, work, health, etc. that lead to meaningful and relevant dialogue among students.

According to Chang (1996), college students are more likely to discuss racial issues when they are part of a diverse body and have the opportunity to participate in conversations with racially diverse groups.

In order for students to truly embrace each other's diversity and differences, instructors are often forced to step outside of their comfort zones.

Ladson-Billings (2001) states that cultural competence us present in classrooms where "the teacher understands the culture and its role in education." The teacher must take responsibility for learning students' culture and community. The teacher uses student culture as a basis for learning and promotes a flexible use of students' local and global culture (p. 98).

The goals of providing students with a "multicultural education" are:

- Gain a greater self-understanding by viewing themselves from the perspective of other cultures.
- Develop greater respect and tolerance through acquaintance and understanding of others
- Provide students with a greater cultural and ethnic alternative.

Instructors can use technology to incorporate more visuals and culturally responsive practices so that language is not the primary way to assess a student's progress and mastery of the material.

WEBQUESTS AND 21ST CENTURY LEARNING

Instructors must discover, create, and implement methods to facilitate ongoing interaction with students. Smaldino, Lowther, and Russell (2012), suggested teacher-led and student-led strategies including teacher presentation and demonstration, student presentation, text, illustrations, live or recorded voice, and full-motion images. Learning must continue online, just as the learning would occur in a face-to-face, traditional environment.

A survey of over 2,000 companies conducted by Corporate Voices for Working Families (2012), found that, "employers are seeking candidates with a clear understanding of 21st-centuryworkplace demands, including the ability to work in teams, the need for wide-ranging communications skills and the aptitude to solve complex problems" (p.4). In another survey initiated by the Conference Board, Corporate Voices for Working Families, The Partnership for 21st Century Skills, and the Society for Human Resource Management (2006), found that the top five skills employers desired new entrants to possess were professionalism, team work, oral communication, ethical and moral responsibility, and reading comprehension. The same study alleged that new entrants were deficient in all of these essential skills.

In 2012, a study was conducted by the International Summit on the Teaching Profession (The Summit), hosted by the United States Department of Education and the Organization for Economic Cooperation and Development (OECD), to identify the 21st century skills educational institutions worldwide would need to incorporate into their curriculum in order to better prepare learners for the global workforce. The Summit involved more than 250 researchers and 60 institutions. The compulsory 21st century skills identified were classified into four categories, as shown in Table 1.

According to the survey conducted by the Conference Board, Corporate Voices for Working Families, The Partnership for 21st Century Skills, and the Society for Human Resource Management (2006), surveyed respondents stated that 42.4% of high school graduates are overall deficient in workforce readiness skills, 69.6% in critical thinking and problem solving, 70.3% in professionalism and in work ethic, 80.9% in written communication, 38.4% in reading comprehension, and 72% in basic grammar and spelling.

Table 1. 21st century skill categories

Category	Skills
Ways of Thinking	Creativity, critical thinking, problem-solving, decision-making and learning.
Ways of Working	Collaboration and communication.
Tools for Working	Information and communications technology and information literacy.
Skills for Living in the World	Citizenship, life and career, and personal and social responsibility.

Another study conducted by the Manpower group (2012) interviewed over 38,000 employers globally and found that 33% of applicants lacked technical competencies/hard skills to perform. These hard skills include: industry specific qualification and knowledge, operation of equipment, computer/information technology skills, speaking/verbal skills, and the ability to speak a second language. The "soft skills' deficits these global employers discussed were: interpersonal skills, motivation, team work/collaboration, professionalism, adaptability, problem solving/decision making, and attention to detail.

As a result of this data, it can be determined that educational institutions are not properly equipping students with the necessary 21st century skills for the global workforce. Webquests, if properly created and developed, can be used as an effective pedagogical tool to facilitate this. In order to appropriately integrate Webquests into a school's curriculum, best practices for implementing them must be followed.

The 21st century workforce skills are defined as the following: collaboration, team work, communication (written and verbal), creativity/innovation, critical thinking and problem solving, Information and Communication Technology (ICT) literacy, field- based knowledge acquisition and mastery, professionalism/work ethic (motivation, completion of tasks, maintaining deadlines, attendance, punctuality, and possessing a positive attitude), adaptability, reading comprehension, and responsible/accountable global citizenry.

Webquest best practices should try to emulate as many of these skills as possible. In order for Webquests to serve as a method of teaching 21st century work force skills, they should employ the following eight best practices:

1. Create Collaborative and Cooperative Tasks

Webquests should assign group-oriented tasks, where there is a common goal amongst its members, yet everyone must participate in order to achieve the means to the end. According to Kozar (2010), differentiates the differences of collaborative and cooperative learning by stating, "cooperation can be achieved if all participants do their assigned parts separately and bring their results to the table; collaboration, in contrast, implies direct interaction among individuals to produce a product and involves negotiations, discussions, and accommodating others' perspectives (p.17)." Since collaboration is one of the requisite 21st century skills employers feel new entrants need but lack, Webquests should develop and foster this skill.

2. Invoke and Foster Critical Thinking for Creative Problem Solving and Innovative Ideas

According to Scriven and Paul (1987), critical thinking is:

Critical thinking is the intellectually disciplined process of actively and skillfully conceptualizing, applying, analyzing, synthesizing, and/or evaluating information gathered from, or generated by, observation, experience, reflection, reasoning, or communication, as a guide to belief and action. In its exemplary form, it is based on universal intellectual values that transcend subject matter divisions: clarity, accuracy, precision, consistency, relevance, sound evidence, good reasons, depth, breadth, and fairness (para.1).

Critical thinking skills are incorporated into problem solving. Problem solving includes identifying the problem, analyzing the problem, devising possible solutions, evaluating potential solutions, selecting the best solution, and reevaluating and reflecting upon the selected solution. The Webquest task should include a challenging problem where these critical thinking skills are engaged. Creativity plays an integral role as well. Creative thinking is subsumed in this application. According to Harris (2012), creative thinking is "the ability to generate new ideas by combining, changing, or reapplying existing ideas…the ability to accept change and newness, a willingness to play with ideas and possibilities, a flexibility of outlook, the habit of enjoying the good, while looking for ways to improve it" (para. 1).

In order for learners to cultivate this skill, the task must require them to generate new ideas, think "outside the box," and consider alternative ideas and suggestions. This can be accomplished with a Webquest that asks students to formulate their own solution to a problem rather than providing it for them or asking them to choose from teacher-generated choices.

3. Incorporate Written and Oral Communication within the Task

Webquests can require students to produce both a written product and an oral presentation. The guidelines and rules for both of these can be specified in a rubric. The presentation must also demonstrate visual components utilizing Web 2.0 tools.

Oral communication skills are also essential to embed into curricula for the 21st century work force. Webquests should include more practice with public presentations. This can be in the form of a debate, student-led class discussion, or formal presentation.

4. Integrate and Require ICT Skills from Beginning to End

According to the Education Testing Services, Webquests should include research skills. Students should have knowledge of effective internet research, utilizing search engines, evaluating a source's credibility, validity, and reliability, collecting and analyzing the data's objectivity, determining the purpose of the website's perspective, and awareness of copyright laws and learning how to properly cite in order to avoid plagiarism.

Students require the skills necessary to communicate asynchronously and synchronously, utilizing technology, such as email, videoconferencing, like Skype, listservs, wikis, blogs, chat groups, and social networks, like Facebook, Twitter, and LinkedIn.

Learners should also possess the skills to use and create various Web 2.0 tools, such as: podcasts, videos, webpages, blogs, wikis, avatars, videoconferencing, social networks, Webquests, and online presentation tools, like Tiki-Toki, Prezi, visual.ly, and SlideRocket. Students require time and practice in order to successfully execute and employ these modes of media. Instructors can facilitate this learning by incorporating assignments where students are required to create a product using a few selected Web 2.0 tools.

5. Implement Relevant and Real World Tasks

Webquest tasks should emulate scenarios, problems, or events that are happening in the world today. The more genuine and relatable the tasks are to students and the more they have the opportunity to apply them to other contexts, the better they will be able to cognitively transfer this knowledge to memory (Darling-Hammond & Austin, n.d.; Willis, 2006) and behaviorally perform and incorporate these skills into the 21st century workforce (Lombardi, 2007

6. Embed Individual and Global Accountability and Responsibility into the Task

According to 21st century skills, employers stated that professionalism, work ethic and responsible global citizenry are essential 21st century skills for new work entrants. Since many of our students are lacking these 21st century skills, incorporating them into Webquests is vital and can be accomplished by embedding individual and global accountability and responsibility into the assignment through shared reflection in the Webquest or a hyperlink to a blog, wiki, etc.

Global responsibly can also be built into a Webquest. Webquests can accommodate this by requiring students to consider, compare, locate, and evaluate global issues and events and relate them to the topic.

Webquests are increasingly becoming a more utilized learning tool, but only if properly designed and employed through incorporation of best practices. Students must be prepared for the 21st century global work force and utilizing Webquests makes this goal attainable.

WEB 2.0 TOOLS

The use of Web 2.0 teaching tools has begun to infiltrate online learning. Students and faculty alike are utilizing these tools to enhance learning, comprehension and overall retention of course topics and objectives. The following Web 2.0 tools highlight student and faculty uses, along with relevant pedagogical implementation strategies:

Animoto (http://animoto.com)

Animoto is a video production tool that allows still photos, videos and music to be integrated into a classroom or other document. Animoto can be used in the online classroom in the following ways:

- **Digital Scrapbook:** Create a digital scrapbook of an event or trip.
- **Oral Presentation:** Students can record an assigned oral presentation and add it as music to an Animoto production that contains desired images. This can add depth to any oral presentation online.
- **Promo:** Students can create a production giving background information, project construction photos, vide, and research questions. Animoto creates a visual interest and draws visitors into the project.

Audacity (http://audacity.sourceforge.net/)

Audacity is a free, easy to use and multilingual audio editor and recorder. Audacity can be used by students and faculty in the online classroom in the following ways:

- Producing a recording of music.
- **Audio Scrapbook:** Record classroom-delivered oral presentations and create an audio scrapbook of all the presentations.
- **Radio Show:** Students can create a radio show for the class or school.

BrainShark (www.brainshark.com)

BrainShark allows students and faculty to add voice to Power Point, narrate a document, upload video, make a photo album, or produce a podcast. It can be used in the online classroom in the following ways:

- **Video Autobiography:** Students and faculty can upload their autobiography and share with the class. This is an excellent way to connect distance students and give them a sense of community in the class.
- **Podcast:** Students can select a topic covered in a recent unit and record a podcast explaining the key ideas and vocabulary of the assigned topic. The podcasts can be distributes to the class for use as a study guide.
- **Photo Album:** Students can upload photos of a recent trip to share with the class or school.

Creately (http://creately.com/)

Creately is an online diagramming application that's built for collaboration. It can be used in the online classroom in the following ways:

- **Map It:** Students can use Creately to mind map notes from a lesson. Online learners can benefit from using this tool to break down written course notes or lectures.
- **How To:** Students can use Creately for delivering an oral presentation online. They will provide the class with process map generated in Creately.
- **Lesson Map:** Faculty can use Creately to create a lesson maps for the upcoming school year. They can also be easily updated.

Croak.It (http://croak.it/)

Croak.It is an audio production tool that allows you to speak rather than type. It can be used in the online classroom in the following ways:

- **Summary Study Notes:** Students can record summaries of their class notes in preparation for upcoming notes or quizzes.
- **Audio:** Faculty can assign students topics relevant to the weekly topics and have them prepare a "Tweet" on the topic and post them online.
- **Audio List:** Faculty can use it to keep personal notes and lists relevant to their class.

Crocodocs (http://crocodoc.com)

Crocodocs is a free online document sharing and collaboration tool. It can be used in the online classroom in the following ways:

- **Group Projects:** Students can use Crocodocs to collaborate on a major project online without emailing or saving to an in-house server. Students can utilize Crocodocs synchronously or asynchronously.
- **Building Collaboration:** Faculty can use Crocodocs to facilitate collaboration among student group assignments.

Delicious (http://delicious.com)

Delicious is a place to collect and showcase your favorite videos, tweets, pictures, blog posts, or articles. It can be used in the online classroom in the following ways:

- **Link up a Project:** Students can use Delicious to find, tag and store links for a project.
- **Lesson Plan Catalogue:** Faculty can upload and tag links related to relevant topics.

Digital Storytelling

Have students assume the persona of an individual with a stigmatized group, such as homeless, pregnant teen, immigrant, obese, disabled, etc. and incorporate evidence-based knowledge, best practices guidelines, and community resources to support or refute their knowledge, beliefs, values, attitudes, assumptions, and judgments that influence the individual. The instructor can pose an example of a question such as "what did you learn about the individual you portrayed and the factors that influence that individual that you did not know prior to this assignment?"

Dropbox (https://www.dropbox.com/)

Dropbox allows students and faculty to save files to a computer, phone and the Dropbox website. It works online or offline. It can be used in the online classroom in the following ways:

- **Classroom Connection:** Students can begin an assignment or project, save in Dropbox, and complete another time.
- **Teacher Gradebook:** Faculty can save their gradebook to Dropbox and access it from anywhere-including a smart phone.

Evernote (http://evernote.com)

Evernote is a free tool that allows students and faculty to capture and save information from anywhere to your phone, computer or tablet. It can be used in the online classroom in the following ways:

- **Research:** Students can use Evernote to save resources for a paper as they find them.
- **Classroom Notes:** Students can capture images, text, and web sites that are discussed in class.
- **Meeting Preparation:** Faculty can capture and store images, text or web pages to use at a meeting.

EyeJot (http://corp.eyejot.com/)

EyeJot allows the user to create and receive video messages without installation. It can be used in the online classroom in the following ways:

- **Video Messages:** Faculty can create video messages to post in their online classroom, giving a more personal touch and sense of community to the online classroom.

Flipsnack (http://flipsnack.com)

Flipsnack is an online flipping book software that allows you to convert PDF documents into Flash page flip digital publications. Once created, the flipping book collection can be embedded or downloaded. It can be used in the online classroom in the following ways:

- **Report or Project:** Students and faculty can use FlipSnack to create a flipping book of a report or project. It can then be emailed to recipients.

Jing (http://www.techsmith.com/jing.html)

Jing allows the user to capture an image from a computer monitor or record up to 5 minutes of onscreen video. It can used in the online classroom in the following ways:

- Students can create video lessons to teach concepts to classmates. It can be used to review for upcoming tests or quizzes.
- **Grading:** Faculty can use Jing to provide feedback for major assignments. They can record a personalized video for each student.
- **Problem-Solving:** Faculty can use Jing to demonstrate to students how to solve complex problems and post them for student to review.

Join Me (http://Join.Me)

Join.Me is an online sharing tool that can be used to share documents, demos, or meetings. It can be used in the online classroom in the following ways:

- **Study Group:** Students can use Join.Me to participate in scheduled study groups. Students can share their screens with one another for group projects. They can also share notes, pictures, and web sites.
- **Feedback:** Faculty can use Join.Me to share their screen with students who have questions about grades or as assignment.

LiveBinders (http://livebinders.com/)

LiveBinders is a 3-ring binder for the Web that allows the user to store and present information. It can be used in the online classroom in the following ways:

- **Notes:** Students can use LiveBinders to create an online notebook for each class.
- **Project:** Students can gather and store resources on an assigned topic or project.
- **Unit Plans:** Faculty can collect resources needed for a unit plan, organize and save it for future use.

Loom- www.useloom.com

Loom is a free web-based screen capture with audio-video recording capability

- Similar to a digital overhead projector
- Using a laptop camera/microphone you can record and share content on computer screen
- Provide relevant and meaningful feedback students
- Personalize announcement/lectures

Movie Maker (http://windows.microsoft.com/en-US/windows-live/movie-maker-get-started)

Students and faculty can import and edit slideshows and videos, edit soundtracks, and share movies online. It can be used in the online classroom in the following ways:

- **Historical Reenactment:** Students can use Movie Maker to reenact a historic event.
- **Video:** Students can film themselves teaching a lesson and share it with the class.
- **Re-Teaching:** Faculty can use Movie Maker to make a movie and upload it to the class to reiterate hard concepts or present new material in a friendly and clear manner.

Omeka (http://omeka.org)

Omeka is a free, flexible and open source web-publishing platform for the display of scholarly collections and exhibitions. It can be used in the online classroom in the following ways:

- **Art or Science:** Students can create original works of art or upload documents and photos of science project to create an online archive.
- **Literary History:** Students can research the historical context of pieces of literature and create and exhibit it online to share with others.

Padagogy Wheel

Developed by Allan Carrington, the Padagogy Wheel is designed to connect Bloom's Taxonomy with Apple iPad applications. The Padagogy Wheel was designed to target engagement through immersive learning (Carrington, 2012). It can be used regularly from planning curriculum to writing learning objectives and designing student-centered activities that focus on the specific needs of students.

The Padagogy Wheel is divided into five segments that relate directly to the cognitive domains of Bloom's Taxonomy. The wheel allows teachers to develop outcome-oriented lessons by choosing an outcome, activity, and form of analysis or creativity.

Apply: Students Demonstrate the Ability to Implement Learned Procedures

- Ustream
- Explain Everything
- Keynote
- Sonic Pics
- Articulate
- Google Docs
- Evernote
- Audioboo
- Adobe Connect
- Perfectly Clr
- Quick Voice
- Animation Creation

Create: Students Have the Opportunity to Generate Ideas, Design/Plan in Order to Produce a Product

- uTimeLapse Pro
- Easy Release
- Wordpress
- ScreenChomp
- iMovie
- Voicethread
- Prezi
- Garageband
- Toontastic
- Nearpod
- Fotobabble
- Interview Assistant
- Aurasma
- Creative Book Builder

Remember/Understand: Students Have the Opportunity to Explain the Ideas and Concepts Through an Open-Ended Format

- iAnnotate
- iThought
- Facebook
- Google Search
- Twitter
- Bump
- DocsToGo
- Blog Docs

- ◦ MentalCase
- ◦ Mapini
- ◦ Quizcast
- ◦ FeedderRSS

Analyze: Students Demonstrate the Ability to Differentiate Between Relevant and Irrelevant Material in Order to Recognize the Organization of the Content

- ◦ MindMash
- ◦ Bento
- ◦ iCarSort
- ◦ Numbers
- ◦ Pages
- ◦ Popplet
- ◦ SurveyPro
- ◦ MiniMash

Evaluate: Students Demonstrate the Ability to Judge the Reliability and Accuracy of Learned Concepts in Order to Reach Informed Decisions

- ◦ Wikinodes
- ◦ WEB to PDF
- ◦ ShareBoard
- ◦ Prompster Pro
- ◦ Evernote Peek
- ◦ Notability
- ◦ Skype
- ◦ Edmodo
- ◦ Google+
- ◦ Studentpad

Photosnack (http://www.photosnack.com)

Photo Snack is a free app that allows students and faculty to add photos, create slideshows with music and share with the class. It can be used in the online classroom in the following ways:

- **Portfolio or Project:** Students and faculty can take digital photos for a project or portfolio and create a slide show that can be uploaded and shared with the class.

Prezi (http://prezi.com/)

Prezi is a cloud-based presentation tool that enables student to explore ideas and make connections between them. It can be used in the online classroom in the following ways:

- **Outline:** Students and faculty can use Prezi to create the sequential thoughts of an outline.
- **Project:** Students can use the rotation feature in Prezi to provide the necessary information for a debate. They can also post their project or assignment to the class for permanent viewing by classmates.

Remind101 (https://www.remind101.com/)

Remind 101 is a website that provides a safe way for teachers to text message or email a student. Teachers add his/her class, which generates a unique code that us shared with students. Faculty can utilize Remind101 to remind students of impending due dates for major project or homework, or restate critical information to the whole class by text message.

Screencast-o-Matic (http://www.screencast-o-matic/)

Screencast-o-matic is an online screen recorder that requires no installation. It can be used in the online classroom in the following ways:

- **Share a Project:** Students can capture the screens of their classroom presentation and upload them to You Tube for viewing by other classmates.
- **Teaching Tool:** Students and faculty can capture screen shots to demonstrate how to use a new software tool. They can then be shared with colleagues or classmates.
- **Lesson Preservation:** Faculty can use Screen-o-matic to preserve a lesson and upload it to You Tube for others to view.

Screenleap (http://screenleap.com/)

Screenleap is a screen sharing tool that can be shared with 100 others. It requires no installation, downloads, or sign-ins. It can be used in the online classroom in the following ways:

- **Groups:** Students can use Screenleap to share the screen of a group project so they can collaborate from anywhere.
- **Teacher Lessons:** Faculty can share their lesson screen with their class.

Skitch (http://skitch.com)

Skitch is a free tool that allows the user to capture and save information from anywhere to a phone, computer or tablet. It can be used in the online classroom in the following ways:

- **Group Project:** Students can use Skitch to provide peer feedback to other group members on a project, improving collaboration.
- **Visual Grading:** Faculty can use Skitch to add annotations to submitted students work.

Skype (http://www.skype.com)

Skype provides a free, convenient way to make computer-to-computer, video calls and instant chat. Multi-user video conferencing is also available. It can be used in the online classroom in the following ways:

- **Lecture:** Faculty can use the multi-user video conferencing to deliver real-time classroom lectures or lessons to distance students.

- **Collaboration:** Students and faculty can use Skype to connect with colleagues or group members around the globe.

Slideshare (https://www.slideshare.net)

Faculty and students can upload documents to Slideshare to share ideas, conduct research and connect with others. It can be used in the online classroom in the following ways:

- **Collaboration and Meetings:** Students and faculty can use Slidehshare to hold a meeting for a group project, trade research data and ideas with colleagues.
- **Lesson Presentation:** Faculty can use Slideshare to post lesson presentations. The analytic tools in Slideshare allows faculty to know if the presentation was viewed.

Slidesnack (http://www.slidesnack.com/)

SlideSnack is a presentation sharing tool that enables faculty and students to easily upload and share presentations online. There are several customizable templates that convert PDF files to presentations. SlideSnack also allows the user to record audio and overlay comments with a presentation. SlideSnack can be used in the online classroom in the following ways:

- **Oral Presentation:** Students upload their reports to SlideSnack. The reports are converted to presentations for sharing with the class. Classmates can follow along on school-approved mobile devices so no printing is required.
- **Teacher Professional Development:** Use SlideSnack to convert notes for the next professional development seminar intoa great looking presentation. The presentation is accessible on the web, so participants can follow along on their tablets or other mobile devices instead of using printed handouts.

VoiceThread (http://voicethread.com/)

With VoiceThread, group conversations are collected and shared in one place from anywhere in the world. All with no software to install. VoiceThread is a collaborative, multimedia slide show that holds images, documents, and videos and allows people to navigate slides and leave comments in 5 ways - using voice (with a mic or telephone), text, audio file, or video (via a webcam). Share a VoiceThread with friends, students, and colleagues for them to record comments too. VoiceThreads can even be embedded to show and receive comments on other websites and exported to MP3 players or DVDs to play as archival movies. Voice Thread can be used in the online classroom in the following ways:

- **Online Discussion:** Students can use Voice Thread to record an audio post to a discussion topic.
- **Peer Review:** Students can create projects in Prezi and post the projects on the class page in VoiceThread. Students can review each other's work and leave voice comments for their peers.
- **Audio Grade:** Faculty can leave audio comments on each learner's project and record the project grade privately in the grade book - not on the website.

Wiffiti (http://wiffiti.com/)

Unlike many new media applications designed for viewing content streams online, Wiffiti was designed for the "Lean Back" experience of viewing user-generated content from a distance as well as the "Lean Forward" experience online or via text messaging. New Wiffiti messages are instantly displayed center screen and are easily viewable from a distance. Older messages then fade back and move as an animated cloud, providing enough ambient activity to continually stimulate audience attention and encourage engagement.

Interactivity is multi-modal - it can happen at the location via mobile phones, or online via easily embeddable website widgets. Incoming content streams and web and mobile messages update across all instances of the addressed Wiffiti screen automatically.

Wiffiti can be used in the online classroom in the following ways:

- **Discussion:** Students can use Wiffiti to post comments to their classmates.
- **Quick Quiz:** Faculty can check for understanding by asking a question and asking students to respond using Wiffiti.

YouTube (http://www.youtube.com/)

YouTube allows billions of people to discover, watch, and share originally-created videos. YouTube provides a forum for people to connect, inform, and inspire others across the globe and acts as a distribution platform for original content creators and advertisers large and small.

YouTube can be used in the online classroom in the following ways:

- **Group Projects:** Students can upload group project presentations to You Tube and embed the YouTube videos into the online class for easy viewing by others.
- **Content:** Faculty can embed topically-relevant videos for use in the online classroom.

Wunderlist (http://www.wunderlist.com/)

Wunderlist is a free easy-to-use task manager for Windows, Mac, iPhone, iPad, Android and the Web. The lists sync automatically over the air and lists can be shared with family, friends and colleagues.

Wunderlist can be used in the online classroom in the following ways:

- **Top 10:** Students can Wunderlist to create "top 10" lists related to classroom content and to share them with classmates.
- **Assignment Planner:** Wunderlist can sync assignment lists to a smart phone and other computer for better assignment organization.
- **Teacher Planner:** Wunderlist can sync an agenda and calendar to a tablet, smart phone, destop and laptop.

Students may have an abundance of experience with online social technologies, but little knowledge on how to use these tools and methods for course learning. Over 80% of students use Facebook (Anderson Analytics, 2008), 40% use MySpace (Anderson Analytics) and many use instant messaging, discussion boards, chat rooms and groups through Google, Yahoo and MSN. However, many do not have the expertise to utilize these technological skills in their online course learning. With the training, practice and support of the instructor and fellow classmates, students can better access and utilize the tools available in order to enhance the learning process. Schools and universities must also offer regular training for students outside of class time on utilizing these web tools. The instructor and fellow students can serve as a support in this area, but in order for students to feel comfortable with the tools, formal training is necessary.

CONCLUSION

Learner interaction is critical in creating s strong learning community (Conrad, 2005; Gorsky, 2004). Online etiquette is at the forefront of a student's success with collaboration with other learners. Just as there are rules for face-to-face communication, cyberspace also contains its own set of etiquette rules. Messages and postings can easily be misconstrued due to the lack of face-to-face and non-verbal cues in the conversation. Patience is also important. Most online classes are asynchronous, so waiting for a message back can take longer than expected or anticipated. It is important for online learners to abide by the following guidelines:

- Be cognizant of the text use-do not use all uppercase letters or strong punctuation in an online forum.
- Write concisely-Online learning requires an abundance of reading, so others will be more apt to read your posts if they are concise and to the point, yet meaningful.
- Do not post a message without checking for spelling, punctuation and sentence structure. Avoid using acronyms or vocabulary that others may not understand.
- Instructors and other learners are looking to read "substantive" quotes, which add depth and variety to the dialogue.
- Respond to others and post frequently. The electronic conversation is the only conversation the class will have, so being active and involved in discussions adds depth and a sense of community to the classroom.
- Regularly check out the technology you are using. Group members and other learners expect that everyone will be up-to-date with their technology and able to utilize the functions the class brings without glitches or often technological issues.

In addition to learner communication and dialogue, it is important for students to interact with the instructor on a regular basis. Swan (2002) found that the interaction with the instructor played a large role in the student's perception of the course. An instructor must find multiple ways to communicate and establish a connection with students. When students see the efforts of their instructor to create a strong presence in the online classroom, their sense of community can improve (Shea et al., 2005). Lowry and colleagues (2000) recommended that members of an online community set deadlines to help them stay motivated. Incorporating a group member agreement can helps set norms, guidelines, choose a group leader and set expectations early on in the process.

The success of an online community depends on the efforts of the students to build it. As Palloff and Pratt (2003) wrote: "The virtual student needs to accept the different role of the instructor online and recognize that the deepest learning in an online course comes from interacting with everyone involved. Reaching that level of understanding, and being willing to take on responsibility for creating the learning community as a result, is critical to its formation." (p. 20).

According to Grudin (1991), the ability for students to collaborate demonstrates maturation that students develop as they move away from working in isolation to working within a larger group. Peer collaboration can be used to enhance academic performance and better performance on a variety of academic tasks. Peer collaboration can be valuable for promoting discussions that foster multiple perspectives or require advanced problem-solving techniques that some, but not all students may possess. More emphasis has been placed on the student and instructor to move the traditional discussions of a brick and mortar school to the online environment. Northrup (2002) indicated four variables that serve as an indicator of student interaction in their online classroom:

- Content interaction which includes pacing, structure, and use of various delivery techniques and strategies by students.
- Dialogue and collaboration through peer interaction and participation in their learning community.
- Self-monitoring techniques such as notetaking guides, and advanced organizers.
- Support through tutorials, mentors and timely correspondence with the instructor.

Virtual learning communities are based on the interactions through discussions. Instructors must consider not the number of posts a student makes, but rather the depth and meaning the student adds to the discussion based on the course objectives. An instructor serves as a model for quantitative postings by students. Modeling includes initiative, attention to detail, relevance of the student's post in the discussions, how well the opinions and ideas are expressed within the post and what contributions the learner is giving to the community.

FUTURE RESEARCH

While there is a growing body of research that contributes grounded theory in community-building communication in the online learning environment, there is not a palpable mass of longstanding set of proven theories which guide effective practices for accredited online advanced degrees. There is a need for additional research on online terminal degree students' sense of community, isolation, and defining instructional strategies that increases student connection with classmates and instructor. There is also a need to conduct studies on the influence social media can have on students' sense of community in online learning. Nevertheless, research has rather conclusively demonstrated that students' heightened sense of community correlates negatively with indicators such as isolation, retention, student course satisfaction, and effective teaching strategies (Drouin, 2008; Ouzts, 2006). There is also a need to conduct studies on the influence social media can have on students' sense of community in online learning. Nevertheless, research has rather conclusively demonstrated that students' heightened sense of community correlates negatively with indicators such as isolation. There is a need to conduct studies to understand the perceptions of online participants toward community building in order to get them to buy into community building goals and activities. There is a need to examine the interaction effect of technology and pedagogy within community building. There is also a need to further study the development of the three levels of communities (group, class, and beyond class) and the tools that specifically help first time students in an online learning environment.

REFERENCES

Allen, E., & Seaman, J. (2005). *Growing by degrees: Online education in the United States, 2005*. Boston, MA: The Sloan Consortium.

Allen, I. E., & Seaman, J. (2010). *Learning on demand: Online education in the United States, 2009*. Babson Survey Research Group. Retrieved from http://sloanconsortium.org/publications/survey/pdf/learningondemand.pdf

Allen, E., & Seaman, J. (2017). Digital Learning Compass: Distance Education Enrollment Report 2017: Babson Survey Research Group, e-Literate.

Angelino, L. M., Williams, F. K., & Natvig, D. (2007). Strategies to engage online students and reduce attrition rates. *The Journal of Educators Online*, *4*(2).

Aron, A., Aron, N. A., & Smollan, D. (1992). Inclusion of the other in the self scale and the structure of interpersonal closeness. *Journal of Personality and Social Psychology*, *63*(4), 596–612. doi:10.1037/0022-3514.63.4.596

Bawane, J., & Spencer, J. (2009). Prioritization of online instructor roles: Implications for competency-based teacher education programs. *Distance Education*, *30*(3), 383–397. doi:10.1080/01587910903236536

Carr, S. (2000). As distance education comes of age, the challenge is keeping the students. *The Chronicle of Higher Education*, *46*(23), A39–A41.

Conference Board, Corporate Voices for Working Families, The Partnership for 21st Century Skills, and the Society for Human Resource Management. (2006). *Are they ready to work? Employers' perspectives on the basic knowledge and applied skills of new entrants to the 21st century U.S. workforce*. Retrieved from http://www.p21.org/storage/documents/FINAL_REPORT_PDF09-29-06.pdf

Carrington, A. (2012). Padagogy Wheel. Retrieved from www.http://tinyurl.com/padwheel

Chan, M. (1996). Racial Diversity in Higher Education: Does a Racially Mixed Student Population Affect Educational Outcomes? (Unpublished doctoral dissertations, University of California, Los Angeles).

Corporate Voices for Working Families. (2012). *A talent development solution: Exploring business drivers and returns in learn and earn partnerships*. Retrieved from http://corporatevoices.org/system/files/LearnEarn_Report2_web.pdf

Craig, A., Goold, A., Coldwell, J., & Mustard, J. (2008). Perceptions of roles and responsibilities in online learning: A case study. *Interdisciplinary Journal of Knowledge & Learning Objects*, *4*, 205–223.

Darling-Hammond, L., & Austin, K. (n.d.). *Session 11: Lessons for life: Learning and transfer*. Retrieved from http://www.learner.org/courses/learningclassroom/support/11_learning_transfer.pdf

Dennen, V., Darabi, A., & Smith, L. (2007). Instructor-learner interaction in online courses: The relative perceived importance of particular instructor actions on performance and satisfaction. *Distance Education, 28*(1), 65–79. doi:10.1080/01587910701305319

Dickey, M. (2004). The impact of web-logs (blogs) on student perceptions of isolation and alienation in a web-based distance-learning environment. *Open Learning, 19*(3), 279–291. doi:10.1080/0268051042000280138

Drouin, M. (2008). The relationship between students' perceived sense of community and satisfaction, achievement, and retention in an online course. *Quarterly Review of Distance Education, 9*(3), 267–284.

Durrington, V. A., Berryhill, A., & Swafford, J. (2006). Strategies for enhancing student interactivity in an online environment. *College Teaching, 54*(1), 190–193. doi:10.3200/CTCH.54.1.190-193

Education Testing Services. (n.d.). *ICT literacy assessment: Information and communication technology*. Retrieved from http://www.ncahlc.org/download/annualmeeting/05Handouts/GSUN0145k_Egan.pdf

Gaytan, J., & McEwen, B. (2007). Effective online instructional and assessment strategies. *American Journal of Distance Education, 21*(3), 117–132. doi:10.1080/08923640701341653

Gibson, S. G., Harris, M. L., & Colaric, S. M. (2008). Technology acceptance in an academic context: Faculty acceptance of online education. *Journal of Education for Business, 83*(6), 355–359. doi:10.3200/JOEB.83.6.355-359

Harris, R. (2012). *Introduction to creative thinking*. Retrieved from http://www.virtualsalt.com/crebook1.htm

Ice, P., Curtis, R., Phillips, P., & Wells, J. (2007). Using asynchronous audio feedback to enhance teaching presence and students' sense of community. *Journal of Asynchronous Learning Networks, 11*(2), 3–25.

Institute for Learning Styles Research. (1996). *Overview of the seven perceptual styles*. Retrieved from http://www.learningstyles.org/index.html

Johnson, D. W., & Johnson, R. (1989). *Cooperation and competition: Theory and research*. Edina, MN: Interaction Book Company.

Kozar, O. (2012). Towards better group work: Seeing the difference between cooperation and collaboration. *English Teacher Forum, 2*. Retrieved from http://exchanges.state.gov/englishteaching/forum/archives/docs/files-folder111111/48_2-etf-towards-better-group-work-seeing-the-difference-between-cooperation-and-collaboration.pdf

Laffey, J., Lin, G., & Lin, Y. (2006). Assessing social ability in online learning environments. *Journal of Interactive Research, 17*(2), 157–165.

Ladson-Billings, G. (2001). *Crossing over to Canaan*. San Francisco, CA: Jossey-Bass.

Lin, S. Y., & Overbaugh, R. C. (2007). The effect of student choice of online discussion format on tiered achievement and student satisfaction. *Journal of Research on Technology in Education, 39*(4), 399–415.

Liu, X., Magjuka, R., Bonk, C., & Lee, S. (2007). Does sense of community matter? An examination of participants' perceptions of building learning communities in online courses. *Quarterly Review of Distance Education, 8*(1), 9–24.

Lombardi, M. M. (2007, May). *Authentic learning for the 21st century: An overview*. Educause Learning Initiative Paper. Retrieved from http://net.educause.edu/ir/library/pdf/eli3009.pdf

Loom. (2019). Retrieved from www.useloom.com

Manpower Group. (2012). *2012 talent shortage survey research results*. Retrieved from http://www.manpowergroup.us/campaigns/talent-shortage-2012/pdf/2012_Talent_Shortage_Survey_Results_US_FINALFINAL.pdf

Maslow, A. H. (1954). *Motivation and personality*. New York, NY: Harper and Row.

McMillan, D. W., & Chavis, D. M. (1986). Sense of community: A definition and theory. *Journal of Community Psychology*, *14*(1), 6–23. doi:10.1002/1520-6629(198601)14:1<6::AID-JCOP2290140103>3.0.CO;2-I

Misanchuk, M., & Anderson, T. (2001). *Building community in an online learning environment: Communication, cooperation, and collaboration*. Paper presented at the Mid-South Instructional Technology Conference, Murfreesboro, TN.

O'Leary, P. F., & Quinlan, T. J. (2007). Satisfaction and achievement of online students. *Education*, *21*(3), 133–143.

Office for Economic Cooperation and Development. (2012, March). *Preparing teachers and developing leaders for the 21st century: Lessons from around the world*. Retrieved from http://www.oecd.org/site/eduistp2012/49850576.pdf

Ouzts, K. (2006). Sense of community in online courses. *Quarterly Review of Distance Education*, *7*(3), 285–296.

Patterson, B., & McFadden, C. (2009). Attrition in online and campus degree programs. *Online Journal of Distance Learning Administration*, *12*(2). Retrieved from http://www.westga.edu/distance/ojdla/summer122/patterson112.html

Rovai, A. P. (2002a). Building sense of community at a distance. *International Review of Research in Open and Distance Learning*, *13*(1).

Rovai, A. P. (2002b). Sense of community, perceived cognitive learning, and persistence in asynchronous learning networks. *The Internet and Higher Education*, *5*(4), 319–332. doi:10.1016/S1096-7516(02)00130-6

Rovai, A. P. (2003). Sense of community in higher education television-based distance education programs. *Educational Technology Research and Development*, *51*(2), 5–16. doi:10.1007/BF02504523

Rovai, A. P., Wighting, M. J., & Liu, J. (2005). School climate: Sense of classroom and school communities in online and on-campus higher education courses. *The Quarterly Review of Distance Education*, *6*(4), 361–374.

Schwier, R. (2002). *Shaping the metaphor of community in online learning environments*. (Unpublished Manuscript).

Scriven, M., & Paul, R. (1987). *Defining critical thinking*. Retrieved from http://www.criticalthinking.org/pages/defining-critical-thinking/766

Shea, P., Sau Li, C., & Pickett, A. (2006). A study of teaching presence and student sense of learning community in fully online and web-enhanced college courses. *The Internet and Higher Education*, *9*(3). doi:10.1016/j.iheduc.2006.06.005

Sher, A. (2009). Assessing the relationship of student-instructor and student-student interaction to student learning and satisfaction in web-based online learning environment. *Journal of Interactive Online Learning*, *8*(2), 102–120.

Smaldino, S. E., Lowther, D. L., & Russell, J. D. (2012). *Instructional technology and media for learning* (9th ed.). Reading, MA: Allyn & Bacon.

Smith, S. D., & Caruso, J. B. (2010). *The ECAR study of undergraduate students and information technology, 2010* (Research Study, Vol. 6). Boulder, CO: EDUCAUSE Center for Applied Research. Retrieved from http://www.educause.edu/ecar

Swan, K., & Shih, L. (2005). On the nature and development of social presence in online course discussions. *Journal of Asynchronous Learning Networks*, *9*(3), 115–136.

Willis, J. (2006). *Research based strategies to ignite student learning*. Alexandria, VA: Association for Supervision and Curriculum Development.

Wilson, B. G., Ludwig-Hardman, S., Thornam, C., & Dunlap, J. C. (2004). Bounded community: Designing and facilitating learning communities in formal courses. *International Review of Research in Open and Distance Learning*, *5*(3).

Young, S. (2006). Student views of effective online teaching in higher education. *American Journal of Distance Education*, *20*(2), 65–77. doi:10.120715389286ajde2002_2

ADDITIONAL READING

Allen, I. E., & Seaman, J. (2010). *Learning on demand: Online education in the United States, 2009*. Babson Survey Research Group. Retrieved from http://sloanconsortium.org/publications/survey/pdf/learningondemand.pdf

Angelino, L. M., Williams, F. K., & Natvig, D. (2007). Strategies to engage online students and reduce attrition rates. *The Journal of Educators Online*, *4*(2). Retrieved from http://www.thejeo.com/Archives/Volume4Number2/Angelino%20Final.pdf

Blackwell, R., Channell, J., & Williams, J. (2001). Teaching circles: a way forward for part-time teachers in higher education? *The International Journal for Academic Development*. doi:10.1080/13601440110033652

Bosch, T. E. (2009). Using online social networking for teaching and learning: Facebook use at the University of Cape Town. *Communication: South African Journal for Communication Theory & Research*, *35*(2), 185–200.

Brookfield, S. D. (1995). *Becoming a critically reflective teacher*. San Francisco: Jossey-Bass.

Burdett, J. (2003). Making Groups Work: University Students' Perceptions. *International Education Journal, 4* (3), Retrieved from: http://ehlt.flinders.edu.au/education/iej/articles/v4n3/Burdett/paper.pdf.

Cameron, B., Morgan, K., Williams, K., & Kostelecky, K. (2009). Group projects: Student perceptions of the relationship between social tasks and a sense of community in online group work. *American Journal of Distance Education, 23*(1), 20–33. doi:10.1080/08923640802664466

Christiensen, E., & Dirkinick-Holmfeld, L. (1995). *Making distance learning cooperative.* Retrieved May 19, 20013, from http://vbn.aau.dk/research/making_distance_learning_collaborative(125626)/.

Craig, A., Goold, A., Coldwell, J., & Mustard, J. (2008). Perceptions of roles and responsibilities in online learning: a case study. [Retrieved from Academic Search Complete database.]. *Interdisciplinary Journal of Knowledge & Learning Objects, 4*, 205–223.

Daradoumis, T., & Xhafa, F. (2005). Problems and Opportunities of Learning Together in a Virtual Learning Environment. In T. S. Roberts (Ed.), *Computer-Supported Collaborative Learning in Higher Education* (pp. 218–233). Hershey, PA: Idea Group Publishing.

Dennen, V., Darabi, A., & Smith, L. (2007). Instructor-learner interaction in online courses: The relative perceived importance of particular instructor actions on performance and satisfaction. [Retrieved from ERIC database.]. *Distance Education, 28*(1), 65–79. doi:10.1080/01587910701305319

Dickey, M. (2004). The impact of web-logs (blogs) on student perceptions of isolation and alienation in a web-based distance-learning environment. *Open Learning, 19*(3), 279–291. doi:10.1080/0268051042000280138

Geoghegan, M. W., & Klass, D. (2007). *Podcast solutions: The complete guide to audio and video podcasting* (2nd ed.). New York, NY: Springer. doi:10.1007/978-1-4302-0473-2

Harasim, L., Hiltz, S. R., Teles, L., & Turoff, M. (1995). *Learning Networks- a Field Guide to Teaching and Learning Online*. Cambridge, MA: The MIT Press.

Jonassen, D., Davidson, M., Collins, M., Campbell, J., & Haag, B. (1995). Constructivism and computer mediated communication in distance education. *American Journal of Distance Education, 9*(2), 7–25. doi:10.1080/08923649509526885

Kozar, O. (2012). Towards better group work: Seeing the difference between cooperation and collaboration. *English Teacher Forum, 2*. Retrieved from http://exchanges.state.gov/englishteaching/forum/archives/docs/files-folder111111/48_2-etf-towards-better-group-work-seeing-the-difference-between-cooperation-and-collaboration.pdf.

Liu, X., Magjuka, R., Bonk, C., & Lee, S. (2007). Does sense of community matter? An examin-ation of participants' perceptions of building learning communities in online courses. [Retrieved from ERIC database.]. *Quarterly Review of Distance Education, 8*(1), 9–24.

Palloff, R. M., & Pratt, K. (2005). *Collaborating online: Learning together in community*. San Francisco, CA: Jossey-Bass.

Picciano, A. G. (2002). Beyond student perceptions: Issues of interaction, presence, and performance in an online course. *Journal of Asynchronous Learning Networks, 6*(1), 21–40.

Roberts, T. S. (2004). *Online Collaborative Learning in Higher Education*. Hershey, PA: Information Science. doi:10.4018/978-1-59140-408-8

Salmon, G. (2000). *E-Moderating: The key to teaching and learning online*. London: Kogan Page Limited. doi:10.4324/9780203465424

Shea, P., Li, C. S., Swan, K., & Pickett, A. M. (2005). Developing learning community in online asynchronous college courses: the role of teaching presence. *Journal of Asynchronous Learning Networks, 9*. Retrieved from http://www.sloanorg/publications/jaln/v9n4/pdf/v9n4_shea.pdf

Sher, A. (2009). Assessing the relationship of student-instructor and student-student interaction to student learning and satisfaction in Web-based Online Learning Environment. [Retrieved from EBSCO*host*.]. *Journal of Interactive Online Learning*, *8*(2), 102–120.

Simonson, M., Smaldino, S., Albright, M., & Zvacek, S. (2012). *Teaching and learning at a distance: Foundations of distance education* (5th ed.). Boston, MA: Pearson.

Swan, K. (2001). Virtual interaction: Design factors affecting student satisfaction and perceived learning in asynchronous online courses. *Distance Education*, *22*(2), 306–331. doi:10.1080/0158791010220208

Swan, K., Shen, J., & Hiltz, S. R. (2006). Assessment and collaboration in online learning. *Journal of Asynchronous Learning Networks*, *10*(1), 45–62.

Tallent-Runnels, M., Thomas, J. A., Lan, W. Y., & Cooper, S. (2006). Teaching courses online: A review of the research. *Review of Educational Research*, *76*(1), 93–135. doi:10.3102/00346543076001093

Weiss, M., & Hansen-Baldauf, D. (2009). Email in academia: Expectations, use, and instructional impact. *EDUCAUSE Quarterly*, *1*, 42–50.

Young, S. (2006). Student views of effective online teaching in higher education. *American Journal of Distance Education*, *20*(2), 65–77. doi:10.120715389286ajde2002_2

Zhu, E., & Kaplan, M. (2010). Technology and teaching. In Sviniki & McKeachie (13th ed), McKeachie's Teaching Tips (pp. 252). Belmont, CA: Wadsworth.

KEY TERMS AND DEFINITIONS

Audio Recordings (Podcasts): Podcasting includes the use of streaming video and web players, and/or the downloading of media using syndication. The information is always portable and available for students to access.

Community: In order for students to have an increases satisfaction with their course and a feeling of connection to their instructor and other learners, students must have a perceived sense of community. Community encompasses the components of values, trust, and mutual support.

Isolation: Reducing the feeling of being alone in the online learning environment. It can be measured by the student's connectedness to the instructor and other learners in the online classroom.

Multimedia: Audiovisual technology that has the possibility to appeal to multiple senses and transform the learner's experience from solitary to collaborative.

Online Group Learning: Students in an online classroom are placed in small groups to complete assignments. The use of multimedia tools is essential for group learning to be successful and meaningful.

Video-Enhanced Chat: Video-enhanced chats can be accomplished using synchronous presentation tools like Adobe Connect, Elluminate, Wimba and Skype. These methods are effective for small groups and for collaboration on group projects. The intent of the integration is to build a sense of community for online students and help to diminish the feeling of isolation or solitude.

Video Recordings: Video recordings in an online classroom is to allow students the opportunity to follow along interactively. Instructors and students can use web cameras or video recording software that can be downloaded and run from a computer.

Chapter 13
Learning Together:
Confucius and Freire Collaborate to Redefine a Community of Learning

Sue K. Park
Claremont Lincoln University, USA

ABSTRACT

In this chapter, the writer unfolds and develops a fundamental praxis of collaboration. Drawing on the wisdom of Freire and Confucius, the author of this chapter on collaboration delineates it from three different perspectives: liberative, practical, and philosophical. Through these three perspectives, she discusses collaboration as a necessary component of online education and offers key principles to shape effective and successful collaborative efforts. Confucian humanism lays the foundation and context for Freire's liberative pedagogy in education; the writer brings these two theoretical practitioners into conversation to offer practical principles for collaboration between educators and students in online spaces.

INTRODUCTION

In this chapter, the writer unfolds and develops a fundamental praxis of collaboration. She comes from a practical and constructive point of view in regard to epistemology and pedagogy; therefore, she will approach the boundaries of collaboration from practical and constructive perspectives. While collaboration in any educational setting demands common understanding among those involved, collaboration in online educational and online professional settings calls for a particular set of agreed-upon and shared commitments. Much can be said about the power and impact collaboration has on pedagogy, didactics, and learning, and collaboration is used in different contexts and fields to work toward a similar goal: to achieve symbiotic reslts. The unique context of online education is that, unlike participants[1] in on-ground education or on-ground institutions, participants in online education and online institutions do not have the physical proximity to their peers to collaborate. This aspect makes collaboration tricky and necessitates participants communicating more carefully and frequently than participants in physical classrooms. Communication modes and methods for online collaboration are important to consider, but the foci of this chapter are more fundamental matters than communication in collaboration.

DOI: 10.4018/978-1-5225-9814-5.ch013

This chapter is divided into three major sections that address fundamental principles involved in a praxis of collaboration. In the first major section, the writer claims that collaboration in education, not only in online education but education in general, must be liberative. The liberative task of collaboration includes being rooted in the community of which the members are a part. All educative efforts must speak to, challenge, inform, and transform communities, because learning is a communal task. The communal aspect of education also entails an awareness of power and privilege. Without understanding and becoming aware of power and privilege in the world, collaborative efforts cannot be liberative. Thus, the first part of this chapter will conclude by grappling with the liberative aspect of collaboration as it is related to power and privilege.

The second major section offers practical guidelines, principles, and examples of collaboration in an online setting with specific methods and modes of exchange. These methods include not only communication modes, but also what online collaboration might look like in praxis. Utilizing the reflection-action cycle to draw boundaries and to practice praxis, the writer borrows ideas from Reg Revans' (1982) Action Learning Model to redefine the roles of educators and students as well as learning.

The third section of this chapter addresses probably the most fundamental commitment in collaboration: honoring the intrinsic goodness of humanity. Readers may wonder why this section is placed last, since an understanding of human goodness needs to undergird the liberative task of collaboration. The first two sections, in which the author unpacks the dimensions of power, privilege, and community with regard to liberation and offers practical suggestions and an understanding of collaboration, will give both the breadth and depth needed for considering this philosophical presupposition. Therefore, the commitment to human goodness is placed last, not first.

BACKGROUND

Collaboration is a broad concept that needs concrete definitions and boundaries. In this chapter, the broad boundary for collaboration is all types of work done by two or more people in an educational setting, whether traditional or nontraditional. Traditional educational settings include any higher education institutions (both online and on-ground), professional learning and training sessions, and continuing education for professionals. Nontraditional educational settings encompass any community-organized training sessions, workshops led by faith and civic organizations, and any type of learning gathering outside a formal educational institution. The narrow boundaries for collaboration discussed in this chapter include classroom discussions, online higher education discussion boards, student projects (written or using other media), conference participation that involves working in groups (e.g., panel presentations, committees, and organizing), publishing with one or more partners, professional projects completed by educators and researchers, and lectures and lessons taught in physical classrooms and online courses.

The author purposely includes on-ground situations in the definition of collaboration because many of the concepts and principles that guide on-ground and in-person collaboration transfer to the online setting. In addition, online technology is often incorporated into on-ground and in-person collaboration. So, it is crucial that no definite demarcation between online and on-ground collaboration is made; the lines have been blurred between them, as most communication takes place online via emails, video conferencing, and cloud or online document sharing programs (like Google docs, Dropbox, and learning management services), whether in-person contact is possible or not.

Most of the offerings found in this chapter come from practical and constructive perspectives. The writer is an educator deeply rooted in constructivist theories and pedagogies, which subscribe to the idea that knowledge is built and layered, not necessarily transmitted or transferred (Albers, 2008). In light of knowledge being constructed, constructivist educators view themselves as both facilitators of dialogue and as managers of knowledge pieces; they are not necessarily people with full authority and knowledge. So, pedagogical approaches are geared toward eliciting curiosity and promoting discussion as they highlight and uphold interactive methods of engagement. In this context of building knowledge and layering meaning together, this author approaches collaboration from practical perspectives that center and value the lived experiences of participants (and humanity at large), thus borrowing ideas from practical theology. Therefore, in discussing collaboration, various contexts and cultures (which make education diverse) will play a significant role, because educators with practical perspectives center their praxis on lived experience.

Insofar as practical understanding of collaboration is concerned, it is germane to detail the term *context*. According to Courtney Goto (2018), a prominent Asian American practical theologian, the term *context* is commonly and routinely used in four different ways: to designate a social milieu, a framing device, a background story, or a locus of concern (p. 86–88). In this chapter, the writer does not deviate from the way *context* is used in practical theology. Separating these four senses of *context* is a difficult task, since they are related. So, when the writer uses the term *context*, she may refer to any one of the four senses, depending on the topic at hand. She talks about the contexts of individuals to refer to their background story; for example, when she discusses the necessity of understanding the sociopolitical and cultural contexts of scholars, research participants, educators, and collaborators, she is referring to each one's narrow and particular situation, including their history. A background story or context includes this writer's own interpretation of the particular situations and will provide a full picture for the readers. The background stories of individuals or communities, however, cannot be separated from their social milieu because the latter "serves as the backdrop for understanding" the background of the individual being considered (p. 88). In its second sense as a framing device, the word *context* is used to denote the circumstances that illuminate the topic of this essay, collaboration. For example, the context from which this chapter arises is practical and liberative, so the author makes claims about the liberative aspects of collaboration. The fourth meaning of the word *context*, a locus of concern, refers to "a particular place/ time in all its complexity" (p. 89). In this chapter, the writer discusses the online educational context and the age of digital media and technology; she uses the word *context* here to mean a setting "*in a moment in time*" (p. 89). Given that context has complexities and takes on different meanings in different situations and circumstances, these four boundaries will help readers decipher what the writer intends when she uses *context* in her claims.

The practical and constructivist perspectives provide an interesting intersection for the works of Paulo Freire and Confucius (Kong-Zi), which offer foundational and critical insights into human collaboration in terms of philosophy and pedagogy. Confucius and Freire shared their concept of what is foundational and what the proper context for education is. Both educators understood the lived experiences of their students to be fertile ground for transformative education. Furthermore, they recognized human connectedness, especially in communities, to be an integral part of education. It is rather surprising that these two scholars from vastly different cultures and times have found their way into collaborating in this chapter to inform those involved in digital collaboration. Neither of these men knew anything about the digital world, yet they offered valuable lessons that are relevant today.

Both Freire's and Confucius's powerful work on liberation lead the writer to bring them together to illuminate the journey of collaboration and to contribute symbiotic energy to academia. Their philosophical understandings of learning can enlighten students of all ages and show them that education is deeply rooted in community and is contextualized. By context, Freire and Confucius both meant the communities that shape, form, and develop the identities of learners. As the topic at hand is learning, working, and interacting together to create new communities of collaboration, the writer feels strongly that these two seemingly unrelated scholars and activists—yes, this author believes Confucius was an activist—shared common fundamental ideas and understandings about collaboration.

PART 1: THE LIBERATIVE TASK OF COLLABORATION

Education is a communal task. As it takes a village to raise a child, it takes a village for an individual to learn; it also takes a village to show the fruits of education. Those involved in education, however, find themselves not in the village, but in their caves working on their projects, research, and classes alone. Academia has been deemed a lonely place, especially in the 21st century with the advancement of digital technology, because education and research can take place in front of a computer without any human interaction. Those in education seek to find community through digital technology and media, yet one of the problems of the digital world, despite the multitude benefits of social media, online education, and web-based communication, is that it easily creates a sense of community without having the foundations for community. This is not to say that there cannot be genuine community online, for the purpose of this chapter is to provide understanding and foundations to create such genuine community in the web space; however, with digital technology and media, it is rather easy to mimic community without having substance, which can lead to individuals feeling isolated and lonely. This sense of isolation then causes students and educators to be less engaged in the learning process.

Collaborating in the virtual space may be appealing to those involved in online education because it allows them to build communities, share ideas, and put their efforts together to alleviate the problems of academic silos and loneliness. These problems, however, are not only rooted in a lack of human interaction, they are also due to people experiencing injustice and inequality when working together with others. Therefore, to uphold the spirit of collaboration and to alleviate academic loneliness for everyone involved, collaboration must be liberative. If collaboration does not include liberation, it may create even more isolation for some as they find themselves experiencing injustice via unequal distributions of power and privilege or via denial of their humanity within the collaborating group. Collaboration itself is not the final solution for the problem of isolation; it also needs to be a site of liberation through which participants experience healthy power dynamics and validation of one another, regardless of the nature of their work. This liberative approach to collaboration will allow participants to become aware of the interconnectedness of their communities and how the societal dynamics of power and privilege affect their collaborating community.

In this chapter, *liberation* refers to finding freedom from injustice, inequality, and oppression on all levels. When liberation is not included and stressed in education, the impact education has in the world is diminished. Education is a practice of freedom, and in this freedom, humans find their worth, dignity, and agency (Freire, 2011). Through liberative education, students are empowered as they learn to name and articulate oppression as they see it. Therefore, no form of communication, interaction, or engagement will enhance the quality of collaboration and education unless it is rooted in promoting liberation.

Teaching and learning with liberation at the core take place in communities, where people experience oppression and liberation together.

Freire and Confucius poured their efforts into cultivating contextual and cultural understandings of education. They saw education as a communal task, despite the sociopolitical contexts in which they worked: Freire's world was filled with poverty, inequality, and oppression of the weak, and Confucius's world was a society with a strict hierarchy and limited access to education for those belonging to the lower working class.

In Freire's groundbreaking work, *Pedagogy of the Oppressed*, he fought against the "practice of domination" in education that views humanity as "abstract, isolated, independent and unattached to the world" (1968/2011, p. 81). He explained further that "authentic reflection considers neither abstract [humans] nor the world without people but people in their relations *with* [emphasis added] the world" (p. 81). Humans need to be fully situated in their community when they approach education for two reasons: communities cultivate people's communal self-awareness and provide fertile grounds for effective learning, and communities receive the outcomes of the knowledge and transformations people gain and go through during the learning process (Tu, 1993, p. 38). Understanding the Chinese character for humanity, *jen* (仁), will help the reader see the correlation between the self and the community. Jen (仁) is made up of two different characters, "the character for person (人) next to the character for two," and "the 'two' is crucial, for it is symbolic here for the Confucian conviction that humans are irreducibly social" (Conroy, 1990, p. 30). Humans cannot become humans alone; they must be in community with others to reach the ultimate goal of becoming human. Becoming human, in other words, means *learning* to be human.

Confucius believed in individualized plans and pedagogies designed according to people's contexts and communities, because a community is the very place that influences and shapes an individual's communal self-awareness (Tu, 1993, p. 38). Honoring each community and context of an individual translates into the individual taking an active role in designing the course of study to improve the self and to cultivate the self, for self-cultivation was one of the most important components in Confucius's philosophy. The idea of cultivating the self stems from Confucius's anthropology. He placed each human "at the centre of a nexus of relationship, not an isolated monad," and in these nexuses of relationships that humans form and sustain, they develop and mature (Tu, 1993, p. 38). One may glean from Confucius's views on humans an indication of the importance of intersections in life as well as of the interconnected web of life. Scholarship becomes a participatory endeavor in the intersections and the interconnected web as scholars find themselves in "a confluence of many life streams" (Tu, 1993, p. 38). Confucius advocated for all of his students to give back to the communities from which they came because those communities had played an important role in their formation and self-cultivation. Thus, Confucius emphasized the need to view the learning process as "an act of service to the communities" (Tu, 1993, p. 41). Education, with all its processes, guides one to become aware of one's role in one's immediate and larger community. Education also has an obligation to develop a philanthropic sense in students, so they will share their knowledge and transformative experiences with their communities as a way to return the favor they received from those communities. Both Freire's and Confucius's emphasis on the communal aspect of education teaches those living in the 21st century how to approach education in the digital age.

Although the contexts are different, those involved in education in the 21st century are still enriched by their communities and the cultures their communities inform. So, the contents and the modes of education arise out of people's contexts and cultures, and they place humans in relationship with the world. As Freire and Confucius both affirmed, without being firmly grounded in community, education fails to liberate its participants. The lived experiences of individuals inform educators about what and how to teach and learn together. According to culturally relevant pedagogy, "Learning may differ across cultures and teachers can enhance students' success by acquiring knowledge of their cultural backgrounds and translating this knowledge into instructional practice" (Irvine, 2009, p. 58). Students' contexts, which include culture, language, socioeconomic status, religion, and age, inform those in teaching roles about their pedagogy and style. In the same vein, collaboration with many individuals from various backgrounds and contexts requires a certain level of cultural awareness and competency, especially in the digital age. Without such an awareness, collaboration fails to be liberative and communal, which is contrary to the very definition of collaboration.

In view of navigating through cultural terrains with all of their complexities and nuances, participants in education, especially in collaborative settings, must be mindful of the interconnected web of life. Freire's focal point was always the community of people who have the least power. Confucius, though his world demanded demarcation between people according to their birthrights, saw education as an opportunity to develop equality across these lines. He also had the flexibility to teach according to each person's context and needs, for he himself was situated in community for the sake of communities (Ng, 2000). The Chinese culture in which Confucius found himself had a clear hierarchy for all relationships, with definitive power differentials and forced honor systems. Contrary to his own cultural context, Confucius took the power that was given to him as an educated, upper-class male, whose main role in the society was to teach, to blur the lines of power and privilege (Ng, 2000, p. 312).

Through transnationalism and globalization, cultural lines have become and continue to become less rigid, and both Eastern and Western societies are finding it difficult to essentialize their cultures. With the current amalgamation of cultures and belief systems, education must raise humans' awareness of their connectedness rather than their separation. When collaborating with individuals who have different worldviews, beliefs, cultures, languages, practices, and so on, participants need to have the same commitment to appreciating the diversity within the group. Collaboration in education, whether it is online or on-ground, brings together humans with all their intersections and webs of life to produce a greater good that has a synergetic energy. Thus, the lines that divide and separate must be blurred so individuals and groups who participate in collaboration can experience liberation. It needs to be reiterated that not "all highly participatory discussions and collaborative learning strategies are liberative," and they "can be nonliberative if they do not help participants to question existing realities" (Ng, 2000, 317). Participants must move forward to question the power dynamics of the world, which will help them reflect on the power dynamics within their collaborative group.

Given Freire's sociopolitical context, he saw a great need for collective efforts among the poor to help them claim their agency and authority and to blur the lines of class, wealth, and privilege. He emphasized the dialogical nature of liberation: liberation involves the process of naming power and privilege as people experience it. Dialogue takes place between those living in the world as they seek "to name the world," and it cannot happen unless these people are on the same page about naming the world (Freire, 2011, p. 88). The dialogical nature of liberation alludes to the idea that power differentials between people prevent individuals and communities from finding their voice, authority, and even dignity as human beings.

Power is directly related to oppression, isolation, and injustice. Those who are serious about crossing the lines of power, privilege, and wealth in the world must translate that commitment into action that aids the groups in which they are involved. If education is a communal task with liberation at its center, a natural by-product of education is to fight and stand for justice for *all*. Note that people should fight for justice for *all* and not only for their particular communities. All injustices are equal, and one cannot see one's own injustice and oppression as more detrimental than others'. Hence, the liberative task of collaboration must include acknowledging the multitude of disadvantages and inequalities that exist in the world and seeking to empower the larger community, not simply the individuals who are involved in collaboration. Human connectedness is highlighted through this understanding of oppression: if one is concerned about freeing oneself from one's own oppression, one must also be aware of others living with oppression and promote others' liberation. The liberative educator will guide the community of learners to recognize their connection with all who experience oppression. Furthermore, in a globalized (and globalizing) world, one must be aware of the multiple belongings and the intersectionality of individuals' identities across global contexts (Killick, 2018, p. 1429). This idea of living in a global and globalizing world will be revisited in part 3.

As has been said earlier, collaboration in and of itself cannot provide solutions to isolation and loneliness, which have become the lived experience for those in the academy. If collaborators simply replicate the power dynamics of the world in their group, they are failing to recognize the liberative power collaboration potentially has, and this will eventually lessen the effectiveness of their collaboration. The synergy collective efforts create cannot be achieved if members of the group view their collective work as a competition; collaboration is neither about getting ahead by exercising power and privilege one has nor about usurping power from someone else.

In the spirit of a genuine exchange of ideas, perspectives, theories, and experiences, collaborators must carefully navigate the complexity of what is normative in terms of power and privilege. In the United States and, more broadly, the West, white Christian narratives, experiences, and perspectives are accepted as the norm, but, due to the diverse nature of the population, collaborative groups must be able to critique their own practices, assumptions, and values. Thus, the power dynamics and differentials in collaborative groups must be unpacked and given proper attention; if participants are serious about their collaborative efforts, they must first be self-aware and reflective. Unpacking power and privilege can be rather tricky in collaborative situations, especially with so many intersections of power and disadvantage in this world. The intersections of power and disadvantage may consist of any combination of race, gender, religion, socioeconomic status, and education. Without self-awareness, it is easy to miss these intersections and dwell only on power or disadvantage and categorize one's self as either powerful or disadvantaged, but not both. Hence, self-reflection must be an ongoing practice as groups constantly negotiate the roles of their members in different situations as they strive to find an equitable balance of power. Participants' commitment to the equality and empowerment of all members must be reflected in their interactions and engagement with one another. Through the careful practice of self-reflection, each member of the group must come to share a similar, if not identical, commitment to equality and justice.

PART II: THE PRACTICAL TASK OF COLLABORATION

In order to discuss the practical aspect of collaboration, the roles of educators and students must be (re)defined. According to the traditional sense of their roles, "the teacher teaches and the students are taught," which implies that the authority on the knowledge being transmitted is the teacher (Freire, 2011, p. 73). It is easy to find literature that debunks the traditional roles of teachers and students; however, what is still commonly accepted is that teachers are the final authorities and students are not. While it is understandable to give educators more authority, for they have more experience with research and more formal education, it is not always true to claim that students do not have any experience and knowledge to share with others. Confucius, in a slightly different tone, sided with the understanding that people learn from everyone, saying, "Since we learn from both positive and negative examples, every human being is potentially our teacher" (Tu, 1993, p. 41). When education is understood as a process of educators and students gaining insight mutually, the traditional sense of the teacher-student relationship no longer seems appropriate. In this section, the writer does not totally strip authority from educators in educational or collaborative settings, but she is claiming that the traditional hierarchy between students and educators needs to be revisited.

The liberative task of collaboration shapes the roles of educators and students; furthermore, it influences the roles of collaborators who may not have an obvious hierarchy that has been formally set. To maintain the liberative aspect of collaboration, educator-student dynamics have to take on a different look. Educators come with more power and privilege to the educational setting, and they must be willing to journey with their students in questioning and challenging their reality together. Educators "cannot think for [their] students, nor can [they] impose [their] thoughts on them," but they can dialogue and communicate with their students so that "authentic thinking, thinking that is concerned about reality" may emerge (Freire, 2011, p. 77). This image of the educator stands in contrast to the image of the authoritarian educator who simply treats students as passive beings (banks) whose main role in the educative process is to receive the information that is being "deposited" or transmitted to them. More often than not, in Western higher education settings, educators expect their students to absorb the information and knowledge they choose to offer and to digest it without much critical thinking.

The commonly accepted line between educators and students needs to be blurred so that everyone in the educative process may gain a sense of community and build knowledge together. This line can only be blurred when all parties involved in education collectively and collaboratively work to grow together; it is not only students who learn and transform in the process of education, but teachers also gain much in the journey. Womanist educator bell hooks (1994) claimed that "engaged pedagogy does not seek simply to empower students. Any classroom that employs a holistic model of learning will also be a place where teachers grow, and are empowered by the process" (p. 21). In order for holistic transformation to take place in the educative process, educators must reframe their thinking about their roles and the relationships they have with their students as they approach pedagogy. In liberative pedagogical settings, students work together, sharing their life experiences and ideas and becoming vulnerable to each other; educators, likewise, need to take a risk and become vulnerable by sharing their life experiences and ideas so that everyone in the classroom practices being present holistically (hooks, 1994). Becoming vulnerable may not be easy for those with authority and power, and for educators who interact with their students frequently, this may need to become an intentional practice as they enter into educational spaces where they are given more authority and power. Reflection is key in practicing vulnerability, and as educators envision their roles in learning, they must include intentional self-reflection as an almost spiritual practice. Freire (2011) claimed that teaching in the form of dialogue "cannot exist in the absence of a profound love for the world and for people," and "Love is at the same time the foundation of dialogue and dialogue itself" (p. 89). Educators must reinterpret their roles to include being deeply committed to loving their students and the world around them; this will allow them to become actively vulnerable with their students. Leading by example, they will help students create a world that is more equitable and just.

If the roles of educators are to learn, grow, and create a just world together with students, students' roles must resemble those of educators. Collaborating together to construct meaning, find new perspectives, broaden horizons, and stretch one another, students naturally become teachers and vice versa. As the writer has suggested earlier, the line between the educator and the student needs to be blurred as they share and switch traditional roles. It may be appropriate to add that *roles*, understood in terms of boundaries between educators and students, refers to a sociological construct consisting of a set of behaviors appropriate for a certain position in a group or society (Kendall, Murray, & Linden, 2000). For both educators and students, understanding and assuming new roles in learning environments can be done through socialization, and it may require time to adjust to different ways of being (Garrison, Cleveland-Innes, & Fung, 2004). Yet, when students witness and experience educators' displays of vulnerability, they may begin to understand that their roles may evolve to assume and share the role of the educator.

According to Reg Revan's action learning model, students become teachers through peer teaching; the model upholds "the notion that peers are valuable resources for learning how to solve the problems encountered" in shared types of situations, such as workplaces and classroom settings (Albers, 2008, p. 79). When students are learning the same subject together, they can share their experiences, reflections, and ruminations to stretch one another's views and understanding of the material. Since knowledge is constructed collectively, it only makes sense to bring those involved in the process together to build knowledge from various contexts. In problem-solving situations, peers can interact with one another while addressing the given task, and they can "successfully identify and implement solutions" because "the experience of colleagues provides a potential source of knowledge" and experience with tackling problems and issues (Albers, 2008, p. 79).

In the same vein, student-led discussions utilize the experiences and knowledge of peers to further learning in forms of dialogue (Hambacher, Ginn, & Slater, 2018). Hambacher et al. (2018) defined learning in terms of dialogue and asserted that the nature of dialogue pushes learners beyond themselves each time they present their arguments and counterarguments. In this dialogic framework of learning, the authors claimed that their student-led discussion model, "the 'first responder/connector' model (FR/C)," allows students to facilitate discussions without the direct involvement of educators (p. 2). In the FR/C, the designated first responder responds to the prompt each week, and the connectors present their thoughts and understandings in dialogue with the first responder. This model allows students to teach one another within the boundaries of content-based discussion prompts. When students lead such discussions, they not only blur the lines of the traditional roles of educators and students, they also bring their whole selves into the learning community to build knowledge together as a collective group.

In collaborative settings, peers, colleagues, or students are placed in groups, either on their own or by assignment, and they will have enough contextual knowledge to contribute to the larger task. In the practice of collaboration, there is not one teacher or leader who has more authority; rather, everyone shares the roles of teacher or leader and students or committed members of the group. In other words, everyone involved in a collaborative endeavor shares a common end goal and commits to learning from one another, to influencing and being influenced by the group, and to carefully negotiating the differences that may arise. This sharing of the roles of an educator in collaborative settings may disrupt the structures of hierarchal and power differentials that may exist in education, thus leading those involved to experience liberative education.

The success of educative collaboration is contingent on the members' willingness and commitment to share their reflections. Reflection is "a way of analyzing personal experience, to increase understanding of a situation" (Albers, 2008, p. 82). Reflection must be included in collaboration and in a safe space that allows participants to freely reflect and share. Swan, Garrison, and Richardson (2009) asserted that reflection takes place somewhere in between the individual's private world and the community's shared world. In an online learning setting, the collaborative group must carve out a time and space for its members to share their private worlds and to juxtapose them into their shared world. These safe spaces may be in the form of discussion forums, small group video conference sessions, or partner conversations. In the task of sharing reflections, students or participants assume the role of teacher and influencer; each person offers unique perspectives and interpretations of his or her experiences as well as of the content of the collaboration, and each will shape others' understanding of the material. The biblical book of Proverbs illuminates the impact a person has on another's development: "Iron sharpens iron, and one person sharpens the wits of another" (Proverbs 27:17, NRSV). To learn from one's experiences, one needs to engage in conscious observation and analysis of one's actions. For this reason, collaborators must engage themselves in reflection regardless of the topic at hand; whether they are collaborating on a physics project or a sociology project, each person needs to be an active constructor and interpreter of human experiences. Participants are not passive learners or gatherers of knowledge. Therefore, all "knowledge and theory become personalized, relevant to, and fully integrated into [their] practice" (Zuber-Skerritt, 2001, p. 10).

The integration of one's reflection into practice requires some form of action, and the holistic process of working collaboratively and constructing knowledge leads to taking action based on this reflection (Zuber-Skerritt, 2001, p. 2). The praxis of collaboration is a cycle of reflection and action; participants must understand that they are asked to reflect on a topic, to share their reflections, and to take action following the collective sharing of reflections. Action is an integral part of successful collaboration since it leads participants to enter back into reflection. It is an organic part of wrestling with and constructing knowledge because those involved in the knowledge building will see the need for change in the world based on their newly gained knowledge. Actions cannot be predicted in advance, for the "determination of what to change grows out of reflection with peers," and "strategies for implementing change can also emerge from collaboration" (Albers, 2008, p. 83). Therefore, successful and effective collaboration must include space for praxis and tools to implement ideas into action.

A safe place for individuals to reflect is a must in collaboration. As was defined earlier, collaboration can take place in many different settings in education. Here, the practical aspects of collaboration will be discussed mainly in terms of online education, and the methods and modes of engagement will be briefly considered. Confucius saw education in terms of self-cultivation, yet claimed it was not a private matter. For Confucius, humans experience personal development and growth through education while helping others to do the same; he believed "a human person, wishing to establish his [or her] character, also establishes the characters of others and wishing to enlarge himself [or herself], also helps others to enlarge themselves" (*Analects* 6:30). The idea of enlarging one's self *and* others seems counterintuitive for those living in the 21st century. How is one to practice this concept of enlarging oneself and others at the same time in an online space?

Online adult education, which refers mainly to higher education settings, uses discussion boards and forums to exchange ideas among students, and these discussions are often facilitated by a teacher. Teachers neither claim full authority on the knowledge being constructed nor exercise absolute power over these discussions or classroom interactions. With their experience in a scholarly field as well as a pedagogical understanding of discussion boards, teachers should facilitate in ways that show vulnerability, thoughtfulness, and a yearning for justice in the world. The facilitating role given to teachers does not mean their special gifts, experiences, and expertise are neglected, yet such facilitation does highlight and acknowledge the contributions of each member of the learning community (Ng, 2000, p. 316). Thus, everyone involved in an online learning community understands the importance of their presence and engagement.

Discussion boards are appropriate conduits for practicing liberative, personalized, and authentic collaboration because they provide a safe space to reflect and share reflections. The asynchronous nature of discussion boards allows students time to reflect and mull over the words of one another as well as time to craft their responses and reflections, being mindful of the expressions, words, and phrases they choose to use. Some have argued that this type of interaction on discussion boards lacks the spontaneity that conventional learning environments provide (Patel & Patel, 2006). What these researchers may not be taking into consideration is the communal commitment necessary on the part of students and teachers to bring about these spontaneous moments of discussion and exchanges of ideas in such environments. It is commonly assumed that in an on-ground learning environment, students and teachers can exchange their ideas with much spontaneity and have liberty as far as the structure of discussions is concerned. Spontaneity may lead to the emergence of new ideas that stem from colleagues' ideas shared in classroom discourse and discussions. Though Patel and Patel (2006) believed that this spontaneity is hindered in the online setting, the online setting provides the irreplaceable time and space for the incorporation of others' reflections into one's own. The lack of spontaneity does not translate into a lack of emergence of new ideas and perspectives, for these ideas may be refined and developed further with the depth of attention more time allows.

The intention of comparing online to on-ground classroom settings is not to favor on-ground classrooms, rather, it is to provide a point of reference. If on-ground learning settings are accepted as the norm, then the claim that is being made here is that online learning settings also provide fruitful engagement and interaction, so online learning communities must receive the acknowledgment they deserve for cultivating genuine community. Patel and Patel (2006) claimed that "the online learning system requires a more formal and structured approach which is likely not to allow instructors to bring in the human touch" (p. 35). Online education has evolved and advanced since 2006, when Patel and Patel wrote this. Online learning communities, despite the seeming impersonal nature of online spaces, are now places where genuine and authentic interaction occurs, especially on discussion boards. When students post and respond to their colleagues, they read one another's comments and posts, engage with them authentically, and incorporate their colleagues' thoughts and reflections into their posts. In the writer's experience as an online educator, she has seen genuine and authentic interaction in discussion boards that resembled on-ground classroom discussions. Authentic and genuine interaction online includes responding to colleagues' posts with ideas and suggestions for further research, posing questions to challenge another person's views, and simply including others' ideas into their own reflections. Such discussions create warmth and provide the human touch, something Patel and Patel (2006) seemed to have found lacking in online learning environments.

Though participants in online courses may not see each other regularly, they develop relationships and comradery over the time period they engage in discussions. This has been the case for most of the author's students who have been in the same degree program and taken multiple classes together. Not having face-to-face time in a traditional classroom setting does not mean they cannot develop relationships. Online educators assign collaborative projects for which students have to spend time communicating with each other in order to complete the assignment. When they are placed in small groups, they video-conference, call, or email each other to work on their assignments. It is in these settings that students develop relationships, and it is in these small-group collaboration settings that they need to be mindful of power and privilege.

As was discussed in the previous section, participants need to be mindful of commonly accepted norms, generalizations, and stereotypes. In order for students to work collaboratively in small groups, everyone must commit to fighting against the preference for white normativity and to honoring the members' diverse contexts. Holding the multiple perspectives in a group may seem like a difficult task, and working with diverse members requires everyone in the group to be critically conscious of their own cultures as well as the dominant culture at large (Killick, 2018). Inclusiveness must be included in the design of the groups and learning environments to allow varying perspectives to be incorporated. Participants' critical appreciation of their own cultures contributes to a shared critical consciousness of diversity within the working group. This shared consciousness of diversity will strengthen the members' commitment to fight against white normativity and to honor and value the diversity of the group. Furthermore, a shared consciousness of diversity will lead to the shared identity of the group (i.e., challenging the status quo and fighting against white normativity together), which will lead to strong cohesion (Garrison, Anderson, & Archer, 2010). Group cohesion is foundational to building trust among group members, thus creating a sense of safety and assurance that encourages reflection to take place.

Once a group successfully collaborates and completes the group's assignment, members must be given the time and space to discuss the collaborative process they experienced as well as the knowledge they constructed. They need to reflect and share together what they experienced as well as what they observed. From this discussion, the members of a collaborative group may envision an action plan to improve their world; they may observe a need for more justice and diversity, for space to discuss the take-away from the project, and for time to envision how they can make the knowledge they constructed a part of the bigger narrative of their field. This is the action part of praxis. Whether students gained knowledge about technology or the social sciences, there needs to be room provided for groups to reflect together to come up with an action plan. Meaningful, effective, and successful collaboration *must* include this part of praxis: how can this knowledge be applied in the world to change the world? This is an integral and synergetic part of collaboration.

PART III: THE PHILOSOPHICAL TASK OF COLLABORATION

Honoring the liberative task of collaboration, the philosophical task of collaboration addresses fundamental views of humanity. Participants in collaboration, whether they are teachers, students, or peers, must be committed to valuing and having faith in the intrinsic goodness of humanity. Without faith in humanity, collaboration fails to be liberative and loses its power to inspire genuine engagement, resulting in less-than-ideal synergy. For collaboration to reach its full potential to create a productive community of peers, students, and teachers, its members need to trust that everyone has the capacity to do good and to contribute to the task at hand, and members need to treat one another with dignity. Confucius's humanism steers collaboration to affirm everyone's humanity and dignity because these delineate "the ultimate meaning of human existence" (Tu, 1993, p. 1). Confucius firmly believed "in the perfectibility of human nature through self-effort, as an answer to the dehumanizing tendencies of the historical moment in which he was inalienably circumscribed," and he "directed his energies to the transformation of the world from within" (Tu, 1993, p. 3). Drawing from Confucius's understanding of human nature and its innate perfectibility, the writer claims that collaborators must be committed to two broad ideologies: humans are intrinsically good and self-cultivation is needed for humans' goodness to become evident.

A little background in Confucian philosophy is necessary in order to grasp the relationship between human goodness and self-cultivation. Confucius's faith in human goodness was foundational to his teachings and his life. The social and educational architecture Confucius devised placed self-cultivation at its center. Self-cultivation was central to Confucius because he saw it as a way for people to reach their full humanity, which is intrinsically good. If self-cultivation leads humanity to perfection (e.g., sages, saints, and enlightened ones) a lack of self-cultivation results in the demise of humanity. He turned no one away from learning except those who were "not bursting with eagerness to learn to be human" (Conroy, 1990, p. 29).

Learning to be human means seeking virtue, developing character, and living in harmony and communion with others (Conroy, 1990; Tu, 1993; Tu, 1985). This learning, as portrayed during Confucius's time period (the classical period), "involves five interrelated visions: poetic, political, social, historical and metaphysical," and with these five visions comes "a comprehensive project to retrieve the deep meaning of human civilization" (Tu, 1993, p. 5). These five visions suggest a beautiful collaborative portrait of a harmonious and peaceful kingdom whose members seek to reach their full potential as human beings. Through the poetic vision, Confucius pointed "to the commonality of human feelings and to the mutuality of human concerns," and Mencius, a student of Confucius's grandson, claimed that "no man is devoid of a heart sensitive to the suffering of others," for humans are born with the capacity to extend compassion to each other (Tu, 1993, p. 5). The political vision and the social vision take the mutuality of the poetic vision and apply it to the moral and political sense of duty humans have to one another; furthermore, this sense of duty translates into a sense of belonging as people find the boundaries of human community empowering and motivating (Tu, 1993). Harmonious communal living leads to the historical vision, which calls for individuals to gather their collective memory to leave as a legacy for later generations to use as wise counsel (Tu, 1993). The burden for the historical vision is that it is a powerful and nuanced task, but this has the potential to be the very space in which a community finds a shared identity. The last vision, the metaphysical vision, boils Confucian humanism down to a set of relationships: a trinitarian interaction of heaven, earth, and humans toward transformation. People have an active role in uniting humans and heaven; becoming human "entails the possibility of going beyond the anthropological realm" as well as investing "continuous effort to transcend anthropocentrism" (Tu, 1993, p. 8). Humans are able to reach their full humanity when they can envision a world that is beyond them and can participate in that world.

Confucian humanism speaks volumes to liberative collaboration. Learning as a whole leads humans to reach their full humanity, which is a union of humans and heaven. Therefore, learning is sacred, and if learning is sacred, collaboration, which is an integral part of learning, is also sacred. Perceiving collaboration as sacred may seem more difficult than it is in reality. For many, *sacred* conveys a religious aspect, but in this context, *sacred* simply means something that holds life and breathes life, whether one is religious, spiritual, or neither. Confucius's humanism allows room to expand the idea of what is sacred to include philosophy and practices that refine virtue, develop character, and lead to peaceful living. Therefore, when collaborating with other human beings, each person has to acknowledge human sacredness and the goodness of human beings. Trusting and honoring everyone's full humanity in a way that transcends spiritual and religious differences between group members with different belief systems calls for an understanding of human nature that is a shared view within the group. This is not to say that everyone has to accept the idea that humans are intrinsically good, but there needs to be a common posture and attitude toward one's collaborators and partners that presumes good intentions on the part of others. One's approach in working groups should be one of openness and respect as well as trust that everyone is searching for perfectibility in this life, whether it is possible or not. Confucius himself posed this as a dilemma:

The creative tension between the ontological reality that we are intrinsically sages and the existential fact that we can never become sages defines the human condition in a most vivid way: we are not what we ought to be, as dictated by our moral sense of rightness, but we learn to become what we ought to be by taking as our point of departure what we are here and now (Tu, 1993, p. 39).

Because humans are caught in between wanting to become perfect (e.g., sages, saints, and enlightened ones) and difficult to reach that goal in this life, credit is given to those who strive for perfection. Mencius presents the other side of the same argument: despite the goodness of human beings, humans become bad because of the influence of their environments and their lack of attention to cultivating their good natures (Oh, 2000, p. 84). Thus, it is crucial that human beings put forth their best efforts. When individuals are interacting with one another in group settings, they must first do their best (self-cultivation) to accomplish the task at hand and to give others the benefit of the doubt. Evaluating and measuring how much effort each member puts forth in a group setting may be an impossible task. Trusting each member of the group to bear the same load and weight may be an even more daunting task in a collaborative setting. Even before a group is formed to work together, the facilitator or educator who creates the group needs to establish the tone of trust that will tie the members together. Though trust is built over time, it can be accelerated in an online learning setting because almost all the members have enrolled with the common expectation of being actively engaged in learning. Through shared expectations and goals of learning together in a virtual community, educators, facilitators, and students may develop trust over a short period of time as they assume the best in each other. Allowing room for the benefit of the doubt signals one's commitment to the idea that people are striving to reach perfection, according to each person's idea and definition of perfection. In other words, collaborators need a shared commitment to contributing to the best of their abilities and to trusting that everyone else is doing the same.

Putting faith in humanity's ability to make strides toward perfection encompasses honoring individuality. Each person is born into and nurtured in a different context, and if the characteristics of that context are neglected, ignored, or dominated by those of another context, then individuals fail to practice freedom. The importance of understanding, appreciating, and celebrating diversity in our global and globalizing world cannot be stressed more; individuals and groups of learners must become competent at recognizing (at the very least) and operating with people of diverse cultural contexts. Cultural competency is not developed overnight and must, therefore, be part of an ongoing commitment and process in collaboration groups.

The commitment to cultivating cultural competency may look different for different groups, but it has to include a component of reflection and of having safe space for it. Reflection leads to action, as was discussed earlier. The action part of developing cultural competency through collaboration involves fostering inclusive work environments. Collaborative environments must be "designed to be inclusive," so members learn to "value and understand their own cultures and the cultures of their peers" (Killick, 2018, p. 1429). Without such environments that are conducive to honoring diversity in groups, collaborative efforts lose their effectiveness to alleviate the problems of academic loneliness and silos. When group members engage with all their complexities, they are able to empower one another to practice freedom with the knowledge they construct. This is not to say that collaborative efforts must be perfect in hitting these marks of diversity, inclusiveness, justice, and praxis. Each person's posture, however, must be one of openness and of actively seeking to reach perfection in these listed areas. Agreeing that humans are intrinsically good will help shift perspectives, which will open people up to seeking perfection.

This theoretical and philosophical understanding of collaboration points to a constant struggle with the reality of the world, which is full of oppression and inequality. Though Confucius lived 2,500 years ago, the problems of the world remain similar, and Confucian philosophy remains relevant. Those living in the 21st century can follow in Confucius's footsteps by seeing human beings as good and as capable of reaching perfection through self-cultivation. The concept of human goodness found in Confucius's work provides a fundamental understanding of human nature that is crucial for liberative collaboration to take place. Recognizing the goodness in humans, however, is not enough to encourage people to seek and labor toward liberation; human self-cultivation must be coupled with this ideology. Collaboration will reach its full effectiveness in solving issues of academic loneliness when everyone involved commits to valuing human dignity and goodness as they struggle to find freedom from oppression.

FUTURE RESEARCH DIRECTION

Online learning will continue to evolve as the demand for online continuing education and higher education continues to grow strong. Though many scholars and practitioners of online education research and develop methods and modes of communication and engagement in online learning environments, gaps exist in the fundamental philosophy and posture in online interactions. In this chapter, the author addresses the need for a liberative component in online collaboration and the importance of having shared goals and an understanding of the diversity that exists within collaborative groups. Rooted in the understanding this chapter offers on liberative collaboration, models of online learning communities that embody the liberative philosophy can be drawn and tested. Confucius, in this theories and pedagogies, had shown, taught, and lived out contextual learning as well as honoring human goodness. Further research on the philosophy of Confucius may yield wisdom in discovering and forming creative methods of engagement that are both liberating and affirming of individuals' contexts and goodness. Far too often will communities of learning forget that they are made up of humans who bring differences and similarities to the online space; both culturally competent and sensitive pedagogies will need to be cultivated and implemented.

CONCLUSION

The application of Confucius's humanism and Freire's critical pedagogy to collaboration boils down to two main ideas: (1) be generous to people involved in one's collaborative group because they are by nature good people who are struggling to reach perfection and (2) be critical of the world, which is oppressive and unjust. Confucius viewed himself not as a sage, but as a perpetual learner, and those in academia must adopt this self-description, since they are also on a journey of discovery. This chapter outlined three distinct and yet interrelated topics that are integral parts of collaboration. Confucius's understanding of human perfection and Freire's pedagogy of liberation inform those involved in academic collaboration about the goals collaborators seek to accomplish. Both the liberative and practical tasks are deeply rooted in a philosophical understanding of human nature, because one must be committed to the goodness of people before one can work together with others to fight against oppression.

REFERENCES

Albers, C. (2008). Improving pedagogy through action learning and scholarship of teaching and learning. *Teaching Sociology*, *36*(1), 79–86. doi:10.1177/0092055X0803600110

Conroy, F. (1990). Learning to be human: Confucian resources for person-centered education. *Persons and Education*, *6*(1), 27–49.

Freire, P. (2011). *Pedagogy of the oppressed* (M. B. Ramos, Trans.). New York, NY: Continuum. (Original work published 1968)

Garrison, D. R., Anderson, T., & Archer, W. (2010). The first decade of inquiry framework: A retrospective. *Internet and Higher Education*, *13*(1-2), 5–9. doi:10.1016/j.iheduc.2009.10.003

Garrison, D. R., Cleveland-Innes, M., & Fung, T. (2004). Student role adjustment in online communities of inquiry: Model and instrument validation. *Journal of Asynchronous Learning Networks*, *8*(2), 61–74.

Hambacher, E., Ginn, K., & Slater, K. (2018). From serial monologue to deep dialogue: Designing online discussions to facilitate student learning in teacher education courses. *Action in Teacher Education*, 1–14. doi:10.1080/01626620.2018.1486753

Hooks, B. (1994). *Teaching to transgress: Education as the practice of freedom*. New York, NY: Routledge.

Irvine, J. J. (2009). Culturally relevant pedagogy. *Teaching Tolerance*, 57–61.

Kendall, D., Murray, J., & Linden, R. (2000). *Sociology in our times* (2nd ed.). Scarborough, Canada: Nelson.

Killick, D. (2018). Critical intercultural practice: Learning in and for a multicultural globalizing world. *Journal of International Studies*, *8*(3), 1422–1439.

Ng, G. A. W. (2000). From Confucian master teacher to Freirean mutual learner: Challenges in pedagogical practice and religious education. *Religious Education (Chicago, IL)*, *95*(3), 308–319. doi:10.1080/0034408000950307

Oh, K. H. (2000). *Dimensions of Chong in Korean Christians*. (Unpublished doctoral dissertation). Northwestern University. Evanston, IL.

Patel, C., & Patel, T. (2006). Exploring a joint model of conventional and online learning systems. *e-Service Journal*, *4*(2), 27–46. doi:10.2979/esj.2006.4.2.27

Swan, K., Garrison, D. R., & Richardson, J. C. (2009). A constructivist approach to online learning: The Community of Inquiry framework. In C. R. Payne (Ed.), *Information Technology and Constructivism in Higher Education: Progressive Learning Frameworks* (pp. 43–57). Hershey, PA: IGI Global. doi:10.4018/978-1-60566-654-9.ch004

Tu, W. M. (1993). *Wei, learning, and politics: Essays on the Confucian intellectual*. Albany, NY: State University of New York Press. Retrieved from http://web.a.ebscohost.com.dtl.idm.oclc.org/ehost/detail/detail?vid=0&sid=9b40b11c-2843-4af0-92f4-3c9281d00b9d%40sdc-v-sessmgr05&bdata=JnNpdGU9ZWhvc3QtbGl2ZSZzY29wZT1zaXRl#db=nlebk&AN=8603

Tu, W. M. (1998). Confucius and Confucianism. In W. H. Slote, & D. A. DeVos (Eds.), *Confucius and the family* (pp. 3–36). Albany, NY: State University of New York Press.

Zuber-Skerritt, O. (2001). Action learning and action research: Paradigm, praxis and programs. In S. Sankara, B. Dicks, & R. Passfield (Eds.), *Effective change management through action research and action learning: Concepts, perspectives, processes and applications* (pp. 1–20). Lismore, Australia: Southern Cross University Press.

ADDITIONAL READING

Akcaoglu, M., & Lee, E. (2016). Increasing social presence in online learning through small group discussions. *The International Review of Research in Open and Distributed Learning*, *17*(3), 1–17. doi:10.19173/irrodl.v17i3.2293

Dewey, J. (1938). *Experience and Education*. New York, NY: Collier Books.

Garrison, D. R., Anderson, T., & Archer, W. (2001). Critical thinking, cognitive presence, and computer conferencing in distance education. *American Journal of Distance Education*, *15*(1), 7–23. doi:10.1080/08923640109527071

Garrison, D. R., & Cleveland-Innes, M. (2005). Facilitating cognitive presence in online learning: Interaction is not enough. *American Journal of Distance Education*, *19*(3), 133–148. doi:10.120715389286ajde1903_2

Hewitt, J. (2005). Toward an understanding of how threads die in asynchronous computer conferences. *Journal of the Learning Sciences*, *14*(4), 567–589. doi:10.120715327809jls1404_4

Kincheloe, J. L. (2012). Critical pedagogy in the twenty-first century: Evolution for survival. *Counterpoints*, *422*, 147–183.

Lipman, M. (2003). *Thinking in education* (2nd ed.). New York, NY: Cambridge University Press. doi:10.1017/CBO9780511840272

Mayberry, M. (1998). Reproductive and resistant pedagogies: The comparative roles of collaborative learning and feminist pedagogy in science education. *Journal of Research in Science Teaching*, *35*(4), 443–459. doi:10.1002/(SICI)1098-2736(199804)35:4<443::AID-TEA14>3.0.CO;2-A

Ng, G. A. W. (1996). Asian sociocultural values: Oppressive and liberating aspects from a woman's perspective. In D. Ng (Ed.), *People on the way: Asian North Americans discovering Christ, culture, and community* (pp. 63–103). Valley Forge, PA: Judson Press.

KEY TERMS AND DEFINITIONS

Collaboration: An act of working together both face-to-face and virtually.

Constructivism: A school of thought that sees knowledge as layered and built rather than transferred or acquired.

Context: Any circumstances that situate an issue, topic, or theory.

Inclusive: Including and embracing human diversity, including but not limited to ability, color, culture, ethnicity, gender, sexual orientation, and language.

Liberative: Any theory, action, or effort contributing and related to bringing justice in the world. It requires one to intentionally and actively change the status quo to bring positive change to result in justice.

Praxis: A reflection-action cycle of applying theories into practice, in which both theories and practices may experience change.

Reflection: A deep internal thought process in which one considers implications and logic of theory, situation, and context of an issue in relation to one's own experience and context. It may be iterated.

ENDNOTE

1 *Participants* includes, but is not limited to, students, administrators, and educators.

Chapter 14
If You Build It, They Will Come: Student Clubs in the Digital World

Elizabeth Donnellan
Purdue University Global, USA

ABSTRACT

Students attending traditional or online universities will benefit from membership in student-run virtual clubs. This chapter provides specific information about tools used to create, administer, and motivate participation in virtual university clubs. To enhance the club experience, suggestions are offered for creating interactive clubrooms, utilizing specific social media tools, and providing unique club events all as a virtual experience. A case study is included to demonstrate how students of a major online university participate in virtual club events. Results of this case study indicate a correlation between students who can easily access club tools and events with participation. Further, students who participate in clubs report greater satisfaction with their overall university experience and increased confidence in professional skills.

INTRODUCTION

When online universities built their first campuses twenty years ago, the focus was on providing a unique space for students and their professors to exchange messages and assignments. These learning environments were primitive as they mostly consisted of asynchronous chat boards. There was no way for students and professors to customize their experience of the classroom or to use it to socialize in it. Over the past twenty years, these learning environments have transformed from primitive chat boards to rich, interactive tools that provide opportunities for asynchronous and synchronous experiences. Whereas earlier learning environments were not technically advanced enough to support activities outside of the classroom, newer environments do. Many technological advances, even in the past five years, have created opportunities for professors and their students to develop online virtual clubs using both synchronous and asynchronous tools (Dede & Barab, 2018). The future of virtual clubs is exciting as some university club advisors utilize three-dimensional spaces (avatar learning) and embed social media tools (e.g. Facebook chat for club meetings).

DOI: 10.4018/978-1-5225-9814-5.ch014

Most studies and articles of online learning focus on strategies for building strong online learning communities in the classroom and on tools for student retention. Most of these works describe strategies for creating active learning experiences. Further, much current research explores the use of social media as a communication tool for classrooms and by extension, student organizations. However, few studies suggest best practice strategies for the development and growth of virtual online student organizations using newer technologies and social media tools (Wang, Woo, Quek, Yang, & Liu, 2012). These concepts will be discussed through a review of the research literature, including a case study from one large online virtual student organization, and a discussion of newer technologies and strategies for employing them.

This chapter will introduce readers to best practices in the use of social media for creating a community that transcends classroom borders. The information can be used as a guide for creating new or strengthening existent organizations. The specific sub-sections will provide the reader with information related to components of online student organizations, use of social media as communication and retention tool, practical guide to types of social media tools, online security consideration, best practice strategies, psychology of virtual community participation and discussion of research into the future of online student communities.

Creating strong student organization has been shown to increase club retention, build community in a department, and strengthen student and faculty morale (Stewart, Goodson, Meirtschin, Norwood, & Ezell, 2013). Understanding how to bolster student participation by offering easy to access synchronous and asynchronous activities is important to the creation of a strong organization. The sections of the chapter will provide specific strategies to do this.

BACKGROUND

With the advent of online learning, students and their professors worked together to create learning communities in their classrooms. Most universities grappled with how to create authentic learning experiences in the abstract of virtual classrooms (Shea & Bidjerano, 2010; Smart & Cappel, 2006). To address this, many universities adopted a standard classroom structure that mimicked traditional classrooms. The structure of these classrooms included tools for collaborative learning such as discussion board, live chat areas (both synchronous and asynchronous), and areas for document storage (Zhu, 2012). Most universities who offer distance-learning classes purchase platform services from virtual learning companies who provide the framework for classroom shells. The arrangement of the components is selected and supported by these companies. Therefore, there is not much opportunity for rearranging course structure. Over time, online students and faculty gained comfort interacting within these conceptual spaces in the classroom despite their lack of control of the creation of it (Zhu, Valcke, & Schellens, 2008).

With the expanded use of virtual classes and the inception of online universities, more students warmed to the idea of creating a virtual, academic life. Many students developed relationships with their classmates based solely on virtual interaction creating new possibilities for collaboration (Smith, Coldwell, Smith, & Murphy, 2005). Like pioneers in a new world, college officials studied and proposed tweaks to the online format and course delivery (Veerman & Veldhuis, 2001). The goal was to create interactive experiences that felt like those of a traditional university. Most officials found that student and faculty satisfaction increased with the implementation of innovations that created a sense of personal control over learning (Santhanam, Sasidharan, & Webster, 2008). These innovations enhanced the student's ability to access synchronous (e.g. live lecture) and asynchronous (e.g. discussion threads) features of the class. Popularity with online learning grew rapidly as more adults living outside major metropolitan areas enrolled in virtual classes and major universities embraced the cheaper delivery of virtual classes.

Students attending online universities expressed interest in participating in traditional college experiences like the ones offered by traditional universities. University officials in the early days of online learning struggled to meet this challenge. The main obstacle was in creating a community that could be used by students to host events, communicate ideas, and still be monitored by school officials (Santhanam, et al., 2008). Membership in virtual clubs was mostly restricted to the most tech savvy and enthusiastic students, many of whom were of traditional college age.

As classroom platform technologies advanced, officials were able to create classroom shells for club members to use. Still, membership was low since many students struggled to balance family, work, and school responsibilities. Other problems were related to accessibility as many students relied on dial-up internet service to access the virtual rooms. Students did not have much free time to wait for additional classrooms to load. Due to these early restrictive connection technologies, many students did not actively participate in clubs due to the necessary addition time that it took to participate.

It was not until 2008, when many students traded their dial-up modems for cable and broadband access, that clubs reported increased memberships. During this time, social media sites grew in popularity helping to train students to think of virtual reality as a social gathering place. With the emergence of these sites and new hardware technologies (e.g. smart phones and tablets), students had more choices for access and were able to access the internet away from their home computers. Despite there being better access to wireless technologies, not all students are familiar with them. Online students are a unique population as the range of age for students is from 18 to 60 years. The range of interest, knowledge of technologies, sophistication of hardware, and speed/type of connection differs greatly as a result (Riley, 2008). The challenge was for university officials to create an experience that is accessible to most students regardless of technical knowledge, hardware capability, and desired level of participation in classes and clubs.

Some online universities began to offer subject specific professional clubs that were like those offered at traditional universities. There are many challenges that came with the creation of student clubs, most of which are like those reported by student life staff at traditional universities. One challenge is in recruiting a core membership who commits to leading and monitoring club activities. Not much research has been conducted in this area, as student club membership in many online universities is not yet significant (Smart & Cappell, 2006). The reasons for lack of membership have as much to do with the age of the student population as it does with the type of college (e.g. online vs traditional). The average age of online college students is 34 years of age while traditional college students are 20 years of age (Aslanian & Clinefelter, 2012). In general, older students have more responsibilities that preclude them from attending evening and/or weekend meetings regularly. Therefore, creating momentum for participation in online clubs requires innovation and strategic planning.

Other challenges include how to hold meetings, create interesting activities, and work on collaborative projects in a space dedicated solely to club activities. Ideally, planned activities should be accessible to all members of the club regardless of technological knowledge or hardware. This will continue to be challenging as there is a marked shift in popularity of online courses among younger students. Many of these students are practiced with using virtual tools while their older classmates may not be.

From 2008 to 2018, many public universities and liberal arts colleges have added online courses and degree programs to their regular schedule of classes. More traditional college aged students (18-24 years) are enrolling in online degree programs to reduce student housing costs and transportation hassles. In 2012, about 24% of traditional aged students were enrolled in at least one online course and by 2016, that number increased to 44% (Allen & Seaman, 2017). Online classes are also attractive to adult students who need a flexible schedule and who prefer to study from home. Younger students who were raised in the digital world report feeling comfortable using online technologies including online learning, while their older counterparts report less comfort. This has created a widening technological knowledge gap between older and younger generations not so much in basic use of internet usage, but in knowledge of how to use specific technologies tied to social media and online learning (van Deursen & van Dijk, 2010). Another significant development during these 10 years is the increase in popularity of mobile devices. Many learning platforms have been modified to accommodate mobile access making classrooms and clubrooms easier to use potentially widening the appeal of club participation (Rambe & Bere, 2013). Meeting each of these challenges can seem overwhelming for administrators, student life staff, and faculty sponsors. However, with a plan and effective use of web tools, clubs can grow into a very useful collaborative tool for the university and students alike.

Building A Club: Case Study- Major University Psychology Club

A four-year case study of a large online university student club provides insight into the benefits and challenges of offering virtual student clubs. The psychology department of a large online university started a student club in 2008 with no plan and few students. Some students asked a faculty member to sponsor a club so that they could meet outside of their classes to discuss different field related topics that were not explored in their classes. The university provided a class shell for the club and the club began with a membership of fifteen students and one faculty advisor. At the time, the plan was to monitor involvement and create a model for sustained membership if interest grew.

The clubroom was a classroom shell like those used for university courses including an area for live chats, asynchronous discussion, announcements, email, and document sharing. The advisor could post announcements, add discussion topics, and post items in the document sharing area, but not change the dynamics of the room. Further, the advisor could not update the club membership roster, which created challenges in contacting active members. At the time, there was no mechanism for allowing club advisors to maintain an active list of participants. That task could only be handled at the course administrator level, of which professors did not have.

The club members elected a board of officers to provide leadership for the club. As the club expanded its membership, committee Chair positions were added. However, with few active members, there was no real interest in developing or participating in committee work. The officers were left with the bulk of the responsibility for planning and sponsoring activities. The club members met once a month to hear guest speakers and to discuss club business. After the first few meetings, membership grew to over fifty students, though most did not actively participate in meetings or activities. The faculty advisor reported dissatisfaction with the lack of regular student participation and inability to customize the club space. Students complained that it felt too much "like class and I have enough of those." The challenges mounted.

At the beginning of the second year, active membership had dropped by 45% and the faculty advisor left the club. A new advisor was assigned, and a new panel of officers was elected in 2009. During that year, the advisor actively recruited new members increasing membership by 70%. However, no additional activities were added to the club schedule leaving members with few choices for participation. The membership numbers plummeted as students did not attend meetings or participate in idea sharing discussions in the clubroom. To study the declining participation, the officers and advisor decided to survey the active members to determine the reasons for the lack of participation in the club. The data was collected and evaluated using a qualitative method. The results revealed that a core group of fifteen to eighteen members were attending most of the events with few other members attending occasionally. Discouraged by the continued lack of participation from most of the membership, the officers stopped volunteering to sponsor events leaving most of the club responsibilities to the President of the club. To evaluate the specific reasons for the decline in club participation despite increased enrollment, the club advisor developed an analysis plan to study effective methods for recruiting and maintaining members.

This plan steered the data collection for the remaining years of the study. Members participated in a survey that was used to determine the main issues that were causing the decline in membership and participation. Of note, 78% of active members responded to the survey and returned it by the deadline making the survey the first successful activity of the club. The problems were that the officers were not trained (e.g. resulting in personality clashes), days/times for scheduled activities were not convenient for many students (e.g. members spanned five time zones), and complaints of lack of knowledge of how to use some of the tools in the clubroom. Interestingly, the strengths of the organization were that recruiting seemed to successful, meetings were informative, active members enjoyed the camaraderie and opportunity to learn from department professors. Clearly, students found value in participation in the club activities. The problems were distilled to the need for leadership training for student leaders, providing a better variety of club activities, and making club activities more accessible to students, including those with weaker technological skills.

Within the first two months of the third year, the faculty advisor resigned, and all the officers graduated. A new advisor was assigned, and a new board of officers were elected creating a surge of enthusiasm amongst the psychology department and club members. Membership expanded to 267 students with still only approximately 18 members attending monthly meetings. Armed with the results of the survey, the club members and new faculty advisor decided to create a plan to increase overall participation that included using a new forum for club meetings and adding new activities. Before implementing the changes, it was important to gain a better understanding of the characteristics of students who were participating in club activities. To do this, members completed another survey that surveyed computer/technological knowledge, habits of technology use, responsibilities (personal and professional), and interest in psychology topics. The following section in an explanation of that study.

STUDY: STUDENT PREFERENCE IN ONLINE CLUB SETTINGS (PSYCHOLOGY CLUB)

Researchers at a major online university decided to explore students' motivations for participating in online club events. The purpose of the study was to explore trends in participation in events, motivation for participation, obstacles in participation, and trends related to the age/responsibilities (e.g.to form a profile of users). The method was a single case study using the club as the single "member" in the study utilizing a time measured approach to data collection. Data was collected using three sources: anonymous survey of membership (with an average of 78% the membership participation), randomized interview (e.g. 25 participants were randomly selected using a computer program to select participants for each administration), and observation of participation using online tools (e.g. embedded in the clubroom). Following data collection and analysis, changes in club events and technologies were made to create a more user-friendly experience for club members. Though these tweaks were minor, there were improvements in the reporter used experience from years one to two and from year one to four.

Figure 1.

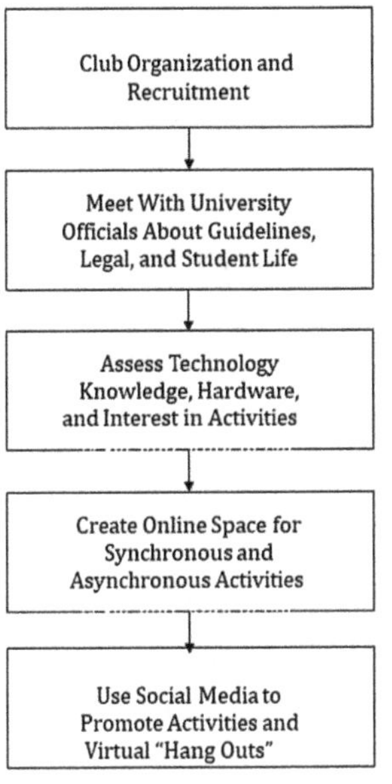

Method

Participants

Participants in the study were official members of the psychology club who were all invited to participate in the study. One of the challenges of this study was that the membership numbers were quite dynamic changing constantly from graduations and new enrollments. For that reason, the individual group of participants were treated as one entity- the club. In the first year of the study, there were no official participants as the data that was collected was completely anonymous and averaged to provide information about patterns of participation. Also, during the first year, only undergraduate students were offered membership in the club, so no information about graduate student participation was collected. In year two, graduate students could join and so, the membership needs changed somewhat with new activities added to accommodate graduate student interests. Over the course of the four-year study, 1,454 total students may have participated in surveys or structured interviews. Participants range in age from 18 to 68 years of age with 82% female and 18% male participation.

Participants lived in forty-three different states (United States) with many students were from the Chicago area with the next greatest concentration from the south, Texas, and the Pacific Northwest. Fewer participants lived in the northeast or Atlantic coastal states. Participants also reported living in seven different countries with the Caribbean islands accounting for most of that population. Other participants reported military deployment as a reason for living in Europe, Africa, and Asia. This is important as a consideration since students were logging into synchronous events from many different time zones.

Most participants reported use of dial-up connection during the first year of the study (2008). By the end of the study, most participants were using some form of high-speed connection. There was a significant shift in type of internet connection used between years two and three of the study (2009-2010).

Data Collection

For this study, three methods of data collection were used over the four-year period. Baseline measures for the first year were taken in the first month of club as undergraduate students were invited to join the club. Data was collected again for the next four years at six-month intervals. Participants were asked to complete a consent form and log onto the survey site (only one survey response was allowed per respondent). At the end of the survey, participants were invited to write comments about the club and were debriefed. Participation was completely anonymous, and responses were not individually correlated.

For this study, 810 undergraduate and 644 graduate students participated in an online self-report survey. Participants completed a thirty-item survey covering several topics related to reasons for participating in the club, frequency of attendance at club-sponsored events, motivation for attending events, ease of access to events and clubroom, career goals, and demographic information. Participants were age 18-68 years living in forty-three states and seven countries. Participants signed consent forms, received passwords (one-time use only), and logged onto the site to complete the survey. When finished, the participants received an email from the researchers inviting feedback about survey and debriefing. The email repeated the debriefing message including information about the purpose of the study and further steps for making suggestions about future club events.

During each administration of the survey, fifty participants were invited to complete a structured interview. Selection for participation in the structured interview was generated randomly using a randomizing feature in the online survey site. Participants were asked at the end of their online survey if they would be willing to participate in the structure interview activity. Approximately 58% of total participants agreed and of those, twenty-five were selected. No participant could complete the structured interview more than ones, though. Data gathered from the structured interview helped to contextualize the responses from the online survey.

Participants who agreed to complete the structured survey met with a researcher in a virtual Adobe Connect room and signed in using the moniker "participant # _." Each member was assigned a number by another researcher (not the interviewer) who explained the study and collected the written consent before the interviewer entered the virtual room. This method helped protect the anonymity of each participant to protect confidentiality and reduce bias.

There were only seven questions on the structured survey; however, they were open-ended allowing for unique responses. Participants answered questions related to the preferred use of social media, access issues/solutions, time online in academic related activities, and motivation for attending club activities. The interviewer recorded responses to each question using the recording function in the virtual room (participants were aware of the recording). After the interviews were completed, two research assistants coded each of the responses on grid sheets focusing on the main information provided in the response. Differences between coding sheets were resolved by a third researcher. Inter-rater agreement for this project was 95%, so disagreement was not a significant issue.

The third method of data collection was observation of user data collected from the clubroom itself. Tools embedded in the clubroom allowed researchers to collect specific information on overall monthly usage of the collective membership, individual usage by member, specific rates of log-in, identification of type of log-in (e.g. book club, announcements, threaded discussions, chat rooms, and other activities). These data helped to provide better context for understanding user preferences of asynchronous and synchronous events. Club meetings were held in a designated Adobe Connect room that also provided valuable data about how many members attended meetings, average time of attendance, and number of comments posted in response to the speaker. These data suggested how interested participants were in activities and speakers.

Results

The results revealed that the age of the student did not predict his/her participation in activities as much as technological knowledge did. The overall average of responses for the survey showed frequency of participation in club events: 35% (n =508) attended at least 9 events, 52% (n = 757) attended at least five events, 11% (n =160) attended at least two events, and 2% (n = 29) attended one to no events. These data represent the total results for each of the seven administrations of the survey. Further, the results from the interviews demonstrated that students who participated in club events did so because of their interest in working as a psychology professional upon graduation. Others attended specific events from academic interest in the topic (e.g. cognitive psychology: memory lecture). Most participants (92%) had and used Facebook accounts at least once in the past month of the survey administration. Approximately 52% had and used Twitter accounts at least once in the past month of survey administration too. No other social media site/tool was used by many of the participants during the study. Of note, those who had Twitter accounts, also reported having Facebook accounts with only 8% of participants only using Twitter.

Results of the clubroom usage data showed that most use of the clubroom was in the discussion threads, most notably in the committee workrooms (68% on online time total). Data from the three methods were correlated to determine the relationship between technology knowledge, motivation for participating in student clubs, ease of access of clubroom, and frequency of participation. Participants used the live chat area least (only 6% of the online time was devoted to live chat). Participants used the other areas including the book club and announcement area also. This access seemed to be purposeful in that participants logged in and went directly to those areas without spending much time there. However, there was trend showing an increase in usage of the club room from years one to four (58% increase overall) with the largest growth seen between years three and four (34% increase). The only other significant result was that same user rates increased steadily between years two and four. However, that increase appeared to be correlated to the frequency of posting of new material in the clubroom.

Discussion

The significant findings of this study show that participation increased as more students gained access to high-speed internet, mobile devices, and social media sites. Further, participation was highest among those who had fewer nonacademic responsibilities and age was not predictive of responsibility load. Most students who participated in at least nine events a year reported that they had fewer to no family responsibilities than students who participated in fewer events. Interview results supported the survey results that indicated that those who participated frequently identified college as their primary focus. Those who identified family as being of equal or greater value than academics tended to attend between two and five annual events. This outcome could be significant for universities trying to create activities that will be well attended by club members. Those members who are mostly focused on academic work might be interested in attending more events focused on academic-themed topics.

Of further note, club members who reported having the most knowledge of internet tools related to social media and communication, were apt to attend more online events than those who reported little knowledge of those technologies. Most "expert" users reported attending at least five club events annually regardless of family responsibilities. The strongest correlation for attendance was technological knowledge followed by level of family responsibility. Therefore, members who self-reported as expert users and who did not have family responsibilities were predicted to attend at least five club events annually.

Overall, members who participated in club events reported interest in working in the psychology field following graduation and believed that club participation would increase their professional knowledge and career opportunities. This was the overwhelming response to the question about motivation for club participation. While this was an expected outcome, it helped to drive planning for club events. Rather than focus on providing social opportunities, members requested more lectures, professional networking opportunities, academic themed book club, and opportunities to work in study groups. These results revealed low interest among many respondents for social activities. Prior to analyzing these data, the club leaders planned many social events thinking that members wanted more of these opportunities. Between years three and four, the leaders changed the focus of activity planning to reflect these outcomes. The result was increased participation in club activities overall.

Since the findings suggested that participation in events correlated to technological knowledge, club leaders began holding seminars for members who wanted to increase knowledge of the clubroom's online tools. Those who reported low levels of technological knowledge were not attending live meetings or using the clubroom. Besides that, members requested assistance with creating Power Point presentations, using Skype and other communication tools, and using survey creation tools. These seminars were surprisingly well-attended with members reporting increased confidence with their skills. Prior to the study, the leaders of the club mistakenly assumed that all members knew how to access various online tools.

A notable trend in the data indicated that many students did not participate because of access issues. Some reported inability to download certain plug-ins or programs that were required to run the club activity. For example, some reported that the Adobe Connect plug-in would not install on their computer and after trying a few times, students stopped trying to enter meetings. Others reported a lack of knowledge as to how to access club activities, and so, did not bother trying to do so. Still others reported that the scheduling of activities was problematic. At that time, club activities were mostly offered synchronously creating scheduling problems for them.

Once the trends from the survey were analyzed, it became clear that there are four types of students who participate in virtual organizations. To help the researchers to understand the how students engage with virtual clubrooms, a model of user profiles was created. These profiles were created according to online behaviors, preferences, interests, and use of hardware.

TECHNOLOGY USE PROFILES: COLLEGE STUDENT USERS

1. **Neophytes**: These students are new to online learning and usually to the more sophisticated online tools (have not used social media much).
2. **Casual Users**: These students use technology and know how to use most tools, but only use them occasionally.
3. **Experienced Users**: These students are tech savvy, often using smart phones, tablets, and netbooks to access class and feel comfortable working in a variety of mediums.
4. **Expert User**: These students are "tech forward" in their knowledge of technologies, hardware, sites, and enjoy creating the tech experience for others. These students like the full video/audio experience and have the equipment to support it.

These categories helped the faculty advisor and club members to conceptualize the problem of designing activities and club structure to accommodate more members. After review of the data, the officers determined that one of the chief problems of inspiring participation in activities was that they were suited for experienced and expert users. Unfortunately, those users were only about one third of the club's membership overall. The realization was that the club membership was mostly unable to participate in the sponsored events.

Immediately, the officers and advisor developed a plan to provide opportunities for all members to interact regardless of the level of technological knowledge. Two volunteers designed short training sessions for students who did not know how to use certain programs that were required for basic club activities. The advisor redesigned the clubroom to include threads for sponsored asynchronous activities. Activities that had been synchronous could now be accessed asynchronously as well. For example, a faculty member sponsored monthly book club meetings. According to the results of the study, only experienced and expert users were attending the live book chat (e.g. five members only). The book club discussions became a discussion thread allowing neophytes to participate in the discussion. An unintended benefit was realized soon after the creation of this thread in that students from different time zones began to participate. Activity in the clubroom increased by 34% in a month (usage was monitored using administrative tools).

The advisor also customized discussion threads to include separate committee work areas, Q&A area, study groups (e.g. undergraduate statistics), job board, and activity suggestion area. Data from the structured surveys showed that students wanted the club to use social media to create an informal gathering place for students. University officials were contacted, and an official Facebook page was created for members to use. Overnight, the page gained over 345 members including students from the department who were not yet club members.

In the fourth year of the study, membership increased to its highest level including both undergraduate and graduate students who actively participated in synchronous and asynchronous activities. New activities required the use of additional technologies, so recorded instructions were added to the clubroom announcement area to aid neophyte users.

For example, the activities committee sponsored monthly "teach-ins" that offered students opportunities to teach other members about a topic or skill in a twenty-minute period. Teach-ins were held in an Adobe Connect room so that presenters could use Power Point, show their desktop, or use their video camera for the presentation. Clearly, these presentations were designed for experienced and expert users of technology, so many students who were intimidated by the technology did not volunteer to participate. To provide an alternate presentation activity, the advisor added a presentation discussion thread to the clubroom where students could present asynchronously. All presenters, both synchronous and asynchronous loaded their presentations to that thread providing an interesting discussion area.

There are many lessons in this study for leaders of virtual clubs. Clubrooms and events need to be easily accessible (defined as number of steps required to access events) by all members. New tools used by the club should be explained to members in written directions with screenshots when appropriate. Club activities should be offered in both synchronous and asynchronous forms so that members can create a customized interactive experience with the club. With these adjustments to the club structure, it is anticipated that participation will continue to increase.

Limitations

A limitation of the study was that membership of the club changed continually, including the addition of graduate students in the second year. This limitation was handled by using a N=1 case study method where the club was the primary unit of analysis. Still, this model did not allow the researchers to fully grasp some of the trends in the data. Some students who participated in the structured interview were double sampled because they participated in both their undergraduate and graduate student years, though the number is quite low (n=10), the data was still added to the overall analysis. There was not a way for researchers to identify these participants until after they had participated, and their data was co-mingled with the total data. Further, students who participated in the survey are more likely to represent those who had been participating in events. Those who did not complete the surveys, are predicted to represent those who did not participate in any club events. When members do not respond to surveys or requests for feedback, it is impossible to fully evaluate the club experience. This limits the modifications that can be made to enhance the club experience, especially for non-participating members.

BUILDING VIBRANT ONLINE STUDENT ORGANIZATIONS

Overall, the results of the case study lead to some very interesting outcomes that were used to update the club experience. The case study demonstrated the problems of creating an active online space where club members can create a meaningful experience for themselves. It is difficult to create a multi-use space that is useful to adults of various levels of technological knowledge. By providing both synchronous and asynchronous activities, members reported satisfaction and increased sense of ownership of the space than when the study began. The membership grew 478% in four years' time and participation in activities has increased three-fold. Challenges still exist in how to balance the use of social media with official university tools (e.g. all university activities must occur inside of their sponsored space). This case study will be referenced in the following subsections as an example of the problems and solutions to building online student clubs.

Each of the next sections introduces some aspect of collaborative communities using a variety of tools. Further, there are suggestions about the use of social media, guidelines for security, and speculations about the future of virtual student organizations.

Components of Online Student Organizations

When designing virtual organizations, the planners must consider the mission of the organization and target audience. The mission of most student clubs is to unite students together to share their interest in a subject or activity (Foubert & Urbanski, 2006). In the example above, the mission of the club was to provide a professional experience for psychology students through a variety of activities. The club eventually sponsored many events for networking, learning, organizing charity work, and developing career interests.

The basic components of virtual student organizations are membership, meeting space, regular meeting times, shared commitment (e.g. reason for club), advisor, and opportunities for student directed activities. While these components are similar to those of traditional college student organizations, there are different challenges in implementation.

Membership

Most student run clubs begin with a core group of interested students who enlist the support of a faculty member to sponsor the club. These beginning members eagerly advocate for resources such as a clubroom and if lucky, a budget for activities. There are often student life guidelines and legal requirements that must be met before the club can gain official status. Universities must approve student membership and oversee activities, to ensure compliance with Family Educational Rights and Protection Act (FERPA) and other regulations. As the club gains exposure, usually through casual means, more students join. Clubs that sponsor a variety of professional and academic activities ten to create a sustainable core membership base especially in consideration of the needs of undergraduate and graduate student participants (Prakash & Potoski, 2007). A part of that experience is in the establishment of a dedicated clubroom.

Meeting Space

To encourage members to use the room, invite students to add to the club page through participation in asynchronous discussion threads (e.g. welcome/introduction thread). For example, some clubs hold logo and slogan design contests that encourage members to take ownership of a part of the club. Once members vote on a slogan and logo, load them into the room and add them to the social media sites. One of the key elements to creating a collaborative experience is to give as much ownership to members as possible. Studies suggest that when members of an online community add something personal to the communal space, they feel a deeper connection to it (Aslanina & Clinfelter, 2012; Zhu, 2012). This is asking to having club members create a mural during a meeting at a traditional university club meeting and hanging it in the meeting space.

In the past ten years, personal mobile devices have undergone such technical transformations that many adults prefer to use them over their personal computers. University students favor mobile devices over laptops because of the advanced ability of mobile phones to act like computers. Many students perceive mobile phone learning to be as effective as traditional computer-based learning, so club rooms should be modified so that mobile devices can easily navigate the site (Iqbal, Khan, & Malik, 2017). Students will be more apt to access the club room to add a comment or idea when those occur to them rather than having to wait until they are logged into the room from a laptop. Mobile devices have revolutionized the way that students interact with virtual spaces. Studies suggest that students raised in the digital age perceive virtual classrooms in the same way as they do traditional ones meaning that to them, a virtual space can feel as intimate and vital as a traditional space does. To them, there is no real difference between "virtual" and "real" environments due to continued enhancements to virtual classroom spaces (Saunders, Rutkowski, van Genuchten, Vogel, & Orrego, 2012). This is an advantage for online clubs that strive to create an active virtual clubroom as it will entice those who favor mobile device use to use it as they would their social media sites- as a tool for communication and learning.

Scheduling Meetings

An important and oft overlooked component is scheduling regular meeting times for the general membership. Most universities now enroll students from across the country and perhaps, even the world. It is difficult to schedule convenient meetings times, which can discourage those who cannot attend from overall participation (Oztok, Zingaro, Brett, & Hewitt, 2013). Of course, surveying students about convenient times helps to narrow the possibilities. Then, members can vote on the specifics from a list of the most popular. Depending on the membership, it might be best to alternate days and times of monthly meetings so that more members could attend, even if occasionally. If the membership is large, to avoid confusion, it is better to hold regular meetings on the same day and time each month. Use Facebook, Instagram, and Snapchat to advertise meetings right up to the start time of the meeting and participation in the meeting will increase. In the case study, the club saw over a 100% increase in meeting participation when a social media blast was instituted a half hour before the start of the meeting. Many students reported that they saw the reminders on their social media (often as pop-up messages) and began to rely on them for meeting reminders.

Shared Commitment

Research suggests that when groups of people share the same goals, there is a greater sense among members of group identification (Yang & Chiu, 2011). Formation of a group identity is critical to fostering group membership and participation. Students who feel as if they are a part of a bigger group report increased desire to support and conform to group norms (Cota, Evans, Dion, Kilik, & Longman, 1995). Therefore, to create a strong group identity, club members and their advisor should create a mission statement and focus activities on that mission. For example, professional student groups often offer opportunities for their members to develop their career specific and overall professional skills. Clubs might offer opportunities for members to present topics at a meeting or provide networking experiences (both virtual and in person). Academic clubs might develop opportunities for members to conduct research studies or participate in webinars hosted by professors.

To create a strong group identity, there should be opportunities for all club members to contribute something towards the overall mission of the club. If meetings are scheduled during times when some members cannot attend, it would be useful to create asynchronous threads in the clubroom that house recordings of the live meetings and related discussions. Members who were unable to attend a live meeting would then still be able to contribute ideas and opinions so that they feel included in the decision-making process. Other asynchronous tools include online survey sites and social media. Use of these tools can remind members of the club's mission, their identity as part of the club, and provide opportunities for members to participate regardless of their schedule.

Student Directed Activities

Successful virtual student clubs can offer a customized experience that those in traditional universities cannot experience unless a virtual club is created for them. Therefore, it is important to use the synchronous and asynchronous tools to create student directed activities. These activities should be varied between long-term continuous and short-term time limited ones.

Some activities that were sponsored by the club mentioned in the case study include long-term continuous activities such as regular club meetings, book club meetings, teach-in events, and committee meetings. Short-term activities included charity drives, networking events, sponsored lectures, and other creative activities that were suggested by members.

Long-term ongoing activities provide opportunities for members to make club participation a regular part of their monthly experience. Besides attending regular club meetings, some members look forward to discussing new ideas with classmates. A popular activity is to sponsor a book club that focuses on the mission of the club. Students meet monthly, read a book chosen by club members and either meet live for a chat and/or discuss aspects of the book on a discussion thread in the club room. Members can access the discussion when it is convenient to them using their mobile device (maybe even the one used to read the book). To enhance the experience, the advisor can post virtual field trip links on the discussion board so that students can learn more about the subject.

Teach-ins or student presentations provide members with the opportunity to teach others about a subject that interests them and matches the club mission. These do not need to be academic subject focused but might be. The key to this activity is that any member of the club may be granted twenty minutes to make a presentation during a teach-in live event. Members of the club provide valuable feedback about the presentation while learning. Faculty members should be invited to events too as both presenters and audience members. It is recommended that these events be held monthly so that members can comfortably add the event to their schedules.

Clubs should offer members the opportunity to work collaboratively in committee settings. Often, members propose ideas for projects and committees develop from those suggestions. Committees can work asynchronously using discussion board threads and email. They can also meet synchronously using third-party rooms such as those offered by Skype and AnyMeeting. Depending on the type of course platform used by the university, there might be a live chat function available in the clubroom too. As with any group work, scheduling convenient meeting times can be challenging. Committee work often fails because of a lack of structured communication system, so members must agree to a communication plan including tools, schedule, and focus of work prior to beginning work.

Some short-term or occasional activities are also suggested for clubs. One such popular activity is the virtual charity drive. Many charities recognize the value of online giving and work with university clubs to create dedicated club "giving pages". These charity drives are very popular with students because it provides a sense of doing a community service project while sitting at their computers. Options include collecting money for a cause related to the club mission or participating in local charity volunteer experiences and logging those hours online. An example of a volunteer drive is for club members from different regions of the country to compete against each other to see who can volunteer the most hours in a month or give the most blood during blood drives. To do this, members report the number of pints of blood donated in that month on an interactive grid (e.g. Google tools) making it a fun challenge to see which region can donate the most in that month. These activities help local communities while building group cohesion in the club.

Each component of the club is important to the continued growth of club participation and pride. Attention to the overall structure of the club can provide students with an enriched experience that promotes interest in both the club mission and use of new technologies. Club members will benefit from the opportunities to learn from each other, direct activities using innovative technologies, and develop leadership skills through active participation. A key to this success is in the creative use of social media to build and strengthen the community. Before endeavoring into social media use, however, it is critical that the advisor and club officers understand the basic principles of secure computing.

1. Members report their level of comfort with the basic tools in the clubroom (discussion board and chat room) and type of internet connection.
2. Members report their level of comfort using more advanced technologies such as Aol or Google Chat, Facebook chat, AnyMeeting or other online meeting room, Skype, or Oovoo. They should also report the equipment that they have and feel comfortable using (e.g. microphone or webcam).

3. Members should provide a schedule of available times for synchronous work.
4. Compare user technology levels, equipment, and time availability of members.
5. Then, write a specific plan for scheduled synchronous and asynchronous activities and specify which technologies will be used.
6. Create a Plan B for any time that a synchronous activity is not fully accessible for all members (e.g. move to the course chat area if Oovoo does not work).

Each component of the club is important to the overall continued growth of the club. Attention to the overall structure of the club can provide students with an enriched experience that promotes interest in both the focus of the club and in using new technologies. Club members will benefit from the opportunities to learn from each other, to direct activities using innovative technologies, and to develop leadership skills through participation of club activities. A key to this success is in the creative use of social media to build and strengthen the club community.

Security Considerations

Before expanding club activities beyond the scope of the university sponsored clubroom, it is important to understand some key legal and security principles. There are laws that protect the privacy of student information. While most clubs will not have to worry about protecting the private information of their members, it is still advisable to understand the applicable laws. Members should be educated on basic security measures too, such as not sharing or downloading documents unless they have first scanned them for viruses.

Family Educational Rights and Privacy Act (FERPA)

The Family Educational Rights and Privacy Act (FERPA) is a federal law that requires all personnel of educational institutions to protect the private information of students. This includes specific demographic information, grades, social security numbers and any other important data related to mental and physical health. However, institutions have permission to publish directories that include student addresses, phone numbers, date of birth, and place of birth. Students must be given the right to opt out of this release of information though. To control the unnecessary access to personal information, university officials prohibit the release of student email addresses or other personal information within the confines of the university. Most universities require faculty and staff to use caution when communicating with students to protect their privacy.

Many universities provide professors have access to their students emails through the course/club room shell. To reduce this potential for problems with unintentional disclosure of personal information, professors are encouraged to use the “bcc” option when sending out club related emails. Students will receive the email but will not have access to other students’ email addresses. Of course, students can opt to share personal email addresses with each other, but the club cannot do it indiscriminately. This level of caution is recommended as it not only protects students from unwanted contact, but also from being victimized by spam email blasts or worse.

Virus Protection

While most computers and mobile devices are sold with virus protection software installed, occasionally viruses elude those protections and infect documents shared by club members. To reduce the potential, students should be reminded to scan all documents before submitting them to the club or before sharing them with other club members in email. If this is not a secure enough option, documents could be sent to a designated member who has the latest online security for scanning. When documents have been scanned and certified as safe, they can be added to the club room in the public file access area. If an infected file is uploaded, it can have a devastating effect when club members download the document and open it on their own computers. Remember that not all students will have updated computers, software, or online security knowledge. Too, many students use a variety of mobile devices that may not be appropriately protected.

If possible, the club should hold periodic training workshops on safe online practices to teach students how to participate in club activities safely. Often, students are not aware of laws or tools designed to protect their privacy and are appreciative of learning about them. The training should include information about FERPA guidelines so that students learn to protect their own data, virus protection, and safe computing practices. Students do not always have time to update their virus protection programs or to consider the safety of submitting a document to a public area, so reminders in those public areas is helpful. Once students understand these safe practices, there is less chance of members accidentally infecting their computers and the club platform.

Monitoring Social Media

Before clubs establish social media accounts, a plan for monitoring use on those sites is advised. Typically, only the faculty advisor and a student life representative will have administrative rights to the account. The content on the account should be closely monitored to ensure proper use. Most universities have hired social media specialists to oversee virtual activities of clubs and departments, but not all have. Social media specialists do not monitor daily use of each site though, so advisors will have to do so. Certain parameters are advisable for preserving the university's reputation, protecting the internal platform from viruses, and monitoring student activities for appropriateness. As with any university sponsored activity, virtual clubs must be closely monitored by student life staff, the club advisor, and student leadership since activity on these sites will be likely throughout the day. Often, universities have policies that dictate the use of third-party sites, especially social media ones. There are too many potential problems with having students administer these sites including frequent turn-over of officers, need for constant monitoring, and careful adherence to FERPA guidelines. Further, personal issues often erupt on social media sites, requiring the intervention of an advisor.

Another suggested policy is to limit club activities to the university-sponsored club room to ensure that actual members participate (instead of those who are not vetted members of the club). Not all club members will want to participate in club activities on social media sites as membership to those sites is required. These policies and procedures should be delineated in the club by-laws of the club's charter and reiterated during training for student leaders and members.

Social Media and Community Building

Faculty advisors and student life representatives can build strong clubs by utilizing social media tools. It is essential to know how to employ these tools to inform, engage, and evaluate club activities. This section proposes activities that clubs can sponsor on social media sites exclusively, in the club shell (housed in the university platform), or a combination of both. Specific activities include instant messages as reminders, mentor programs, retention alerts, polls, asynchronous meetings, and synchronous opportunities for socialization.

Many studies demonstrate that online community building depends on a few important factors (Park & Choi, 2009; Riley, 2008; Book, 2006). Ease of access is consistently cited as being the most important factor in community building since the community exists only when members access it. Club sponsors should periodically evaluate the room and its tools to ensure that members are accessing and utilizing them. Adding announcements with important reminders or information about events can entice students to check the room often. Members who attend sponsored events and who independently use the clubroom resources will encourage other members to participate as well.

Many universities allow their clubs to promote club activities on a Face Book and Snap Chat pages that are often monitored by student life staff. The page can help build a sense of community that most university clubrooms as members post pictures of themselves, ask each other for advice, share ideas, and stories in real time. Since the average age of adults using Facebook and/or Snap Chat falls within the typical online college student range, these are useful tools for community building since many members will already be members. It can also be a crutch, if the club activities gravitate away from the clubroom to Facebook or Snap Chat. Most universities require that university sponsored activities be conducted in the virtual university space. The university needs to monitor the activities for legal reasons. Additionally, not all members of the club will want to participate in Facebook or Snap Chat activities, which would mean that these members would be excluded from club events. Therefore, the best use of Facebook or other social media sites are in building excitement for club activities, and in developing a larger community of members. Used in this manner, social media can be valuable for building community away from the official clubroom.

Another popular social media source is Twitter, which has gained popularity over the last five years as people use it to report real time news. Clubs can use a Twitter account to announce breaking club news such as meeting links and times. Members can easily send links to research articles, breaking news stories, or pictures to other members using Twitter. Clubs can also use these sites to advertise fundraising drives, which reaches a large group of people quickly by retweeting the announcement on various sources.

Other social media tools used by many people may or may not be effective for promoting club activities. For example, Pinterest and Instagram are useful for sharing pictures from club events. These sites are mostly image based as users add their pictures (either originals or ones taken from the web that represent interests) to an individual page. Image based sites are particularly useful to members of art-based clubs who like to meet and solicit suggestions for art projects. Depending on the average age of the members and type of club, other social media sites might be better suited for use as a communication tool for the club. Regardless of the specific social media site, it is important to post the link to those sites in the clubroom so that members can easily find the site link.

Clubs that are business or network oriented might create a club age o LinkedIn or other professional networking sites. These types of sites allow the user to create connections inside of a secure server that are used specifically to find jobs or to connect to people in certain industries. There are many other sites that provide users with one place to stream media from other sources while serving as a networking vehicle. Club members can post information about their work experience and education so that perspective employers can find them. Then, club members can add each other to their network with hopes of creating a large web of connections over time.

Practical Guide for Social Media Tools

This section will present an overview of specific social media tools, technical requirements, considerations of use, and potential obstacles for use. Categories of tools to be presented include quick access tools, platform-based tools, communication/chat tools, and non-university-based clubrooms. Each type of tool will be explained and coupled with suggestions for activities.

Quick Access Tools

Quick access tools include those that deliver a message quickly to a target group of members as a reminder of upcoming events or meetings. Twitter is a social media tool that limits messages to 280 characters making it easy to read quickly. It is available in both standard and mobile format (e.g. smart phones, tablets, and other mobile devices). Even computers that are still using slower connection speeds can download and upload Twitter messages quickly. Another quick access tool is any messenger-based program that is either embedded in email (Google chat) or is a stand-alone application like Whats App. The main providers of the university student email might have an included live chat feature that allows students to chat with each other or in groups. Many younger students prefer to use standalone applications like Whats App or Facebook messenger. The messenger services provide tools for inviting members to join a discussion or to participate in an asynchronous discussion. Members can save discussions and even send them to other members making them valuable for impromptu synchronous and asynchronous meetings.

Another class of social media tools that offer quick access to information and members, are called social media management tools. These tools are designed specifically to aid in monitoring several different social media accounts at once. These programs are free and provide a dashboard to control the flow of information between accounts. A club officer might post a meeting announcement on the Facebook page and use the management tool to also post it on all other social media sites. Club members can use the message scheduling and usage analysis tools to schedule the release of reminders and track access/usage of each media site. The most popular of these programs are Hootsuite, Buffer, Tweetdeck, and SocialOOmph all of which have free levels of use that are appropriate for clubs. Overall, club leaders can use these quick access tools to reach their membership efficiently to remind them of events or meetings.

Platform Based: Web Conferencing

Platform based web conferencing sites are valuable tools for clubs to use when hosting large meetings or events that require webcam, audio, and presentation features. Most universities do not have that capability built into their class sites because of the great expense of these programs. However, there are free sites that provide users with a secure meeting area where discussions with small or large groups can meet to share ideas. Many universities recommend the use of Google chat, which can be accessed by members even if they do not have a Google account. Another option is AnyMeeting which offers a secure meeting area where discussions with small or large groups can meet to share ideas. These platforms are often used by clubs for general membership meetings or other formal events (e.g., career fair). The platform holds many participants who can use microphones and even webcams to communicate with each other. Further, members can share their desktop images, upload documents, and even Power Point presentations.

Examples of free web-conferencing sites include Google chat, AnyMeeting, Zoom, Uberconference, TokBox, and Big Blue Button (specifically for university students). Many universities encourage the use of Google chat and Big Blue Button. Clubs might prefer to use these free rooms as they are easily accessible, support webcam use, and have live presentation tools that are easy to use. Members who would like to speak during meetings need to have basic microphone capabilities and if they do not, some platforms offer a phone-in option (e.g. Google chat). Most smart phones and tablets are compatible with these meeting programs, so students who are unable to be at a computer can phone in or watch from a remote area. Most new devices include built in microphones and cameras that are supported by the listed programs. Overall, students report that they enjoy attending meetings using these platforms because of the interactive experience.

Communication Tools

Often, members do not need use of a full web conferencing site to hold committee meetings, study groups, or casual meetings. For those meetings, members can utilize communication programs that are designed to connect a limited number of people together so that each has speaking capabilities. In the past few years, many families have dropped home phones in favor of cell phones or web-based phones. Powerful communication programs such as Skype, Google chat, and Face Time allow users to connect using audio and/or video on computers, mobile devices, and smartphones. This is particularly useful for committee meetings, especially since the sites offer instant messaging and video recording features that can be used to take notes during the meetings.

If members do not have a working webcam, or have slow internet connections, it might be better to hold meetings using of the many phone conferencing services. A few of these companies offer free voicemail and email notifications for calls (e.g. Google Voice). Some of the most popular conference calling programs are Google Chat, Free Conference Call and Rondee. Most of these companies offer either free basic service or premium service with many options. Clubs that have members who live in different time zones, might benefit from using a teleconferencing service for meetings instead of a web-based one. Some of the services offer an outside conference call line and web-based platform so that members who do not have computer access can still join. Providing multiple levels of access will increase the effectiveness of club meetings.

Third Party Sites: Virtual Clubrooms

If the university cannot supply extra virtual space for a clubroom, one can be developed off-site using several hosting services. Some universities have paid for space on third-party platforms such as Kitley and Second Life. These platforms require members to join the site and customize avatars to represent them in the virtual world. The possibilities for use of this space are endless as many presentation tools can be used inside the site like Power Point presentations. For example, a university sponsored architecture club could build virtual structures in the club space and hold meetings in them. Clubs that have inexperienced users would not benefit from use of these sites as advanced technological knowledge is required to use them properly. Sites like these can create a strong sense of community as members can chat with each other "face to face." These platforms are particularly intriguing to members of university computer clubs.

If virtual reality sites are too difficult for members to access or manipulate, there are companies that offer free limited space for group use. Be cautioned that the amount of space available would not accommodate a larger club. Further, there is no guarantee of privacy for the members or activities. The purpose of these sites is to allow universities to create open source materials for anyone to use. While the key function of these platforms is for offering classes, some of the sites can be used to create a clubroom. Some of the most popular sites are Moodle, RCampus, and Udemy. Members who are not able to access the advanced virtual reality sites will find the open source easy to navigate.

Overall, use of these tools can increase membership, retention, and participation in student run clubs. Most of the tools are free and should be approved by university officials before being implemented. Many universities want to manage the use of social media of official university clubs. Though members might differ in technology knowledge and computing capabilities, they all share a common interest in learning more about their major. Use of clubrooms and social media can bring members together in meaningful ways. The key to success is in knowing how to use available online tools to create collaborative communities.

FUTURE AREAS OF STUDY

Across the world, college students demonstrate interest in increasing their knowledge about professions, hobbies, the arts, and sports. Many studies suggest that the future of online collaborative computing in virtual worlds will expand in popularity as more universities adopt virtual technologies in their course platforms (Akyol, Garrison, & Ozden, 2009). With enhanced technologies, students can utilize tools that are built into these platforms to customize their interactive experience making it easier to collaborate with peers during club activities. While many studies have explored strategies for enhancing the online experience and effectiveness of learning in online environments, few have explored the effectiveness of online environments and college student club participation. The following are suggestions for areas of research that could help university club advisors optimize the club experience for student members.

Three-Dimensional Presence: Avatars

It is possible that universities will create and maintain their own virtual worlds within their formal platform so that students will attend class as avatars. Avatars are three-dimensional representations of the student which he/she can manipulate using a computer keyboard inside of a simulated space like a classroom or laboratory (Mkrttchian, Kataev, Hwang, Bedi, & Fedotova, 2014). Research suggests that students feel connected to virtual spaces more when they adopt an avatar-like body (Peterson, 2011). Avatars provide opportunities for students to interact with learning materials inside of a computer-simulated environment which can seem as stimulating as learning in live classrooms (Petrakou, 2010).

While there are studies of the effect of avatar adoption in learning settings, there has not been much done exploring the use of avatar adoption to strengthen online communities.

Psychological studies suggest that as students create and adopt an avatar for online presence that there is a transference of "self-identity" to the image, regardless of intended activity for the avatar. Through a sense of ownership of the avatar, the student can feel as engaged in an activity (e.g. attending a club meeting) as if he/she was present in person (Scarborough & Bailenson, 2014). Most of these studies either discuss the effectiveness of learning through avatar mediated models or discuss the increase in student use of learning communities (as a measure of desire to use the environment). There are few studies that investigate the potential correlation between use of avatar mediated environments and satisfaction (participation) in university club activities. This is a potential area for further study.

Utilization of Social Media: Enhanced Club Experience

The popularity of virtual student clubs will increase as younger generations comfortable in virtual settings enroll in college courses. Many of these students, often called digital natives, report comfort with learning and engaging in virtual environments likely from their use of social media platforms. Their engagement with these platforms is critical to their overall social development as adolescent socialization patterns have transformed in the past thirty years from primarily face-to-face interactions to primarily virtual ones (Best, Maktelow, & Taylor, 2014). This shift comfort with socializing in virtual spaces can make participation in student clubs can be a natural extension of their social life (which is the purpose of university clubs offered in traditional settings).

Their heavy reliance on social media predicts their adoption of virtual space for learning and club participation (Jacobsen & Forste, 2011). However, more research is required to understand how they will want to use club access as part of their virtual daily life. Adults who attend virtual club meetings now are not, as a group, as technologically savvy as those raised in the digital age. Therefore, a paradigm shift is likely in the next decade as college classes continue to be added to mobile platforms. The popularity of using virtual spaces will continue to increase, however, research is required to understand its most effective application. It is possible that students will be overwhelmed from so much virtual space use that clubs feel like more work instead of a tool. Currently, the focus of most virtual learning research is on the efficacy of learning in virtual spaces and not on the benefits of participation in virtual clubs (Bers & Chau, 2010). It is suggested that future research in the field of virtual club participation explore how students perceive and use virtual club spaces, how that influences retention and learning, and how club sponsors can increase the use of emerging technologies to enhance the club experience.

CONCLUSION

As more digital natives enroll in university courses and online technologies advance, the potential for club engagement in virtual settings is unlimited. Students who grow up using digital technologies as a natural part of their lives will find comfort and benefit in online settings, especially in peer interactions (Thompson, 2013). University clubs exist to stimulate and support student interests by allowing them to create collaborative communities. Students who participate in club activities report feeling better connected to the university and to their classmates. Further, students who participate in virtual clubs demonstrate increased technological and professional skills than their non-participating peers (Stuart, Lido, Morgan, Solomon, & May 2011). A goal of many universities is to establish a brand that promotes an image of learning and community. Members of university clubs often participate in research conferences, artistic performances, and sporting events helping to increase the university's visibility. Therefore, it behooves universities to support the mission and growth of student directed clubs, especially those that meet virtually.

With the continued advancement in social media and online meeting tools, students have many opportunities to develop club activities, fundraisers, and socials. In the past twenty years, online student clubs developed from campus-based ones to standalone ones that reach beyond the traditional campus to provide students with opportunities to network with professionals outside of their communities, to explore research or other cultures (e.g. interact with students in other university clubs), and to continue to develop their technological skills. It is possible that in the next twenty years that students will participate in student clubs in three-dimensional platforms as avatars or holograms (Mkrttchian, et al., 2014). As online technologies continue to advance (e.g. avatars, virtual reality platforms), so do opportunities for rich student experiences (Schubert & Weibert, 2014).

Overall, virtual clubs provide rich, interactive experiences that are always accessible to members. With more universities offering online courses, students will view virtual club membership as a natural extension of their education. Universities will save money by not having to provide evening facilities for club meetings while simultaneously offering a quality club experience to unlimited members. By all accounts, virtual clubs offer faculty members and students an enhanced platform for creating collaborative communities without the traditional hassles of having to coordinate schedules.

REFERENCES

Akyol, Z., Garrison, D. R., & Ozden, M. Y. (2009). Online and blended communities of inquiry: Exploring developmental and perceptional differences. *The International Review of Research in Open and Distributed Learning*, *10*(6), 65–83. doi:10.19173/irrodl.v10i6.765

Allen, I. E., & Seaman, J. (2017). *Distance education enrollment report 2017*. Wellesley, MA: Babson.

Aslanina, C. B., & Clinefelter, D. L. (2012). Online college students 2012: Comprehensive data on demands and preferences. New York, NY: Learning House Online Pub.

Bers, M., & Chau, C. (2010). The virtual campus of the future: Stimulating and simulating civic actions in a virtual world. *Journal of Computing in Higher Education*, *22*(1), 1–23. doi:10.100712528-009-9026-3

Best, P., Manktelow, R., & Taylor, B. (2014). Online communication, social media, and adolescent well-being: A systematic narrative review. *Children and Youth Services Review*, *41*, 27–36. doi:10.1016/j.childyouth.2014.03.001

Cota, A. A., Evans, C. R., Dion, K. L., Kilik, L., & Longman, R. S. (1995). The structure of group cohesion. *Personality and Social Psychology Bulletin*, *21*(6), 572–580. doi:10.1177/0146167295216003

Dede, C., & Barab, S. (2018). Emerging technologies for learning science: A time of rapid advances. *Journal of Science Education and Technology*, *28*(4), 301–304. doi:10.100710956-009-9172-4

Foubert, J. D., & Urbanski, L. A. (2006). Effects of involvement in clubs and organizations on psychosocial development of first-year and senior college students. *NASPA Journal*, *43*(1), 166–182. doi:10.2202/0027-6014.1576

Hoffman, M., Richmond, J., Morrow, J., & Salomone, K. (2003). Investigating sense of belonging in first-year college students. *Journal of College Student Retention*, *4*(3), 227–256. doi:10.2190/DRYC-CXQ9-JQ8V-HT4V

Jacobsen, W. C., & Forste, R. (2011). The wired generation: Academic and social outcomes of electronic media use among university students. *Cyberpsychology, Behavior, and Social Networking*, *14*(5), 115–125. doi:10.1089/cyber.2010.0135 PMID:20961220

Mkrttchian, V., Kataev, M., Hwang, W., Bedi, S. S., & Fedotova, A. (2014). Using plug-avatars "hhh" technology education as service-oriented virtual learning environment in sliding mode. The Handbook of Research on Emerging Priorities and Trends in Distance Education: Communication, Pedagogy, and Technology, 12(1), 1-13.

Oztok, M., Zingaro, D., Brett, C., & Hewitt, J. (2013). Exploring asynchronous and synchronous toll use in online courses. *Computers & Education*, *60*(1), 87–94. doi:10.1016/j.compedu.2012.08.007

Park, J., & Choi, H. J. (2009). Factors influencing adult learner's decision to drop out or persist in online learning. *Journal of Educational Technology & Society*, *12*(4), 207–217.

Peterson, M. (2011). Towards a research agenda for the use of three-dimensional virtual worlds in language learning. *CALICO Journal*, *29*(1), 67–80. doi:10.11139/cj.29.1.67-80

Petrakou, A. (2010). Interaction through avatars: Virtual worlds as a context for online education. *Computers & Education*, *54*(4), 1020–1027. doi:10.1016/j.compedu.2009.10.007

Prakash, A., & Potoski, M. (2007). Collective action through voluntary environmental programs: A club theory perspective. *Policy Studies Journal: the Journal of the Policy Studies Organization*, *35*(4), 23–29. doi:10.1111/j.1541-0072.2007.00247.x

Rambe, P., & Bere, A. (2013). Using mobile messaging to leverage participation and transform pedagogy at a South African University of Technology. *British Journal of Educational Technology*, *44*(4), 36–44. doi:10.1111/bjet.12057

Santhanam, R., Sasidharan, S., & Webster, J. (2008). Using self-regulatory learning to enhance e-learning-based information technology training. *Information Systems Research*, *19*(1), 26–47. doi:10.1287/isre.1070.0141

Saunders, C., Rutkowski, A. F., van Genuchten, M., Vogel, D., & Orrego, J. M. (2012). Virtual space and place: Theory and test. *Management Information Systems Quarterly*, *36*, 1–20.

Scarborough, J. K., & Bailenson, J. N. (2014). Avatar psychology. In M. Grimshaw (Ed.), *The Oxford Handbook of Virtuality* (pp. 129–144). New York, NY: Oxford University Press.

Schubert, K., & Weibert, A. (2014). How the social structure of interculture 'come_IN' computer clubs fosters interactive storytelling. *International Journal of Arts and Technology*, *7*(1), 55–63. doi:10.1504/IJART.2014.058944

Shakeel, I., Khan, M. N., & Malik, I. R. (2017). Mobile phone usage and students' perception towards m-learning: A case of undergraduate students in Pakistan. *International Journal of E-Learning & Distance Education*, *32*(1), 2–17.

Shea, P., & Bidjerano, T. (2010). Learning presence: Towards a self-efficacy, self-regulation, and the development of a communities of inquiry in online and blended environments. *Computers & Education*, *55*(4), 1721–1731. doi:10.1016/j.compedu.2010.07.017

Smith, P. J., Coldwell, J., Smith, S. N., & Murphy, K. L. (2005). Learning through computer-mediated communication: A comparison of Australian and Chinese heritage students. *Innovations in Education & Training International, 42*(2), 123–134. doi:10.1080/14703290500062441

Stewart, B. L., Goodson, C. E., Miertschin, S. L., Norwood, M. L., & Ezell, S. (2013). Online student support services: A case based on quality frameworks. *Journal of Online Learning and Teaching / MERLOT, 9*(2), 1–14.

Stuart, M., Lido, C., Morgan, J., Solomon, L., & May, S. (2011). The impact of engagement with extracurricular activities on the student experience and graduate outcomes for widening participation populations. *Active Learning in Higher Education, 12*(3), 203–215. doi:10.1177/1469787411415081

Thompson, P. (2013). The digital natives as learners: Technology use patterns and approaches to learning. *Computers & Education, 65*, 12–23. doi:10.1016/j.compedu.2012.12.022

van Deursen, A., & van Dijk, J. (2011). Internet skills and the digital divide. *New Media & Society, 13*(6), 893–911. doi:10.1177/1461444810386774

Veerman, A., & Veldhuis-Diermanse, E. (2001). Collaborative learning through computer-mediated communication in academic education. In P. Dillenbourg, A. Eurelings, & K. Hakkarainen (Eds.), *European Perspectives on Computer-Supported Collaborative Learning: Proceedings.*

Wang, Q., Woo, H. L., Quek, C. L., Yang, Y., & Lie, M. (2012). Using Facebook group as a learning management system: An exploratory study. *British Journal of Educational Technology, 43*(3), 428–438. doi:10.1111/j.1467-8535.2011.01195.x

Yang, Z., & Chiu, C. (2011). Goal commitment and alignment of personal goals predict group identification only when goals are shared. *Group Processes & Intergroup Relations, 15*(3), 425–437.

Zhu, C. (2012). Student Satisfaction, Performance, and Knowledge Construction in Online Collaborative Learning. *Journal of Educational Technology & Society, 15*(1), 127–136.

Zhu, C., Valcke, M., & Schellens, T. (2008b). Collaborative learning in a social constructivist e-learning environment: A crosscultural study. *Proceedings of the 13th Annual Conference of the European Learning Styles Information Network*, 617–630.

ADDITIONAL READING

Bugawa, A. M., & Mirzal, A. (2018). The impact of web 2.0 technologies on the learning experience of students in higher education. *International Journal of Web-Based Learning and Teaching Technologies, 13*(3), 1–17. doi:10.4018/IJWLTT.2018070101

Chapman, C., Ramondt, L., & Smiley, G. (2005). Strong community, deep learning: Exploring the link. *Innovations in Education and Teaching International, 42*(3), 217–230. doi:10.1080/01587910500167910

Clem, C., & Junco, R. (2015). The future of technology in education. *Psychology. Technology, and Society*, 514–532.

Lohfink, M. M., & Paulsen, M. B. (2005). Comparing the determinants of persistence for first-generation and continuing-generation students. *Journal of College Student Development*, *46*(4), 409–428. doi:10.1353/csd.2005.0040

Park, J., & Choi, H. J. (2009). Factors influencing adult learner's decision to drop out or persist in online learning. *Journal of Educational Technology & Society*, *12*(4), 207–217.

Renn, K., Ozaki, A., & Casey, C. (2010). Psychosocial and leadership identities among leaders of identity-based organizations. *Journal of Diversity in Higher Education*, *3*(1), 14–26. doi:10.1037/a0018564

Weigel, V. B. (2002). Deep learning for a digital age: Technologies untapped potential to enrich higher education. San Francisco, CA: Jossey-Bass pub.

Yee, N., Bailenson, J. N., Urbanek, M., Chang, F., & Merget, D. (2007). The unbearable likeness of being digital: The persistence of nonverbal social norms in online virtual environments. *Cyberpsychology & Behavior*, *10*(1), 115–121. doi:10.1089/cpb.2006.9984 PMID:17305457

Compilation of References

Abamu, J. (2018). *The number of students taking online courses is quickly rising, but perceptions are changing slowly.* Retrieved from https://www.edsurge.com/amp/news/2018-06-12-the-number-of-students-taking-in-online-courses-is-quickly-rising-but-perceptions-are-changing-slowly

Aboujaoude, E., Savage, M. W., Starcevic, V., & Salame, W. O. (2015). Cyberbullying: Review of an old problem gone viral. *The Journal of Adolescent Health*, *57*(1), 10–18. doi:10.1016/j.jadohealth.2015.04.011 PMID:26095405

Abrams, Z. (2019). Interpersonal Communication in Intracultural CMC. In N. Arnold, & L. Ducate (Eds.), *Engaging language learners through CALL. From theory and research to informed practice*. Sheffield, UK: Equinox Publishing.

Adams, S., Brown, M., Dahlstrom, E., Davies, A., DePaul, K., Diaz, V., & Pomerantz, J. (2018). *NMC Horizon Report: 2018 Higher Education Edition*. Louisville, CO: EDUCAUSE.

Airey, J. (2011). The disciplinary literacy discussion matrix: A heuristic tool for initiating collaboration in higher education. *Across the Disciplines: A Journal of Language, Learning, and Academic Writing*. Retrieved from http://wac.colostate.edu/atd/ clil/airey.cfm

Akcaoglu, M., & Bowman, N. D. (2016). Using instructor-led Facebook groups to enhance students perceptions of course content. *Computers in Human Behavior*, *65*, 582–590. doi:10.1016/j.chb.2016.05.029

Akyol, Z., Garrison, D. R., & Ozden, M. Y. (2009). Online and blended communities of inquiry: Exploring developmental and perceptional differences. *The International Review of Research in Open and Distributed Learning*, *10*(6), 65–83. doi:10.19173/irrodl.v10i6.765

Albers, C. (2008). Improving pedagogy through action learning and scholarship of teaching and learning. *Teaching Sociology*, *36*(1), 79–86. doi:10.1177/0092055X0803600110

Aldrich, H. (2017). *Guidelines for Reducing Implicit Bias in Your Grading.* Retrieved from https://howardaldrich.org/2017/07/guidelines-for-reducing-implicit-bias-in-your-grading/

Allen, E., & Seaman, J. (2017). Digital Learning Compass: Distance Education Enrollment Report 2017: Babson Survey Research Group, e-Literate.

Allen, I. E., & Seaman, J. (2010). *Learning on demand: Online education in the United States, 2009.* Babson Survey Research Group. Retrieved from http://sloanconsortium.org/publications/survey/pdf/learningondemand.pdf

Allen, I., & Seaman, J. (2016). Online report card: Tracking online education in the United States. ERIC Document. ERIC Number: ED572777.

Allen, E., & Seaman, J. (2005). *Growing by degrees: Online education in the United States, 2005.* Boston, MA: The Sloan Consortium.

Allen, I. E., & Seaman, J. (2017). *Distance education enrollment report 2017*. Wellesley, MA: Babson.

Al-Mashaqbeh, I. F. (2015). Social media practice: The challenges of using Facebook in higher education. *Malaysian Journal of Distance Education, 17*(2), 37–50. doi:10.21315/mjde2015.17.2.3

Alvarez-Torres, M. J. (2001). On "chatting" in the foreign language classroom. *The Clearing House: A Journal of Educational Strategies, Issues and Ideas, 74*(6), 313–316. doi:10.1080/00098650109599216

American Nurses Association (ANA). (2011). *American nurses association fact sheet*. Retrieved from www.NursingWorld.org

Angelino, L. M., Williams, F. K., & Natvig, D. (2007). Strategies to engage online students and reduce attrition rates. *The Journal of Educators Online, 4*(2).

Arbaugh, J. B., Cleveland-Innes, M., Diaz, S. R., Garrison, D. R., Ice, P., Richardson, J., & Swan, K. P. (2008). Developing a community of inquiry instrument: Testing a measure of the community of inquiry framework using a multi-institutional sample. *The Internet and Higher Education, 11*(3-4), 133–136. doi:10.1016/j.iheduc.2008.06.003

Arbaugh, J., & Hwang, A. (2006). Does "teaching presence" exist in online MBA courses? *The Internet and Higher Education, 9*(1), 9–21. doi:10.1016/j.iheduc.2005.12.001

Aristotle. (2011, Sept. 27). *Aristotle's Rhetoric*. (L. Honeycutt, Ed.) Retrieved from http://rhetoric.eserver.org/aristotle/index.html

Arnold, N., & Ducate, L. (2015). Contextualized views of practices and competencies in CALL teacher education research. *Language Learning & Technology, 19*(1). Retrieved from http://www.lltjournal.org/item/2880

Aron, A., Aron, N. A., & Smollan, D. (1992). Inclusion of the other in the self scale and the structure of interpersonal closeness. *Journal of Personality and Social Psychology, 63*(4), 596–612. doi:10.1037/0022-3514.63.4.596

Aslanina, C. B., & Clinefelter, D. L. (2012). Online college students 2012: Comprehensive data on demands and preferences. New York, NY: Learning House Online Pub.

Austen, J. (2000). *The collaboration challenge: How nonprofits and business succeed through strategic alliances*. San Francisco, CA: Jossey-Bass.

B'Far, R. (2005). Mobile computing principles: Designing and developing mobile applications with UML and XML. Cambridge, UK: Cambridge University Press.

Bailey, D., & Koney, K. M. (2000). *Strategic alliances among health and human services organizations: From affiliations to consolidations* [ABRIDGED]. Thousand Oaks, CA: Sage. doi:10.4135/9781483328546

Baker, C. (2010). The impact of instructor immediacy and presence for online student affective learning, cognition, and motivation. *The Journal of Educators Online, 7*(1), 1–19. doi:10.9743/JEO.2010.1.2

Baldwin, R. G. (2007). *Academic civility begins in the classroom*. Center For Teaching and Learning. Retrieved from http://teaching.uchicago.edu/;d/pod2/97-98/baldwin.htm

Barab, S. A., Baek, E., Schatz, S., Scheckler, R., & Moore, J. (2008). Illuminating the Braids of Change in a Web-Supported Community: A Design Experiment by Another Name. In A. Kelly, R. Lesh, & J. Baek (Eds.), Handbook of Design Research Methods in Education: Innovations in Science, Technology, Engineering, and Mathematics Learning and Teaching. London, UK: Routledge.

Barab, S. A., Kling, R., & Gray, J. H. (2004). *Designing for virtual communities in the service of learning*. New York, NY: Cambridge University Press. doi:10.1017/CBO9780511805080

Barab, S., & Squire, K. (2004). Design-Based Research: Putting a Stake in the Ground. *Journal of the Learning Sciences*, *13*(1), 1–14. doi:10.120715327809jls1301_1

Barger, K. (2008, July). *Ethnocentrism.* Retrieved from http://www.iupui.edu/~anthkb/ethnocen.htm

Barnes, N., & Lescault, A. (2012). Social media adoption soars as higher-ed experiments and reevaluates its use of new communications tools. Retrieved from http://www.umassd.edu/cmr/studiesandresearch/socialmediaadoptionsoars/

Baron-Nixon, L. (2007). *Connecting non full-time faculty to institutional mission.* Sterling, VA: Stylus.

Bawane, J., & Spencer, J. (2009). Prioritization of online instructor roles: Implications for competency-based teacher education programs. *Distance Education*, *30*(3), 383–397. doi:10.1080/01587910903236536

Beattie, G. (2013). *Our Racist Heart? An exploration of unconscious prejudice in everyday life.* New York, NY: Routledge. doi:10.4324/9780203100912

Beck, M., Bradley, H. B., Cook, L. L., Leasca, J. B., Lampley, T., & Gatti-Petito, J. (2018). A paradigm shift from brick and mortar: Full-time nursing faculty off campus. *Nursing Education Perspectives*, *39*(2), 107–109. doi:10.1097/01.nep.0000000000000211

Bender, T. (2012). *Discussion-based online teaching to enhance student learning: Theory, practice, and assessment.* Sterling, VA: Stylus.

Berge, Z. (2008). Changing instructor's roles in virtual worlds. *Quarterly Review of Distance Education*, *9*(4), 407–414.

Bers, M., & Chau, C. (2010). The virtual campus of the future: Stimulating and simulating civic actions in a virtual world. *Journal of Computing in Higher Education*, *22*(1), 1–23. doi:10.100712528-009-9026-3

Best, P., Manktelow, R., & Taylor, B. (2014). Online communication, social media, and adolescent well-being: A systematic narrative review. *Children and Youth Services Review*, *41*, 27–36. doi:10.1016/j.childyouth.2014.03.001

Betts, K. (2009). Lost in translation: Importance of effective communication in online education. *Online Journal of Distance Learning Administration*, *12*(2).

Biesenbach-Lucas, S. (2007). Students writing email to faculty: An examination of e- politeness among native and non-native speakers of English. *Language Learning & Technology*, *11*(2), 59–81.

Biro, S. C. (2005). *Adjunct faculty perceptions about their preparation, support, and value as online instructors.* (Ed.D. doctoral dissertation). Harrisburg, PA: Widener University. Retrieved from http://proquest.umi.com/pqdweb?did=1317311891&Fmt=7&clientId=65345&RQT=309&VName=PQD

Bloch, J. (2008a). Integrating the computer and internet. In *Technologies in Second Language Composition Classroom.* Ann Arbor, MI: University of Michigan Press.

Bloch, J. (2008b). Issues in using technology in the L2 composition classroom. In *Technologies in Second Language Composition Classroom.* Ann Arbor, MI: University of Michigan Press.

Bova, B., & Kroth, M. (2001). Workplace learning and generation X. *Journal of Workplace Learning*, *13*(2), 57–65. doi:10.1108/13665620110383645

Boyd, D. (2011, Sept. 22). Why Cyberbullying Rhetoric Misses The Mark. *The New York Times.* Retrieved from http://www.nytimes.com/2011/09/23/opinion/why-cyberbullying-rhetoric-misses-the-mark.html?scp=2&sq=cyberbullying&st=cse

Boyd, D. M., & Ellison, N. B. (2008). Social networking sites: Definition, history, and scholarship. *Journal of Computer-Mediated Communication, 13*(1), 210–230. doi:10.1111/j.1083-6101.2007.00393.x

Boyer, R. (2016, July 16). Great colleges to work for 2016. *The Chronicle of Higher Education*. Retrieved from https://www.chronicle.com/specialreport/Great-Colleges-to-Work-For/47

Bradley, L. J., Hendricks, B., Lock, R., Whiting, P., & Parr, G. (2011). Email communications: Issues for mental health counselors. *Journal of Mental Health Counseling, 33*(1), 67–79. doi:10.17744/mehc.33.1.05208025375v03r7

Braxton, J. M. (2004). Addressing faculty and student classroom improprieties. *New Directions for Teaching and Learning*, 89–95.

Brooks, D. J., & Greer, J. G. (2007). Beyond negativity: The effects of incivility on the electorate. *American Journal of Political Science, 51*(1), 1–16. doi:10.1111/j.1540-5907.2007.00233.x

Brosnan, K., & Burgess, R. (2003). Web based continuing professional development - a learning architecture approach. *Journal of Workplace Learning, 15*(1), 24–33. doi:10.1108/13665620310458794

Brownstein, M. (2015, Feb. 26). *Implicit Bias.* Retrieved from https://plato.stanford.edu/entries/implicit-bias/

Burke, K. (1969). *A Rhetoric of Motives. Berkley, CA*: University of California Press.

Burton, L. (2017). *What is unconscious bias in recruitment?* Available at https://www.highspeedtraining.co.uk/hub/types-of-unconscious-bias/

Byrk, A. (2016). Accelerating how we learn to improve. *Educational Researcher, 44*(9), 467–477. doi:10.3102/0013189X15621543

Byrk, A. S., & Schneider, B. (2004). *Trust in schools.* New York, NY: Russell Sage Foundation.

Byron, K. (2008). Carrying too heavy a load? The communication and miscommunication of emotion by email. *Academy of Management Review, 33*(2), 309–327. doi:10.5465/amr.2008.31193163

Cain, J., & Policastri, A. (2011). Using Facebook as an informal learning environment. *American Journal of Pharmaceutical Education, 75*(10), 1–8. doi:10.5688/ajpe7510207 PMID:22345726

Cameron, D. (2000). Small Incivilities. *Critical Quarterly, 42*(2), 127–131. doi:10.1111/1467-8705.00293

Carrington, A. (2012). Padagogy Wheel. Retrieved from www.http://tinyurl.com/padwheel

Carr, S. (2000). As distance education comes of age, the challenge is keeping the students. *The Chronicle of Higher Education, 46*(23), A39–A41.

Carter, H. L., Foulger, T. S., & Ewbank, A. D. (2008). Have you Googled your teacher lately? Teachers' use of social networking sites. *Phi Delta Kappan, 89*(9), 681–685. doi:10.1177/003172170808900916

Cassidy, J. (2006). Me media: How hanging out on the internet became big business. *The New Yorker, 82*(13), 50.

Chan, M. (1996). Racial Diversity in Higher Education: Does a Racially Mixed Student Population Affect Educational Outcomes? (Unpublished doctoral dissertations, University of California, Los Angeles).

Chang, C. K., Chen, G. D., & Li, L. Y. (2006). Constructing a community of practice to improve coursework activity. *Computers & Education, 50*(1), 235–247. doi:10.1016/j.compedu.2006.05.003

Chao, R., Jr. (2009). Understanding the Adult Learners Motivation and Barriers to Learning. Retrieved from https://www.academia.edu/1267765/

Chen, C. C., Jones, K. T., & Xu, S. (2012). The communication methods of today's students. *The CPA Journal*, *82*(11), 66–71.

Chen, J., Belkada, S., & Okamoto, T. (2004). How a Web-based course facilitates acquisition of English for academic purposes. *Language Learning & Technology*, *8*(2).

Chen, Y., Chen, N.-S., & Tsai, C.-C. (2009). The use of online synchronous discussion for web-based professional development for teachers. *Learning with ICT: New Perspectives on Help Seeking and Information Searching*, *53*(4), 1155–1166. doi:10.1016/j.compedu.2009.05.026

Cherry, R. D. (1998). Ethos Versus Persona. *Written Communication, 15*(3), 384. Retrieved from http://link.galegroup.com/apps/doc/A53994287/PPCM?u=nm_a_wnmu&sid=PPCM&xid=4b7a0469

Ching, C. C., & Hursh, A. W. (2014). Peer modeling and innovation adoption among teachers in online professional development. *Computers & Education*, *73*, 72–82. doi:10.1016/j.compedu.2013.12.011

Chinowsky, P. S., & Rojas, E. M. (2003, July). Virtual Teams: Guide to Successful Implementation. *Journal of Management Engineering*, *19*(3), 98–106. doi:10.1061/(ASCE)0742-597X(2003)19:3(98)

Coghlan, M. (2002, September). *Facilitating online learning.* Retrieved from http://users.chariot.net.au/~michaelc/olfc.html

Colliander, J., & Dahlen, M. (2011). Following the fashionable friend: The power of social media weighing publicity effectiveness of blogs versus online magazines. *Journal of Advertising Research*, *51*(3), 313–320. doi:10.2501/JAR-51-1-313-320

Collins, C. (2008, Sept. 15). Looking to the future: Higher education in the metaverse. *Educause Review.* Retrieved from http://www.educause.edu/ero/article/looking-futurehigher-education-metaverse

Conference Board, Corporate Voices for Working Families, The Partnership for 21st Century Skills, and the Society for Human Resource Management. (2006). *Are they ready to work? Employers' perspectives on the basic knowledge and applied skills of new entrants to the 21st century U.S. workforce.* Retrieved from http://www.p21.org/storage/documents/FINAL_REPORT_PDF09-29-06.pdf

Connelly, R. J. (2009). Introducing a Culture of Civility In First Year College Classes. *JGE: The Journal of General Education*, *58*(1), 47–64. doi:10.1353/jge.0.0029

Conner, M. L. (1997-2004). *Andragogy and Pedagogy.* Ageless Learner. Retrieved from http://agelesslearner.com/intros/andragogy.html

Conroy, F. (1990). Learning to be human: Confucian resources for person-centered education. *Persons and Education*, *6*(1), 27–49.

Cooper, C., & Boyd, J. (n.d.). *Schools as Collaborative Learning Communities.* Retrieved at http://www.vision.net.au/~globallearning/pages/lfs/clc_artcle.html

Cooper, L. E., & Booth, B. A. (2011). The adjunct faculty handbook. Thousand Oaks, CA: Sage: eBook Collection. Retrieved from EBSCOhost.

Corporate Voices for Working Families. (2012). *A talent development solution: Exploring business drivers and returns in learn and earn partnerships.* Retrieved from http://corporatevoices.org/system/files/LearnEarn_Report2_web.pdf

Cota, A. A., Evans, C. R., Dion, K. L., Kilik, L., & Longman, R. S. (1995). The structure of group cohesion. *Personality and Social Psychology Bulletin*, *21*(6), 572–580. doi:10.1177/0146167295216003

Coto, M. (2010). *Designing for Change in University Teaching Practices. The case of UNAgora: A community of Practice Approach to Facilitate University Teacher Professional Development in ICT and Project-Oriented Problem Pedagogy.* (Doctoral dissertation). Aalborg Universitet, Institut for Kommunikation, Aalborg, Denmark.

Coto, M. (2014). A Distributed Community of Practice to Facilitate Communication, Collaboration, and Learning among Faculty. In C. N. Stevenson, & J. C. Bauer (Eds.), *Building Online Communities in Higher Education Institutions: Creating Collaborative Experience* (pp. 327–368). doi:10.4018/978-1-4666-5178-4.ch018

Coto, M., & Dirckinck-Holmfeld, L. (2008). Facilitating Communities of Practice in Teacher Professional Development. In *Proceedings of the 6th International Conference on Networked Learning*. Greece: Lancaster University. Retrieved from http://www.networkedlearningconference.org.uk/abstracts/Coto.htm

Craig, A., Goold, A., Coldwell, J., & Mustard, J. (2008). Perceptions of roles and responsibilities in online learning: A case study. *Interdisciplinary Journal of Knowledge & Learning Objects*, *4*, 205–223.

Cranton, P. (2006). Fostering authentic relationships in the transformative classroom. *New Directions for Higher Education*, *109*, 5–14.

Crawford, K. (2008). Continuing professional development in higher education: The academic perspective. *The International Journal for Academic Development*, *13*(2), 141–146. doi:10.1080/13601440802076657

Creswell, W. (1998). *Qualitative inquiry and research design; choosing among five traditions*. Thousand Oaks, CA: Sage.

Crossman, A., & Lee-Kelley, L. (2004). Trust, commitment and team working: The paradox of virtual organizations. *Global Networks*, *4*(4), 375–390. doi:10.1111/j.1471-0374.2004.00099.x

Cruickshank, K., Chen, H., & Warren, S. (2012). Increasing international and domestic student interaction through group work: A case study from the humanities. *Higher Education Research & Development*, *31*(6), 797–810. doi:10.1080/07294360.2012.669748

Cummings, J., & Haas, M. (2012). So many teams, so little time: Time allocation matters in geographically dispersed teams. *Journal of Organizational Behavior*, *33*(3), 316–341. doi:10.1002/job.777

Cummings, L. L., & Bromiley, P. (1996). The Organizational Trust Inventory (OTI): Development and validation. In R. Kramer, & T. Tyler (Eds.), *Trust in organizations* (pp. 302–330). Thousand Oaks, CA: Sage. doi:10.4135/9781452243610.n15

Cushman, E. (2008). Toward a rhetoric of self-representation: Identity politics in Indian country and rhetoric and composition. *College Composition and Communication*, *60*(2), 321–365.

Dabney, J. (2008). *Show me that you care: the presence of relational trust between a principal and teachers in an urban school*. Columbus, OH: Ohio State University.

Dahlstrom, E. (2012). *ECAR study of undergraduate students and Information technology, 2012*. Retrieved from http://net.educause.edu/ir/library/pdf/ERS1208/ERS1208.pdf

Darling-Hammond, L., & Austin, K. (n.d.). *Session 11: Lessons for life: Learning and transfer.* Retrieved from http://www.learner.org/courses/learningclassroom/support/11_learning_transfer.pdf

De Felice, D. (2013). *A phenomenological study of teaching endangered languages online: Perspectives from Nahua and Mayan educators*. Retrieved from ProQuest Dissertations and Theses. (1317032973)

De Felice, D. (2012). Nahuatl as a classical, foreign, and additional language: A phenomenological study. *Qualitative Report*, *7*(78), 1–23. Retrieved from http://www.nova.edu/ssss/QR/QR17/defelice.pdf

Debiec, P. (2018). Effective learner-centered approach for teaching an introductory digital systems course. *IEEE Transactions on Education*, *61*(1), 38–45. doi:10.1109/te.2017.2729498

Debucquoy-Dodley, D. (2011, Sept. 27). *New York looks to 'modernize' cyberbullying laws*. Retrieved from http://www.cnn.com/2011/09/27/politics/new-york-cyberbullying/index.html

Decker, J. C., Beltran, V., Matzaganian, M., Walker, N. T., & Elzarka, S. (2014). Creating a collaborative community in online environments. In C. N. Stevenson, & J. C. Bauer (Eds.), *Building online communities in higher education institutions* (pp. 369–387). Hershey, PA: IGI Global. doi:10.4018/978-1-4666-5178-4.ch019

Dede, C., & Barab, S. (2018). Emerging technologies for learning science: A time of rapid advances. *Journal of Science Education and Technology*, *28*(4), 301–304. doi:10.100710956-009-9172-4

Dennen, V., Darabi, A., & Smith, L. (2007). Instructor-learner interaction in online courses: The relative perceived importance of particular instructor actions on performance and satisfaction. *Distance Education*, *28*(1), 65–79. doi:10.1080/01587910701305319

Denning, P. (1993). A World Lit By Flame. *Communications of the ACM*, *36*(12), 170. doi:10.1145/163298.163353

Derver, M. (2016). Four drivers to enhance global virtual teams. *Industrial and Commercial Training*, *48*(1), 1–8. doi:10.1108/ICT-08-2015-0056

Design-Based Research Collective. (2003). Design-Based Research: An Emerging Paradigm for Educational Inquiry. *Educational Researcher*, *32*(1), 5–8. doi:10.3102/0013189X032001005

Dewey, J. (1916). *Democracy and education*. London, UK: MacMillan.

Dickey, M. (2004). The impact of web-logs (blogs) on student perceptions of isolation and alienation in a web-based distance-learning environment. *Open Learning*, *19*(3), 279–291. doi:10.1080/0268051042000280138

Dickinson, A. (2017). Communicating with the online student: The impact of email tone on student performance and teacher evaluations. *The Journal of Online Educators*, *14*(2), 1–10.

Dietz-Uhler, B., Fisher, A., & Han, A. (2008). Designing online courses to promote student retention. *Journal of Educational Technology Systems*, *36*(1), 105–112. doi:10.2190/ET.36.1.g

Dirckinck-Holmfeld, L., Jones, C., & Lindström, B. (2009). Analysing Networked Learning Practices in Higher Education and Continuing Professional Development. Rotterdam, The Netherlands: Sense Publishers.

Diversity & Social Justice Teaching Guide Website. (2014). *Understanding and Overcoming Implicit Bias in Higher Education*. Retrieved from https://www.youtube.com/watch?v=FW0XLnvFvgo

Diversity Abroad. (2016). *Unconscious bias in study abroad?* Retrieved from https://www.diversitynetwork.org/blog-post/1437725/253300/Unconscious-Bias-in-Education-Abroad

Doctors explain why teens bully, offer advice . (2011, Dec. 6). Retrieved from http://drdrew.blogs.cnn.com/2011/12/06/doctors-explain-why-teens-bully-offer-advice/

Donathan, L. N., Dotson, A. T., & Hanks, M. (2017). Minimizing incivility in the online classroom. *Radiologic Technology*, *89*(1), 88–91. PMID:28904163

Donegan, R. (2012). Bullying and cyberbullying: History, statistics, law, prevention and analysis. *The Elon Journal of Undergraduate Research in Communications*, *3*(1), 33–42.

Doran, G. T. (1981). There's a S.M.A.R.T. way to write management's goals and objectives. *Management Review*, *70*(11), 35–36.

Drouin, M. (2008). The relationship between students' perceived sense of community and satisfaction, achievement, and retention in an online course. *Quarterly Review of Distance Education*, *9*(3), 267–284.

Ducate, L. C., & Lomicka, L. L. (2008). Adventures in the blogosphere: From blog readers to blog writers. *Computer Assisted Language Learning*, *21*(1).

DuFour, R., & Eaker, R. (1998). *Professional Learning communities at work: Best practices for enhancing student achievement*. Alexandria, VA: Association for Supervision and Curriculum Development.

DuFour, R., Eaker, R., & Eaker, R. (2005). *On common ground: The power of Professional Learning Communities*. Bloomington, IN: Solution Tree.

Duggan, M., & Brenner, J. (2012). *The demographics of social media users-2012*. Retrieved from http://pewinternet.org/~/media//Files/Reports/2013/ PIP_SocialMediaUsers.pdf

Dumford, A. D., & Miller, A. L. (2018). Online learning in higher education: Exploring advantages and disadvantages for engagement. *Journal of Computing in Higher Education*, *30*(3), 452–465.

Durnford, V. (2010). *An examination of teacher-student trust in middle school classrooms*. Amherst, MA: University of Massachusetts.

Durrington, V. A., Berryhill, A., & Swafford, J. (2006). Strategies for enhancing student interactivity in an online environment. *College Teaching*, *54*(1), 190–193. doi:10.3200/CTCH.54.1.190-193

Duryea, E. D. (2000). Evolution of the university. In M. C. Brown (Ed.), *Organization and governance in higher education* (5th ed.). Boston, MA: Pearson Custom Publishing.

Dwyer, C. (2018). *12 Common Biases that affect how we make everyday decisions*. Retrieved from https://www.psychologytoday.com/us/blog/thoughts-thinking/201809/12-common-biases-affect-how-we-make-everyday-decisions

Dymock, D. (2007). *Engaging Adult Learners*. Canberra, Australia: Adult Learning Australia.

Ede, L., & Lunsford, A. (1984). Audience addressed/Audience invoked. In V. Villanueva (Ed.), *Cross talk in comp theory: A reader* (2nd ed., pp. 77–95). Urbana, IL: NCTE.

Education Testing Services. (n.d.). *ICT literacy assessment: Information and communication technology*. Retrieved from http://www.ncahlc.org/download/annualmeeting/05Handouts/GSUN0145k_Egan.pdf

Eib, B. J. (2002). Online learning and professional development. *Principal Leadership*, *3*, 61–64.

Eisner, E. W. (1991). *The enlightened eye: Qualitative inquiry and the enhancement of educational practice*. New York, NY: Macmillan Publishing Company.

Engeström, Y. (1987). *Learning by Expanding - an activity theoretical approach to developmental research*. Helsinki, Finland: Orienta-konsultit. Retrieved from http://communication.ucsd.edu/MCA/Paper/Engestrom/expanding/toc.htm

Engeström, Y. (2001). Expansive Learning at Work: Toward an activity theoretical reconceptualization. *Journal of Education and Work*, *14*(1), 133–156. doi:10.1080/13639080020028747

Engeström, Y. (2014). *Learning by expanding*. Cambridge, UK: Cambridge University Press. doi:10.1017/CBO9781139814744

Estus, E. L. (2010). Using Facebook within a geriatric pharmacotherapy course. *American Journal of Pharmaceutical Education, 74*(8), 145. doi:10.5688/aj7408145 PMID:21179256

Everett, M. R., & Kincaid, L. D. (1982). Communication networks: Towards a new paradigm for research. *Social Forces, 61*(1), 325–327. doi:10.2307/2578109

Faculty Focus. (2011). *Social media usage trends among higher education faculty*. Retrieved from http://www.facultyfocus.com/free-reports/social-media-usage-trends-among-higher education-faculty/

Falls, I., Bahhouth, V., Chuang, C. M., & Bahhouth, J. (2014). Factors influencing students' perceptions of online teamwork. *SAGE Open*, 1–9. doi:10.1177/2158244014525415

Farnham, A. (2014). Fighting telemarketers: When do-not-call list fails, these strategies work, *ABC News*, Jan. 21. Retrieved from http:// abcnews.go.com/Business/best-ways-turn-tables-telemarketers/story?id=21534413; and www.donotcall.gov

Felder, R. M., & Brent, R. (2001). Effective strategies for cooperative learning. *Cooperation & Collaboration in College Teaching, 19*(2), 69–75.

Ferguson, S. (2014). *Privilege 101: A Quick and Dirty Guide.* Retrieved from https://everydayfeminism.com/2014/09/what-is-privilege/

Ferrazzi, K. (2012). Candor, criticism and teamwork. *Harvard Business Review*. Retrieved from http://hbr.org/2012/01/candor-criticism-teamwork/ar/1

Ferrazzi, K. (2014). Getting virtual team right. *Harvard Business Review*. Retrieved from https://hbr.org/2014/12/getting-virtual-teams-right

Fonseca, J. W., & Bird, C. P. (2007, October). Under the radar: Branch campuses take off. *University Business Solutions for Higher Education Management.* Retrieved from http://www.universitybusiness.com/article/under-radar-branch-campuses-take

Foral, P. A., Turner, P. D., Monaghan, M. S., Walters, R. W., Merkel, J. J., Lipschultz, J. H., & Lenz, T. L. (2010). Faculty and student expectations and perceptions of email communication in a campus and distance doctor of pharmacy program. *American Journal of Pharmaceutical Education, 74*(10), 10. doi:10.5688/aj7410191 PMID:21436932

Fortenbaugh, W. W. (1992). Aristotle on Persuasion through Character. *Rhetorica, 10*(3), 220. doi:10.1525/rh.1992.10.3.207

Fotouhi-Ghazvini, F., Earnshaw, R. A., & Haji-Esmaeili, L. (2009, September). Mobile assisted language learning in a developing country context. In *2009 International Conference on CyberWorlds* (pp. 391-397), Bradford, UK. Piscataway, NJ: IEEE. 10.1109/CW.2009.28

Foubert, J. D., & Urbanski, L. A. (2006). Effects of involvement in clubs and organizations on psychosocial development of first-year and senior college students. *NASPA Journal, 43*(1), 166–182. doi:10.2202/0027-6014.1576

FoxNews.com. (2012, Jan. 17). *Supreme Court declines to take up cases involving online attacks by students on school officials, other students.* Retrieved from http://www.foxnews.com/politics/2012/01/17/us-supreme-court-passes-on-rulings-for-cases-involving-online-attacks-by/

Freire, P. (2011). *Pedagogy of the oppressed* (M. B. Ramos, Trans.). New York, NY: Continuum. (Original work published 1968)

Frontier, T. (2012, June 15). *Windows on intelligence*. Presented at Summer Institute 2012 of Cardinal Stritch University, Milwaukee, WI.

Gajda, R. (2004). Utilizing collaboration theory to evaluate strategic alliances. *The American Journal of Evaluation, 25*(1), 65–77. doi:10.1177/109821400402500105

Galanek, J., Gierdowski, D. C., & Brooks, D. C. (2018). *ECAR Study of Undergraduate Students and Information Technology, 2018.* Retrieved from https://library.educause.edu/ resources/2018/10/2018-students-and-technology-research-study

Galbraith, D., & Mondal, S. (2018). The road to graduation: On-line or classroom. *Research in Higher Education*, 35.

Gallant, G. (2000). Professional development for Web-based teaching: Overcoming innocence and resistance. In E. J. Burge (Ed.), *New directions for adult and continuing education* (pp. 69–78). San Francisco, CA: Jossey-Bass. doi:10.1002/ace.8807

Gamie, S. (2017). Ethos Construction, Identification, and Authenticity in the Discourse of AWSA: The Arab Women's Solidarity Association International. In M. Folk, & S. Apostel (Eds.), *Establishing and Evaluating Digital Ethos and Online Credibility* (pp. 163–189). Hershey, PA: IGI Global. doi:10.4018/978-1-5225-1072-7.ch009

Garrison, D. R., Anderson, T., & Archer, W. (2000). Critical inquiry in a text-based environment: Computer conferencing in higher education. *The Internet and Higher Education, 2*(2-3), 87–105. doi:10.1016/S1096-7516(00)00016-6

Garrison, D. R., Anderson, T., & Archer, W. (2010). The first decade of inquiry framework: A retrospective. *Internet and Higher Education, 13*(1-2), 5–9. doi:10.1016/j.iheduc.2009.10.003

Garrison, D. R., Cleveland-Innes, M., & Fung, T. (2004). Student role adjustment in online communities of inquiry: Model and instrument validation. *Journal of Asynchronous Learning Networks, 8*(2), 61–74.

Gaytan, J., & McEwen, B. (2007). Effective online instructional and assessment strategies. *American Journal of Distance Education, 21*(3), 117–132. doi:10.1080/08923640701341653

Giang, V. (2015). *The growing business of detecting unconscious bias.* Retrieved from https://www.fastcompany.com/3045899/the-growing-business-of-detecting-unconscious-bias

Gibbs, G., & Coffey, M. (2004). The impact of training on university teachers on their teaching skills, their approach to teaching and the approach to learning of their students, 5 (1) 87-100. *Active Learning in Higher Education, 5*, 87–100. doi:10.1177/1469787404040463

Gibson, S. G., Harris, M. L., & Colaric, S. M. (2008). Technology acceptance in an academic context: Faculty acceptance of online education. *Journal of Education for Business, 83*(6), 355–359. doi:10.3200/JOEB.83.6.355-359

Glater, J. (2006, Feb. 21). To: Professor@University.edu Subject: Why it's all about me. *New York Times*. Retrieved from http://www.nytimes.com/2006/02/21/education/21professors.html?_r=1&oref=slo gin.

Glendinning, M. (2006). Email: Boon or bane for school leaders? *Phi Delta Kappan, 88*(1), 83–86. doi:10.1177/003172170608800115

Godwin-Jones, R. (2005). Emerging technologies: Messaging, gaming, peer-to-peer sharing: Language learning strategies & Tools for the millennial generation. *Language Learning & Technology, 9*(1), 17–22.

Goldback, E. (2017). *Diversity Toolkit: A Guide to Discussing Identity, Power, and Privilege.* University of Southern California's Suzanne Dworak-Peck School of Social Work. Available at https://msw.usc.edu/mswusc-blog/diversity-workshop-guide-to-discussing-identity-power-and-privilege/#icebreaker

Goleman, D. (1995). *Emotional Intelligence Why It Can Matter More Than IQ.* New York, NY: Bantam Books.

González, G., & Skultety, L. (2018). Teacher learning in a combined professional development intervention. *Teaching and Teacher Education, 71*, 341–354. doi:10.1016/j.tate.2018.02.003

Gonzalez, V., & Lopez, E. (2001). The age of incivility: Countering disruptive behavior. *AAHE Bulletin, 55*(8), 3–6.

Goodyear, P. Jones, C., Asensio, M., Hodgson, V., & Steeples, C. (2001). Effective networked learning in higher education: notes and guidelines. Lancaster, UK: Centre for Studies in Advanced Learning Technology. Lancaster University.

Goold, A., Augar, N., & Farmer, J. (2006). Virtual teams: Exploring the student experience. *Journal of Information Technology Education, 5*, 477–490. doi:10.28945/260

Grannan, C. (2019). *What's the difference between emoji and emoticons?* Retrieved from www.britannica.com

Granovetter, M. (1983). *The strength of weak ties: A network theory revisited.*

Green, N. C., Edwards, H., Wolodko, B., Stewart, C., Brooks, M., & Littledyke, R. (2010). Reconceptualising higher education pedagogy in online learning. *Distance Education, 31*(3), 257–273. doi:10.1080/01587919.2010.513951

Gullo, G., & Beachum, F. (2017). *The negative effects of implicit bias in schools.* Retrieved from https://whyy.org/articles/essay-the-negative-effects-of-implicit-bias-in-schools/

Gupta, N. (2012). Email etiquettes: Dos and dont's. *The IUP Journal of Soft Skills, 6*(1), 29–37.

Gurley, L. E. (2018). Educators' preparation to teach, perceived teaching presence, and perceived teaching presence behaviors in blended and online learning environments. *Online Learning, 22*(2), 197–220. doi:10.24059/olj.v22i2.1255

Guzdial, M., & Turns, J. (2000). Effective discussion though a computer-mediated anchored forum. *Journal of the Learning Sciences, 9*(4), 437–469. doi:10.1207/S15327809JLS0904_3

Hackman, J. R. (2012). From causes to conditions in group research. *Journal of Organizational Behavior, 33*(3), 428–444. doi:10.1002/job.1774

Hadar, L., & Brody, D. (2010). From isolation to symphonic harmony: Building a professional development community among teacher educators. *Teaching and Teacher Education, 26*(8), 1641–1651. doi:10.1016/j.tate.2010.06.015

Hambacher, E., Ginn, K., & Slater, K. (2018). From serial monologue to deep dialogue: Designing online discussions to facilitate student learning in teacher education courses. *Action in Teacher Education*, 1–14. doi:10.1080/01626620.2018.1486753

Hampton, K., Goulet, L., Rainie, L., & Purcell, K. (2011). *Social networking sites and our lives: How people's trust, personal relationships, and civic and political involvement are connected to their use of social networking sites and other technologies.* Retrieved from http://pewinternet.org/Reports/2011/Technology-and-social-networks.aspx

Han, S. Y., & Hill, J. R. (2007). Collaborate to learn, learn to collaborate: Examining the roles of context, community, and cognition in asynchronous discussion. *Journal of Educational Computing Research, 36*(1), 89–123. doi:10.2190/A138-6K63-7432-HL10

Hardeman, K. T. (2010). *Students and communication competence: A call to professors for establishing appropriate communication boundaries.* Retrieved from http://www.unco.edu/ae-extra/2010/2/hardeman.html

Harrington, S., & Floyd, K. (2009). *Enhancing engagement and the value of the course to the student through course organization and active learning.* Online Classroom.

Harris, R. (2012). *Introduction to creative thinking.* Retrieved from http://www.virtualsalt.com/crebook1.htm

Harrison, T. (2015). Virtuous reality: moral theory and research into cyber-bullying. *Ethics and Information Technology, 17*(4), 275–283. Retrieved from https://link.springer.com/article/10.1007%2Fs10676-015-9382-9

Heath, C., & Heath, D. (2017). *The power of moments: Why certain experiences have extraordinary impact*. New York, NY: Simon and Schuster.

Hendrix, K. (2007). "She must be trippin": The secret of disrespect from students of Color toward faculty of Color. *New Directions for Teaching and Learning*, *110*(110), 85–96. doi:10.1002/tl.277

Henttonen, K., & Blomqvist, K. (2005). Managing distance in a global virtual team: The evolution of trust through technology-mediated relational communication. *Strategic Change*, *14*(2), 107–119. doi:10.1002/jsc.714

Hepburn, A. (2010, March 22). Facebook: Facts and figures for 2010 [Web log post]. *Digital Buzz*. Retrieved from http://digitalbuzzblog.com/facebook-facts-figures-2010

Hepburn, A. (2011, Jan. 18). Facebook statistics: Stats and facts for 2011 [Web log post]. *Digital Buzz*. Retrieved from http://digitalbuzzblog.com/facebook-statistics-stats-facts-2011

Hetland, H., Skogstad, A., Hetland, J., & Mikkelsen, A. (2011). Leadership and learning climate in a work setting. *European Psychologist*, *16*(3), 163–176. doi:10.1027/1016-9040/a000037

Hill, C. (n.d.). *Why So Few? Women in Science, Technology, Engineering, and Mathematics*. Retrieved from https://www.aauw.org/research/why-so-few/

Hipp, K. K., & Huffman, J. B. (2010). *Demystifying professional learning communities: School leadership at its best*. Lanham, MD: Rowan & Littlefield Education.

Hirsh, A. (2017). How to use technology to support remote teams. Society for Human Resource Management. Retrieved from https://www.shrm.org/hr-today/news/hr-magazine/1017/pages/how-to-use-technology-to-support-remote-teams.aspx

Hoang, H. (2009). Campus racial politics and a "rhetoric of injury.". *College Composition and Communication*, *61*(1), 188.

Hoffman, M., Richmond, J., Morrow, J., & Salomone, K. (2003). Investigating sense of belonging in first-year college students. *Journal of College Student Retention*, *4*(3), 227–256. doi:10.2190/DRYC-CXQ9-JQ8V-HT4V

Hogarth, H. (n.d.). Students at a lecture. *Hogarth's Graphic Works*. London, UK: Heath Edition.

Hooks, B. (1994). *Teaching to transgress: Education as the practice of freedom*. New York, NY: Routledge.

Houser, C., & Lemmons, K. (2018). Implicit bias in letters of recommendation for an undergraduate research internship. *Journal of Further and Higher Education*, *42*(5), 585–595. doi:10.1080/0309877X.2017.1301410

Howard, G. T. (2010). *Dictionary of rhetorical terms*. Bloomington, IN: Xlibrus Publishing.

Hoy, W. K., & Tschannen-Moran, M. (2003). The conceptualization and measurement of faculty trust in schools: The omnibus T-Scale. In W. K. Hoy, & C. G. Miskel (Eds.), *Studies in Leading and Organizing Schools* (pp. 181–208). Greenwich, CT: Information Age Publishing.

Huang, X., & Hsiao, E. (2012). Synchronous and asynchronous communication in an online environment: Faculty experiences and perceptions. *Quarterly Review of Distance Education*, *13*(1), 15–30.

Hyde, M. J. (2004). *The Ethos of Rhetoric*. Columbia, SC: University of South Carolina Press.

Ice, P., Curtis, R., Phillips, P., & Wells, J. (2007). Using asynchronous audio feedback to enhance teaching presence and students' sense of community. *Journal of Asynchronous Learning Networks*, *11*(2), 3–25.

Institute for Healthcare Improvement. (2017). *How to Reduce Implicit Bias*. Retrieved from http://www.ihi.org/communities/blogs/how-to-reduce-implicit-bias

Institute for Learning Styles Research. (1996). *Overview of the seven perceptual styles*. Retrieved from http://www.learningstyles.org/index.html

Ioannou, A., & Stylianou-Georgiou, A. (2012). Mashing-up wikis and forums: A case study of collaborative problem-based activity. *Educational Media International*, *49*(4), 303–316. doi:10.1080/09523987.2012.741201

Irvine, J. J. (2009). Culturally relevant pedagogy. *Teaching Tolerance*, 57–61.

IWG. (2018). Retrieved from https://www.cnbc.com/2018/05/30/70-percent-of-people-globally-work-remotely-at-least-once-a-week-iwg-study.html

Jacobsen, W. C., & Forste, R. (2011). The wired generation: Academic and social outcomes of electronic media use among university students. *Cyberpsychology, Behavior, and Social Networking*, *14*(5), 115–125. doi:10.1089/cyber.2010.0135 PMID:20961220

Jarvenpaa, S., & Leidner, D. (1999). Communication and trust in global virtual teams. *Organization Science*, *10*(6), 791–815. doi:10.1287/orsc.10.6.791

Johnson, D. W., & Johnson, R. (1989). *Cooperation and competition: Theory and research*. Edina, MN: Interaction Book Company.

Johnson, D. W., & Johnson, R. T. (2008). Cooperation and the use of technology. In J. M. Spector, M. D. Merrill, J. V. Merrienboer, & M. P. Driscoll (Eds.), *Handbook of research on educational communications and technology* (pp. 401–418). New York, NY: Routledge.

Jones, A., & Issroff, K. (2005). Learning technologies: Affective and social issues in computer-supported collaborative learning. *Computers & Education*, *44*(4), 395–408. doi:10.1016/j.compedu.2004.04.004

Kagan, S. (2001). *Kagan structures: Research and rationale. Kagan Online Magazine*.

Kaptelinin, V., & Nardi, A. B. (2006). Acting with Technology: Activity Theory and Interaction Design. In First Monday, 12, p. 345). doi:10.5210/fm.v12i4.1772

Kárpáti, A. (2009). Web 2 technologies for net native language learners: A "social CALL". *ReCALL*, *21*(2), 139–156. doi:10.1017/S0958344009000160

Kasturi, S. K., & Vardhan, P. B. (2014). Social media: Key issues and new challenges - A study of Nalgonda district, *Global Media Journal*, *Summer Issue*, *5*(1), 1–12.

Keil, M., & Johnson, R. D. (2002). Feedback channels: Using social presence theory to compare voice mail to email. *Journal of Information Systems Education*, *13*(4), 295–302.

Kendall, D., Murray, J., & Linden, R. (2000). *Sociology in our times* (2nd ed.). Scarborough, Canada: Nelson.

Kerr, C. (1963). *The uses of the university*. Cambridge, MA: Harvard University Press.

Kezar, A., & Lester, J. (2009). *Organizing higher education for collaboration*. San Francisco, CA: Jossey-Bass.

Kiffin-Petersen, S. A. (2004). Trust: A neglected variable in team effectiveness research. *Journal of the Australian and New Zealand Academy of Management*, *10*(1), 38–53.

Killick, D. (2018). Critical intercultural practice: Learning in and for a multicultural globalizing world. *Journal of International Studies*, *8*(3), 1422–1439.

Killion, J. (2000). Logon to learn: To reap benefits of online staff development, ask the right questions. *Journal of Staff Development*, 48–53.

King, K. (2005). *Bringing transformative learning to life*. Malabar, FL: Krieger.

King, K. P. (2003). Learning the New Technologies: Strategies for Success. *New Directions for Adult and Continuing Education, 98*(98), 49–57. doi:10.1002/ace.99

King, M. L. Jr, & Washington, J. M. (1986). *A testament of hope: The essential writings and speeches of Martin Luther King, Jr*. New York, NY: Harper Collins.

Kirkman, B. L., & Mathieu, J. E. (2005). The dimensions and antecedents of team virtuality. *Journal of Management, 31*(5), 700–718. doi:10.1177/0149206305279113

Kirkup, G. (2002). Identity, community and distributed learning. In M. R. Lear, & K. Nicholl (Eds.), *Distributed learning: Social and cultural approaches to practice* (pp. 182–195). London, UK: Routledge-Falmer.

Kirwan Institute for the Study of Race and Ethnicity. (2012). *Implicit Racial Bias: Implications for Education and Other Critical Opportunity Domains*. A Presentation to the National Association for the Education of African American Children with Learning Disabilities. Retrieved from http://kirwaninstitute.osu.edu/docs/AACLD_implicit_bias_and_education.pdf

Kirwan Institute for the Study of Race and Ethnicity. (2015). *Understanding Implicit Bias*. Retrieved from http://kirwaninstitute.osu.edu/research/understanding-implicit-bias/

Knowles, M. (1984). *The Adult Learner: A Neglected Species* (3rd ed.). Houston, TX: Gulf Publishing.

Knowles, M. S. (1975). *Self-directed learning*. Chicago, IL: Follet.

Knowles, M. S. (1980). *The modern practice of adult education: From pedagogy to andragogy. Englewood Cliffs*. Cambridge, UK: Prentice Hall.

Koole, M. (2014). Identity and the itinerant online learner. *International Review of Research in Open and Distance Learning, 15*(6), 52–70. doi:10.19173/irrodl.v15i6.1879

Kotler, P., & Armstrong, G. (2016). *Principles of marketing, 16th Global Edition*. San Francisco, CA: Pearson Publication.

Kozar, O. (2012). Towards better group work: Seeing the difference between cooperation and collaboration. *English Teacher Forum, 2*. Retrieved from http://exchanges.state.gov/englishteaching/forum/archives/docs/files-folder111111/48_2-etf-towards-better-group-work-seeing-the-difference-between-cooperation-and-collaboration.pdf

Kruger, J., Epley, N., Parker, J., & Ng, Z. (2005). Egocentrism over email: Can we communicate as well as we think? *Journal of Personality and Social Psychology, 89*(6), 925–936. doi:10.1037/0022-3514.89.6.925 PMID:16393025

Kumar, S., & Ritzhaupt, A. D. (2014). Adapting the Community of Inquiry survey for an online graduate program: Implications for online programs. *E-Learning and Digital Media, 11*(1), 59–71. doi:10.2304/elea.2014.11.1.59

Kunz, M. B., & Hackworth, B. A. (2011). Are consumers following retailers to social networks. *Academy of Marketing Studies Journal, 15*(1), 1–23.

Kupritz, V., & Cowell, E. (2011). Productive management communication: Online and face-to-face. *Journal of Business Communication, 48*(1), 54–82. doi:10.1177/0021943610385656

Ladson-Billings, G. (2001). *Crossing over to Canaan*. San Francisco, CA: Jossey-Bass.

Laffey, J., Lin, G., & Lin, Y. (2006). Assessing social ability in online learning environments. *Journal of Interactive Research, 17*(2), 157–165.

Lampe, C., Ellison, N., & Steinfeld, C. (2006). In P. Hinds, & D. Martin (Eds.), A Face(book) in the crowd: Social searching vs. social browsing. *Proceedings of the 2006 20th anniversary conference on Computer supported cooperative work* (pp. 167-170). New York, NY: Association for Computing Machinery.

Lampman, C., Bancroft, S., & Beneke, M. (2009). Contrapower Harassment in Academia: A Survey of Faculty Experience with Student Incivility, Bullying and Sexual attention. *Sex Roles*, *60*(5/6), 331–346. doi:10.100711199-008-9560-x

Langhorst, E. (2009). You are here. No budget for travel? Try video chat. *School Library Journal*, *55*(6).

Lanius, C. (2017). Telling the Quants from the Quacks: Evaluating Statistical Arguments in Debates Online. In M. Folk, & S. Apostel (Eds.), *Establishing and Evaluating Digital Ethos and Online Credibility* (pp. 1–21). Hershey, PA: IGI Global. doi:10.4018/978-1-5225-1072-7.ch001

Lantz-Andersson, A., Lundin, M., & Selwyn, N. (2018). Twenty years of online teacher communities: A systematic review of formally-organized and informally-developed professional learning groups. *Teaching and Teacher Education*, *75*, 302–315. doi:10.1016/j.tate.2018.07.008

LaRue, E. M. (2012). Using Facebook as a course management software: A case study. *Teaching and Learning in Nursing*, *7*(1), 17–22. doi:10.1016/j.teln.2011.07.004

Lave, J., & Wenger, E. (1991). *Situated learning: legitimate peripheral participation*. Retrieved from http://www.loc.gov/catdir/description/cam024/91010450.html http://www.loc.gov/catdir/enhancements/fy0702/91010450-t.html

Lawler, P. A., & King, K. P. (2001). *Refocusing faculty development: The view from an adult learning perspective*. Presented at the *Pennsylvania Adult and Continuing Education Research Conference*

Layard, R., & Dunn, J. (2010). *A good childhood, searching for values in a competitive age*. London, UK: Penguin.

Layne, J., Froyd, J., Simpson, N., Caso, R., & Merton, P. (2004). *Understanding and improving faculty professional development in teaching*. Presented at the *34th ASEE/IEEE Frontiers in Education Conference*. 10.1109/FIE.2004.1408683

Ledell, G. H., & Scott, R. (1925). Arete. Retrieved from *A Greek-English Lexicon*: http://www.perseus.tufts.edu/hopper/text?doc=LSJ%20a)reth/&lang=original

Lederman, D. (2018). *New data: Online environments grow, and share of overall enrollment grows faster.* Retrieved from https://www.insidehighered.com/print/digital-learning/article/2018/11/07/new-data-online-enrollments-grow-and-share-overall-enrollment

Lee, A. J., Ngampornchai, A., Trail-Constant, T., Abril, A., & Srinivasan, S. (2016). Does a case-based online group project increase students' satisfaction with interaction in online courses? *Active Learning in Higher Education*, *17*(30), 249–260. doi:10.1177/1469787416654800

Legg, A. M., & Wilson, J. H. (2009). Technology and teaching: Email from professor enhances student motivation and attitudes. *Teaching of Psychology*, *36*, 205–211. doi:10.1080/00986280902960034

Levine, J., & Hogg, M. (2010). *Encyclopedia of group processes & intergroup relations*. Thousand Oaks, CA: Sage. doi:10.4135/9781412972017

Light, G., & Calkins, S. (2008). The experience of faculty development: Patterns of variation in conceptions of teaching. *The International Journal for Academic Development*, *13*(1), 27–40. doi:10.1080/13601440701860227

Ligoria, M. B. (2001). Integrating communication formats: Synchronous versus asynchronous and text-based versus visual. *Computers & Education*, *37*(2), 103–125. doi:10.1016/S0360-1315(01)00039-2

Lim, V. K., & Chin, J. Y. (2006). Mind Your E-Manners: Impact of cyber incivility on justice, emotions, and individual responses. *66th Annual Academy of Management Meeting.* Atlanta, GA.

Lim, C., & Putnam, R. D. (2010). Religion, social networks, and life satisfaction. *American Sociological Review*, *75*(6), 914–933. doi:10.1177/0003122410386686

Lim, V. K., Thompson, S. H., & Chin, J. (2008). Bosses and their E-Manners. *Communications of the ACM*, *51*(12), 155–158. doi:10.1145/1409360.1409391

Lin, F., Lin, S., & Huang, T. (2007). Knowledge sharing and creation in a teachers' professional virtual community. *Computers & Education*, *50*(3), 742–756. doi:10.1016/j.compedu.2006.07.009

Lin, S. Y., & Overbaugh, R. C. (2007). The effect of student choice of online discussion format on tiered achievement and student satisfaction. *Journal of Research on Technology in Education*, *39*(4), 399–415.

Lin-Sommer, S., & Lucek, S. (2015). The Dangerous Mind: Unconscious Bias in Higher Education. *Brown Political Review.* Retrieved from http://www.brownpoliticalreview.org/2015/04/the-dangerous-mind-unconscious-bias-in-higher-education/

Li, Q. (2010). Cyberbullying in high schools: A study of students' behaviors and beliefs about this new phenomenon. *Journal of Aggression, Maltreatment & Trauma*, *19*(4), 372–392. doi:10.1080/10926771003788979

Litwiller, B., & Brausch, A. (2013). Cyber Bullying and Physical Bullying in Adolescent Suicide: The Role of Violent Behavior and Substance Use. *Journal of Youth and Adolescence*, *42*(5), 675–684. doi:10.100710964-013-9925-5 PMID:23381779

Liu, X., Magjuka, R. J., Bonk, C. J., & Lee, S. (2007). Does sense of community matter? An examination of participants' perceptions of building learning communities in online courses. *The Quarterly Review of Distance Education*, *8*(1), 9–24.

Liu, X., Magjuka, R., Bonk, C., & Lee, S. (2007). Does sense of community matter? An examination of participants' perceptions of building learning communities in online courses. *Quarterly Review of Distance Education*, *8*(1), 9–24.

Lock, J. V. (2006). A new image: Online Communities to Facilitate Teacher Professional Development. *Journal of Technology and Teacher Education*, *14*, 663–678.

Lohr, K. D., & Haley, K. J. (2018). Using biographical prompts to build community in an online graduate course an adult learning perspective. *Adult Learning*, *29*(1), 11–19. doi:10.1177/1045159517735597

Lombardi, M. M. (2007, May). *Authentic learning for the 21st century: An overview.* Educause Learning Initiative Paper. Retrieved from http://net.educause.edu/ir/library/pdf/eli3009.pdf

Loom. (2019). Retrieved from www.useloom.com

Loughran, J. (2014). Professionally Developing as a Teacher Educator. *Journal of Teacher Education*, *65*(4), 271–283. doi:10.1177/0022487114533386

Lunsford, A. (2006). Writing, technologies, and the fifth canon. *Computers and Composition*, *23*(2), 169–177. doi:10.1016/j.compcom.2006.02.002

Lwin, M., Li, B., & Ang, R. P. (2012). Stop bugging me: An examination of adolescents' protection behavior against online harassment. *Journal of Adolescence*, *35*(1), 31–41. doi:10.1016/j.adolescence.2011.06.007 PMID:21767872

MacDonald, J., Atkin, W., Daugherity, F., Fox, H., MacGillivray, A., Reeves- Lipscomb, D., & Uthailertaroon, P. (2003). *Let's get more positive about the term "lurker."*

Macià, M., & García, I. (2016). Informal online communities and networks as a source of teacher professional development: A review. *Teaching and Teacher Education, 55*, 291–307. doi:10.1016/j.tate.2016.01.021

MacPhail, A., Patton, K., Parker, M., & Tannehill, D. (2014). Leading by Example: Teacher Educators' Professional Learning Through Communities of Practice. *Quest, 66*(1), 39–56. doi:10.1080/00336297.2013.826139

Madden, M., & Fox, S. (2006). Riding the waves of "Web 2.0:" More than a buzzword but still not easily defined. Retrieved from http://www.pewinternet.org/ Reports/2006/Riding-theWaves-of-Web-20.aspx

Madden, M., & Zickuhr, K. (2011). *65% of online adults use social networking sites.* Retrieved from http://pewinternet.org/~/media//Files/Reports/2011/PIP SNSUpdate-2011.pdf

Magee, R. (2015). *How mindfulness can defeat racial bias.* Retrieved from https://greatergood.berkeley.edu/article/item/how_mindfulness_can_defeat_racial_bias

Manpower Group. (2012). *2012 talent shortage survey research results.* Retrieved from http://www.manpowergroup.us/campaigns/talent-shortage-2012/pdf/2012_Talent_Shortage_Survey_Results_US_FINALFINAL.pdf

Martins, L. L., Gilson, L. L., & Maynard, M. T. (2004). Virtual teams: What do we know and where do we go from here? *Journal of Management, 30*(6), 805–835. doi:10.1016/j.jm.2004.05.002

Marzano, R. J. (2007). *The art and science of teaching.* Virginia: ASCD.

Marzano, R. J., Pickering, D. J., & Pollock, J. E. (2001). *Classroom instruction that works. Research-based strategies for increasing student achievement.* Alexandria, VA: Association for Supervision and Curriculum Development.

Maslow, A. H. (1954). *Motivation and personality.* New York, NY: Harper and Row.

McCall, M., Spencer, E., Owen, H., Roberts, N., & Heneghan, C. (2018). Characteristics and efficacy of digital health education: An overview of systematic reviews. *Health Education Journal, 77*(5), 497–514.

McMillan, D. W., & Chavis, D. M. (1986). Sense of community: A definition and theory. *Journal of Community Psychology, 14*(1), 6–23. doi:10.1002/1520-6629(198601)14:1<6::AID-JCOP2290140103>3.0.CO;2-I

McTavish, J. (2010). The Ethos of the Practice of Rhetoric. *PHILIPPINIANA SACRA, 45*(133), 66–78.

Means, B., Toyama, Y., Murphy, R., Bakia, M., & Jones, K. (2010). *Evaluation of Evidence-based practices in online learning: A meta-analysis and review of online learning studies.* Washington, DC: U. S. Department of Education.

Mefolere, K. F. (2015). WhatsApp and information sharing: Prospects and challenges. *International Journal of Social Science and Humanities Research, 4*(1), 615–625.

Merriam, S. B., & Simpson, E. L. (2000). *A guide to research for educators and trainers of adults.* Malabar, FL: Krieger Publishing.

Meyer, P. J. (2003). *"What would you do if you knew you couldn't fail? Creating S.M.A.R.T. Goals". Attitude is everything: If you want to succeed above and beyond.* Meyer Resource Group.

Mezirow, J. (1991). *Transformative dimensions of adult learning.* San Francisco, CA: Jossey-Bass.

Mezirow, J. (Ed.). (2000). *Learning as transformation: Critical perspectives on a theory in progress.* San Francisco, CA: Jossey-Bass.

Mgbeahurike, O. (2015). Social media: To build and to destroy. *Archcardinal's Blog on Economic and Burning Issues in Nigeria.* Retrieved from https: archardinal.wordspress.com/2015/06/05/socialmedia-to-build-and-to-destroy/

Milkman, K. L., Akinola, M., & Chugh, D. (2015). What Happens Before? A Field Experiment Exploring How Pay and Representation Differentially Shape Bias on the Pathway into Organizations. *The Journal of Applied Psychology, 100*(6), 1678–1712. doi:10.1037/apl0000022 PMID:25867167

Mindful.org. (2014). *What is Mindfulness?* Retrieved from https://www.mindful.org/what-is-mindfulness/

Minton-Eversole, T. (2013). Society for Human Resource Management. Virtual teams used most by global organizations, survey says. Retrieved from http://www.shrm.org/hrdisciplines/orgempdev/articles/Pages/VirtualTeamsUsedMostbyGlobalOrganizations,SurveySays.aspx

Misanchuk, M., & Anderson, T. (2001). Building community in an online learning environment: Communication, cooperation and collaboration. Proceedings of the *Sixth Annual Mid-South Instructional Technology Conference*, Murfreesboro, TN, Middle Tennessee State University. Retrieved from http://kevinmcmanamon.files.wordpress.com/2012/01/building-community-in-an-online-learning-environment.pdf

Misanchuk, M., & Anderson, T. (2001). *Building community in an online learning environment: Communication, cooperation, and collaboration.* Paper presented at the Mid-South Instructional Technology Conference, Murfreesboro, TN.

Mkrttchian, V., Kataev, M., Hwang, W., Bedi, S. S., & Fedotova, A. (2014). Using plug-avatars "hhh" technology education as service-oriented virtual learning environment in sliding mode. The Handbook of Research on Emerging Priorities and Trends in Distance Education: Communication, Pedagogy, and Technology, 12(1), 1-13.

Mohr, S. C., & Shelton, K. (2017). Best practices framework for online faculty professional development: A delphi study. *Online Learning, 21*(4), 123–140.

Montoya-Weiss, M. M., Massey, A. P., & Song, M. (2001). Getting it together: Temporal coordination and conflict management in global virtual teams. *Academy of Management Journal, 44*(6), 1251–1262.

Morris, S. A., Marshall, T., & Kelleyrainer, R. (2002). Impact of user satisfaction and trust on virtual team members. *Information Resources Management Journal, 15*(2), 2–30. doi:10.4018/irmj.2002040103

Morrow, A., & Downey, C. (2013). Perceptions of adolescent bullying: Attributions of blame and responsibility in cases of cyber-bullying. *Scandinavian Journal of Psychology, 54*(6), 536–540. doi:10.1111jop.12074 PMID:24111682

Most Popular Websites. (2011). *Most popular websites on the internet.* Retrieved from http://mostpopularwebsites.net/

Moustakas, C. (1994). *Phenomenological research methods.* Thousand Oaks, CA: Sage.

MSNBC. (2012, Jan. 24). *Clergy voice support for student in prayer banner case.* Retrieved from http://www.msnbc.msn.com/id/46122620/ns/local_news-providence_ri/t/clergy-voice-support-student-prayer-banner-case/

Myers, D. (2011). *Myers' Psychology for AP*. New York, NY: Worth Publishers.

National Center for Education Statistics, Institution of Education Sciences. (2011). *Digest of education statistics, 2011.* Retrieved from http://nces.ed.gov/fastfacts/display.asp?id=98

National Center for Education Statistics, Institution of Education Sciences. (2018). *The Condition of Education, 2018.* Retrieved from https://nces.ed.gov/pubs2018/2018144.pdf

Newman, N., Levy, D. A. L., & Nielsen, R. K. (2015). Reuters institute digital news 2015: tracking the Future of News. Reuters Institute for the Study of Journalism. Oxford, UK: University of Oxford. doi:10.2139srn.2619576

Ng, G. A. W. (2000). From Confucian master teacher to Freirean mutual learner: Challenges in pedagogical practice and religious education. *Religious Education (Chicago, IL), 95*(3), 308–319. doi:10.1080/0034408000950307

O'Connor, E. (2012). Next generation online: Advancing learning through dynamic design, virtual and Web 2.0 technologies, and instructor attitude. *Journal of Educational Technology Systems, 41*(1), 3–24. doi:10.2190/ET.41.1.b

O'Leary, P. F., & Quinlan, T. J. (2007). Satisfaction and achievement of online students. *Education, 21*(3), 133–143.

Ödalen, J., Brommesson, D., Erlingsson, G. Ó., Schaffer, J. K., & Fogelgren, M. (2019). Teaching university teachers to become better teachers: The effects of pedagogical training courses at six Swedish universities. *Higher Education Research & Development, 38*(2), 339–353. doi:10.1080/07294360.2018.1512955

Office for Economic Cooperation and Development. (2012, March). *Preparing teachers and developing leaders for the 21st century: Lessons from around the world.* Retrieved from http://www.oecd.org/site/eduistp2012/49850576.pdf

Oh, K. H. (2000). *Dimensions of Chong in Korean Christians.* (Unpublished doctoral dissertation). Northwestern University. Evanston, IL.

Ollila, M., & Simpson, A. (2004). Dimensions of Design: A Comparison of Professional Development in Two On-Line Learning Communities. *Proceedings of the IEEE International Conference on Advanced Learning Technologies,* 271–275. 10.1109/ICALT.2004.1357417

Olson, D. (2001). *The world on paper.* New York, NY: Cambridge University Press.

Ortega, L. (2017). New CALL-SLA research interfaces for the 21st century: Towards equitable multilingualism. *CALICO Journal, 34*(3), 285–316. doi:10.1558/cj.33855

Ouzts, K. (2006). Sense of community in online courses. *Quarterly Review of Distance Education, 7*(3), 285–296.

Oztok, M., Zingaro, D., Brett, C., & Hewitt, J. (2013). Exploring asynchronous and synchronous toll use in online courses. *Computers & Education, 60*(1), 87–94. doi:10.1016/j.compedu.2012.08.007

Palen, L., & Liu, S. B. (2007, April). Citizen communications in crisis: Anticipating a future of ICT-supported public participation. In *Proceedings of the SIGCHI conference on Human factors in computing systems* (pp. 727-736). New York, NY: ACM. 10.1145/1240624.1240736

Palen, L., Vieweg, S., Sutton, J., Liu, S. B., & Hughes, A. (2007). Crisis informatics: Studying crisis in a networked world. In *Third International Conference on e-Social Science* (7-9).

Palen, L., Vieweg, S., Sutton, J., Liu, S. B., & Hughes, A. (Oct. 2010). Crisis informatics: studying crisis in a networked world. In *Third International Conference on e-Social Science* (pp. 7-9).

Palloff, R., & Pratt, K. (2005). *Online learning communities revisited.* Presented at the *21st Annual Conference on Distance Teaching and Learning.*

Pallof, R., & Pratt, K. (2001). *Lessons from the cyberspace classroom: The realities of online teaching.* San Francisco, CA: Jossey-Bass.

Parker, K., Lenhart, A., & Moore, K. (2011). *The digital revolution and higher education: College presidents, public differ on value of online learning.* Retrieved from http://www.pewinternet.org/~/ media//Files/Reports/2011/PIP-Online Learning.pdf

Park, J., & Choi, H. J. (2009). Factors influencing adult learner's decision to drop out or persist in online learning. *Journal of Educational Technology & Society, 12*(4), 207–217.

Patel, C., & Patel, T. (2006). Exploring a joint model of conventional and online learning systems. *e-Service Journal, 4*(2), 27–46. doi:10.2979/esj.2006.4.2.27

Patterson, B., & McFadden, C. (2009). Attrition in online and campus degree programs. *Online Journal of Distance Learning Administration*, *12*(2). Retrieved from http://www.westga.edu/distance/ojdla/summer122/patterson112.html

Patton, K., & Parker, M. (2017). Teacher education communities of practice: More than a culture of collaboration. *Teaching and Teacher Education*, *67*, 351–360. doi:10.1016/j.tate.2017.06.013

Paulsen, M. (1995). Moderating educational computer conferences. In A. Berge, & M. Collins (Eds.), *Computer-mediated communication and the on-line classroom in distance education*. Cresskill, NJ: Hampton Press.

Pawar, K. S., & Sharifi, S. (1997). Physical or virtual team collocation: Does it matter? *International Journal of Production Economics*, *52*(3), 283–290. doi:10.1016/S0925-5273(97)89241-9

Pearson, C. M., & Porath, C. L. (2005). On the nature, consequences and remedies of workplace incivility: No time for "nice.". *Executive*, *19*, 7–18.

Pentland, A. (2012, April). The new science of building great teams. *Harvard Business Review*. Retrieved from http://hbr.org/2012/04/the-new-science-of-building-great-teams

Perception Institute. (n.d.). Retrieved from https://perception.org/research/explicit-bias/

Perception.org. (n.d.). *Transforming Perception: Black Men and Boys*. American Values Institute. Retrieved from http://perception.org/wp-content/uploads/2014/11/Transforming-Perception.pdf

Persico, D., Pozzi, F., & Sarti, L. (2009). Design patterns for monitoring and evaluating CSCL processes. *Computers in Human Behavior*, *25*(5), 1020–1027. doi:10.1016/j.chb.2009.01.003

Peterson, M. (2011). Towards a research agenda for the use of three-dimensional virtual worlds in language learning. *CALICO Journal*, *29*(1), 67–80. doi:10.11139/cj.29.1.67-80

Petrakou, A. (2010). Interaction through avatars: Virtual worlds as a context for online education. *Computers & Education*, *54*(4), 1020–1027. doi:10.1016/j.compedu.2009.10.007

Plaisance, P. (2013). Virtue ethics and digital flourishing: An application of Philippa foot to life online. *Journal of Mass Media Ethics*, *28*(3), 91–102. doi:10.1080/08900523.2013.792691

Plank, S. B., McDill, L., McPartland, J. M., & Jordan, W. J. (2001). Situation and Repertoire: Civility, Incivility, Cursing and Politeness in an Urban High School. *Teachers College Record*, *103*(3), 504–524. doi:10.1111/0161-4681.00125

Plonsky, L., & Ziegler, N. (2016). CALL-SLA interface: Insights from a second-order synthesis. *Language Learning & Technology*, *20*(2), 17–37. Retrieved from http://llt.msu.edu/issues/june2016/plonskyziegler.pdf

Porter, J. (2009). Recovering delivery for digital rhetoric. *Computers and Composition*, *26*(4), 207–224. doi:10.1016/j.compcom.2009.09.004

Poulin, R., & Straut, T. (2016). WCET Distance Education Enrollment Report. Retrieved from https://files.eric.ed.gov/fulltext/ED570525.pdf

Powell, C. G., & Bodur, Y. (2019). Teachers' perceptions of an online professional development experience: Implications for a design and implementation framework. *Teaching and Teacher Education*, *77*, 19–30. doi:10.1016/j.tate.2018.09.004

Prakash, A., & Potoski, M. (2007). Collective action through voluntary environmental programs: A club theory perspective. *Policy Studies Journal: the Journal of the Policy Studies Organization*, *35*(4), 23–29. doi:10.1111/j.1541-0072.2007.00247.x

Pratt, S. (2016). *9 types of unconscious bias and the shocking ways they affect your recruiting efforts*. Retrieved from https://www.socialtalent.com/blog/recruitment/9-types-of-bias

Preece, J., Nonnecke, B., & Andrews, D. (2004). The top 5 reasons for lurking: Improving community experiences for everyone. *Computers in Human Behavior*, *20*(2), 201–223. doi:10.1016/j.chb.2003.10.015

Prenger, R., Poortman, C. L., & Handelzalts, A. (2017). Factors influencing teachers' professional development in networked professional learning communities. *Teaching and Teacher Education*, *68*, 77–90. doi:10.1016/j.tate.2017.08.014

Project Implicit. (n.d.). Retrieved from https://www.projectimplicit.net/index.html

Quintillian. (2006). *Institutes of oratory.* (L. Honeycut, Ed., & J. Watson, Trans.) Retrieved from http://rhetoric.eserver.org/quintilian/

Rambe, P., & Bere, A. (2013). Using mobile messaging to leverage participation and transform pedagogy at a South African University of Technology. *British Journal of Educational Technology*, *44*(4), 36–44. doi:10.1111/bjet.12057

Rau-Foster, M., & Duthka, P. (2004). Workplace Civility and Staff Retention. *Nephrology Nursing Journal*, *31*(6), 702. PMID:15686340

Reeves, T. C. (2006). Design Research from a Technology Perspective. In J. van den Akker, K. Gravemeijer, S. McKenney, & N. Nieveen (Eds.), *Educational Design Research* (pp. 52–66). London, UK: Routledge.

Reilly, R. B. (2014). Feds to mobile marketers: stop targeting kids, or else, *Venture Beat,* March 27. Retrieved from http://venturebeat. com/2014/03/27/feds-to-mobile-marketers-stop- targeting-kidsor- else-exclusive/.

Reinhardt, J., & Thorne, S. L. (2019). Digital literacies as emergent multifarious repertoires. In N. Arnold, & L. Ducate (Eds.), *Engaging language learners through CALL. From theory and research to informed practice.* Sheffield, UK: Equinox Publishing.

Richardson, J. T. (1999). Centralizing governance isn't simply wrong; it's bad business, too. *Chronicle of Higher Education.* Retrieved from http://chronicle.com/article/Centralizing Governance-Isnt/8672

Richardson, J. C., & Lowenthal, P. (2017). Instructor social presence: Learners' needs and a neglected component of the Communities of Inquiry. In A. L. Whiteside, A. G. Dikkers, & K. Swan (Eds.), *Social Presence in online learning: Multiple perspectives, theories, and practices.* Sterling, VA: Stylus Publishing.

Richardson, J. C., & Swan, K. (2003). Examining social presence in online courses in relation to students' perceived learning and satisfaction. *Journal of Asynchronous Learning Networks*, *7*(1), 68–88.

Rienties, B., Giesbers, B., Tempelaar, D., Lygo-Baker, S., Segers, M., & Gijselaers, W. (2012). The role of scaffolding and motivation in CSCL. *Computers & Education*, *59*(3), 893–906. doi:10.1016/j.compedu.2012.04.010

Robert Wood Johnson Foundation and the Institute of Medicine. (2010). *The future of nursing: Leading change, advancing health. need publisher information or the website.* Author.

Rogers, P., & Lea, M. (2005). Social presence in distributed group environments: The role of social identity. *Behaviour & Information Technology*, *24*(2), 151–158. doi:10.1080/01449290410001723472

Rojano-Caceres, J. R., Ramos-Quintana, F., & Vargas-Cerdán, M. D. (2012). On fostering a co-creative process within a CSCL framework. *Creative Education*, *3*(4), 383–391. doi:10.4236/ce.2012.34061

Rookstool, J. (2007). *Fostering civility on campus.* Washington, DC: Community College Press.

Rorty, A. O. (1980). Structuring Rhetoric. In A. O. Rorty (Ed.), Essays on Aristotle's Rhetoric (p. 9). Berkeley, CA: University Of California Press.

Rosen, L. D., Carrier, L. M., & Cheever, N. A. (2013). Facebook and texting made me do it: Media-induced task-switching while studying. *Computers in Human Behavior*, *29*(3), 948–958. doi:10.1016/j.chb.2012.12.001

Roseth, C., Akcaoglu, M., & Zellner, A. (2013). Blending synchronous face-to-face and computer-supported cooperative learning in a hybrid doctoral seminar. *TechTrends*, *57*(3), 54–59. doi:10.100711528-013-0663-z

Rossman, M. (1999).. . *Journal of Asynchronous Learning Networks*, *3*(2). Retrieved from http://www.aln.org/alnweb/journal/Vol3_issue 2/Rossman.htm

Rourke, L., Anderson, T., Garrison, D. R., & Archer, W. (2001). Assessing social presence in asynchronous, text-based computer conferencing. *Journal of Distance Education*, *14*(3), 51–70.

Rovai, A. P. (2002a). Building sense of community at a distance. *International Review of Research in Open and Distance Learning*, *13*(1).

Rovai, A. P. (2002b). Sense of community, perceived cognitive learning, and persistence in asynchronous learning networks. *The Internet and Higher Education*, *5*(4), 319–332. doi:10.1016/S1096-7516(02)00130-6

Rovai, A. P. (2003). Sense of community in higher education television-based distance education programs. *Educational Technology Research and Development*, *51*(2), 5–16. doi:10.1007/BF02504523

Rovai, A. P., Wighting, M. J., & Liu, J. (2005). School climate: Sense of classroom and school communities in online and on-campus higher education courses. *The Quarterly Review of Distance Education*, *6*(4), 361–374.

Rubio, F., Thomas, J. M., & Li, Q. (2018). The role of teaching presence and student participation in Spanish blended courses. *Computer Assisted Language Learning*, *31*(3), 226–250. doi:10.1080/09588221.2017.1372481

Rudick, M., & O'Flahavan, L. (n.d.). *Set the tone in email: How you say it is as important as what you say.* Retrieved from http://www.hodu.com/email-tone.shtml

Russell, V., & Curtis, W. (2013). Comparing a large- and small-scale online language class: An examination of teacher and learner perceptions. *The Internet and Higher Education*, *16*, 1–13. doi:10.1016/j.iheduc.2012.07.002

Sack, M. D. (2014, May 12). *Destined to Stereotype? How the Mind's Gift for Grouping Gets Us into Trouble.* Retrieved from https://www.huffingtonpost.com/david-sack-md/stereotype_b_4934495.html

Sadeghi, H., & Kardan, A. A. (2015). A novel justice-based linear model for optimal learner group formation in computer-supported collaborative learning environments. *Computers in Human Behavior*, *48*, 436–447. doi:10.1016/j.chb.2015.01.020

Sadker, D. (n.d.). *Some Practical ideas for Confronting Curricular Bias.* The Myra Sadker Foundation. Retrieved from https://www.sadker.org/curricularbias.html

Salmon, G. (2004). E-moderating. The key to teaching and learning online (2nd ed.). Abingdon-on-Thames, UK: Routledge Falmer. doi:10.4324/9780203465424

Sandoval, W., & Bell, P. (2004). Design-Based Research Methods for Studying Learning in Context: Introduction. *Educational Psychologist*, *39*(4), 199–201. doi:10.120715326985ep3904_1

Sannino, A., & Engeström, Y. (2018). Cultural-historical activity theory. *Cultural-historical Psychology*, *14*(3), 43–56. doi:10.17759/chp.2018140305

Santhanam, R., Sasidharan, S., & Webster, J. (2008). Using self-regulatory learning to enhance e-learning-based information technology training. *Information Systems Research*, *19*(1), 26–47. doi:10.1287/isre.1070.0141

Sapkota, K., & Vander Putten, J. (2018). Social media acceptance and usage by business communications faculty. *Business and Professional Communication Quarterly*, *81*(3), 328–350. doi:10.1177/2329490618777818

Saunders, C., Rutkowski, A. F., van Genuchten, M., Vogel, D., & Orrego, J. M. (2012). Virtual space and place: Theory and test. *Management Information Systems Quarterly*, *36*, 1–20.

Savali, K. W. (2015). Throw Away the Script: How Media Bias is Killing Black America. Retrieved from https://www.theroot.com/throw-away-the-script-how-media-bias-is-killing-black-1790860024

Saville, B. K., Lawrence, N. K., & Jakobsen, K. V. (2012). Creating learning communities in the classroom. *New Directions for Teaching and Learning*, *2012*(132), 57–69. doi:10.1002/tl.20036

Scarborough, J. K., & Bailenson, J. N. (2014). Avatar psychology. In M. Grimshaw (Ed.), *The Oxford Handbook of Virtuality* (pp. 129–144). New York, NY: Oxford University Press.

Scheuermann, M. (2010, Feb. 24). *Engaging students with synchronous methods in online courses* [Audio podcast]. Retrieved from http://www.facultyfocus.com/seminars/engaging-students-with-synchronous-methods-in-online-courses/?aa=10502

Schlager, M. S., Fusco, J., & Schank, P. (2002). Evolution of an On-line Education Community of Practice. In K. A. Renninger, & W. Shumar (Eds.), Building virtual communities: Learning and change in cyberspace (pp. 129–158). New York, NY: Cambridge University Press. doi:10.1017/CBO9780511606373.010

Schlager, M. S., & Fusco, J. (2004). Teacher professional development, technology, and communities of practice: Are we putting the cart before the horse? In S. Barab, R. Klin, & J. Gray (Eds.), *Designing for Virtual Communities in the Service of Learning*. Cambridge, MA: Cambridge University Press. doi:10.1017/CBO9780511805080.009

Schneider, A. (1998). Insubordination and intimidation signal the end of decorum in many classrooms. *The Chronicle of Higher Education*, *44*(29), A12–A14.

Schnetter, V. A., Lacy, D., Jones, M. M., Bakrim, K., Allen, P. E., & O'Neal, C. (2014). Course development for web-based nursing education programs. *Nurse Education in Practice*, *14*(6), 635–640. doi:10.1016/j.nepr.2014.06.007

Schubert, K., & Weibert, A. (2014). How the social structure of interculture 'come_IN' computer clubs fosters interactive storytelling. *International Journal of Arts and Technology*, *7*(1), 55–63. doi:10.1504/IJART.2014.058944

Schwier, R. (2002). *Shaping the metaphor of community in online learning environments*. (Unpublished Manuscript).

Scriven, M., & Paul, R. (1987). *Defining critical thinking*. Retrieved from http://www.criticalthinking.org/pages/defining-critical-thinking/766

Seaman, J. E., Allen, I. E., & Seaman, J. (2018). *Grade Increase: Tracking Distance Education in the United States*. Retrieved from https://www.onlinelearningsurvey.com/highered.html

Seaman, J. E., Allen, I. E., & Seaman, J. (2018). *Grade increase: Tracking distance education in the United States*. Retrieved from: http://www.onlinelearningsurvey.com/highered.html

Sedley, D. (2003). *The Cambridge Companion to Greek and Roman Philosophy*. Cambridge, UK: Cambridge University Press. doi:10.1017/CCOL0521772850

Serva, M., & Fuller, M. (2004). Aligning what we do and what we measure in business schools: Incorporating active learning and effective media use in the assessment of instruction. *Journal of Management Education*, *28*(1), 19–38. doi:10.1177/1052562903252648

Sexton, J., & Bollinger, L. C. (2002). Fostering collaboration in higher education. *Bulletin - American Academy of Arts and Sciences*, *55*(3), 59–68. doi:10.2307/3824212

Shakeel, I., Khan, M. N., & Malik, I. R. (2017). Mobile phone usage and students' perception towards m-learning: A case of undergraduate students in Pakistan. *International Journal of E-Learning & Distance Education*, *32*(1), 2–17.

Shea, P., & Bidjerano, T. (2010). Learning presence: Towards a self-efficacy, self-regulation, and the development of a communities of inquiry in online and blended environments. *Computers & Education*, *55*(4), 1721–1731. doi:10.1016/j.compedu.2010.07.017

Shea, P., Sau Li, C., & Pickett, A. (2006). A study of teaching presence and student sense of learning community in fully online and web-enhanced college courses. *The Internet and Higher Education*, *9*(3). doi:10.1016/j.iheduc.2006.06.005

Sheeran, N., & Cummings, D. J. (2018). An examination of the relationship between Facebook groups attached to the university courses and student engagement. *Higher Education*, *76*(6), 937–955. doi:10.100710734-018-0253-2

Sher, A. (2009). Assessing the relationship of student-instructor and student-student interaction to student learning and satisfaction in web-based online learning environment. *Journal of Interactive Online Learning*, *8*(2), 102–120.

Sherer, P. D., Shea, T. P., & Kristensen, E. (2003). Online Communities of Practice: A Catalyst for Faculty Development. *Innovative Higher Education*, *27*(3), 183–194. doi:10.1023/A:1022355226924

Shurville, S., & Browne, T. (2006). ICT-driven change in higher education: Learning from e-learning. *Journal of Organisational Transformation & Social Change*, *3*(1), 245–250.

Simpson, J. (2005). Learning electronic literacy skills in an online language learning community. *Computer Assisted Language Learning*, *18*(4), 327–345. doi:10.1080/09588220500335463

Singel, R. (2005, Oct. 6) Are you ready for Web 2.0? *Wired*. Retrieved from http://www. wired.com/science/discoveries/news/2005/10/69114

Singh, N., Chopra, N., & Kaur, J. (2015). A study to analyse relationship between psychological behavioural factors on WhatsApp addiction among youth in Jalandhar District in Punjab. *Global Advanced Research Journal of Management and Business Studies*, *5*(4), 203–207.

Sipior, J. C., & Ward, B. T. (1999). The dark side of employee email. *Communications of the ACM*, *42*(7), 88–95. doi:10.1145/306549.306591

Sloan Consortium. (2012). *Changing course: Ten years of tracking online education in the United States*. Retrieved from http://sloanconsortium.org/publications/survey /changing_course_2012

Smaldino, S. E., Lowther, D. L., & Russell, J. D. (2012). *Instructional technology and media for learning* (9th ed.). Reading, MA: Allyn & Bacon.

Smith, A., & Anderson, M. (2018). *Social Media Use in 2018: A majority of Americans use Facebook and YouTube, but young adults are especially heavy users of Snapchat and Instagram*. Retrieved from http://www.pewinternet.org/2018/03/01/social-media-use-in2018/

Smith, S. D., & Caruso, J. B. (2010). *The ECAR study of undergraduate students and information technology, 2010* (Research Study, Vol. 6). Boulder, CO: EDUCAUSE Center for Applied Research. Retrieved from http://www.educause.edu/ecar

Smith, P. J., Coldwell, J., Smith, S. N., & Murphy, K. L. (2005). Learning through computer-mediated communication: A comparison of Australian and Chinese heritage students. *Innovations in Education & Training International*, *42*(2), 123–134. doi:10.1080/14703290500062441

Smith, Y. M., & Crowe, A. R. (2017). Nurse educator perceptions of the importance of relationship in online teaching and learning. *Journal of Professional Nursing*, *33*(1), 11–19. doi:10.1016/j.profnurs.2016.06.004

Smyth, R. (2003). Concepts of Change: Enhancing the Practice of Academic Staff Development in Higher Education. *The International Journal for Academic Development*, *8*(1-2), 51–60. doi:10.1080/1360144042000277937

Society for Human Resource Management. (2019). Retrieved from http://www.shrm.org/pages/default.aspx

Solorzano, D., Ceja, M., & Yosso, T. (2000). Critical Race Theory, Racial microaggressions, and Campus Racial Climate: The Experiences of African American College Students. *The Journal of Negro Education*, *69*(1/2), 60.

Sorcinelli, M. D., Austin, A. E., Eddy, P. L., & Beach, A. L. (2006). Creating the Future of Faculty Development: Learning From the Past, Understanding the Future. Bolton, MA: Anker Publishing Co.

Sorcinelli, M. D., & Yun, J. (2007). From mentor to mentoring networks: Mentoring in the new academy. *Change*, *39*(6), 58–61. doi:10.3200/CHNG.39.6.58-C4

Steele, C. M., Spencer, S. J., & Aronson, J. (2002). Contending with group image: The psychology of stereotype and social identity threat. *Advances in Experimental Social Psychology, 34,* 379-440. Retrieved from http://disjointedthinking.jeffhughes.ca/wp-content/uploads/2011/07/Steele-Spencer-Aronson-2002.-Contending-with-group-image.pdf

Stewart, B. L., Goodson, C. E., Miertschin, S. L., Norwood, M. L., & Ezell, S. (2013). Online student support services: A case based on quality frameworks. *Journal of Online Learning and Teaching / MERLOT*, *9*(2), 1–14.

Stott, A., & Mozer, M. (2016). Connecting learners online: Challenges and issues for nurse education—is there a way forward? *Nurse Education Today*, *39*, 152–154. doi:10.1016/j.nedt.2016.02.002

Stuart, M., Lido, C., Morgan, J., Solomon, L., & May, S. (2011). The impact of engagement with extracurricular activities on the student experience and graduate outcomes for widening participation populations. *Active Learning in Higher Education*, *12*(3), 203–215. doi:10.1177/1469787411415081

Sull, E. C. (2010, Oct. 28). Online teaching tips for leveraging students' insights and experiences in online education [Web log post]. Retrieved from http://www.facultyfocus.com/topic/articles/online-education/

Swan, K., Garrison, D. R., & Richardson, J. C. (2009). A constructivist approach to online learning: The Community of Inquiry framework. In C. R. Payne (Ed.), *Information Technology and Constructivism in Higher Education: Progressive Learning Frameworks* (pp. 43–57). Hershey, PA: IGI Global. doi:10.4018/978-1-60566-654-9.ch004

Swan, K., & Shih, L. (2005). On the nature and development of social presence in online course discussions. *Journal of Asynchronous Learning Networks*, *9*(3), 115–136.

Sykes, J. M., Holden, C. L., & Knight, S. W. P. (2019). Communities: Exploring digital games and social networking. Interpersonal Communication in Intracultural CMC. In N. Arnold, & L. Ducate (Eds.), *Engaging language learners through CALL. From theory and research to informed practice*. Sheffield, UK: Equinox Publishing.

Thelin, J. (2004). *A history of American higher education*. Baltimore, MD: The Johns Hopkins University Press.

Thompson, P. (2013). The digital natives as learners: Technology use patterns and approaches to learning. *Computers & Education*, *65*, 12–23. doi:10.1016/j.compedu.2012.12.022

Thorston, K., Vraga, E., & Eckdale, B. (2010). Credibility in Context: How uncivil online commentary affects news credibility. *Mass Communication & Society*, *13*(3), 289–313. doi:10.1080/15205430903225571

Toufaily, E., Zalan, T., & Lee, D. (2018). What do learners value in online education? An emerging market perspective. *E-Journal of Business Education & Scholarship of Teaching*, *12*(2), 24–39.

Trabold, B. (2009). Walking the cliff's edge: The new nation's rhetoric of resistance in apartheid South Africa [Excerpt]. *College Composition and Communication*, *61*(2), 372.

Trevino, L. K. (1986). Ethical decision making in organizations: A person-situation interactionist model. *Academy of Management Review, 11*(3), 601–617. doi:10.5465/amr.1986.4306235

TRUSTe. (2014). 2014 TRUSTe US Consumer Confidence Index, *TRUSTe.* Retrieved from www.truste.com/us-consumerconfidence- index-2014/

TRUSTe. (2014). 2014 TRUSTe US Consumer Confidence Index. Retrieved from www.truste.com/us-consconsumer-confidence- index-2014/

Tschannen-Moran, M. (2001). Collaboration and the need for trust. *Journal of Educational Administration, 39*(4), 308–331. doi:10.1108/EUM0000000005493

Tschannen-Moran, M. (2004). *Trust Matters.* San Francisco, CA: Jossey-Bass.

Tschannen-Moran, M., & Hoy, W. K. (1998). Trust in schools: A conceptual and empirical analysis. *Journal of Educational Administration, 36*(4), 334–352. doi:10.1108/09578239810211518

Tsiotakis, P., & Jimoyiannis, A. (2016). Critical factors towards analysing teachers' presence in on-line learning communities. *The Internet and Higher Education, 28,* 45–58. doi:10.1016/j.iheduc.2015.09.002

Tu, W. M. (1993). *Wei, learning, and politics: Essays on the Confucian intellectual.* Albany, NY: State University of New York Press. Retrieved from http://web.a.ebscohost.com.dtl.idm.oclc.org/ehost/detail/detail?vid=0&sid=9b40b11c-2843-4af0-92f4-3c9281d00b9d%40sdc-v-sessmgr05&bdata=JnNpdGU9ZWhvc3QtbGl2ZSZzY29wZT1zaXRl#db=nlebk&AN=8603

Tu, W. M. (1998). Confucius and Confucianism. In W. H. Slote, & D. A. DeVos (Eds.), *Confucius and the family* (pp. 3–36). Albany, NY: State University of New York Press.

University of Tennessee Knoxville- Teaching & Learning Innovation. (n.d.). *Addressing Implicit Bias & its Impact on Teaching & Learning.* Retrieved from https://teaching.utk.edu/wp-content/uploads/sites/78/2018/03/Addressing-Implicit-Bias-and-its-Impact-on-Teaching-Learning.pdf

Unwin, A. (2015). Developing new teacher inquiry and criticality: The role of online discussions. *British Journal of Educational Technology, 46*(6), 1214–1222. doi:10.1111/bjet.12194

Vallor, S. (2010). Social networking technology and the virtues. *Ethics and Information Technology, 12*(2), 157–170. doi:10.100710676-009-9202-1

van Deursen, A., & van Dijk, J. (2011). Internet skills and the digital divide. *New Media & Society, 13*(6), 893–911. doi:10.1177/1461444810386774

Van Dijck, J. (2013). *The culture of connectivity: A critical history of social media.* Oxford, UK: Oxford University Press. doi:10.1093/acprof:oso/9780199970773.001.0001

Vanderbilt University. (2019). Office of Active Citizenship and Service. *Understanding Privilege and Oppression.* Retrieved from https://www.vanderbilt.edu//oacs/students/meaningful-service-toolkit/

Veerman, A., & Veldhuis-Diermanse, E. (2001). Collaborative learning through computer-mediated communication in academic education. In P. Dillenbourg, A. Eurelings, & K. Hakkarainen (Eds.), *European Perspectives on Computer-Supported Collaborative Learning: Proceedings.*

Vygotsky, L. S. (1978). *Mind in society: The development of higher psychological processes.* Cambridge, MA: Harvard University Press.

Wageman, R., Gardner, H., & Mortensen, M. (2012). The changing ecology of teams: New directions for teams research. *Journal of Organizational Behavior, 33*(3), 301–305. doi:10.1002/job.1775

Wagner, E. D. (2005). Enabling mobile learning. *EDUCAUSE Review, 40*(3), 41–42.

Wake, J. D., Dysthe, O., & Mjelstad, S. (2007). New and Changing Teacher Roles in Higher Education in a Digital Age. *Journal of Educational Technology & Society, 10*, 40–51.

Wall, J. (2013). *A Framework for Academic Professional Development in Higher Education.*

Walmsley, A., & McManemy, J. (2008). College student character dysfunction: It's time we set some expectations for our students that go beyond the syllabus. *Academe, 94*, 1.

Walther, J. B. (1996). Computer-mediated communication: Impersonal, interpersonal, and hyperpersonal interaction. *Communication Research, 23*(1), 3–43. doi:10.1177/009365096023001001

Wang, M. J., & Poole, M. (2004). Nurturing a dynamic online learning community among teens. *International Journal of Learning, 9*, 859–870.

Wang, Q., Woo, H. L., Quek, C. L., Yang, Y., & Lie, M. (2012). Using Facebook group as a learning management system: An exploratory study. *British Journal of Educational Technology, 43*(3), 428–438. doi:10.1111/j.1467-8535.2011.01195.x

Wang, X., Lu, W., Ester, M., Wang, C., & Chen, C. (2016). Social Recommendation with Strong and Weak Ties. *Proceedings of the 25th ACM International on Conference on Information and Knowledge Management*, 5–14. 10.1145/2983323.2983701

Ward, L. (2001). Nobility and Necessity: the problem of Courage in Aristotle's Nicomachean Ethics. *Political Science Review, 95*(1), 71. Retrieved from http://go.galegroup.com/ps/i.do?p=AONE&sw=w&u=nm_a_wnmu&v=2.1&it=r&id=GALE%7CA73021417&asid=b295edb474117734b0f7643af4e2ac8a

Warhurst, R. P. (2006). "We Really Felt Part of Something": Participatory learning among peers within a university teaching-development community of practice. *The International Journal for Academic Development, 11*(2), 111–122. doi:10.1080/13601440600924462

Weidman, R., & Bishop, M. (2009). Using the jigsaw model to facilitate cooperative learning in an online course. *Quarterly Review of Distance Education, 10*(1), 51-64, 89-91.

Weinstock, J. A. (2004). Respond now! Email, acceleration, and a pedagogy of patience. *Pedagogy, 4*(3), 365–383. doi:10.1215/15314200-4-3-365

Welch, K. (1990). Electrifying classical rhetoric: Ancient media, modern technology, and contemporary composition. *Journal of Advanced Composition, 10*(1), 22–38.

Wenger, E. (1998). *Communities of practice : learning, meaning, and identity*. Retrieved from http://www.loc.gov/catdir/description/cam029/98202423.html http://www.loc.gov/catdir/toc/cam026/98202423.html

Wenger, E., McDermott, R. A., & Snyder, W. (2002). *Cultivating communities of practice : a guide to managing knowledge.* Retrieved from http://edrev.asu.edu/reviews/rev405.htm

Wiest, E. A. (2011). Social media in the Egyptian revolution. *International Journal of Communication, 23*(4), 2–3.

Willis, J. (2006). *Research based strategies to ignite student learning.* Alexandria, VA: Association for Supervision and Curriculum Development.

Wilson, B. G., Ludwig-Hardman, S., Thornam, C., & Dunlap, J. C. (2004). Bounded community: Designing and facilitating learning communities in formal courses. *International Review of Research in Open and Distance Learning*, *5*(3).

Wilson, J. M., Straus, S. G., & McEvily, B. (2006). All in due time: The development of trust in computer-mediated and face-to-face teams. *Organizational Behavior and Human Decision Processes*, *99*(1), 16–33. doi:10.1016/j.obhdp.2005.08.001

Wing Lai, K., Pratt, K., Anderson, M., & Stigter, J. (2006). *Literature Review and Synthesis: Online Communities of Practice*. Dunedin, New Zealand: Faculty of Education, University of Otago.

Wolford, J. (2013). Facebook still has a big problem with underage users, and they know it, *WebProNews*, Jan. 24. Retrieved from www.webpronews.com/facebook-still-has-a-big-problemwith- underage-users-and-they-know-it-2013-01

Wright, A. D. (2016). *Experts: Threefold increase in telecommuting is sign of the times.* Retrieved from https://www.shrm.org/resourcesandtools/hr-topics/technology/pages/threefold-increase-in-telecommuting-is-sign-of-the-times.aspx

Yale Poorvu Center for Teaching and Learning. (2018). *Awareness of Implicit Biases.* Retrieved from https://poorvucenter.yale.edu/ImplicitBiasAwareness

Yancey, K. B. (2009). *Writing in the 21st Century*. Urbana, IL: National Council of Teachers of English.

Yang, F., Wang, M., Shen, R., & Han, P. (2007). Community-organizing agent: An artificial intelligent system for building learning communities among large numbers of learners. *Computers & Education*, *49*(2), 131–147. doi:10.1016/j.compedu.2005.04.019

Yang, Z., & Chiu, C. (2011). Goal commitment and alignment of personal goals predict group identification only when goals are shared. *Group Processes & Intergroup Relations*, *15*(3), 425–437.

Yin, R. K. (2011). *Qualitative research from start to finish.* New York, NY: Guilford Press.

Yoon, S. W. (2006). Two group development patterns of virtual learning teams: Linear progression and adaptive progression. *Quarterly Review of Distance Education*, *7*(4), 297–312.

Young, M. D. (1998, April). *Importance of trust in increasing parental involvement and student achievement in Mexican American communities.* Paper presented at the annual meeting of the American Educational Research Association, San Diego, CA. (ERIC Document Reproduction Service No. ED423587).

Young, S. (2006). Student views of effective online teaching in higher education. *American Journal of Distance Education*, *20*(2), 65–77. doi:10.120715389286ajde2002_2

You, X. (2005). Ideology, textbooks, and the rhetoric of production in China. *College Composition and Communication*, *56*(4), 632–653.

Yu, F., & Yu, H. J. J. (2002). Incorporating emails into the learning process: Its impact on student academic achievement and attitudes. *Computers & Education*, *38*(1-3), 117–126. doi:10.1016/S0360-1315(01)00085-9

Zhang, S., & Liu, Q. (2019). Investigating the relationships among teachers' motivational beliefs, motivational regulation, and their learning engagement in online professional learning communities. *Computers & Education*, *134*, 145–155. doi:10.1016/j.compedu.2019.02.013

Zheng, C., Liang, J., Li, M., & Tsai, C. (2018). The relationship between English language learners' motivation and online self-regulation: A structural equation modelling approach. *System*, *76*, 144–157. doi:10.1016/j.system.2018.05.003

Zhu, C. (2012). Student Satisfaction, Performance, and Knowledge Construction in Online Collaborative Learning. *Journal of Educational Technology & Society*, *15*(1), 127–136.

Zhu, C., Valcke, M., & Schellens, T. (2008b). Collaborative learning in a social constructivist e-learning environment: A crosscultural study. *Proceedings of the 13th Annual Conference of the European Learning Styles Information Network*, 617–630.

Zuber-Skerritt, O. (2001). Action learning and action research: Paradigm, praxis and programs. In S. Sankara, B. Dicks, & R. Passfield (Eds.), *Effective change management through action research and action learning: Concepts, perspectives, processes and applications* (pp. 1–20). Lismore, Australia: Southern Cross University Press.

About the Contributors

Carolyn Stevenson is a faculty member of Purdue University Global. The veteran educator and qualitative research expert has over 18 years of teaching and administrative experience in higher education. She holds a Master of Arts degree in Communication, Master of Business Administration, and Doctor of Education with an emphasis in Higher Education. Carolyn Stevenson teaches the bachelor's capstone in the professional studies degree program and also serves as a faculty advisor. She oversees numerous innovations in curriculum, including competency-based degree programs. She previously worked in publishing for five years before going into higher education teaching and administration. She has been cited for her expertise in online learning, open educational resources, and prior learning. Stevenson is also a reviewer for conference papers and has served on various offices and committees for the American Education Research Association. Publications include a chapter entitled: "Leading across Generations: Issues for Higher Education Administrators" published in the Handbook of Research on Transnational Higher Education Management, IGI Global; Technical Writing: A Comprehensive Resource for Technical Writers at all Levels, (Martinez, Hannigan, Wells, Peterson, and Stevenson) Revised and Updated Edition, Kaplan Publishing; Building Online Communities in Higher Education Institutions: Creating Collaborative Experience (with Joanna Bauer), published by IGI Global; Promoting Climate Change Awareness through Environmental Education (with Lynn Wilson), published by IGI Global; Building Sustainability Through Environmental Education (with Lyn Wilson), published by IGI Global; and Enhancing Education through Open Degree Programs and Prior Learning Assessment, published by IGI Global.

Joanna C. Bauer has 20 years of experience teaching and in academic leadership for online and onground modalities in communication, critical thinking, and related areas of higher education. She combines this experience with a business background in communication, online, onground and non-traditional andragogy & instruction, curriculum development, faculty development, student engagement, brand positioning, B2B partnerships, academic strategy, and business development including communication, corporate strategy, special events, and media relations. She earned an MA and a BS in Speech Communication, is currently working on an EdD in Higher Education Leadership, and has been recognized with 15 teaching and curriculum development awards. She is working as a Dean for the MA in Organizational Leadership degree for Claremont Lincoln University in Claremont, CA. Her research interests include gender equity in leadership, curriculum development, andragogy, and cultural communication. She enjoys interacting with diverse students and focuses on combining academic theory with real world application so that students can apply the content learned to professional and personal goals.

* * *

Richard Afedzie is a lecturer in the faculty of Business Administration at Pentecost University College in Accra, Ghana. He is an expert in business ethics.

James Aller is an Assistant Professor specializing in Human Resources at Georgia SouthWestern State University in Georgia. Dr. Aller is an expert in employee performance appraisals.

Ludmila Battista is an adjunct faculty at Claremont Lincoln University and Purdue University Global. She has over 17 years of experience teaching education, professional and personal development courses in the online environment. She is also a certified Reading Specialist supporting special needs students with multisensory instruction. Her research/interests include project-based learning, supporting at-risk learners, and motivating and engaging students in higher education through mindfulness and addressing social justice.

Valerie Beltran has a doctorate in Education and is a Professor of Education at the University of La Verne. In the K-12 field, she has been a teacher, a resource specialist, and a principal. At the university level, she teaches courses in both the teacher-credential and Master's programs. Her research interests include bilingual education, student engagement, and online education.

Benjamin J. Cline lives with his wife, daughter, and pets in the beautiful mountains of Silver City, NM, where he is Associate Professor of Speech and Communication at Western New Mexico University. Through teaching and research, Dr. Cline uses humanities-based thinking to philosophically consider how people can and should interact rhetorically in the contemporary, media-saturated environment in which we live. Dr. Cline has produced more than 40 publications including book chapters, scholarly articles, conference presentations, and other scholarly productions.

Mayela Coto is a professor in Informatics at the Informatics School, Universidad Nacional in Costa Rica. She is the head of the postgraduate studies at the university. She got a master's degree in Computer Science in her country and a PhD in Human Communication Centered Informatics from Aalborg University, Denmark. Her main research interests are engineering education, affective computing, pedagogical approaches, ICT4D, educational software, collaborative learning, and communities of practice.

Wesley Curtis is an experienced language educator with an extensive background in the areas of international education and distributed learning. In his current role as an international education program administrator, he works to support international students whose personal, academic, and professional goals require increased English language proficiency. More broadly, as Director of English Programs for Internationals, he serves as a facilitator of the internationalization efforts of the University of South Carolina. Additionally, Dr. Curtis serves on the Executive Board of the University and College Intensive English Programs consortium.

Dustin De Felice is an experienced educator approaching his second decade on the job. Dustin has a passion for working with teachers, learners, and organizations in creating an environment of success. As a scholar, he has explored language teaching and learning through qualitative inquiries, and he is particularly interested in technology as it relates to the development of materials and its use in traditional and virtual classrooms. His teaching has taken him around the US and Mexico and he regularly advocates for language learning at Michigan State University and beyond. Of course, he is honored to continue the legacy of the past director, Susan Gass, ELC management, faculty, and staff. He looks forward to helping grow the ELC, serve its students and scholars, and work towards a dynamic and sustainable future. Dustin holds a PhD in Second Language Acquisition and Instructional Technology from the University of South Florida, an M.A. in Linguistics with a concentration in TESL from Northeastern Illinois University, and a B.A. in Speech Communication with a minor in Spanish and Linguistics from Northeastern Illinois University.

Jessica C. Decker has a doctorate in education and is an Associate Professor of Education and Director of Teacher Education at the University of La Verne. With a background in elementary education, she has taught courses in writing, technology in education, multiple subject methodology, and current issues in education at both the undergraduate and graduate levels. Her research interests include instructional use of technology and mentoring.

Lone Dirckinck-Holmfeld is professor in ICT and Learning at the Department of Communication and Psychology, Aalborg University, and former Dean of the Faculty of Humanities, Aalborg University, from 2009 to 2015. Her research focuses on ICT as a springboard for transforming education, strengthening teachers' agency, and developing new ways of learning. She is engaged in ICT4D research on transforming education, employing participatory design methods, and is currently involved in a research capacity program in Africa: Building Stronger Universities, supported by DANIDA.

Elizabeth Donnellan is a published author and international and national research presenter who has been teaching college students for over 20 years. She teaches in the psychology department, addiction studies, at Purdue University Global. She is a national trainer for the Association of Addiction Professionals (NAADAC), providing CEU training sessions for professionals in social work, psychology, medical, and addiction fields. She has provided mental health, addiction treatment, and emergency mental health treatment to clients for over 25 years and uses that knowledge to guide her teaching, research, and clinical work. She serves as Associate Editor for the International Journal in Technology and Education Marketing (IGI) as well.

Sammy Elzarka is the Chief Advancement Officer for a law firm in Los Angeles, CA. In this capacity, he applies many of the skills and knowledge gained while he was director of assessment, and then director of faculty development, for the University of La Verne. His research interests include the impact of use of technology on student learning as well as effective curricular designs for greatest student engagement and success.

Janice E. Jones received her Ph.D. in Urban Education with a specialization in Counseling Psychology from the University of Wisconsin-Milwaukee. She is an Associate Dean in the College of Education and Leadership at Cardinal Stritch University in Milwaukee. She is also a certified alcohol and drug counselor and a certified clinical supervisor for alcohol and drug counselors. Dr. Jones's publications include articles and book chapters in the areas of research, adult education, training and supervision, positive psychology, multicultural awareness and training, successful life transitions for people with disabilities, and career and life transitions. She is actively engaged in applying positive psychology to practical problems, and is researching the impact of using positive coping strategies on the academic, career, and life outcomes of diverse, low-income youth.

Justina Kwapy started her educational journey at Rider University in Lawrenceville, NJ, as a communications/journalism major, graduating with a Bachelor of Arts in 1988. She went to Regis University in Denver and obtained an elementary education teaching degree in 1994 and graduated in 1997 with a Master of Arts degree in Special Education. She received a PhD in 2004 from Capella University. Dr. Kwapy enrolled in one of the first online programs in 2000. She has been an online instructor for GCU since 2004, and has also taught Special Education in K-12 for over 20 years. Supporting students of all ages to succeed and reach their dreams is her passion. She is very interested in current research about supporting students with learning disabilities in higher education. She has presented at the State Speech Symposium in Denver on Non-Verbal Learning Disorders and the National Differentiated Instruction Conference in Las Vegas. She is conducting research on "Cultural Competency Teaching Strategies." In her spare time, she enjoys spending time with her grown children, reading, and being involved in her local parish. She has traveled primarily in the US, visiting the East Coast frequently. Dr. Kwapy is a full-time online instructor at Grand Canyon University, teaching classes in the College of Doctoral Studies. Every day, she is grateful for the opportunity to support, guide, and mentor her student through their doctoral journey.

Mark Matzaganian received a Bachelor's Degree in Liberal Studies from Cal Poly Pomona, a Master's Degree in Higher Education from Claremont Graduate University, and a Doctorate in Educational Leadership from the University of La Verne. He served as a college administrator for 10 years before becoming a member of the University of La Verne faculty in 2003. Dr. Matzaganian serves as an Associate Professor in the LaFetra College of Education. His scholarly interests include human motivation, educational assessment, and the role of research in education.

Melissa Miller completed her Ed.D. with an emphasis in Teacher Leadership from Walden University. She holds an M.Ed. from Mary Washington University and a B.A. in Interdisciplinary Studies from Virginia Tech. Dr. Miller's professional and research interests include online learning, professional development, Applied Behavioral Analysis, Autism Spectrum Disorders, and literacy. Dr. Miller works as an Adjunct Faculty member in addition to enjoying her roles as a wife and mother.

Stanford Nartey holds a PhD in Management. He obtained his PhD from the University of Hull Business School in the UK. He also holds an MBA jn Management, BSc in Marketing and various professional certificates in Management and Marketing.

Luz María Ortiz Alcocer is a language teacher and educational researcher with 15 years of experience teaching English and Spanish in high school and college levels. She collaborates on and researches different projects related to learning and teaching languages, application and educational use of Information and Communication Technologies (ICTs) in the classroom, and intercultural education. She is involved with the design of teacher evaluation processes, elaboration of school trajectory studies, syllabus design, and Spanish-English translation. She has published articles, and participated in educational forums, both nationally and internationally.

Sue Park has years of experience teaching both on-ground and online platforms. Her Ph.D. is in Practical Theology in Interreligious Education and her research interests include innovative pedagogy, contextual learning, practical theology, interreligious dialogue, and positive psychology. She is a teaching faculty at Claremont Lincoln University.

Denise Passmore is retired assistant professor at the University of South Florida in Tampa, FL. She began developing online courses while employed with Nielsen Media Research and later went into academics as director of the online program for the college of nursing. Currently, she does freelance writing with a focus on medical writing. She earned her Ph.D. in Adult and Continuing Education in 2010 with a cognate in Qualitative Research and Certificate in Instructional Design.

Shelley Stewart is a career educator and eLearning Specialist. She works with universities and their faculty to transform their content into rich, digital, educational experiences. Shelley does this because education transformed her life for the better and she seeks to pass on this opportunity to constituents across the globe through virtual platforms. Shelley is an expert-level, trained and experienced technologist, having mastered multiple software packages. She is a Quality Matters - Master Reviewer, certifying online and hybrid courses that adhere to international criteria for course design. Shelley holds a Doctor of Philosophy in Instructional Technology and Educational Evaluation from the University of South Florida.

Jim Vander Putten received his Ph.D. in Higher Education and Postsecondary Education from the University of Michigan and is an Associate Professor of Higher Education at the University of Arkansas at Little Rock (UALR). He coordinates the Higher Education doctoral concentration in Faculty Leadership and the Higher Education M.A. concentration in Health Professions Teaching and Learning. He formerly chaired the UALR Institutional Review Board, and his research interests include the influences of social class origins on faculty work life, the college choice process for historically underrepresented students, and the organizational culture and climate for the responsible conduct of human participant research.

Nancy T. Walker is a Professor of Education at the University of La Verne where she teaches courses in literacy and research methods. Dr. Walker also coordinates the Teacher Education Literacy Program. Her research focuses on adolescent motivation, disciplinary literacy, and visual literacy. Dr. Walker is the coauthor of "When Textbooks Fall Short". Her articles can be found in the Reading Teacher and Journal of Adolescent and Adult Literacy.

Jodi Whitehurst holds an Ed.D. in Higher Education with an English composition faculty leadership concentration, an M.A. in Professional and Technical Writing, and a B.S. in Education. She is an Assistant Professor of English Composition at Arkansas State University in Beebe, and advisor for the literary and art magazine, *Uncharted*. Jodi has published in her field and continues to present at local and national conferences. She currently lives in central Arkansas with her husband, Shane, and their three children--O'Neal, Olivia, and Oakleigh.

Lisa Wright has a Bachelor's Degree in Physical Therapy, and a Master's Degree and PhD in Special Education, all from the University of Missouri. Dr. Wright teaches for Mizzou Online in the Graduate School and is a Faculty Leader for the University of Missouri Service Learning program where she leads students in service learning in Chiang Mai, Thailand, and Ho Chi Minh City, Vietnam. In addition, Dr. Wright serves as a reviewer for several professional organizations and journals and is a volunteer Guardian Ad Litem for the state of Florida. She teaches ballet as a volunteer to young children with disabilities, and has published research on interventions for children with autism.

Index

www.ingramcontent.com/pod-product-compliance
Lightning Source LLC
LaVergne TN
LVHW060421300926
849162LV00006B/1492
* 9 7 8 1 5 2 2 5 9 8 1 4 5 *